D0734840

CURRICULUM

READINGS IN
THE PHILOSOPHY
OF EDUCATION

GENERAL SERIES EDITOR, HARRY S. BROUDY

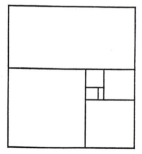

CURRICULUM

EDITED BY MARTIN LEVIT

UNIVERSITY OF ILLINOIS PRESS
URBANA, CHICAGO, LONDON
1971

LB
41
L66

370.1
L666

For Steve and Nancy

GENERAL SERIES PREFACE

Readings in the Philosophy of Education is a series of books each of which reprints significant articles, excerpts from books, and monographs that deal philosophically with problems in education.

The distinctive feature of this series is that the organization of materials is based on the results of a three-year project supported by the U.S. Office of Education and the University of Illinois. A team of philosophers of education with consultants from both philosophy of education and general philosophy scanned thousands of items. Their final selection was presented in a report entitled *Philosophy of Education: An Organization of Topics and Selected Sources* (Urbana: University of Illinois Press, 1967). A supplement to this volume by Christiana M. Smith and H. S. Broudy was issued by the University of Illinois Press in 1969.

Unfortunately, not all college libraries are equally well stocked with the items listed in these reports, and even with adequate library resources, putting the appropriate materials into the hands of students is often a formidable task for the instructor.

Accordingly, several members of the original team that worked on the project agreed to bring out this series. The items in the series are organized in two groups. One group devotes a separate volume to each of the following problems in education: the nature, aims, and policies of education (edited by Adrian Dupuis), teaching-learning (edited by Donald Vandenberg), and curriculum (the present volume, edited by Martin Levit).

The second group is made up of volumes which bring together significant materials from epistemology and metaphysics (edited by Donald Vandenberg), value theory (edited by Philip G. Smith), aesthetics (edited by Ralph A. Smith, now in press), and the philosophy of science.

The first group of books, of which this volume is one, will make available to the student some important and representative statements that philosophers of education, utilizing the resources of epistemology, metaphysics, value theory, etc., have made about problems of education. Used as a set, these volumes are appropriate for the first course in the philosophy of education whether offered to undergraduates or on the master's level. Individually, or in combination, they can also be used in courses in administration, methods, principles, curriculum, and related fields.

Each of the volumes in the second group approaches the problems of education from one of the standard divisions of general philosophy, and individually and in combination are suited to advanced and specialized courses in philosophy of education. Some instructors may wish to use a combination of volumes of both types in their courses.

Martin Levit, editor of this volume, was one of the members of the research team on the Philosophy of Education Project. He is a past president of the Philosophy of Education Society and has authored a number of works in the theory of education. He is especially interested in the relation of the philosophy of science to problems in education.

HARRY S. BROUDY
General Series Editor

CONTENTS

GENERAL INTRODUCTION

In this book of readings, a variety of philosophic concerns, viewpoints, and styles or techniques are brought to bear on basic problems encountered in developing curricula and curricular theory. In the main, the selections deal with broad matters that are relevant to any level of education, to either general or professional education, and to problems of building either a course or a program for a school system.

The text is introductory in two senses. In the first place, the selections deal with elemental issues but in a nontechnical way. Most of the writings were addressed originally to students rather than to philosophers of education. All the selections were judged by several students to be suitable for college students who have had no previous work in philosophy or philosophy of education.

In the second place, the selections are intended to introduce readers to major or representative proponents of a variety of philosophic approaches to curricular problems. Since ways and techniques of philosophizing are extremely varied, and since problems of the curriculum are unpleasantly numerous, only a small sample of connections between philosophy and the curriculum can be presented here. A few selections in general philosophy are not explicitly concerned with the curriculum. However, the implications of these writings for education may be quite significant. In any event, the reader can see, in these cases, both some of the possible uses of general philosophy for curriculum development and some of the difficulties in applying general principles to particular cases.

Selections are organized around certain enduring and pervasive curricular problems—determination of objectives and priorities, selection and organization of subject matter and experiences, reconceptualization of ways of studying the curriculum. The three parts indicated in the table of contents suggest only one general organization of materials that in fact overlap and could be arranged and read in a number of equally justifiable sequences.

This book neither begins nor ends with a capsule definition of the curriculum. No attempt is made to "solve" any problem or to present a single point of view. On a number of key problems, the selections provide alternative or conflicting viewpoints. As critical and persistent reflection on the justification of basic beliefs, philosophy deals with complex and far-reaching issues for which there are no generally accepted "final" answers. At the same time, however, philosophic work can help us move toward increasingly clear and warranted judgments about increasingly significant curricular questions.

Philosophic works should be read in a philosophic manner. A necessarily limited and vague indication of some uses of philosophy in reflecting about curricular problems can be given in the form of a few suggestions about reading the selections in *this* book. The reader might approach each selection with these questions in mind:

1. *What, precisely, is the major question the author asks, and what, precisely, is his answer?* Some writings tend to be descriptions, reports, or exhortations rather than *arguments* (that is, reasoned justification of one or more conclusions). Some writers do not clearly define, for themselves or for readers, the precise question(s) being raised. But where there is argument, search for the "point," the conclusion, and the question to which the conclusion responds. Unless defied by the material, do not be satisfied with merely a "topic sentence" or with a vague question and answer.

2. *What is the argument, the chain or chains of reasoning?* What reasons are given for what conclusions, and what reasons are given to support other reasons? Following a line of reasoning usually is a very difficult matter. Most writers, including many philosophers, do not reason in a neat, formal order. Many pages may separate a reason from a conclusion; reasons and conclusions may be expressed in any order; the same belief may be expressed in numerous grammatical variations as supposedly "different"

reasons. Usually, what is given as an example or instance of a general statement used as a reason is itself a reason for the general statement. Understanding an argument includes the ability to state, as precisely as possible, the relations among reasons and conclusions.

3. *What are the author's basic and general beliefs, including some of his significant implicit assumptions? Basic* beliefs are those which explain or give a reason for other beliefs in a particular argument but are themselves unexplained. Basic beliefs tend to be *general,* to cut across or be used in various disciplines or problems. For example, statements about this or that particular truth, or statements about this or that particular value or goal of education are, in most arguments, not as basic as the criteria or principles used to accept or reject truths and values. Again, the belief that curriculum organization should be determined by psychological rather than logical criteria usually is not as basic or general as the principles that indicate how this belief is known to be true, how psychological matters are to be distinguished from logical matters, and why one set of criteria (psychological) rather than two or more sets should be used in making these decisions about organization.

Logically, basic beliefs are *assumptions;* their truth is taken for granted in a particular argument. Philosophers are especially interested in discerning and examining basic and general beliefs, the logical grounds on which we stand. Of course, no single argument can support or even state all its assumption. Implicit, unexpressed assumptions are especially significant because what is not brought to light cannot be examined.

4. *What are the meanings of the author's key terms or concepts?* Terms may have various kinds of meanings or senses, even in one usage. Moreover, the meanings of a term may vary, sometimes misleadingly, in an argument. Even when a writer makes a point of distinguishing between meaning A and meaning B, probing often reveals that his meanings are complex and his distinctions are not clear. Some philosophers believe that the main business of philosophy should be the clarification of meanings

(examples of this kind of work are included in this volume). In any event, a degree of obscurity is a normal ailment, and the belief that one understands obscurities is a normal ailment. In general, persistent probing is needed to clarify meanings or to uncover dead-end vagueness.

5. *Are the premises credible?* In the light of "all" available evidence—which, of course, need not be confined to what the author cites—do the expressed and implicit reasons seem reasonable? What reasons are there to doubt or believe the reasons given? Philosophic principles and techniques are essential in the analysis and evaluation of arguments in any area of inquiry. At the same time, the data from many fields of inquiry are essential in evaluating the general principles used in philosophic writings.

6. *Is the reasoning sound?* Inconsistencies and irrelevancies may be found, especially when meanings, lines of reasoning, and implicit assumptions are clarified. Emotion-loaded appeals to "individual values" or (by another author) to "social values" or to many other "good" or "bad" things may replace argumentation. In short, like writings in other disciplines, philosophic arguments may be weakened by all kinds of fallacies.

7. *Is the view a comprehensive one that is consistent with cognate views?* Does it explain "all" phenomena of the type it sets out to explain? Does an explanation of "the structure of a subject" explain all kinds of structures for all kinds of subjects? Or does a theory of learning explain not only how facts and generalizations are learned but also how critical thinking and creative abilities are learned? Moreover, does the theory of learning comport well with views—either those of the author or of other experts— about personality development, processes of social change, the behavior of people in different social classes or cultures, biochemical influences on behavior, and so on. For some philosophers, the development of a unified, consistent, and sound "world-view" is the general goal of philosophic inquiry.

8. *What is the credibility of the author's argument when compared with other arguments?* What are or could be some alternative viewpoints? Generally, "pure" eclecticism is not considered

philosophically respectable; it usually signals a lack of coherent principles. But it is always useful to ask whether borrowings or modifications may lead to sounder and more comprehensive and consistent positions. The possible development of views that go beyond existing alternatives should not be lost in the rhetoric of conflict among existing alternatives.

9. *Is the argument about a significant issue, and does it work for and under the influence of desirable values?* Even if a viewpoint is credible, it may be that we should be concerned with other and more important problems. But what are criteria of importance? Are the criteria of a logical, causal, or ethical sort? Or are these rough categories really as different as they seem?

Some writer may propose that educational means and objectives be evaluated largely in terms of their potential contribution to the students' abilities to think critically (logically). The writer may argue that these abilities usually will (causally) bring the (ethically) right decisions and actions. Another person may argue that, for various reasons, other values—such as self-realization or the ability to love other people—are "more important." In any event, questions about values can be rationally discussed.

In preparing this reader, I have received able and much-appreciated assistance from Bruce F. Baker, Mary Louise Bartram, Martha Ann Bunch, Clarence E. Hughes, and Elizabeth Jane Smith. I am grateful, also, for the award of a facilitative research grant by the University of Missouri at Kansas City.

Suggested Reading

Although no previous work in philosophy or philosophy of education is necessary in order to read the selections in this text, understanding would be deepened and analysis sharpened by a study of some of the following works. For further references on the indicated topics and on the relations of philosophy to curricular problems, see Harry S. Broudy *et al.*, *Philosophy of Education: An Organization of Topics and Selected Sources* (Urbana: University of Illinois Press, 1967), and C. M. Smith and H. S. Broudy, *Philosophy of Education: An Organization of Topics and Selected Sources, Supplement, 1969* (Urbana: University of Illinois Press, 1969).

A. Introduction to Philosophy

Beardsley, Monroe C., and Elizabeth Lane Beardsley, *Philosophical Thinking: An Introduction* (New York: Harcourt, Brace and World, Inc., 1965).

Beck, Lewis White, and Robert L. Holmes, *Philosophic Inquiry: An Introduction to Philosophy,* 2nd ed. (Englewood Cliffs, N.J.: Prentice-Hall, Inc., 1968).

Hospers, John, *An Introduction to Philosophical Analysis,* 2nd ed. (Englewood Cliffs, N.J.: Prentice-Hall, Inc., 1967).

Olson, Robert G., *A Short Introduction to Philosophy* (New York: Harcourt, Brace and World, Inc., 1967).

B. Introduction to Philosophical Analysis

Copi, Irvin M., *Introduction to Logic,* 3rd. ed. (New York: Macmillan, 1968). There are a number of other equally suitable practical or applied logic texts, including those written by Monroe C. Beardsley, Max Black, Robert G. Olson, and Lionel Ruby.

Emmett, E. R., *Learning to Philosophise* (New York: Philosophical Library, Inc., 1964). Other editions of this text are available.

Ennis, Robert H., *Logic in Teaching* (Englewood Cliffs, N.J.: Prentice-Hall, Inc., 1969).

McGreal, Ian Philip, *Analyzing Philosophical Arguments* (San Francisco: Chandler Publishing Company, 1967).

Passmore, John, *Philosophical Reasoning* (New York: Charles Scribner's Sons, 1961).

Scheffler, Israel, *The Language of Education* (Springfield, Ill.: Charles C. Thomas, 1960).

C. Introduction to Educational Philosophy

Bowyer, Carlton H., *Philosophical Perspectives for Education* (Glenview, Ill.: Scott, Foresman and Company, 1970).

Brubacher, John S., *Modern Philosophies of Education,* 4th ed. (New York: McGraw-Hill Book Company, 1969).

Burns, Hobert W., and Charles J. Brauner, editors, *Philosophy of Education: Essays and Commentaries* (New York: The Ronald Press, 1962).

Jarrett, James L., editor, *Philosophy for the Study of Education* (Boston: Houghton Mifflin Company, 1969).

Smith, Philip G., *Philosophy of Education: Introductory Studies* (New York: Harper and Row, 1965).

"Symposium: The Aims and Content of Philosophy of Education," *Harvard Educational Review,* 26 (1956).

AIMS OF EDUCATION: CRITERIA AND INTELLECTUAL AND MORAL OBJECTIVES

INTRODUCTION

In varied ways and sometimes from quite different perspectives, the selections in Part One focus on the problem of justifying decisions about curricular objectives. The authors make, defend, explain, or criticize diverse assumptions about man, society, and nature, about what is good or valuable, and about how these things are known. Thus, their arguments bring to light some of the basic criteria that educators may use in accepting or rejecting proposals that certain facts and values are of capital importance in this decision-making process.

Most of the selections are concerned (again, in varied ways) with the relations between value and fact, emotion and reason, attitude and knowledge—the moral and intellectual elements and aims of education. However, most of the papers deal with or at least touch on a variety of topics relevant to determining educational objectives. Thus the selections hardly can be sequentially organized, let alone neatly subdivided. For example, the paper by Broudy (1)* does serve an introductory function in that it surveys different ways of conceiving, using, and determining educational objectives. But the paper also takes positions on a number of issues that connect it, by way of comparison or contrast, with some arguments in selections written by Greene (3), Aristotle (5), Hook (7), Scheffler (8), Dewey (9), and Horne (10).

For many teachers and curriculum-makers, the counsel and conclusions of experts in the disciplines, in subject matter, is a major resource in formulating educational objectives. On the other hand, many educators use this resource with caution, and some consider it of secondary importance. What are the criteria justifying these different statuses of the disciplines and organized subject matter? What should be the relative weight of subject mat-

---

* The number following the reference to the author or paper in the introduction indicates the selection number shown in the table of contents.

ter considerations when compared with other considerations in determining objectives? Are some subjects more important, more basic—in some sense—than other subjects? For example, are scientific procedures and findings more reliable than philosophic procedures and judgments? Are literature, art, and history as important as science? Is knowledge of any subject good in and of itself or is such knowledge merely a means toward higher ends? What subjects, if any, are especially suited for the development of character and moral beliefs? These questions, among many others, come up more or less explicitly in a number of the papers. The selections from Peters (2) and Greene (3) are not focused mainly on the role of subject matter in education. But their arguments do provide contrasting views of this role. This is so because their arguments are based on different beliefs about the nature of meaning, truth, and value, and about the significance of what is "internal," individual, and subjective as compared to what is "external," common, and objective. Among the other selections in Part One which deal with these kinds of questions are those by Broudy (1), Wilson (4), Hook (7), and Scheffler (8). Relevant, also, are some selections in Part Two—especially those by Phenix (12), Levit (14), and Schwab (15).

Suggestions often are put forward that in developing objectives educators should consider both "individual" and "social" factors, both the abilities, interests, and needs of learners and the problems, norms, and needs of society. Most of the selections consider some philosophical problems that are involved in these suggestions. For example, both Greene (3) and Aristotle (5) may be said to focus their discussions on the nature of the learner. But Greene has individual man in mind, and Aristotle has generic man in mind; they relate and evaluate different aspects of man differently, and they make quite diverse assumptions about the causal and ethical relations of man and society. With Dewey (9), man becomes a biosocial creature, and rigid distinctions between individual and social factors collapse. For Dewey, as for Hook (7), man is many-sided and malleable, and because this is so, problems arise in selecting aims and in grounding the criteria of selection. For others, as for Aristotle and Horne (10), certain essential, directive characteristics of man are inherent, and problems arise in defending this view, or defining the characteristics and deducing educational implications from them.

The selections by Broudy (1), Peters (2), Wilson (4), and Scheffler (8) propose various philosophical, logical, and moral criteria for determining aims. In doing so, the authors sometimes conflict with each other and with those who have recourse to what are usually called "individual" or "social" criteria. For instance, it seems that Broudy believes there are more ultimate criteria than individual needs or the scientific and social criteria defended by Hook. Scheffler (8) argues that scientific criteria of critical and comprehensive thought generally are higher than either social reform or individual interest. Dearden's discussion (6) of the concept of "needs" brings together certain individual and social considerations as well as certain empirical and moral questions. The selections from Dewey and Horne represent conflicting positions on a number of issues. Even though the metaphors of "growth" versus "shaping" may not be precisely applicable to Dewey or Horne, Scheffler's cautionary words about metaphors (11) raise questions about the use of many kinds of unanalyzed models or interpretive systems in education.

Scheffler's two papers indicate his belief that goals and values can be evaluated by certain criteria of logic and evidence. All the selections in this part at least touch on problems concerning the relations between moral and intellectual components of education. Diverse views are presented about such matters as whether there is a uniform, unconditioned hierarchy of values and whether there are some things that are good in and of themselves; whether moral and intellectual questions are settled by the same criteria or ways of knowing; whether the individual, society, or some other touchstone is the measure of value; whether knowledge and reason are more causally efficacious or more valuable than attitudes and emotions. These suggested questions are quite incomplete and grossly formulated. It may be misleading, for example, to label Dewey's concept of "growth" and Peter's concept of "disinterested attitude" as having either purely cognitive or purely emotive referents. With Wilson, Aristotle, and some other authors, moral and intellectual aims are related explicitly to questions concerning the roles of habituation, emotion, and reason in the experience of education—kinds of problems discussed in Part Two.

Suggested Reading

Brandt, Richard B., editor, *Value and Obligation: Systematic Readings in Ethics* (New York: Harcourt, Brace and World, Inc., 1961).

Broudy, Harry S., *Building a Philosophy of Education,* 2nd ed. (Englewood Cliffs, N.J.: Prentice-Hall, Inc., 1961), Part II and Ch. 12.

Matson, W. I. "Discussion: Morality Pills," *Ethics,* 72 (1962): 132–36.

Nash, Paul, *Authority and Freedom in Education* (New York: John Wiley and Sons, Inc., 1966).

Peters, Richard, *Authority, Responsibility and Education* (New York: Atherton Press, 1967).

Sayers, E. V., and Ward Madden, *Education and the Democratic Faith* (New York: Appleton-Century-Crofts, Inc., 1959), pp. 239–370.

THE PHILOSOPHICAL FOUNDATIONS OF EDUCATIONAL OBJECTIVES*

Harry S. Broudy

The term "philosophical foundations" implies that there are other types of foundations from which the philosophical ones are to be distinguished. Accordingly, we commonly speak of historical, psychological, and sociological foundations of education, as well as of philosophical ones. "Foundations," however, connotes a special relation between the parent disciplines (psychology, philosophy, etc.) and the study of educational problems. We probably would not speak of architecture or statistics as foundational to education, even though they are very useful to it. To get closer to the meaning of foundational in the sense that it will be used in this paper, it will be useful to dismiss the analogies with the building industry, funding agencies, and the art of corsetry that the word foundations suggests. About the only value these analogies have is that they convey a sense of priority and importance to foundational studies.

It would seem that a foundational discipline can contribute two sorts of things to the practice or study of education:

1. Empirical theories which by translation into observational statements and rules of procedure yield prescriptions for practice. The behavioral sciences in principle can provide theory that could be "applied" to problems of educational practice. One well-known example is the theory of operant conditioning which has been turned into a strategy of teaching; another is John Dewey's description of the complete act of thought.

2. A set of concepts that furnishes a special context for the study of educational problems, but not necessarily a causal hy-

* Reprinted from "The Philosophical Foundations of Educational Objectives," *Educational Theory*, 20 (1970): 3–21. By permission of the author and the editor of *Educational Theory*.

pothesis that can be translated into procedures and techniques. For example, history furnishes a frame of reference for the discussion of education but not rules of practice. Political science and some forms of sociology are also foundational in the sense that they offer distinctive patterns of interpretation.

Philosophy would have to be classed with the interpretative foundational disciplines, and its value is to be estimated not by the rules of procedure it supplies for practice, but rather by the illumination it casts on problems of practice, i.e., whether or not it makes them more intelligible, and the discussions of them more orderly and precise. And the value of such intelligibility, one must suppose, is that the more completely we are aware of the context of a problem, the less likely are we to produce unwanted and unintended side effects in our practice.

The contextual material that philosophy contributes to the consideration of educational objectives is both substantive and critical. It is substantive as a source of ideas about man, society, and nature that figure in the prescriptions for the good life. It is critical by virtue of its concern with the nature of knowledge and the criteria of truth. Philosophy thus assumes jurisdiction over all types of knowledge claims. We shall expect, therefore, to find in the philosophical foundations of educational objectives: (1) references to ideas taken from metaphysics, epistemology (theory of knowledge), ethics, and aesthetics, and (2) analysis of discourse about educational objectives, including the discourse in (1) but not excluding discourse from other contexts and disciplines.

I. Levels of Conceptualization in Educational Objectives

The statement of educational objectives serves several functions. First of all, it may be used as a slogan to solicit support. "The aim of education is growth," for example, invites approbation from right-minded people in general and from those who are unhappy with rigid curricula in particular. Because slogans are often employed for their persuasive efficacy, it is not always profitable to scrutinize them for descriptive accuracy.[1]

Second, the statement of objectives is supposed to help guide the educative process, as a goal or target directs a journey or shot. Because it is believed that choice among ends in education is possible, it is felt that such choice is also necessary, for otherwise means, presumably, could not be selected for relevance and fitness, and failure in this respect would render the whole enterprise irrational, i.e., aimless or vacillating.

In the third place, a statement of objectives is held to be a test to be applied to the educative process. Thus a school with the announced objective of matriculating 75 percent of all its graduates in Ivy League colleges would be condemned out of its own mouth if it placed only 50 percent in such institutions.

To state educational objectives is therefore important. However, it becomes a problem because life, like a big country, offers a wide choice of destinations. Educational objectives may be broad, narrow, remote, or proximate. They can be stated in terms of overt behavior, character traits, developmental tasks, life-styles, learning products, learning processes, tendencies, dispositions, habits; school outcomes, test results, generic operations; attitudinal syndromes and learning strategies; national security, rates of juvenile and adult delinquency, church attendance, and credit ratings. In short, anything anyone regards as desirable can become an educational objective and, not infrequently, a school objective.

The situation is further complicated because educational objectives refer to (1) goals at which school systems do in fact aim, and (2) goals a school system *ought* to aim at. Roughly, the first type is one for the behavioral sciences, sociology, anthropology, and perhaps political science to deal with. The second topic is usually taken to be in the province of philosophy, or that kind of philosophy which has to do with value—sometimes called

[1] B. Paul Komisar and James E. McClellan, "The Logic of Slogans," in *Language and Concepts in Education,* B. O. Smith and R. H. Ennis, eds. (Chicago: Rand McNally, 1961).

axiology. A school system is constrained to deal with both questions at the same time, at all times. It may be appropriate to speculate a moment on why this is so, because it throws light on the mixed character of lists of objectives encountered in the educational literature. Such lists are compiled by school superintendents and every curriculum committee. Some have 10 items; some, 50.

An examination of the history of education, or rather of educational literature, will support the hypothesis that at any given time, in a fairly well-developed culture, a system of instruction exists that purports to prepare its clients for success in that culture. The Egyptian schools at one time turned out scribes and accountants because desirable governmental jobs were available for them; the rhetorical schools of Greece and early Rome graduated men who became eminent because swaying the public was the way to political success. The medieval universities trained men to combine secular scholarship with Christian ideas and service in the ecclesiastical bureaucracy.

However, in every epoch some men criticized the success routes their contemporaries were traveling, and they endorsed or proposed educational designs that would turn men into other routes on the ground that *real* success lay in following these directions. Thus Socrates paid with his life for not using the forensic skills that the Sophists had perfected, and in which he was no doubt adept himself. In arguing and dying for a vision of life in which a transcendental truth, and virtue based on it, were to be the "real success" routes, he was proposing a style of education quite at odds with that of the actual schools of his time. Montaigne, Locke, and others heaped scorn upon the sort of verbalism and pedantry in which the late vestiges of scholasticism and the aberrations of classicism abounded. In our own time there is no dearth of examples. Schools are criticized because they are too devoted to vocational preparation and to the achievement of middle-class values. Ideal schools and ideal people, the critics aver, would be more creative, more spontaneous, more exciting, more "caring," and more relevant, whatever these terms may be taken to mean. So in every age the distinction has to be drawn between that at which schools do aim and that at which their critics say they ought to aim.

This is not to say that the schools uniformly produce the success to which they purport to be the routes. Curricula sometimes persist long after their utility is negated by changed circumstance. For example, the rhetorical curriculum in reduced form lived on long after oratory had ceased to be the road to political success. Today schools still make gestures toward a "liberal" education despite the fact that the Aristotelian notion of leisure, which was its rationale, is no longer—if it ever was—a valid premise for our culture, even for the upper classes. The liberal studies are listed in college catalogues, and some of them are required for undergraduate degrees, even though the liberal spirit—study for and only for the sake of self-cultivation—stipulated by Aristotle is hard to find in the American academic world.

And yet, if one examines the sentiments expressed by the schoolmasters in those diverse ages, one finds them professing ideals not very different from those of their critics. Isocrates, a most successful master of a most successful school of rhetoric, and Quintilian, another famous and successful schoolmaster, entertained high moral expectations for their pupils. The orator, said Quintilian, was the *good* man skilled in speaking and not merely a persuasive and eloquent pleader of causes. The school, however closely it is allied with the values of the dominant class of its time, no matter how tightly it hews to the success route of its day, is still an institution that embodies the professed ideals of the community. This internal division between the actual and the ideal within the school reflects the tension within individual men themselves.

The fact that lists of objectives contain aspirations as well as descriptions makes it impossible to comply with the demand that objectives always be stated in behavioral terms. In the first place, an aspiration aims at a situation that does not exist, and although "having the aspiration" does exist, translating it into behavioral terms presents problems. Second, some of the aspirational objectives are not behaviors at all, but rather dispositions to behaviors, and such dispositions are not easily tested by behaviors. Altruism, for example, is often listed as an outcome to be desired from a good education, but just what behavior is unequivocally and unmistakably a token or sign of altruism? In the third place, some school objectives, such as the formation of democratic attitudes, are not translatable into behavioral objectives because democratic attitudes are postures toward doing a wide variety of things. All of which does not mean that some educational objectives cannot and should not be stated in behavioral terms; rather, it warns against mindless adherence to a dogma that has relevance only in a restricted domain of education, viz., some of the terminal products of a course of instruction.

We can understand also, considering the variety of things men regard as good, why there is such a bewildering plethora of taxonomies of educational objectives. The net effect of this abundance is that, in order to preserve some semblance of clarity or sanity, discussion has to take place within one taxonomic system. Translation of taxonomies one into another is virtually impossible, and every attempt to bring them together into one overarching classification results in just one more taxonomy which no one besides its author feels obliged to consider, much less adopt.

Although there is no way at present of making different taxonomies of objectives comparable or translatable into each other, the chaos of every man with his own taxonomy may be mitigated by trying to sort them into types arranged at various levels of abstraction. After all, we do have to talk to each other about educational problems, and in doing so we cannot avoid talking about objectives. Meaningful communication in educational discourse depends on some uniformity in the connotation and denotation of terms. If A means by an "objective" something on the order of good citizenship and B means "critical thinking" while C means "ability to do problems in algebra," then it is fruitless for them to argue about problems of curriculum, methodology, and the organization of school systems. They pass each other as do vehicles on the multi-level clover-leafs of our modern expressways.

No less important are the consequences of the formulation of objectives for educational research. If objectives are stated as functions of numerous and elusive variables, e.g., good citizenship, growth, democratic living, mental health, then obviously they will resist empirical research. Furthermore, if objectives are too broad, educational research spills over into so many disciplines that it loses any distinctiveness it may claim; it gets lost in the sea of the behavioral sciences and may have to be turned over to them. This may be desirable for all I know, but we had better be fully aware of the possibility.

There is also the risk that research may be irrelevant to educational problems unless communication about objectives among all educational workers is possible. Thus countless studies on animal learning and human rote learning, however relevant and fruitful they are for learning theory, may be of trivial import so far as producing school outcomes are concerned. Contrariwise, research on how school learnings are actually used in nonschool situations may be stimulated, if objectives are formulated in terms of such uses, and if the different uses are distinguished both semantically and operationally. Time taken to conceptualize educational objectives carefully, critically, as precisely as possible is not wasted; casually, almost ritualistically, compiled lists of clichés are not only a waste of time, but a positive source of confusion and mystification.

II. Life Outcomes

Value Patterns as Objectives

Educational objectives are sometimes stated as value schema that are "borrowed" from metaphysics or ethics. Thus one might say that the goal of education is a life characterized by rationality, or virtue, or self-realization. Or with John Dewey it might be said that the aim of education is growth. In an important sense, however, it is not correct to say that education borrows these goals from philosophy, because a philosophical system that puts these characteristics at the top of its value hierarchy is already offering an educational prescription. Conversely, a set of educational aims stated at this level of generality is implicitly a philosophical position and needs only the explication of its arguments to become one. In other words, a general philosophical position does not *imply* a set of educational aims, it already *is* such a set. For such a position states criteria for the real and the true; and to say that one form of life is *more real* and *more true* than another is to say at the same time that it is *better* than another. As we shall have occasion to point out below, there is a school of philosophy that consigns all talk about Being, Substance, Perfection and other metaphysical notions to the limbo of a noncognitive misuse of language, but it is doubtful that this will really stop such talk either in philosophy or education.

The Platonic epistemology and metaphysics, for example, argue for a hierarchy of knowledge that is also a hierarchy of perfection. At the lowest rung is the knowledge we get by means of unstable images of things such as reflections in water or in shadows. Above it is the more stable, but still highly idiosyncratic, perception of individual objects that lies at the basis of belief. Higher on the ladder are the abstractions of science, and above them all are the Ideas themselves, the archetypes of reality apprehended by reason. The Eros, or the desiring element of the soul, follows the same ascending path from beautiful things and persons to the Idea of the Beautiful in itself.[2]

Clearly, such a schema is a prescription for the good life, and insofar as education is concerned with such matters, Plato's philosophical position is relevant to it. Abstraction as the road to perfection is a profound and radical formula that determines the pecking order of academic life. Its potency is felt not only in the prestige hierarchy of the diverse intellectual disciplines, but also, I take it, in all verbal intelligence testing.

Forms of Society as Objectives

At a somewhat lower level of generality, one can ask: What sort of society, what social and institutional arrangements would be needed to educate individual human beings to achieve a certain pattern of value? Could Plato's good life pattern, for example,

[2] *The Republic,* 509D-511E.

have been realized in a democracy? Could Dewey's good life be realized in a totalitarian state? The search for an answer is essentially the work of the social theorist and the political scientist. When an objective is phrased as the preservation of some form of the State or government, it creates demands for certain traits of character and behavior which, presumably, the educational system would either engender or reinforce. In a totalitarian state, obedience clearly has a higher priority than in a democratic one; the tendency to be critical and individualistic will find more reinforcement in a democracy than in a totalitarian state. But when a given form of political organization is challenged, the arguments mount to the first level of objectives, i.e., to some theory about the nature and good of man; some theory of perfection in terms of which the societal form is justified or rejected. For this reason, a set of educational objectives that takes the social or governmental form as an axiom or postulate has to preclude calling that form into question.

We see examples of this whenever questioning of the virtues of democracy brings charges of disloyalty and treason. We are put into the awkward position of having to say either that the principle of democracy prevents calling the principle itself into question, or that there is really no rational way of defending democracy against its critics.

As examples of how justifications for a given form of society are carried to a more general level, let us take the Hegelian argument for the primacy of the state and Dewey's defense of democracy.

Roughly paraphrased, Hegel's argument goes something like this: every human individual is finite, i.e., limited in his power, and to that extent is dependent on other objects or persons to achieve his goals. And to the degree that one is dependent he is unfree, frustrated, and to that degree imperfect. The community is an entity that is more comprehensive, more self-sufficient, more powerful, and therefore more real and more nearly perfect than the individuals who compose it. The individual becomes free, i.e., able to carry out his choices, if he joins his will to that of the community. The community's goals are more stable than those of the individual. By this line of reasoning, it does not take long to make out a case that true individuality is *really* achievable only in the most complete identification of self with the community or the State. The wisdom, the power, the glory, and the immortality of the State confer on each person who identifies with it genuine selfhood, genuine self-sufficiency, genuine individuality. One may quarrel with the argument, but there is sufficient truth in it to make it more than a verbal *tour de force*. Large numbers of men have accepted the doctrine and lived in states that exemplified it. I am not arguing the merits of the doctrine; it is simply an example of the point that one can take his ultimate stand on the preservation of the State and refuse to argue its merits, but if one does want to defend it rationally, it is to some metaphysical or ethical theory that one has to resort for concepts and arguments.[3]

The other example has to do with the way Dewey justifies democracy. In *Democracy and Education,* he argues that the good society is the one which permits the maximum of sharing of experience. Sharing is a key concept for Dewey, because if we did not try to share experience, we would not have to objectify it for communication, and this objectification is at the heart of knowing: knowledge reduces a culture to communicable form. A band of robbers, Dewey notes, is bad not only because of the harm it inflicts, but also because the act of robbing and the organization of robbery are in the nature of the case exclusive. Sharing is also the antidote to conflict and discontinuity, and if there could be absolutes for Dewey, continuity and harmony might well be candidates for that status. So here once more the argument is not that something is good because it is democratic, but rather democratic is an honorific term precisely because it is the means to a more fundamental good—sharing.[4]

The societal type of objective is needed in any full statement of

[3] Georg W. F. Hegel, *Philosophy of Right,* trans. T. M. Knox (Oxford: Clarendon Press, 1942).

[4] John Dewey, *Democracy and Education* (New York: Macmillan, 1961), Ch. 7.

objectives, but it cannot be the final goal of the school. If it is left out, then the list invites the conclusion that any form of government would do equally well in achieving the good life. One cannot rule out this possibility, but the evidence of history is even more against it than that a form of government guarantees the good life.

Even more important is the fact that the form of society conditions the ways in which the good life is achieved, so that to understand its workings, rationale, and one's relation to it is necessarily high on the school's agenda. Since the duties of citizenship are specific to the form of a society, they have to be taught with specific content, and the objectives should draw attention to this.

However, the greater danger is that already alluded to, viz., that the school so formulates its objectives that the form of society operates as if it were the final goal. It is one thing for a study to be prescribed because it is needed to exercise the functions of citizenship; it is quite another for the State to use its own welfare as a criterion of truth. Or to put it differently, it is defensible for the State to require that all pupils study the history of their country, but it is indefensible for the State to decide what constitutes "true" or "good" history. We need not recount the instances in which a State has decided what shall be good genetics, good art, and good literature. The danger lies not so much in whether the State makes good judgments in these matters, for conceivably it might make very good ones, but rather that for it to do so misconstrues the nature of knowledge and the criteria for judging the scholarship that produces it.

For there is no necessary connection between the political power of an idea or a theory and its truth. Ideas may be powerful if and because they are true, but their power is not the reason they are true. The existence of a criterion that is independent of political power, therefore, is essential if knowledge and truth are essential to the good life. The autonomy of the school as a social institution depends on its being able to appeal to the expertise of the scholar against the predilections of this or that group. For if anything can claim to transcend the cultural peculiarities of social groups, it is the tradition of intellectual inquiry.

The current demands of protestors on college campuses for a voice in the governance of the university illustrate the point at issue with sad but piercing clarity. As citizens in a democracy, the protestors have a right to demand a voice in the conduct of an institution that is sanctioned by the society of which they are members. All the rules of the game demand that political policies be settled by the weight of numbers translated into votes. That the students do not know enough to exercise this power is not a convincing excuse for withholding it. Citizens are not given achievement tests before they are allowed to cast their ballots for governors and presidents; why become so finicky in the case of college students wanting a voice in determining the policies of a university, especially a state university?

The proper retort, it seems, is that it depends on the policies under consideration. The limit of participatory democracy is reached when the content of courses and the qualifications of instructors are at issue. Being a student virtually implies lack of expertise in these domains. For these matters are not matters of opinion or desire or expediency in the sense that housing regulations, disciplinary rules, and the control of student organizations are. But if the ultimate criterion is voting power, there is no valid limit to its use, if the participants wish to have no limit. Only when theoretical room is left to question democracy or totalitarianism can there be a possible appeal from them. The autonomy of the school, therefore, is a prime concern when we evaluate educational objectives, and those who are content to derive them from some form of social organization should be quite clear about the price they are paying for it.

In this connection, it is interesting to note that the notions of natural law and natural rights—both metaphysical notions—are escape hatches from the tyranny of the State and the sovereign. In our own case, the Bill of Rights was promptly added to the Constitution for the purpose of enabling men to appeal beyond the law-making powers of the majority and the executive powers of officialdom. The Declaration of Independence speaks of unalienable rights, avowedly limiting the rights of the sovereign power to alienate them. Natural law serves the same purpose.

It may not be amiss, therefore, to suggest to compilers of lists of educational objectives that before they commit their school systems to the ideals of the Declaration of Independence or the Bill of Rights they read carefully the textbooks to be used in the social studies. If they find—as they are likely to—that the authors of the texts deny the validity of natural law and natural rights, the objectives had better carry extensive footnotes to explain the sense in which the ideals are to be understood and taught.

Social Roles as Objectives

It is natural to follow the form of society as an objective with the question: what role is the student expected to play in each of the institutions that make up the society? When linked with the broader objective above it, the requirements of institutional roles become means for attaining that higher objective which, in turn, is supposed to be conducive to the realization of the good life.

In the literature, one not infrequently finds the total list of objectives stated in terms of what it would take for the citizen to play roles in the family, church, government, the economy, etc. In a complex culture, some roles will be common to all members, e.g., being a member of a family, being a citizen, being a consumer; but some are specialized, e.g., that of a bank manager. By analyzing classes of tasks connected with these roles, one finds the skills, knowledge, and attitudes they seem to require, and the school makes these its more immediate objectives and constructs the curriculum accordingly.

Sociologists of education, and perhaps social psychologists, typically undertake this type of analysis. Strictly speaking, at this level, the statement of objectives should be free from normative considerations. Presumably, the social scientists can specify objectively and dispassionately diverse roles and statuses and the obstacles thereto and facilitations thereof. Much more probable is the conjecture that these social scientists and their educational counterparts operate from an implicit vision of the ideal society and the ideal life. The characteristics of the good life are taken as understood, just as the total form of the society is taken for granted. Without repeating the arguments in the previous section, it should be clear that taken as means to the higher objectives this approach makes sense; taken as the complete analysis of objectives it does not. Again it must be noted that institutional roles depend on the form of the good life for their validation, and not the other way around. Furthermore, the specialized roles within a society may change—the case of family roles and vocational roles are obvious examples of the school mistakenly assuming that they would remain constant. The rate of social change has produced an ever greater number of individual differentiations in life needs, but at the same time has made it more and more difficult to anticipate these needs by differentiated instruction. Paradoxically, the greater the variety of social roles and tasks, the greater may be the premium on general education, the sort that really is generalizable.

Life Styles as Objectives

Sometimes it is possible to combine the first three types of objectives in what might be called a life-style. Given the form of society, an ideal of the good life value patterns, and the institutional roles of a given period, there emerges an image of something like the English country squire, the courtier of the Renaissance, the industrial tycoon, or the religious saint, or the rugged, individualistic, honest citizen of frontier days in this country.

In *The Republic,* Plato described the degeneration of the State in terms of the aristocratic man (or his sons), characterized by a love of wisdom, turning into the timocratic man who is dominated by a love of honor, into the oligarchic man, the man whose main motive is wealth, to the democratic man who is in love with his desires, to the tyrannical man whose obsession with power and lust destroys him.[5] "Thus, when nature or habit or both have

[5] 543E-588A.

combined the traits of drunkenness, lust, and lunacy, then you have the perfect specimen of the despotic man."[6]

Aristotle does some similar character typing in the *Nicomachean Ethics* as examples of various combinations of excess and deficiency in the emotional life.[7] Thus the liberal man exemplifies the mean between stinginess and vulgarity in the matter of expenditures, and the brave man exhibits the mean between cowardice and rashness. Plutarch's *Lives* for centuries was a source of life-styles as a basis for character education in the schools. When so described, life-styles are objectives at a high level of abstraction, but when they are personified they become much more concrete. Leonardo da Vinci, for example, is more concrete as a model than the "Renaissance man"; St. Francis more than a "religious saint."

Educationally, the role of such models is not to be underestimated. Such personified images are among our most potent pedagogical resources if they seduce considerable proportions of the younger generation into imitating them. Horatio Alger heroes and Frank Merriwell were seductive models for an earlier generation; without such models, character education limps. To be sure, writers on education do not list "to be like Jackie (Kennedy) Onassis" or "to be like the Beatles" as educational objectives, but who doubts that in children as well as in their parents educational objectives take this form?

The objectives we have been discussing might be called life outcomes rather than school outcomes. The distinction is related to that between education taken in its broad sense and in its narrower sense of schooling or formal instruction. These differences are important not only because the latter is a relatively small part of the former, but also because they are qualitatively different. That is to say, the informal portion of education, in the broad sense of the word, is virtually the same as learning. It goes on with or without the awareness of the learner, and often there is no teacher other than the maze of interactions we call life. Formal education, on the other hand, is structured in terms of means and

6 IX, 572.
7 III, 6–V, II.

ends, and although some learning occurs outside of the teacher's plans or in spite of them, it is what one *means* to do that counts as the criteria of formal schooling.

In the broad sense, education goes on almost from cradle to the grave. The skein of factors that enter into it is a tangle that defies complete analysis. This type of learning is not, to any appreciable extent, within our control. Final estimates of its extent and worth are impossible so long as the subject is still alive—and learning. For these reasons a life-style, a form of society, a value pattern are not school outcomes, nor can we fully identify and isolate the part that schooling will play in their development. Efforts to establish a tight correlation between school inputs and this sort of result are misguided precisely because the end result is the effect of so many causes over which we have no control, many of which we cannot even clearly identify, and of some of which we are totally unaware.

The slogan, "Down with nonbehavioral objectives" has a two-fold effect: first, of creating the illusion that if these life outcomes could be formulated in behavioral terms, we could fashion schooling so as to produce them more efficiently; e.g., if we could "behavioralize" democracy, our schools would produce it without straying from the path leading to the goal, as if our failure to render democracy triumphant is to be blamed on our inability to "point" to it.

In the second place, the slogan, taken literally and seriously, makes the school wary of all life outcomes, precisely because they resist translation into behavioral language, the language of observables. We may be able to avoid both of these consequences if we distinguish the role each type of objective plays in educational thinking.

Life outcomes such as have been described thus far in this paper are schema for the interpretation of life as a whole. They are patterns of action rather than aggregates of behaviors. Granted that for purposes of instruction these patterns need to be broken down into observable behaviors by the teacher; nevertheless the criterion for the success of the analysis is whether or not the total pattern has a certain quality or character. The satisfactory personality or the good looking face has a quality (a *Gestaltqualität*) that is a function of the way elements are put together and not merely the sum of these elements—something that Gestalt psychology insists upon and which ordinary experience supports. Life outcomes stress the relational features, and it is to these that philosophy, especially when done in a certain way, is specially relevant.

To sum up the discussion thus far, life outcomes are to be achieved and used during adult life and presumably to be retained throughout life. This means that they cannot, as they stand, be adopted as immediate objectives for schooling. For one thing, the school has no way of isolating its part in the result; for another, it has no way of checking out whether the result ever accrues. Nor is it clear as to what we shall regard as sufficient evidence for the presence or absence of the result. Metaphysical characteristics, social goals, generic roles, personality types, and life styles are ways of justifying *school* objectives and can be the matrix of them, but they are not to be mistaken for them. The aim of education as a whole, for example, can properly be said to be rational freedom or self-realization, but it is not the aim of any school. On the other hand, if a school is challenged to defend its objectives, it may have to end up with a commitment to self-realization or some equally general quality as its ultimate criterion of goodness.

III. School Outcomes

School outcomes more properly refer to the terminal products of instruction. They are proximate rather than distant and usually do specify the knowledge, skill, or attitude that is supposed to accrue as a result of instruction. Presumably the school has considerable control over the inputs and the relations between them and the expected outputs. For example, if it is said that the aim of the arithmetic course is to enable the student to do decimals or multiply fractions, then presumably the relation between the instruction and the outcome has been established with a high degree of probability.

School outcomes can be arranged in a general-particular continuum in a number of ways. Thus a continuum could be constructed so that the particular end could be represented by content while the general end could be represented by operations, e.g., critical thinking, imagining, etc. Or contents could be sorted into those that have high or low degrees of generalizability, e.g., math, high; names of presidents, low. Or the goals could be stated in terms of the way in which learnings are to be used, e.g., by using them replicatively, i.e., as learned; associatively, as relatively undetermined responses to a class of stimuli; interpretively, as means of organizing stimuli by conceptual or other schemata; applicatively, to solve problems that have not been practiced during instruction.

There is a sense in which school objectives always claim implicitly that the outcomes will function beyond the period of instruction. Critical thinking, use of a subject matter for subsequent thinking or the solving of problems, and even attitudes toward learning or life tasks are supposed to manifest themselves after schooling. Hence the assumption is that there is a relation between doing the school task and performing the life task, such that if the school does something in its instruction, the life tasks will show its effects.

Two quite different problems are involved here, but I shall only mention them. One is establishing the causal connection, and this is, I suppose, the task of educational psychology, teaching methodology, and curriculum construction. The other is analysis of the logical and epistemic relations between a given piece of instruction and the life tasks to which it purports to be relevant. This is essentially a problem for the philosophy of education. For example, what constitutes a proper explanation, a definition, or inference is a philosophical question. It can be raised in the various subject matters of instruction and the uses of those subject matters in thinking about any kind of problem. Lacking full and facile awareness of the logical and the psychological nature of learning and teaching, the teacher has no way of distinguishing among responses symptomatic of rote learning, pseudo-understanding, and of genuine ability to use learning in the applicative and interpretive modes.[8]

It is only after such philosophical and methodological questions are discussed, if not settled, that the objectives can be brought down to the more specific levels that we call course objectives, unit objectives, lesson objectives, and even objectives of episodes within the lesson. That we are far from agreement on the way school learnings are used in life tasks partly explains, to my way of thinking, why our taxonomies of educational objectives are so disparate and why lesson objectives and course objectives lack a credible relationship with the life outcomes to which they purport to be the means.

IV. Philosophy and Educational Objectives

As substantive, philosophy contributes to educational objectives certain ideas about reality, truth, and value as well as arguments for their justification; as critical, philosophy examines the validity of these aguments.

Philosophy has always been both substantive and critical, but in this country and Great Britain during the last half-century professional philosophy has been primarily concerned with the critical side of the enterprise. This has taken two major forms: logical positivism and language analysis.

Logical positivism emanated from the Vienna Circle, a group of philosophers who gathered around Moritz Schlick in the Twenties. These men were interested in science and mathematics, and they hoped to develop by logical analysis a type of philosophizing that would itself be scientifically respectable. Influenced by Ludwig Wittgenstein's *Tractatus logico-philosophicus*,[9] the Circle dedicated itself to showing (*a*) that all human knowledge is built up out of the data of experience, especially sense experience, (*b*) that propositions that could not be reduced to statements about

---

[8] In this connection, see Robert H. Ennis, *Logic in Teaching* (Englewood Cliffs, N.J.: Prentice-Hall, Inc., 1969).

[9] London, 1921: translated, London, 1922.

observable items in experience were both literally and figuratively nonsense, i.e., meaningless, and (c) that philosophy that talked about nonobservables was to be dismissed as disguised expressions of wishes rather than as description of anything.[10]

Ordinary language analysis grew out of the realization that if knowledge was to be restricted to scientific use of language, then most of life and discourse was not scientific. Accordingly, philosophers became curious about the meanings of nonscientific uses of language. Wittgenstein in his later work[11] argued that we used language in many ways. In addition to using it for describing states of affairs, we use it to command, interrogate, and to express feelings. There is no commonality to these uses; they are like games which have only a "family resemblance" to each other. No type of discourse is basic or privileged. Language "games," within which alone words have any meaning, are human activities carried on according to the rules of the particular game being played. The study of these language games, therefore, gives an insight to the culture which produced them.

It followed, therefore, that the task of philosophy was to explicate and clarify the meaning of propositions, exhibit the rules of the game being played, and to get rid of those notions which pretended to describe, but really were doing nothing of the sort. In other words, the substantive type of philosophy could be regarded as a form of language sickness which proper language analysis would diagnose and perhaps even cure. However, according to one writer, Wittgenstein's account of "previous philosophy as pathological does not seem to have been confirmed by much therapeutic success. The problems he aimed to dissolve have obstinately refused to stay dead."[12] This development of philosophy has had its counterpart in educational philosophy. Much of the current writing is in this vein of language analysis.[13]

[10] *The Vienna Circle: Its Scientific World-Conception,* 1929.

[11] *Philosophical Investigations* (London: Oxford, 1953).

[12] A. M. Quinton, "Contemporary British Philosophy," in *A Critical History of Western Philosophy,* D. J. O'Connor, ed. (Glencoe, Ill.: The Free Press, 1964), p. 543.

[13] For a recent bibliography on this approach, see H. S. Broudy, M. J. Parsons, I. A. Snook, and R. D. Szoke, *Philosophy of Education: An Or-*

Substantive views about the nature of reality, of truth, of goodness, and of beauty traditionally have been the concern of metaphysics, ethics, epistemology, and aesthetics. A fully developed philosophical system would have views in each of these departments, and the philosopher would take pains to make his epistemology, metaphysics, ethics, and aesthetics consistent with each other. We think of Plato, Aristotle, Descartes, St. Thomas Aquinas, Kant, Hegel, as examples of the systematic philosopher. Various names have been given to these systems: Platonic Realism, Moderate Realism, Idealism, Stoicism, Pragmatism, and a half-hundred others. These names classify views by identifying them with a leading idea, or an approach, or a style of philosophizing, and like other forms of labeling are justified only by the time and thought they save.

These systematic theories—mixtures of observation, reflection, and speculation—were about the nature of man, his relation to nature, to other men, and to God. Ethics developed principles by which one defined, clarified, and justified what was worthwhile pursuing in life, what was to be judged right and wrong, and the conditions under which men could be held blameworthy and praiseworthy for what they did. For example, Plato could conceive of no better life than that which would result from the complete governance of life and society by Ideas, archetypes of absolute goodness, truth, and beauty. His guardians—the philosopher-statesmen—were to be men in whom a glimpse of these Ideas provided them and the State with sure touchstones for legislation and education.

One could list the systems of philosophy that have flourished in the world, but it is not the purpose of this paper to do so. The relevant point is that these ideas about life have been woven into the fabric of the human mind and consequently become operative when men set about formulating the objectives of education.

Philosophical ideas find their way into educational thinking in several ways. One likely route runs somewhat as follows: the convictions of the common man are subjected to reflective scru-

ganization of Topics and Selected Sources (Urbana: University of Illinois Press, 1967).

tiny by philosophers. The refined versions of these convictions, plus more or less of the reasoning behind them, find their way into the schooling of the educated classes; they produce and read materials that embody the ideas. As a result, the language and concepts of an age reflect these ideas. It has been argued, for example, that our ordinary way of saying that "the grass is green" assumes an Aristotelian metaphysics of a substance "grass" being able to take on the attributes "greenness." Or it may be, as others have charged, that Aristotle's metaphysics merely formalizes the grammatical structure of the Greek language. On either hypothesis, we can understand why analytic philosophers have felt that it was their duty to rid the language of these metaphysical ingredients.

I have already mentioned the deeply ingrained value syndrome that was made explicit in the metaphysics of Plato and Aristotle, viz., that the ladder of perfection paralleled the ladder of abstraction: the more theoretical the activity of man, the better the man. This value scale is still widely accepted, although it has repeatedly been challenged by those who believed that religious faith, strong will, and social action should rank higher than the contemplative life for which Plato and Aristotle reserved the highest rank. Today the dependence of our culture on science and science-based technology has made idea power the basic and ultimate form of power. The intellectual has come into his own.

Another example is furnished by the influence on American thought and education by the philosophy of John Locke. Natural rights, constitutional law, separation of church and state, religious toleration, and empiricism are among the notions that not only impressed the founding fathers but their descendants ever since. To be sure, today Locke is thought of as the arch defender of the middle class, but this tribe is far from extinct, and despite many reasons for believing that his liberalism with its emphasis on private property may no longer fit the requirements of a bureaucratic industrial state, his ideas are still influential, not only in political, but in educational circles.

Said Locke,

. . . I imagine you would think him a very foolish Fellow, that would not value a virtuous or a wise Man infinitely before a great Scholar. Not but that I think Learning a great Help to both in well-dispos-'d minds; but yet it must be confess'd also, that in others not so dispos'd, it helps them only to be the more foolish, or worse Men. I say this, that when you consider of the Breeding of your Son, and are looking out for a School-Master or a Tutor, you would not have (as is usual) Latin and Logick only in your Thoughts. Learning must be had, but in the second Place subservient only to greater Qualities. Seek out somebody that may know how discreetly to frame his Manners: Place him in Hands where you may, as much as possible, secure his Innocence, cherish and nurse up the good, and gently correct and weed out any bad Inclinations, and settle him in good Habits. This is the main Point, and this being provided for, Learning may be hand into the Bargain, and that, as I think, at a very easy rate, by Methods that may be thought on.[14]

The catalogue of the "good" small liberal arts college until recently reflected the objectives of education that were dear to Locke: virtue, wisdom, breeding, and learning. Scholarship, sheer intellectual activity, was put well below good breeding, and this, in turn, below virtue, which was closely tied to religious training, and wisdom, which consisted largely in managing one's affairs with prudence. The advent of the high-powered intellectual onto the staff of this type of college has changed this emphasis, because Ph.D.'s tend to be of the same stripe as far as their evaluation of academic excellence is concerned. But the trustees and alumni of these colleges—many of them private—are reluctant to surrender the college to intellectuals. Virtue, wisdom, and breeding in their book, as in Locke's, are to be at the top; learning could be pursued in the graduate school.

Clearly not all philosophical systems have had equal impact on the formulation of educational objectives. Those philosophers who had things to say about education, naturally, were more likely to be read by schoolmasters and those who wrote for schoolmasters.

However, in the class of men who were both interested in for-

---

[14] *Some Thoughts Concerning Education,* par. 147.

mal philosophy and in problems of education, one would be inclined to mention Rousseau, Froebel, Herbart, and John Dewey as having the most direct and powerful impact on conceptions of education in modern times. By trying to say what education *really* is, i.e., how it should properly be conceived, they were, of course, proposing the life outcomes for which education ought to be responsible.

Bringing such materials to the prospective worker in education, to reiterate a point mentioned earlier, is the function of the philosophical foundations of education, but in addition it is also the function of such workers to formulate educational theories of their own that incorporate ideas from philosophy, and to carry on a critical examination of theories that do so. This criticism is undertaken in an attempt to test the adequacy of a theory in terms of its internal consistency and its systematic completeness. Those who make philosophy of education an academic specialty, therefore, not only teach courses to prospective workers in education—and to anyone else who might be interested—but also bring their scholarship to bear on the materials to be taught.

One might question the need for a specialized personnel in the philosophy of education. After all, schoolmen can read, and they, together with the bulk of classroom teachers, have a bachelor's degree or something approaching it. Surely in these encounters with general education they could have been expected to learn how to read the philosophers on their own, and to extract from them the ideas needed for discourse about education.

Unfortunately, in the first place, having attended a liberal arts college does not guarantee that the student has had formal work in philosophy or more than the minimum required for graduation. In the second and more important place, general philosophers have only side glances for education, whereas what is called for is the reading of philosophy for its relevance to educational problems. Finally, as a result of the sins of omission and commission, the average school worker has acquired a collection of notions about education and life that exhibit little consistency, system, or completeness.

Currently, the substantive and the analytical contributions of philosophy to the formulation of educational objectives are being made by different sets of people, although there may be a few notable exceptions. This is true both in general and educational philosophy. One group talks about the problems of education or educational theory in terms of Idealism, Realism, Pragmatism, Existentialism, etc. This group is also likely to discourse in terms of ideas taken from metaphysics, epistemology, ethics, and social philosophy. The other group elucidates ideas, sorts them into logical types, and assays the meanings that can be properly attributed to them. Not the least part of their job is to convince their readers that much of what the substantive philosophers have had to say about education is either false or meaningless, and that many of the alleged "problems" in education are the results of the misuse of language.

As might be expected, the two groups do not regard each others' work with unrestricted enthusiasm. The substantive philosophers regard the analysts as playing language games that do not really generate any ideas for schooling while tearing down the ideas of others; the analysts regard the substantive philosophers as mixing up metaphysics with science, wishes with fact, and emotive use of language with the descriptive.

Without in any way attempting to settle this controversy or even to make peace between the parties, a few observations may help to clarify the issues:

1. Much is made by the analytical group of the argument that, from traditional philosophical doctrines, nothing can be deduced as to what ought to be done in the way of school policy or practice. For one thing, a philosophical principle, e.g., education is self-realization, is so general that it tells us nothing about the proximate steps that have to be taken to bring self-realization about, nor does it provide a criterion for choosing one method over another. More important, however, is the principle that the way things are does not prove that they ought to be that way; usually they can stand improvement.

Both of these arguments are cogent, but their importance rests on a misunderstanding of the role that philosophical doctrines play in educational thought and practice. One can no more deduce a method of teaching children to read from the principle of self-realization than one can invent a new form of transportation by reciting Newton's laws of motion. One would have to consult the behavioral sciences for rules and principles that would give more specific guidance about what educational procedures would or would not produce self-realization. This does not mean that "self-realization" is useless or meaningless as an educational objective, but it is useful for interpretation rather than for application.

2. This brings us to the second objection, viz., that from the principle, for example, that all beings try to actualize their potentialities, one cannot conclude that they ought to. Perhaps they should not actualize their potentialities for cruelty and stupidity. But again, metaphysical "descriptions" are also descriptions of a value hierarchy; they purport to be value facts and facts about value. One may reject these "descriptions" as unverifiable, but metaphysical statements do not claim empirical verifiability as the evidence for their truth. So it is difficult to see how peace can be achieved on this issue on theoretical grounds. But practically, education must get its value orientations somewhere, and if it does not get them from philosophical doctrines, it has to take them from the *mores* of the group or the customs of the culture. The difficulties of defending such a procedure have already been touched upon; it precludes the possibility of subjecting the basic values of a school system to rational scrutiny. Once put to such a scrutiny, appeal would have to be made to a higher principle of value determination, and one would be back into metaphysical questions once more.

The educational enterprise can utilize both types of philosophizing, and each group would contribute more if it did "its own thing," so to speak, without spending so much time in denigrating what the other was doing. Examples of tasks that the analytical philosophers can help with are sharpening distinctions between teaching and learning, the analysis of subject matters in terms of differential cognitive operations, and the adequacy of various psychological theories for educational theory.[15]

[15] Cf. Smith and Ennis, eds., *Language and Concepts in Education,* passim.

Summary

This paper has tried to identify, exemplify, and justify the role of philosophy in the formulation and discussion of educational objectives. It was thought advisable to do this by first exhibiting the various levels of generality at which objectives could be conceptualized, the relations between them, and the way in which philosophical materials and approaches made their contribution to the objectives at the various levels. It was concluded that (1) substantive philosophy makes its contribution to objectives at their most general level by providing value hierarchies or value schemata that are either made explicit or are implicit in systematic positions on metaphysics, epistemology, and ethics. (2) Analytical philosophy makes its major contribution by clarifying ideas and evaluating their logical and linguistic adequacy in educational discourse. Generally this applies more directly to the lower-level objectives, but all levels of educational discourse are subject to critical analysis. (3) Although the two types of philosophizing tend to be done by different personnel within educational philosophy, both are needed. (4) Because philosophy's contribution to educational objectives is complex, and because it comes into educational literature in so many ways, there is a need for people trained in philosophy of education to do scholarly work in making sure that the ideas and procedures taken from philosophy are used with precision and with some concern for internal consistency and systematic adequacy. (5) Finally, such scholarly work should have a salutary effect in selecting and organizing the materials taught to prospective workers in education.

WORTHWHILE ACTIVITIES*

R. S. Peters

Things, of course, can be good in the sense that they are instrumental to or lead on to other things that are good. Similarly many answers to the question "What ought I to do?" advise on policies and courses of action which will promote what is good or what is in the interest of a particular individual. We are not here concerned with such instrumental or technical judgments but with judgments about the activities or states of affairs which are intrinsically good, from which instrumental or technical judgments derive their normative force. That there must be such judgments about ends is obvious enough. Otherwise giving reasons for actions would be an endless enterprise. It is with judgments such as these, which are answers to the questions "Why do this rather than that?" when instrumental considerations are ruled out, that we are here concerned. In the next chapter we will touch briefly on instrumental judgments about means.

What has to be shown, therefore, is why a person who asks the question "Why do this rather than that?" must pick out activities having certain characteristics rather than others. The first step must be to make explicit what seriously asking this question presupposes, for such reflection about activities is surely something that some do in varying degrees and others scarcely at all. The obvious point to make, first of all, is that asking this question seriously presupposes that the questioner is capable, to a certain extent, of a noninstrumental and disinterested attitude. He can see, in other words, that there are considerations intrinsic to activities themselves which constitute reasons for pursuing them, as distinct from considerations connected with what such activities might lead up to, which usually relate to the satisfaction

* From *Ethics and Education* by R. S. Peters, pp. 80–90. Copyright George Allen and Unwin, Ltd., 1966. Reprinted by permission of Scott, Foresman and Company, George Allen and Unwin, Ltd., and the author.

of what Plato called the "necessary appetites." It is surprising, as a matter of fact, how many people are strangers to this attitude. This type of probing is not pushed very far by the majority of men. Their way of life over and above those things which they do because of their station and its duties, because of general social rules, and because of palpable considerations of their interest is largely the outcome of habit, social pressure, sympathy, and attraction toward what is immediately pleasurable.

What considerations, then, could there be which would induce a man to choose one activity rather than another once he has achieved the degree of disinterestedness and detachment necessary to pose this as a serious question? The answer must be that considerations must derive from the nature of the activities themselves and the possible relations between them within a coherent pattern of life. Insofar as he is capable of asking this question of his life generally, he must also be capable of appreciating that particular activities can be appraised because of the standards immanent in them rather than because of what they lead on to. For how else, in general, could this attitude of disinterestedness be learned save by participating in activities which had their own built-in standards of excellence? It is significant that the Greeks, when they asked this question of their life, turned naturally to the analogy of the arts. They looked at their lives as a whole in ways made familiar to them by engaging in artistic creation and appreciation, which are paradigm cases of disinterested activity. It is, therefore, not surprising that the good life for them was the supreme example of an art. Aristotle's man of practical wisdom is the man who is an artist in shaping his own conative tendencies and giving expression to them in an appropriate manner on the appropriate occasion. One of Socrates' most telling criticisms of Thrasymachus in the *Republic* was his contention that if knowledge is involved in the life of the superman as well as the mere pursuit of power, then there must be, taking the analogy of other practical arts, limits and standards determining right and wrong ways of doing things. If a man is going to be an artist even in something as limited as self-aggrandizement, there must be standards defining skillful and appropriate ways of bringing about even this end which are important to him. Machiavelli obviously admired the "virtue" of the Prince which he displayed in inviting all his enemies to supper and putting them all to death in one masterly stroke.

It has been argued already that to understand characterizations such as elegant, ingenious, shrewd, appropriate, neat, and cogent from the inside is, in a sense, to be positively inclined toward doing things in some ways rather than others. Such considerations must have an appeal to a person who is capable of appraising activities purely from the point of view of what is involved in them. They pick out the pleasures characteristic of these activities. But there are other dimensions of such activities. To ask the question "Why do this rather than that?" cannot be divorced from questions of time and commitment. An activity must go on for a time, and, if one is deciding to spend time in one way rather than another, surely questions relating to boredom must be relevant. From this point of view there must be some kind of preference for activities which are capable of holding a person's attention for a certain span of time and which provide constant sources of pleasure and satisfaction. Washing glasses requires a certain amount of skill and attention; but the thought of spending hours at it must surely appall any reflective person if it is regarded as something which is intrinsically worthwhile rather than as necessary for health or domestic harmony. But blowing glass is quite another matter. When glass has to be shaped, it is resistant and full of surprises in ways that it is not when, in its finished form, it has to be washed. Anyone, therefore, who is thinking seriously about how to spend his time cannot but go for activities which afford rich opportunities for employing his wits, resources, and sensitivities in situations in which there is a premium on unpredictability and opportunities for skill—and a sense of the fitting. Activities based on the satisfaction of the necessary appetites will thus become transformed. Eating will be transformed into elaborate dinners where great skill and taste can be shown in the selection of dishes and drinks and in the opportunities afforded for conversation; sex will become transformed into an elaborate display of skill and sensitivity in the art of courting and making love. Both will be invested with all sorts of skills and standards, and both will be spun out to circumvent their transience. And both, of course, can degenerate into highly civilized perversions.

Another dimension involved in asking the question "Why do this rather than that?" must be that of mutual compatibility. This is where talk of happiness, integration, and the harmony of the soul has application. The question is not whether something should be indulged in *for the sake of* something else, but whether indulging in some activity to a considerable extent is compatible with indulging in another which may be equally worthwhile. A man who wants to give equal expression to his passions for golf, gardening, and girls is going to have problems, unless he works out his priorities and imposes some sort of schedules on the use of his time. And there may be some worthwhile activities that simply cannot be combined in a coherent pattern of life—athletics, for instance, and observing the nocturnal habits of animals. The coherence theory of goodness has obvious application when this dimension of the question "Why do this rather than that?" is opened up. The appeal to coherence, however, may be necessary; but it cannot be sufficient. For trivial activities could be combined in a coherent pattern of life, and it gives no ground for grading activities which might be mutually compatible.

The Case for Curriculum Activities

This defect of the coherence theory might be regarded as a general defect of the argument to date. For no reason has yet been produced to show that the pursuit of science or art is any more worthwhile than playing golf or bridge, which share the character of being disinterested, civilized, and skillful pursuits. Yet it is the former rather than the latter types of activities which feature on the curriculum of schools and universities.

To justify the special importance of curriculum activities, considerations could be produced relating to their point; reference could also be made to the opportunities provided for discrimination and skill. In relation to the first type of consideration philosophers have usually produced strong arguments for theoretical activities. They have claimed, not altogether convincingly, that the objects of most activities have certain obvious disadvantages when compared with the pursuit of truth or the creation of beauty. The ends of eating and sex, for instance, depend to a large extent on bodily conditions which are cyclic in character and which limit the time which can be spent on them; there are no such obvious limitations imposed on theoretical activities. The objects, too, of the life of the politician, of the businessman, or of the philanderer are necessarily competitive. If one man acquires power, riches, or a mistress like Aspasia, this means that others are disappointed; but in theoretical activities, although there are acute rivalries and although fashions exert a terrible tyranny, it is absurd to conceive of the object of pursuit under the aspect of ownership or possession. It is absurd for a man to be jealous of another philosopher in the same sort of way as he might be jealous of his wife's lover, or of a business rival. Questions of scarcity of the object cannot arise either, for no one is prevented from pursuing truth or painting pictures if many others get absorbed in the same quest . . . .

Theoretical activities could also be defended in respect of the unending opportunities for skill and discrimination which they provide. Most activities consist in bringing about the same state of affairs in a variety of ways under differing conditions. One dinner differs from another just as one game of bridge differs from another. But there is a static quality about them in that they both have either a natural or a conventional objective which can be attained in a limited number of ways. In science or history there is no such attainable objective. For truth is not an object that can be attained; it is an aegis under which there must always be progressive development. To discover something, to falsify the views of one's predecessors, necessarily opens up fresh things to be discovered, fresh hypotheses to be falsified. There must therefore necessarily be unending opportunities for fresh discrimination and judgment and for the development of further skills . . . .

Some of these are quite good arguments for pursuing science or philosophy as if they were what we call games or pastimes; but they are unconvincing because science or philosophy or history manifestly are not just pastimes, and it is from the character which they share over and above what they have in common with games and pastimes that the strongest arguments for them derive. The first is the nature of their cognitive concern. Insofar as knowledge is involved in games and pastimes, this is limited to the isolated end of the activity which may be morally indifferent. A man may know a great deal about cricket if he is a devotee of the game; but it would be fanciful to pretend that his concern to find out things is linked with any serious purpose, unless the game is viewed under an aesthetic or moral aspect. Cricket is classed as a game because its end is morally unimportant. Indeed, an end has almost to be invented to make possible the various manifestations of skill. What a cricketer or onlooker knows is therefore harnessed to his intention of playing or judging cricket. If, however, he is interested in cricket as a sociologist or psychologist might be, then his interest is really in the behavior of men as exemplified in cricket, not in judging or playing cricket for its own sake.

It may well be that people in fact come to understand each other better, to cooperate better with them, and to develop fine moral characters as a result of playing cricket. It may, too, be of great social value in the integration of a community. Games may thus be of educational value; indeed, play generally may be regarded as an important vehicle of education because "serious" things may be better assimilated when they are not taught primarily under this aspect. Cricket, too, when seen through the eyes of a Neville Cardus,[1] may acquire an aesthetic dimension. But if the participants in games come to *look on* games as exercises in morality, aesthetic grace, or in understanding others, they cease to be merely games. Often in golf people have to be reminded that it is "only a game." This is tantamount to saying that playing it supremely well or badly, or winning or losing, should not be regarded as significant from the point of view of the universe, or made significant because of a suggestion to play for £5 rather than 5s. Conversely when people say that politics has become

[1] A commentator famous for his lyrical and perceptive writing about cricket.

"merely a game" they imply that an end has been set up like the maintenance of power which has become morally adrift and arbitrarily set aside and isolated from the moral concerns of a community.

Curriculum activities, on the other hand, such as science, history, literary appreciation, and poetry are "serious" in that they illuminate other areas of life and contribute much to the quality of living. They have, secondly, a wide-ranging cognitive content which distinguishes them from games. Skills, for instance, do not have a wide-ranging cognitive content. There is very little to know about riding bicycles, swimming, or golf. It is largely a matter of "knowing how" rather than of "knowing that," of knack rather than of understanding. Furthermore what there is to know throws very little light on much else. In history, science, or literature, on the other hand, there is an immense amount to know, and if it is properly assimilated, it constantly throws light on, widens, and deepens one's view of countless other things.

Some games in which skills are systematized, such as bridge and chess, have considerable cognitive content; but this is largely internal to them. Part of what is meant by calling something a "game" is that it is set apart from the main business of living, complete in itself, and limited to particular times and places. Games can be conceived of as being of educational importance only insofar as they provide opportunities for acquiring knowledge, qualities of mind and character, aesthetic grace, and skills that have application in a wider area of life. Their importance for moral education, for instance, is obvious enough. For virtues such as courage, fairness, persistence, and loyalty have to be exhibited in a pre-eminent degree in many games—especially those that involve teamwork. Others give scope for judgment, coolheadedness, and insight into other people's motives. The presumption of those who believe in the educational importance of games is that the situations which they present, and in which virtues have to be cultivated and exercised, are relevantly similar to situations in life of a less self-contained character.

Science, history, literary appreciation, philosophy, and other such cultural activities are like games in that they are disinterested pursuits. They can be, and to a large extent are, pursued for the sake of values intrinsic to them rather than for the sake of extrinsic ends. But their cognitive concerns and far-ranging cognitive content give them a value denied to other more circumscribed activities which leads us to call them serious pursuits. They are "serious" and cannot be considered merely as if they were particularly delectable pastimes, because they consist largely in the explanation, assessment, and illumination of the different facets of life. They thus insensibly change a man's view of the world. A man who has read and digested Burke finds it difficult to look on Americans in quite the same way; his concept of jealousy develops overtones after seeing Othello. If he is also a trained scientist he scarcely sees the same world as his untrained contemporary, for he is being trained in modes of thought that cannot be tied down to particular times and places. A man who devotes himself to a game, on the other hand, does not thereby equip himself with a cognitive content that spills over and transforms his view of other things in life. He may, of course, regard other activities such as war or politics as if they are games of cricket on a large scale. This may shape his attitude to other activities. But it will not transform his understanding of them in the way that a study of psychology, social science, and history should. It may well be that those who stood their ground resolutely at Waterloo learned to do something very similar on the playing fields of Eton. But they did not learn to reason why there, nor to see in such a battle what Tolstoy saw on the fields of Borodino.

The point, then, about activities such as science, philosophy, and history is that although they are like games in that they are disinterested activities which can be pursued at set times and places, they can never be isolated and confined to such times and places. A person who has pursued them systematically develops conceptual schemes and forms of appraisal which transform everything else that he does. It is possible to conceive of what is being done in an almost infinite number of ways. A Marxist, for instance, who is stirring up strife in a factory or selling horses on a farm in order to buy a tractor does not see himself as just doing these things; he probably sees his actions as moments in the dialectical progression of historical change. There are at least two truths contained in the slogan "Education is for life," depending on how it is interpreted. One is that if people are properly educated, so that they want to go on when the pressures are off, the conceptual schemes and forms of appraisal into which they have been initiated in schools and universities continue to develop. Another is that "living" cannot be separated from the ways in which people have learned to conceive and appraise what they are doing.

Enough has been said, then, to indicate the main characteristics which distinguish activities like science and philosophy from less serious pursuits such as games and pastimes. Why, then, must a person who asks seriously the question "Why do this rather than that?" be more committed to these sorts of activities which have this special sort of cognitive concern and content built into them? The answer is obvious enough—namely, that these sorts of inquiries are all, in their different ways, relevant to answering the sort of question that he is asking. If his question is concerned, as has been shown, with the nature and quality of the possible activities which he can pursue, he has really embarked upon a difficult and almost endless quest. For the description of disinterested activities and hence, the discussion of their value, is not a matter of mere observation. They depend on how he has learned to conceive them. He cannot simply engage in such activities; he has to see what he is doing in a certain way. This will depend very much on how he has been taught to conceive it, on the concept of what science, art, or cookery is in his culture. This has been formed in the main by the differentiated forms of understanding that have been developed. Is the historical or religious or moral dimension to what he is doing emphasized? Is his concept of himself as an artist or a scientist one which emphasizes pleasure or social responsibility or cosmic piety? Does he think of science or art as an ideological superstructure growing out of an economic base or as the expression of unrecognized sexual strivings? Or has he been encouraged to think of such activities as somehow self-contained and unrelated to the rest of his experience as a sentient being? What a man thinks of science, or history, or art *as* will thus depend upon his general conceptual scheme, which is formed by the cross-fertilization of such inquiries with practical experience conducted in the light of deposits of previous inquiries, however embryonic they may be. Thus, to regard such inquiries or creative activities as merely pastimes is to ignore the fact that they are the main determinants of the conceptual schemes picking out all other pastimes, as well as of what is to count as a pastime.

.   .   .   .

Insofar, therefore, as a person seriously asks the question "Why do this rather than that?" he can only answer it by trying this and that and by thinking about what he is doing in various ways which are inseparable from the doing of it. When he stands back and reflects about what it is that he is doing, he then engages in the sorts of activities of which the curriculum of a university is largely constructed. He will find himself embarking upon those forms of inquiry such as science, history, literature, and philosophy which are concerned with the description, explanation, and assessment of different forms of human activity. It would be irrational for a person who seriously asks himself the question "Why do this rather than that?" to close his mind arbitrarily to any form of inquiry which might throw light on the question which he is asking. This is presumably one of the basic arguments for a "liberal education." It is presumably, also, the logical outcome of Socrates' claim that the unexamined life is not worth living.

The force of this argument for curriculum activities might be admitted, but it might be said that introducing this further feature of their cognitive content, in virtue of which any rational man who seriously asks "Why do this rather than that?" must grant their superiority over games, provides an argument only for their *instrumental* value. It does not show that they should be pursued for their own sake, particularly if they are rather boring. This argument, too, also shows the great importance of physical education. For without a fit body a man's attempts to answer the question "Why do this rather than that?" might be sluggish or slovenly. So it provides, it seems, a transcendental deduction of the principle of physical fitness. The seeming correctness of such a deduction does not establish that physical exercise is worthwhile in itself. It shows why a rational man ought to engage both in physical exercise and in theoretical activities; but it does not show that he must necessarily regard the latter as any more worthwhile in themselves than the former . . . .

Is there, then, no further argument which could support the worthwhileness of theoretical speculation or aesthetic exploration? Does their value depend solely either on their instrumentality to answering the question "Why do this rather than that?" or on their possessing to a more pre-eminent degree characteristics such as skill and complexity, which they share with games and in virtue of which they are better *as* games or pastimes? The answer is partly to question the appropriateness of the notion of instrumentality in this context. Thinking scientifically, for instance, is not exactly instrumental to answering the question "Why do those rather than that?" for it transforms the question by transforming how "this" and "that" are conceived. It is built into asking the question as well as into answering it. It is not surprising that it should do this, for this is derivative from a further feature possessed by theoretical activities and not by games or pastimes. This is their "seriousness" in a sense rather different from that already used to bring out a difference between games and theoretical activities. This sense must now be explicated.

Games have to date been regarded as not serious because, as it were, they are isolated from and contribute little to the "business of living"; they are not usually pursued on grounds either of morality or prudence. But they are not "serious" in another slightly different sense.[2] They are isolated from man's curiosity about the world and his awe and concern about his own peculiar predicament in it. Any reflective person who asks the

---

[2] There is thus also an ambiguity in the concept of "worthwhile" here employed. For it can mean worth spending one's time on in the light of intrinsic or instrumental considerations already treated. Or it can mean worth spending one's time on because it contains an unconditioned value like that of concern for truth, which is about to be treated.

question "Why do this rather than that?" cannot arbitrarily limit the context in which this question is asked. If he asks this question seriously, he must answer it in the consciousness that there are regularities in nature, one of them being his own mortality as a man. Whitehead gave expression to this point in his own way when he said: "Religion is what the individual does with his solitariness. . . . In its solitariness the spirit asks, What, in the way of value is the attainment of life? And it can find no such value till it has merged its individual claim with that of the objective universe. Religion is world loyalty." A man's consciousness of possibilities may be highly differentiated in scientific, aesthetic, historical, and religious forms of awareness. Or these possibilities may be only obscurely intimated in an undifferentiated way. But insofar as he can stand back from his life and *ask* the question "Why this rather than that?" he must already have a serious concern for truth built into his consciousness. For how can a serious practical question be asked unless a man also wants to acquaint himself as well as he can with the situation out of which the question arises, and with the facts of various kinds which provide the framework for possible answers? The various theoretical inquiries are explorations of these different facets of his experience. To ask the question "Why do this rather than that?" seriously is therefore, however embryonically, to be committed to those inquiries which are defined by their serious concern with those aspects of reality which give context to the question which he is asking. In brief, the justification of such activities is not purely instrumental because they are involved in *asking* the question "Why do this rather than that?" as well as in answering it.

This attitude is not simply one of curiosity, though this may provide some sort of natural basis for it in the way in which sympathy for others may provide a natural basis for respect. It is rather the attitude of passionate concern about truth that informed Socrates' saying that the unexamined life is not worth living. It lies at the heart of all rational activities in which there is a concern for what is true or false, appropriate or inappropriate, correct or incorrect. Anyone who asks seriously the question "Why do this rather than that?" must already possess it, for it is built into this sense of "serious." It is impossible to give any further justification for it, for it is presupposed in all serious attempts at justification. It is thus the motivational linch-pin not simply of the ethical system here defended but of any system that is based on discussion and argument.

EXISTENTIAL ENCOUNTERS AND MORAL EDUCATION*

. . . Unlike traditional philosophers—from Aristotle to Hegel—
the existential thinker refuses to conceive man as an abstraction,
a category, an "essence." To describe man as a "rational animal,"
as Aristotle did, or to see man in Hegelian fashion as a compo-
nent part of a system of "thought objectified" is, for the existentialist, to eliminate the crux: the existing individual with his own
consciousness of "being," his dread of "nothingness," his need to
create himself. To say that man's "essence" is his rationality is to
say nothing about the existing being, with all his shifting moods,
feelings, impulses, fantasies, who is struggling to cope with the
world. To identify a child by giving his age group, his social class,
or his IQ score is, similarly, to say nothing about the existing child
in his particularity and uniqueness. To identify an individual by
means of a category ("Negro," "disadvantaged," "upper class")
is to give a certain amount of information; but it makes the individual, *qua* individual, "invisible"—to use Ralph Ellison's term.

The existentialist endeavors to break through such categories
and essences when he considers human creatures living in the
world. A physical object, a piece of furniture, a natural phenomenon may be known by means of abstractions: "table" *does* refer to
a set of qualities all tables possess, and that set of qualities may
be used, with certain variations, to define any table on earth. But
if one says "tool-using biped," "symbol-using organism," "social
animal," or even "man," one's terms in no way encompass or account for *this* person or *that* person as he actually exists.

And his existence comes first, his brute being-in-the-world. If
he is to become an identity, he must plunge into action and relate

* Reprinted from *Existential Encounters for Teachers,* edited with
commentaries by Maxine Greene (New York: Random House, 1967), pp.
7–9, 156–65. Copyright 1967 by Random House, Inc. By permission of
the publisher. The selection is taken from Professor Greene's introduction
and epilogue to this book which facilitates "encounters" with existentialists.

himself reflectively to the situations marking his life in time. Also, he must choose. He must create values, and indeed create himself, by choosing the kind of person he is moment by moment, year by year. His essence, that which he "really" is, turns out to be the identity he defines for himself as he lives.

This is, as most existentialists see it, a subjective achievement; and they put much stress on subjectivity. Each existing person, after all, is inwardly conscious of his being. No external categorization, naming, or definition can touch that crucial awareness; each man relates himself to the world around from a perspective that is within. This does not necessarily mean that he must rely upon his nonrational capacities for "knowing." It certainly does not mean that he depends upon his unconscious mind for his existential truths.

He effects relationships with the world and with other men by means of various capacities, including reason and intuition, feeling and (sometimes) "absurd" faith. The important point is that his subjective consciousness of being alive and a "single one" is involved in whatever relationships he achieves. His consciousness of freedom—"dreadful freedom"—is also involved, since he knows that "anything is possible" for the man who cannot will himself *not* to be free. But, complementing the sense of freedom and open possibilities, is the sense of mortality, of his own personal death; and all the choices he makes and the action he takes are shadowed in some fashion by the perception of a "nothingness" which threatens a man's being and achievements every step of the way.

Perhaps paradoxically, this perception—and the moods which accompany it—makes the individual feel more sharply alive than if he believed in his own immortality, or if he denied the fact that nothing is guaranteed. From the subjective vantage point, living is an affair of risks and uncertainties. There are constant challenges; there is always the need to choose without knowing what is absolutely right, which alternative course is "better," which is "worse." If one does not choose or chooses insincerely, one becomes no better than a stone; one denies one's existential reality.

There are, of course, many people who refuse confrontation,

who accede to mere existence as part of a mass or a "crowd." Comfortable, complacent, bland, they live automatically, and indifferently. They follow; they conform; they think in terms of stereotypes; they cannot either learn or become. Out of touch with the natural world, with tools, with crafts, with other human beings, they tend to be "hollow men" or men "without entrails," as Joseph Conrad once put it, men who neither suffer nor rejoice.

Youngsters like these are the youngsters who withdraw from the challenge of learning and growing. They are the sort who must be urged into the disquietude, the sense of crisis in which existential awareness begins. The existentialist suggests that the very drive to become, to launch oneself into the future, is a function of subjectivity and of the often anguished sense of being-in-the-world, of being responsible for one's own destiny.

Not only, then, have existential thinkers been concerned with the individual as a "single one," exploring his own innerness, his own consciousness of being alive. They have been specifically concerned with crisis and unease, with what educators have sometimes called "the sense of problem." A sense of insufficiency, of incompletion, has been a prevalent response to the modern age as it affects the private person; and the peculiarly contemporary ring of existential writing may be attributed to the contemporary nature of the dislocations to which existentialists respond.

· · · ·

Too often, those who study the subject called "education" consider the processes and phenomena to which that word refers from without. They talk and write about "education" without any feeling of responsibility for what happens in any particular school. This may be appropriate for behavioral scientists, asked to describe the institutional patterns of a society or a group. It may be appropriate, on occasion, for historians and anthropologists.

But the situation of the teacher is as different from these as is the situation of the psychotherapist from that of the statistician. No matter how deliberately, how rationally the teacher guides what happens in his classroom, he personally is involved in it; and almost everything that occurs is affected by his presence there, by his moods and gestures, his expectations and explanations, his responses to those who are trying to learn. A "true," a reliable account of a teaching situation is the one presented from that vantage point, since it is the only one which can take intention into account—the intention of the living individual who is making choices, guiding discoveries, identifying possibilities.

There is a sense, then, in which both an "inner" and an "outer" vision is required. There is a sense in which the multiple facets of the educational process can be described from both perspectives; and when one perspective is taken, the facets seen from the other need be neither eroded nor denied. This means that, if one looks existentially upon the act of teaching—taking choosing into account, and freedom, and being *there*—the strategies devised by the teacher, the tasks he identifies as learning, or the materials he uses, continue to be as consequential and "real" as the physical classroom itself.

It is important to see this after reading existential literature. It is important, too, to think about the ways in which the subjectivity of the teacher may sustain his rationality, and about the ways in which a decision to be intelligent may sustain the struggle to be.

There is no reason, therefore, to suspect dichotomy; there are no necessary either/ors where human existence is concerned. The person who is a teacher may be conscious of his own condition, his own fearful freedom, and at once behave strategically at his work. The major difference between the "inner" and the "outer" lies in the relationship between idea and action in each dimension: one can draw logical inferences from theory for teaching behavior; one can define no implications for behavior in general from encounters with existentialists.

Since this means that we can posit no existential theory or philosophy of education, given or derived, it leads us back to our earlier question: how can we put our encounters to use? We have said that they may move the one who experiences them to renewed consciousness of his life's commitment, but this gives little promise of help, if help is conceived in general, prescriptive terms. The very notion of doctrine is excluded by the existential view. Prescription is excluded by the centrality of free choice. All we can say is what we said originally: if the individual who engages with existential writers is committed to the study of teaching and learning, and to the action which is teaching, he—or she—cannot but see education with new eyes when the reading is, for the moment, done.

And he—or she—can say how it looks after such an experience. Saying, such a person will at least indicate possibilities; and these possibilities may be acted upon by others who are seeking their own vision, their own enhanced awareness of themselves. This, it is hoped, will be the response to the commentaries placed among the foregoing readings. They are personal statements; they are neither deductions nor explications. They were written by one committed to being an educator, and so they have to do with education. But there still exists a world of things to say by the others, the many others, who may also choose to see.

Education, for many people, signifies a process of unfolding. The teacher's function, according to this view, is to make it possible for a child to realize his inborn potentialities, to actualize himself. Whether this is accomplished through deliberate efforts to arouse activity in the child, through the creation of an "educative" environment, or through some nondirective, intuitive approach, the objective is to permit the child to be whatever he has it in him to be. Those who conceive education in this way are those who prize spontaneity and difference, who hope to see a society composed of autonomous individuals, each of whom is committed to his own form of "excellence," all of whom are committed to a common good.

Education, for other people, signifies a process of rearing, of deliberately cultivating certain tendencies and discouraging others, depending upon what the cultural situation demands. The end of education so conceived is productive membership. The individual, properly reared, is equipped with the beliefs, skills, and techniques of thought which are meant to enable him to function adequately in his society. Achieving identity through participation in a culture and a heritage, he is ready to take his place in history. He has been taught, and presumably he has chosen, to act upon values which are communal, to forge in the midst of the many a significant personal life.

Education, for still others, signifies a course of initiation, through which young people are enabled to form the inchoate world of experience by means of the cognitive disciplines and the arts. The primary aim of education, in this view, is to liberate and sensitize young minds for cognition, vision, innovative thought. Properly taught, they will be expected to find pleasure in the subject matters that they will discover as their store of concepts grows and as their perspectives diversify and expand. And, although there will never be an end to their learning, they will be increasingly free and competent when it comes to ordering the substance of their lives.

The emphases shift as the generations pass and the earth turns. In all the important views of education, however, there is concern for the diffuse and multiple energies of the child. There is an interest, always, in the ways in which particular children may be stimulated to learn, in the curricula conducive to the patterns of growth considered valuable, and in the human world where the child will perform his adult tasks.

Clearly there are points of contact between each of these views and the responses aroused by the readings in this book. The integrity of the individual seems central to the view of education as unfolding. Being-in-the-world seems focal to the conception of education as rearing. And those who speak in terms of initiation are concerned with the learner's own responsibility for enlarging his vision and achieving growth.

None of these views, however, seems to summon up an image of the contemporary learner under the conditions of the present age. An encounter with existentialism makes such an imaging crucial for the person choosing himself to be a teacher at this time. The import of "this time," this particular historic moment, cannot be overlooked by the one who tries to see, even for an instant, through an existential glass.

It is *now* that our teaching is to be carried on, *now*, in the second half of the twentieth century. Conscious of the now, we may consider the very process of learning to be a rebellion against the forces which abstract and depersonalize. How, having read what we have read, can we forget what these forces have done to persons? How can we overlook what it means to resign oneself to a "crowd"? We see the individual struggling against the incursions of that crowd when he is a child and when he is grown. We see ourselves as teachers goading him on to "live dangerously" for his own sake, to combat inertia, to take the risks of growth. We see a student choosing to learn only as he commits himself to achieve his own reality, only as he defines his own "fundamental project," which is to act on his own possibilities.

The principle of mere unfolding begins to seem alien, once we confront the obstacles to being: the neutrality of nature, the essential indifference of the world. But we agree that each person must act upon his own possibilities, recognizing them as such. And he must be held responsible for his choice. He must ache to learn and to grow; and we must welcome his aching and unease. We must welcome the anguish he may feel, the guilt before his own refusals. There may be no sin so great as the sin of refusing to become, to be.

Responsible as we are for indicating possibility to him, we know that all we can do is enable him to will his own freedom and make his own choices. As teachers, we can provide curricula rich enough and diverse enough to excite all sorts of youngsters to attempted mastery. We can provide a ground for the "lurch" into teachability. When the individual learner begins moving restlessly, when he shows signs of abandoning formlessness and prereflective "slime," we can acknowledge each small advance he makes, so long as it is in the direction decided on by the youngster himself with the knowledge that he is being given his single chance on earth, that he will never pass this way again.

No matter how many students we have in our classrooms, we will not (having read what we have read) treat the individual as a "specimen." We will not objectify him or make him an object of study, even when we consult the assessments made of what he can do or what he has achieved. Knowing we are "other" with respect to him, we can nonetheless work for encounters with him—for the sake of his authenticity and our own. We may succeed in entering an "I-Thou" relationship; we may dare to engage in dialogue with him and open ourselves to him as he opens himself to us. But we recognize, if we do this, that we are opening the way to tensions and anxieties, the disquietude that is so essential to growth.

We engage in relationships with young people, as with our contemporaries, in an effort to release the "single one." No one of our pupils is likely to live as an isolate, not in a world where others are always present; therefore we must make it somehow possible for each to live among those others while remaining authentically himself. He will be threatened constantly by the appraising "look," the stare that demeans and objectifies. His sincerity will be put to the test by the social games he and others must continually play. But classroom situations can be made occasions for strengthening his will to be authentic and free—if, that is, we who teach are willing to open ourselves sufficiently to be *present* there. If we are, if we can stand forth as existing selves while we teach, we can transform our classrooms into exemplary places where presentness and objectivity coexist.

We can exert ourselves to see through the eyes of the student "other," to take his perspective, his vantage point, even while we concern ourselves deliberately with objective things. We can, while working with the structures of subject matters, with the tasks that must be performed if our students are to learn, create an atmosphere of intersubjectivity. Tranquillity will not pervade such an atmosphere; the members of the class will not be put at ease. But neither will they be dealt with as objects, cases, specimens. Engaged as subjectivities as well as minds, they may discover the possibility of being with others and at the same time being themselves. They may learn that one is not doomed to be a thing in an objective, public domain, so long as one ventures out of coolness and separateness—so long as one rebels through questioning and forming, and insists on the right to grow.

· · · ·

As teachers, we became concerned not with *what* he knows but with *how* he comes to know, how the truths of the world and of consciousness are revealed to the "single one." We endeavor to keep ourselves and the child in touch with concrete life situations, since these represent the dimensions of the world-to-be-known. The individual comes to know as he achieves appropriate relationships with various aspects of his life situations; sometimes he relates himself as a scientist would to empirical phenomena; sometimes, as an artist would to forms which are deeply felt; sometimes, as a statesman would to the practical strategies of life.

This, too, is an area where dichotomies have no place. The object is not to choose between the intuitive and the rational-empirical, the aesthetic and the discursive, the emotive and the logical. Nor is it to establish priority for one way of knowing above all others. The teacher's concern must be for the way in which each student chooses his relationship with the various situations which arise; for if knowing is conceived as a relationship with a variety of concrete situations, the student will not be likely to take refuge in the propositions of "pure" reason and disembodied intellect. As seeker, as knower, he will be participant. He will construct orders and define meanings as he chooses to do so, as he acts upon and challenges his world.

Only as he chooses can he achieve a continuity of identity and a continuity of knowing. As a free individual, he must take his choices seriously and commit himself in the space he discovers between his limitations and his possibilities. If not, he will flounder "in the possible"; and the project which is his selfhood will become abstract and finally meaningless.

And so we who teach must give him "care" and intense concern. We must foster the freedom that he can attain as he moves dialectically between necessity and fulfillment, between the ineradicable qualities of his particular situation and the thus-far-unrealized capacities which are his. "Cast into the world" though he may have been, the individual has grown up in situations: of slum life, perhaps, of poverty, of parental dominance, of rootlessness. These need not determine him; they certainly do not define him; but they do compose the frame of reference in which his becoming must take place. He cannot make decisions in a vacuum; he cannot define his possibilities if he is unaware of limitations, of necessities.

He is caught in a dialectical movement, therefore, when he acts to learn and to create himself; and, inevitably, he will feel strain, he will suffer as he struggles to become. It is in that suffering, however, that he experiences the pain of willing and the intensity of consciousness which make a person feel himself to be an existing creature—sharply and painfully alive. And it is in the midst of such intensity that he will be moved to shape values as he lives, to create his "ethical reality."

Values may be arbitrary at some level, but they do not appear in a vacuum. The individual must feel himself to be a distinctive person, confronting negations, caught up in the situations which give content to his life. These situations, as we teachers know, are social and political; they are economic, recreational, religious; occasionally they are situations of love, passion, friendship, faith. And they are, always, temporal situations, conditioned by history and by transiency.

The meaning and the impact of such situations are determined by the individual who encounters them; and one of our commitments as teachers is to enable him to confront them and choose appropriate action when he does. This is another reason for teaching for the widest, most varied perspectives: the young person must be equipped to perceive himself imaginatively in multiple predicaments, against diverse backgrounds. He must be, as he learns, a seeker and a wanderer. He must be adventurous enough to break repeatedly with the conventional. He must image himself in the great reaches of time and in continually expanding space. And at climactic moments of decision, he must experience the "boundary situations," where he can confront the "Encompassing," or the unanswerable, or non-being, or the absurd.

On the one hand, this implies a necessity for the most "general" curriculum, at least in the early years of his life. If he is to relate himself to novel situations as he chooses his future, he must experience himself thinking now like a scientist, now like an artist, now like a strategist. He must be given opportunities to manipulate, to experiment, to hypothesize, to test. He must be offered possibilities, as well, for knowledgeable appreciation of art forms, for vicarious identification with literary figures. He must find himself occasions for appropriating ideas, ideals, visions of possibility from a heritage made contemporary with him.

On the other hand, the prospect of confronting strange situations ought to lead the individual student to rehearse encounters with absurdity. He must not be protected, therefore, from inequity, injustice, suffering, and death—nor from the frequently unanswerable questions to which they give rise. It is only as he confronts the existence of "plague," only as he intensifies his own consciousness of "dread," that he may be moved to commitments which are ethical.

We cannot indoctrinate him with moral regulations if we intend to nurture his freedom. We cannot impose a ready-made value system upon him if we want him to choose himself. We can, however, open the way to the confrontations which will require him to make choices, choices involving conceptions of "good" and "right." In his freedom, then, he will shape a conscience for himself; he will construct a morality. And if the situations of his life (including the ones we have made) permit him to act on the possibilities he perceives, he will commit himself to the moral ideals that he has chosen. Taking responsibility, he will have achieved the hope of meaning at that point; he will have become a rebel for a cause. . . .

MORALITY, REASON, AND EDUCATION*

John Wilson

. . . Valuing, choosing, commending, etc., are certainly different from stating, describing, or noting facts. But they are not arbitrary activities: they have their own criteria of success. Consequently we are bound to direct our attention toward sketching those rules, principles, or standards in virtue of which we can say that one moral belief is better than another. The words which we should most naturally use, in making this sort of judgment, would include "reasonable," "rational," "unprejudiced," "sensible," "wise," and "sane." I shall in fact make most use of the word "rational," and attempt to outline the senses in which we can say that one moral belief is more rational than another, or that one person is more rational than another in the sphere of morality. My purpose in doing this should be plain. For although we cannot hope to establish a full set of immediate, first-order moral values, we may be able to establish a set of second-order principles or norms, by reference to which we can assess the merits of a moral belief or believer, and hence be able to describe one person as more "morally educated" than another.

People, Not Only Beliefs, Can Be Called Rational

From the point of view of the moral educator, it is natural to begin by trying to consider what we mean when we call *people*, rather than *beliefs*, rational or irrational. When we describe somebody as "irrational," "unreasonable," "intolerant," "prejudiced," "insane," etc., we do not (or should not) refer primarily to the truth or falsehood of his beliefs. A man may hold beliefs which are perfectly correct in an unreasonable, intolerant, prejudiced, or insane

* Reprinted from John Wilson, Norman Williams, and Barry Sugarman, *Introduction to Moral Education* (Baltimore: Penguin Books, Inc., 1967), pp. 73–79, 128–31, 133–36, 138–40. Copyright 1967 by The Farmington Trust. By permission of The Farmington Trust and the author.

manner—and, of course, vice versa. We are talking about the *way in which* or the *reasons for which* he comes to believe, and continues to believe, rather than *what* he believes. A "reasonable" man is not essentially a man who believes *x*, *y*, and *z*, but a man who is prepared to listen to argument, attend to the facts, to logic, to the meanings of words, and so on. We tend to assume that certain beliefs, being so obviously false, could only be held by somebody who was unreasonable or prejudiced or insane: for instance, it seems to most of us that anyone who thought the earth was flat, or that all those of Aryan blood were superior to all non-Aryans, must have failed to attend to the evidence. But we must not be tempted to suppose that it is the belief itself which justifies our charge of unreasonableness. Plenty of inventors and scientists have been thought unreasonable or insane because their views did not find favour at the time: and afterwards they were found to be correct. It is the sort of reasons a man has for his beliefs which count. . . .

Rules of Procedure

What is it, then, to be "good" at morality? I am suggesting that we ought not to try to answer this question by saying "Holding the right moral views." If we say this, we shall find ourselves asking next "But what *are* the right moral views?"; and to this question we may fail to find an answer. We may fail for two reasons: first, because we may be in doubt about the sense, if any, in which we can talk at all about the "right" moral views, since morality seems to be in some degree a matter of choice; and second, because we still might not know which actual views were right, even if we knew what we meant by calling a view "right"—we might, for instance, not have enough factual information to decide between conflicting views. We should rather ask "What are the rules of procedure, or the canons of relevance, which we actually use to assess the merits of a moral view?" or "What sort of demands do we make on a person who puts forward a moral view, when we want him to justify it?" I don't think it should worry us too much to realize that, even if and when we have established the rules of procedure for morality, we still cannot in a strict sense *prove* this or that specific moral view to be "right" beyond any possible doubt.

After all, we are in a not very dissimilar position as regards scientific views. We have a fairly good idea of what rules and criteria govern the activity of science, and how scientific arguments and justifications are supposed to work. But this does not mean that we never hold mistaken scientific beliefs, however careful we try to be in attending to the rules and criteria—we may have overlooked some vital fact, or our instruments may not be good enough to collect all the evidence we need. . . .

With some of the rules of procedure in morality we are perfectly familiar, because they are rules which enter into other activities besides morality. Briefly they are:

(*a*) That we should stick to the laws of logic;
(*b*) That we should use language correctly;
(*c*) That we should attend to the facts.

Many examples have been given of these kinds of rationality; they may be found elsewhere, and I will not repeat them here. We all know that if, during a moral argument, a person contradicts himself, or disregards some fact which is relevant to his opinion, or plays fast and loose with the meanings of words, he is behaving irrationally. This may seem somewhat dogmatic, but we shall have more to say about it later.

Other People's Interests

These particular rules of procedure, however, are not peculiar to morality, even though they enter into it. In our search for other rules of procedure, it seems most profitable to begin by one account of a certain type of thinking which has a right to be called "moral," and which can be defined *formally* rather than in terms of *content*. These formal criteria may not be sufficient to give us everything we need for the concept of a "morally educated" person, but they will at least serve to distinguish some kinds of moral thought and action from nonmoral thought and action, without forcing us to assign a particular content to morality. The close analysis of moral language on which this account rests, and which is required to elucidate these criteria, has been done elsewhere, and I need not repeat it here at length.

We may summarize the criteria which a man's opinions must satisfy if they are to count as moral opinions, under five headings: (1) They must be autonomous (freely held). (2) They must be rational. These two criteria we have discussed already. (3) They must be impartial as between persons. (4) They must be prescriptive. One might very roughly express the last two criteria as follows: if someone expresses a moral opinion ("It is wrong to steal," "It is a good thing to keep one's promises," or whatever), then (i) he is laying down a principle of behaviour, not just for one particular person or occasion, but for all people on all similar occasions, (ii) he commits himself to acting on that principle (though of course he may sometimes lack the means or the will-power so to act); that is, a moral opinion does not just make an *observation* about what is good or bad, but (if sincerely held) *prescribes* for the person, or commits him to, a certain type of behaviour. (5) They must be overriding: that is, they must take precedence over his other opinions.

There are a number of questions which may be raised about this account; but the most important for our present argument is the notion of the impartiality of moral judgements ([3] above). The account suggests that, in making moral judgements, we consider other people as being on an equal footing with ourselves: what goes for us, goes for them too, and vice versa. Without this, it is suggested, the whole business of morality and interpersonal rules could not get started. Moreover, if a man's moral opinions have to *prescribe* conduct for others as well as for himself ([4] above), the implication is that he regards them as equals: one might think that he could not advance these opinions with any show of reason, or with much chance of success, unless he so regarded them. But what is it to accept other people as equals? Do we have to accept *all* other people as equals? Or only some? Or only to accept that our moral judgments apply in principle to other people—that is, that they would apply if other people were in the same position as ourselves, which perhaps in fact they are not? Or is it rather that the onus lies on us to show that they are not—to point out relevant differences between their case and ours? And anyway, whatever is demanded by the notion of equality or impartiality, are there any reasons for accepting this notion?

Despite these philosophical difficulties, many of us (at least in this society) would perhaps accept some such notion without serious hesitation. Partly for this reason, I shall delay a consideration of the (very complex) issues involved. . . . Now though the account itself defines moral judgments in purely formal terms, the implication of the underlying notion of equality suggests at least one obvious procedural principle for at least one area that we usually call "moral": perhaps the most important, or the most typical, area. This is the area of interpersonal morality: that is, the area where the wants and interests of individuals living in society conflict, or may conflict. The procedural principle is simply that the *sort of justification* needed for a moral view in this area must relate to the feelings and interests of other people (just as the sort of justification needed for a scientific view must relate to observed empirical facts, experimental results, and so forth). This is not to say *either* that moral or scientific views must have a particular content—that we can dismiss a priori certain specific views as not moral, or not scientific—*or* that you can rationally hold any moral view you like. It is simply to say that a moral view, to count as rational, must be backed up by certain kinds of reasons.

Thus, suppose a man said that he believed that we ought to kill everyone whose name began with a Q on Tuesday night, while they were sleeping. He might hold this in a way which satisfied all the formal criteria for a moral view; yet in itself it seems a very odd view to hold. But now suppose he explains as follows: "Well, you see, I happen to know that every Wednesday from now on Martians will descend and torture everyone whose name begins with Q—Martians don't have the letter Q in their language, and they hate it so much that they can't stand hearing it spoken: and the torture will be so horrible that it would be better for them if they were killed painlessly in their sleep on Tuesday night." Now this becomes intelligible as a moral view. What makes it intelligible is that he is relating it to the interests of other people, those whose names begin with Q. It is ultimately because they have those interests—because they would prefer to die painlessly rather than under Martian torture—that he holds the view, not *just* because it is a Tuesday or because their names begin with Q. . . .

Educational Practice Must Be Justified by the Standards

. . . I want to make it absolutely clear that the criteria of rationality of which I have made so much are not the be-all and end-all in moral education. There is even a sense in which these criteria may not be the most important feature; but we must be clear about what this sense is. Suppose we are trying to educate people in science. Then we must start by being clear about what science is, and what criteria and rules of procedure we must use to arrive at and judge the merits of scientific beliefs; and we need a rough definition of an ideally "scientifically educated" person in terms of those criteria. Now there is a sense in which this is the most important feature of "scientific education"; that is, we have constantly to refer our educational methods to this goal—we have to try to produce people who are as "scientifically educated" as possible, as defined by these criteria. But there is also a sense in which these criteria may not play a predominant part in our educational *practice*, in the actual arrangements we make for teaching children. The arrangements must be geared to, or focused on, this end; but we might in fact spend most of our time doing things which had no direct or obvious relationship to the end.

To use another parallel: if we want to teach someone to play football, we have to be clear about what counts as playing football and what counts as playing it well. If we are not clear about this, we simply do not know what we are doing. But the largest part, in a sense the most "important" features, of "football education" would not necessarily consist of explaining the rules of football or giving the child a grasp of tactics. They might rather consist of making the child take plenty of exercise, preventing him from smoking and drinking, giving him the right sort of equipment and playing fields, and so forth. In deciding exactly what to do in practice, we should have to defend our arrangements by showing that they were necessary to produce a person who could play football well; but most of our time would be spent on the arrangements themselves, and not on explaining the rules of football.

I hope this will lessen the temptation to misinterpret what we have said about rationality, or to think (as I suppose somebody still might) that we have been talking about *how* you should educate children morally, instead of about *what it means* to educate children morally, and how one would have to *justify* various methods and arrangements for moral education. Of course the child needs what we might call training, conditioning, enforced rules, a firm framework, and so on: he needs to accept—indeed, in his early years he can probably do no other than accept—a certain code of behavior, parental commands, traditional rules, etc. The child also needs other things, such as love, emotional security, food, warmth, enough sleep, and so forth. All these things, as well as a framework of rules, are necessary if we are going to be able to produce people who are "morally educated" in the sense already described.

. . . Preventing a child from smoking and drinking may be a necessary arrangement if he is to play football well, but would hardly be properly called "education in football" or "physical education." It is, rather, a *precondition* which is necessary if our physical education is going to succeed. In the same way the early training, emotional security, and so forth, which we need to give children may best be regarded as preconditions rather than as educational processes in themselves. This does not make them less important, but it puts them in a different category.

It would, of course, be extremely silly for educationalists in any field to disregard some essential precondition on the purely linguistic grounds that the precondition is not, strictly speaking, an *educational* process. Certainly we shall include all the preconditions—whatever they may be, for we cannot know what they are without further research—under the general title of "moral education". . . .

The crucial point is that, in considering what preconditions to establish or what arrangements to make in moral education, our criteria of justification must be taken from a neutral and non-partisan definition of a morally educated person *and from no-where else*. When children are young, we make them do various things—we give them toilet training, make them sit up at table, tell them to say "please" and "thank you," prevent them from hitting each other, and so forth; we may also say things like "It's wrong to tell lies," or "It's breaking the law to steal"; and we may punish them if they hit each other, or tell lies, or are dirty. Now how do we justify these arrangements? Briefly, we must *not* try to justify them by saying, "It's obviously bad to tell lies or be dirty," or "All decent societies tell the truth and are clean." This would put us right back to square one, where we are trying to justify certain specific *first-order* moral beliefs or actions. What we must do is to inspect the arrangements, and ask whether these arrangements generate those preconditions which are necessary for producing people who are morally educated in the *second-order* sense of being rational, sane, "reality-orientated," autonomous, capable of loving, or whatever general descriptive expression we care to use.

Whether a precondition is necessary is emphatically *not* a matter of whether we ourselves happen to approve of it. It is not a matter of counting heads, or going by the majority verdict; in morality, just as in science, weight of numbers goes no way at all toward establishing truth. It is a matter of whether or not the *facts show* that a particular arrangement does actually result in giving the child a piece of essential equipment. This is why it is important to regard these arrangements as preconditions rather than as educational processes, or morally educational processes. For if we give them the latter description, we shall be tempted to think that we can judge our arrangements on some first-order, partisan basis. For instance, suppose we are deciding whether to allow children to bite their nails or not. We have not to decide whether nail-biting is in itself "good" or "bad," but rather to decide whether by stopping it or allowing it we shall best be able to increase the child's security, his capacity for moral thought and action, the strength of his ego, his ability to relate to other people and consider their interests, etc.

This example will show that very often we simply do not know the right course; but this will vex only those people who expect moral education to be easy. There will of course be many cases where we can feel confident that our arrangements are substantially correct, and do generate necessary preconditions; but even here it is difficult to know what *sort* of preconditions are the crucial ones. It is an open question, for instance, how far some kind of "moral training," in the sense of getting children to obey rules and regard certain actions as "wrong" or "naughty," is important, as against those preconditions which might be generally described as giving emotional security, regularity of life, opportunities for personal attachment and imitation, and so forth. Those who are impressed with the notions of "ethics" or "a moral code" may instinctively favor one line; those whose orientation is psychoanalytic, another. The important thing is to realize our own ignorance.

. . . The child whose moral education has been successful will, of course, end up with a particular set of moral principles. By using the relevant skills which we have called by the general title of "rationality," he will reach particular conclusions, such as, "Stealing is wrong," "One ought not to tell lies," etc. If we like, we can call these "the right answers." It is a little dangerous to do so, because we may be tempted to suppose that as long as the child gives the "right answers" it does not matter how he arrives at them—and this would be as silly as a mathematics master who did not mind about how his pupils got the right answers to their sums (even if they looked them up in the back of the book), so long as they wrote them down. But, in cases where we are quite sure about the rationality of a particular moral principle, there is no harm in saying, as it were, "Look, this is the answer you'll almost certainly get, if you apply the moral skills correctly," or "Well, an awful lot of rational people think your answer is wrong, we'd better go over the working again." There are parallels here with teaching science or history or most other subjects. We don't *just* want the pupils to get the right answers; but we recognize also that we can *use* what are commonly taken as the right answers to educate the children in the relevant skills.

. . . .

The extent to which it is profitable to make children "go through the motions" in other subjects, e.g., by making them learn lots of facts by heart in science, is nowadays regarded as very doubtful by many educationalists; and in the case of morality we need to preserve an even more open mind. Thus, for many maladjusted children, notions like "obedience" or "moral training," in the sense of making the child obey a set of what are (from the adult viewpoint) moral rules, seem to be out of place; whereas the child's emotional relationship to adults, and the ways in which we can help him to handle his inner life of anxiety, fear, guilt, aggression, and so forth seem to be much more important. Over-simple notions of "moral training" may be tacitly based on naïve pre-Freudian views of the "natural child" whose mind is a "tabula rasa," who needs only to be taught to make moral motions, as it were, and who (as a potentially rational being) will naturally come to understand the point of them later. But on any serious psychological view, the emotional development of even the youngest child is so complex that such "training" may not be the only, nor even the most important, requirement.

The comparison with learning methods in other fields is an interesting one, and, though much more research is needed before any specific conclusions can be drawn, it is worth our while to pursue it briefly from the conceptual point of view. Consider, for instance, the teaching of mathematics or science. Here we may contrast two general types of methods:

(*a*) those which we might call "drill," "rules of thumb," "making children go through the motions," "learning by heart," etc., e.g., parrot-learning of the multiplication tables, reciting Boyle's Law, and so on.

(*b*) those designed to give the children understanding of what they are doing, and of why the truths of mathematics and science are true.

Now (*pace* some very "progressive" educationalists) it would be doctrinaire to say that we should *only* use the methods in (*b*). For there are obviously many occasions on which it is extremely useful for the child to be able to calculate automatically, in his head and on the spot, without the use of blocks, colored rods, or adding machines, and without taking time off to wonder why the right answer is right. The child will need to be able to make sure he gets the right change, to know what happens if he joins two electric wires together, and so forth; it is not necessary to enter on these occasions into the conceptual foundations of mathematics or the real nature of electricity. It *may* be that the methods in (*b*) will enable him to do these simple, habit-based things just as well as those in (*a*), but this has to be shown. But the *reasons why* we may need (*a*)-type methods are of two quite different kinds:

1. They may be useful, as initial drill movements, to give the child a proper basis for being "mathematically educated" or "scientifically educated" in the sense that (*b*)-type methods aim to achieve.

2. They may be useful for reasons that have nothing at all to do with *education,* but rather (as hinted above) with quite practical objectives, like getting the right change or not getting electric shocks.

In just the same way, habits, drill, or "going through the motions" may be useful in education:

1. As psychologically essential groundwork for becoming "morally educated" later on.

2. For other reasons, such as to keep the child out of trouble, prevent him from coming up before the magistrates, stop him from offending his elders, and so on. These *need* not have anything to do with moral *education,* any more than teaching someone not to touch electric wires has anything to do with scientific education.

In both cases, we can see that there are other objectives in bringing up children besides strictly educational ones: we want the child to remain healthy, not to be cheated, not to be put in prison, and so forth. Only a very silly and doctrinaire person would regard these as unimportant. But we can also see that the dangers of not teaching the child habits that will enable him to avoid these misfortunes can be minimized, if the misfortunes turn out to be partly of our own making. Thus, if you have an irrational monetary or spelling system, or unsafe electrical equipment that gives you a shock if you touch it, then you will have to work quite hard to give children the right habits; whereas if you change to a decimal system and reform the spelling, it becomes easier. Similarly, if we have to teach children a lot of complicated moral habits simply because the adult world reacts irrationally, then we shall waste a lot of time that might be better spent elsewhere.

But what the comparison chiefly shows is that success in using *any* methods is heavily dependent on knowing what we are trying to do and knowing what counts is doing it well. It is chiefly because we *know how to do* mathematics and science that we can experiment successfully with various educational methods and techniques; and the child, too, can get the hang of the general aims, logic, and criteria of the subject at a fairly early age—partly because we ourselves are clear about them. We can say, "Put down so-and-so, and such-and-such, and I'll show you why and how it works in a minute." But in moral education, although we can certainly *say,* "Do *x, y,* and *z,* and when you're older I'll show you why it's reasonable," do we really feel any confidence about being able to show this? The fault does not lie with morality; it lies with ourselves, unless and until we have worked hard enough to get as clear about the methodology of morals as we are about the methodology of science. At present we are still in the "alchemy" stage of morals; and it is not surprising that we tend to convey to our children an impression of a field of discourse where much may be reasonable, but much also arbitrary, relativistic, tyrannical, or just plain feeble-minded.

. . . .

Is "Moral Education" a Subject?

People ask questions like "Is moral education a subject?" "Do we teach it by itself or do we smuggle it into other subjects (such as religious instruction or English)?" "Is it suitable for children of all ages?" "Is it something you can teach at all?" and so forth.

If we are now clearer about what we mean by a morally educated person, we may at this point be able to tidy up some of the muddles that underlie these questions. Many of the muddles are the result of very deep-seated confusions which I have not space to deal with fully; but the following points may be of some help.

Suppose a "morally educated" person is someone who has abilities or characteristics $a, b, c,$ and d (for instance, someone who considers the interests of others, knows what they feel, makes up moral rules appropriate to the situation, and abides by those rules). Then a particular educational context (A) might be ideal for developing one of these characteristics (a); and this context might already exist in our curriculum. "English literature," for instance, might be ideal as it stands for developing awareness of other people's feelings (a). But for the development of another characteristic (b) we might need to invent a new context (B); thus the subject that we call "ethics" or "religious instruction" might be very bad for helping children to make up moral rules. We might find that teaching the children anthropology or psychology, or giving them personal experience of social classes or groups different from their own, or making them play certain kinds of games, was much more efficient. Or we might find that it did not much matter what you taught them, but the way in which you taught them was very important. Or we might even find that no *direct* attempt to develop these characteristics was much good—that their existence depended more on how the school was organized, or the personality of the teacher, or how much their mothers had loved them in infancy. Hence we might end up with a lot of contexts or arrangements $(B, B1, B3$ etc., $C1, C2$ etc.), some of which might be the same as existing subjects, or parts of existing subjects, some of which represented quite new subjects, and some of which were not subjects at all.

In other words, some of the most important factors which *produce* a morally educated person may have little to do with any *direct process* of moral education, or even with any *educational* process at all. Those that can be institutionalized into an educational process may fit some already existing subjects or disciplines, or they may not; or they may partly fit and partly not fit;

or they may fit if the subject or discipline were to be taught in a different way, but not fit as the subject is taught at present. Suppose—purely for the sake of example—that we can list the following factors as necessary for producing a morally educated person:

(i) That he should be of certain physical type, or have a certain minimum IQ;

(ii) That his mother should love him in infancy, or that his schoolteachers should be of a certain personality type;

(iii) That he should be taught to read;

(iv) That he should be taught English literature;

(v) That he should be taught history, but in an unusual way;

(vi) That he should be taught some new (intellectual) subject, (say) psychology;

(vii) That he should be taught some nonintellectual skills, already institutionalized, (say) mime or painting;

(viii) That he should be taught some nonintellectual skills which we have not institutionalized: i.e. we need to introduce some new activity, perhaps some new kind of game, or psychotherapeutic sessions, or social work, or whatever.

Now of these, (i) is something we can as yet do nothing at all about, either by education or anything else. We can do something about (ii), but it would not count as education. (iii) is education, but would not normally count as specifically *moral* education. (iv)-(viii) might count as moral education, but their variety shows that we cannot assume any particular correlation (or lack of correlation) either with existing subjects or disciplines as against ones we have to invent, or with intellectual subjects or disciplines as against nonintellectual skills.

Any educational process can count as moral education if it is a deliberate process and directed toward producing (or perhaps just produces) the skills or characteristics of a morally educated person. Suppose English, as normally taught, produces one of these skills. Then a question like "Shall we teach the children English or morally educate them?" is silly, because teaching them English *is* morally educating them; just as it is silly to say, "Shall we have pigs or animals?" To the extent that an existing subject or discipline morally educates, teaching that subject or discipline is moral education. Again, if I try to make people think logically, then what governs my teaching is the laws of logic; I try to get children to follow these laws and *thereby* (incidentally) contribute to their moral education. Even if we have to change the style of certain subjects, or invent quite new ones, it might still be misleading to *call* them "moral education." For each subject or discipline would still be trying to develop its own particular skills or abilities, so that (from the point of view of someone doing or teaching the subject) it is in a sense accidental that these skills are characteristic of a morally educated person. We have to rid ourselves of the temptation to think that there is a *thing called* "moral education" which exists over and above particular activities designed to elicit particular skills.

MAN'S NATURE AND THE INTELLECTUAL AND MORAL VIRTUES*

Aristotle

Book I

[1094ª] 1. Every art and every inquiry, and similarly every action and pursuit, is thought to aim at some good; and for this reason the good has rightly been declared[1] to be that at which all things aim. But a certain difference is found among ends; some are activities, others are products apart from the activities that produce them. Where there are ends apart from the actions, it is the nature of the products to be better than the activities. Now, as there are many actions, arts, and sciences, their ends also are many; the end of the medical art is health, that of shipbuilding a vessel, that of strategy victory, that of economics wealth. But where such arts fall under a single capacity—as bridle-making and the other arts concerned with the equipment of horses fall under the art of riding, and this and every military action under strategy, in the same way other arts fall under yet others—in all of these the ends of the master arts are to be preferred to all the subordinate ends; for it is for the sake of the former that the latter are pursued. It makes no difference whether the activities themselves are the ends of the actions, or something else apart from the activities, as in the case of the sciences just mentioned.

2. If, then, there is some end of the things we do, which we desire for its own sake (everything else being desired for the sake of this), and if we do not choose everything for the sake of something else (for at that rate the process would go on to infinity, so that our desire would be empty and vain), clearly this must be

* Reprinted from "Nichomachean Ethics," trans. W. D. Ross, in *The Basic Works of Aristotle,* ed. Richard McKeon (New York: Random House, 1941), pp. 935–38, 941–43, 950–54, 1104. By permission of The Clarendon Press, Oxford. The original source is *The Oxford Translation of Aristotle,* ed. W. D. Ross, vol. 9, 1925.
[1] Perhaps by Eudoxus; cf. 1172b9.

the good and the chief good. Will not the knowledge of it, then, have a great influence on life? Shall we not, like archers who have a mark to aim at, be more likely to hit upon what is right? If so, we must try, in outline at least to determine what it is, and of which of the sciences or capacities it is the object. It would seem to belong to the most authoritative art and that which is most truly the master art. And politics appears to be of this nature; for it is this that ordains which of the sciences [1094^b] should be studied in a state, and which each class of citizens should learn and up to what point they should learn them; and we see even the most highly esteemed of capacities to fall under this, e.g., strategy, economics, rhetoric; now, since politics uses the rest of the sciences, and since, again, it legislates as to what we are to do and what we are to abstain from, the end of this science must include those of the others, so that this end must be the good for man. For even if the end is the same for a single man and for a state, that of the state seems at all events something greater and more complete whether to attain or to preserve; though it is worthwhile to attain the end merely for one man, it is finer and more godlike to attain it for a nation or for city-states. These, then, are the ends at which our inquiry aims, since it is political science, in one sense of that term.

3. Our discussion will be adequate if it has as much clearness as the subject matter admits of, for precision is not to be sought for alike in all discussions, any more than in all the products of the crafts. Now fine and just actions, which political science investigates, admit of much variety and fluctuation of opinion, so that they may be thought to exist only by convention, and not by nature. And goods also give rise to a similar fluctuation because they bring harm to many people; for before now men have been undone by reason of their wealth, and others by reason of their courage. We must be content, then, in speaking of such subjects and with such premises to indicate the truth roughly and in outline, and in speaking about things which are only for the most part true and with premises of the same kind to reach conclusions that are no better. In the same spirit, therefore, should each

type of statement be *received;* for it is the mark of an educated man to look for precision in each class of things just so far as the nature of the subject admits; it is evidently equally foolish to accept probable reasoning from a mathematician and to demand from a rhetorician scientific proofs.

Now each man judges well the things he knows, and of these he is a good judge. And so the man who has been educated in a subject is [1095^a] a good judge of that subject, and the man who has received an all-round education is a good judge in general. Hence a young man is not a proper hearer of lectures on political science; for he is inexperienced in the actions that occur in life, but its discussions start from these and are about these; and, further, since he tends to follow his passions, his study will be vain and unprofitable, because the end aimed at is not knowledge but action. And it makes no difference whether he is young in years or youthful in character; the defect does not depend on time, but on his living, and pursuing each successive object, as passion directs. For to such persons, as to the incontinent, knowledge brings no profit; but to those who desire and act in accordance with a rational principle, knowledge about such matters will be of great benefit.

These remarks about the student, the sort of treatment to be expected, and the purpose of the inquiry, may be taken as our preface.

4. Let us resume our inquiry and state, in view of the fact that all knowledge and every pursuit aims at some good, what it is that we say political science aims at and what is the highest of all goods achievable by action. Verbally there is very general agreement; for both the general run of men and people of superior refinement say that it is happiness, and identify living well and doing well with being happy; but with regard to what happiness is they differ, and the many do not give the same account as the wise. For the former think it is some plain and obvious thing, like pleasure, wealth, or honour; they differ, however, from one another—and often even the same man identifies it with different things, with health when he is ill, with wealth when he is poor;

but, conscious of their ignorance, they admire those who proclaim some great ideal that is above their comprehension. Now some[2] thought that apart from these many goods there is another which is self-subsistent and causes the goodness of all these as well. To examine all the opinions that have been held were perhaps somewhat fruitless; enough to examine those that are most prevalent or that seem to be arguable.

Let us not fail to notice, however, that there is a difference between arguments from and those to the first principles. For Plato, too, was right in raising this question and asking, as he used to do, "Are we on the way from or to the first principles?"[3] There is a difference, as there is in a race course between the course from the judges to the turning point and the way back. For, while we must begin with what [1095^b] is known, things are objects of knowledge in two senses—some to us, some without qualification. Presumably, then, *we* must begin with things known to *us*. Hence any one who is to listen intelligently to lectures about what is noble and just and, generally, about the subjects of political science must have been brought up in good habits. For the fact is the starting point, and if this is sufficiently plain to him, he will not at the start need the reason as well; and the man who has been well brought up has or can easily get starting-points. . . .

5. Let us, however, resume our discussion from the point at which we digressed. To judge from the lives that men lead, most men, and men of the most vulgar type, seem (not without some ground) to identify the good, or happiness, with pleasure, which is the reason why they love the life of enjoyment. For there are, we may say, three prominent types of life—that just mentioned, the political, and thirdly the contemplative life. Now the mass of mankind are evidently quite slavish in their tastes, preferring a life suitable to beasts, but they get some ground for their view from the fact that many of those in high places share the tastes of Sardanapallus. A consideration of the prominent types of life shows that people of superior refinement and of active disposition

2 The Platonic School.
3 Cf. *Republic,* 511B.

identify happiness with honor; for this is, roughly speaking, the end of the political life. But it seems too superficial to be what we are looking for, since it is thought to depend on those who bestow honour rather than on him who receives it, but the good we divine to be something proper to a man and not easily taken from him. Further, men seem to pursue honor in order that they may be assured of their goodness; at least it is by men of practical wisdom that they seek to be honored, and among those who know them, and on the ground of their virtue; clearly, then, according to them, at any rate, virtue is better. And perhaps one might even suppose this to be, rather than honor, the end of the political life. But even this appears somewhat incomplete; for possession of virtue seems actually compatible with being asleep, or with lifelong inactivity, and, further, with the greatest [1096ᵃ] sufferings and misfortunes; but a man who was living so no one would call happy, unless he were maintaining a thesis at all costs. But enough of this, for the subject has been sufficiently treated even in the current discussions. Third comes the contemplative life, which we shall consider later.[4]

.   .   .   .

7. Let us again return to the good we are seeking, and ask what it can be. It seems different in different actions and arts; it is different in medicine, in strategy, and in the other arts likewise. What then is the good of each? Surely that for whose sake everything else is done. In medicine this is health, in strategy victory, in architecture a house, in any other sphere something else, and in every action and pursuit the end; for it is for the sake of this that all men do whatever else they do. Therefore, if there is an end for all that we do, this will be the good achievable by action, and if there are more than one, these will be the goods achievable by action.

So the argument has by a different course reached the same point; but we must try to state this even more clearly. Since there are evidently more than one end, and we choose some of these

4 1177ᵃ 12–1178ᵃ 8, 1178ᵃ 22–1179ᵃ 32.

(e.g., wealth, flutes, and in general instruments) for the sake of something else, clearly not all ends are final ends; but the chief good is evidently something final. Therefore, if there is only one final end, this will be what we are seeking, and if there are more than one, the most final of these will be what we are seeking. Now we call that which is in itself worthy of pursuit more final than that which is worthy of pursuit for the sake of something else, and that which is never desirable for the sake of something else more final than the things that are desirable both in themselves and for the sake of that other thing, and therefore we call final without qualification that which is always desirable in itself and never for the sake of something else.

Now such a thing happiness, above all else, is held to be; for this we choose always for itself and never for the sake of something else, [1097^b] but honour, pleasure, reason, and every virtue we choose indeed for themselves (for if nothing resulted from them, we should still choose each of them), but we choose them also for the sake of happiness, judging that by means of them we shall be happy. Happiness, on the other hand, no one chooses for the sake of these, nor, in general, for anything other than itself.

From the point of view of self-sufficiency, the same result seems to follow; for the final good is thought to be self-sufficient. Now by self-sufficient we do not mean that which is sufficient for a man by himself, for one who lives a solitary life, but also for parents, children, wife, and in general for his friends and fellow citizens, since man is born for citizenship. But some limit must be set to this; for if we extend our requirement to ancestors and descendants and friends' friends we are in for an infinite series. Let us examine this question, however, on another occasion;[7] the self-sufficient we now define as that which when isolated makes life desirable and lacking in nothing; and such we think happiness to be; and further we think it most desirable of all things, without being counted as one good thing among others— if it were so counted it would clearly be made more desirable by the addition of even the least of goods; for that which is added becomes an excess of goods, and of goods the greater is always

[7] i. 10, 11, ix, 10.

more desirable. Happiness, then, is something final and self-sufficient, and is the end of action.

Presumably, however, to say that happiness is the chief good seems a platitude, and a clearer account of what it is is still desired. This might perhaps be given, if we could first ascertain the function of man. For just as for a flute-player, a sculptor, or any artist, and, in general, for all things that have a function or activity, the good and the "well" is thought to reside in the function, so would it seem to be for man, if he has a function. Have the carpenter, then, and the tanner certain functions or activities, and has man none? Is he born without a function? Or as eye, hand, foot, and in general each of the parts evidently has a function, may one lay it down that man similarly has a function apart from all these? What then can this be? Life seems to be common even to plants, but we are seeking what is peculiar to man. Let us [1098ª] exclude, therefore, the life of nutrition and growth. Next there would be a life of perception, but *it* also seems to be common even to the horse, the ox, and every animal. There remains, then, an active life of the element that has a rational principle; of this, one part has such a principle in the sense of being obedient to one, the other in the sense of possessing one and exercising thought. And, as "life of the rational element" also has two meanings, we must state that life in the sense of activity is what we mean, for this seems to be the more proper sense of the term. Now if the function of man is an activity of soul which follows or implies a rational principle, and if we say "a so-and-so" and "a good so-and-so" have a function which is the same in kind, e.g., a lyre player and a good lyre player, and so without qualification in all cases, eminence in respect of goodness being added to the name of the function (for the function of a lyre player is to play the lyre, and that of a good lyre player is to do so well): if this is the case, [and we state the function of man to be a certain kind of life, and this to be an activity or actions of the soul implying a rational principle, and the function of a good man to be the good and noble performance of these, and if any action is well performed when it is performed in accordance with the appropriate excellence, if this is the case,] human good turns

out to be activity of soul in accordance with virtue, and if there
are more than one virtue, in accordance with the best and most
complete.

But we must add "in a complete life." For one swallow does not
make a summer, nor does one day; and so too one day, or a short
time, does not make a man blessed and happy.

．　．　．　．

13. Since happiness is an activity of soul in accordance with perfect virtue, we must consider the nature of virtue; for perhaps we
shall thus see better the nature of happiness. The true student of
politics, too, is thought to have studied virtue above all things;
for he wishes to make his fellow citizens good and obedient to
the laws. As an example of this we have the lawgivers of the
Cretans and the Spartans, and any others of the kind that there
may have been. And if this inquiry belongs to political science,
clearly the pursuit of it will be in accordance with our original
plan. But clearly the virtue we must study is human virtue; for
the good we were seeking was human good and the happiness
human happiness. By human virtue we mean not that of the body
but that of the soul; and happiness also we call an activity of
soul. But if this is so, clearly the student of politics must know
somehow the facts about soul, as the man who is to heal the eyes
or the body as a whole must know about the eyes or the body; and
all the more since politics is more prized and better than medicine; but even among doctors the best educated spend much labor
on acquiring knowledge of the body. The student of politics, then,
must study the soul, and must study it with these objects in
view, and do so just to the extent which is sufficient for the questions we are discussing; for further precision is perhaps something more laborious than our purposes require.

Some things are said about it, adequately enough, even in the
discussions outside our school, and we must use these; e.g., that
one element in the soul is irrational and one has a rational principle. Whether these are separated as the parts of the body or
of anything divisible are, or are distinct by definition but by na-

ture inseparable, like convex and concave in the circumference of a circle, does not affect the present question.

Of the irrational element one division seems to be widely distributed, and vegetative in its nature, I mean that which causes nutrition and growth; for it is this kind of power of the soul that one must assign to [1102ᵇ] all nurslings and to embryos, and this same power to full-grown creatures; this is more reasonable than to assign some different power to them. Now the excellence of this seems to be common to all species and not specifically human; for this part or faculty seems to function most in sleep, while goodness and badness are least manifest in sleep (whence comes the saying that the happy are no better off than the wretched for half their lives; and this happens naturally enough, since sleep is an inactivity of the soul in that respect in which it is called good or bad), unless perhaps to a small extent some of the movements actually penetrate to the soul, and in this respect the dreams of good men are better than those of ordinary people. Enough of this subject, however; let us leave the nutritive faculty alone, since it has by its nature no share in human excellence.

There seems to be also another irrational element in the soul— one which in a sense, however, shares in a rational principle. For we praise the rational principle of the continent man and of the incontinent, and the part of their soul that has such a principle, since it urges them aright and toward the best objects; but there is found in them also another element naturally opposed to the rational principle, which fights against and resists that principle. For exactly as paralyzed limbs when we intend to move them to the right turn on the contrary to the left, so is it with the soul; the impulses of incontinent people move in contrary directions. But while in the body we see that which moves astray, in the soul we do not. No doubt, however, we must none the less suppose that in the soul too there is something contrary to the rational principle, resisting and opposing it. In what sense it is distinct from the other elements does not concern us. Now even this seems to have a share in a rational principle, as we said;[21] at any rate in the continent man it obeys the rational principle—and

[21] l. 13.

presumably in the temperate and brave man it is still more obedient, for in him it speaks, on all matters, with the same voice as the rational principle.

Therefore the irrational element also appears to be twofold. For the vegetative element in no way shares in a rational principle, but the appetitive, and in general the desiring element in a sense shares in it, insofar as it listens to and obeys it; this is the sense in which we speak of "taking account" of one's father or one's friends, not that in which we speak of "accounting" for a mathematical property. That the irrational element is in some sense persuaded by a rational principle is indicated also by the giving of advice and by all reproof and exhortation. And if this element also must be said to have a rational principle, [1103ª] that which has a rational principle (as well as that which has not) will be twofold, one subdivision having it in the strict sense and in itself, and the other having a tendency to obey as one does one's father.

Virtue too is distinguished into kinds in accordance with this difference; for we say that some of the virtues are intellectual and others moral, philosophic wisdom and understanding and practical wisdom being intellectual, liberality and temperance moral. For in speaking about a man's character we do not say that he is wise or has understanding, but that he is good-tempered or temperate; yet we praise the wise man also with respect to his state of mind; and of states of mind we call those which merit praise virtues.

Book II

1. Virtue, then, being of two kinds, intellectual and moral, intellectual virtue in the main owes both its birth and its growth to teaching (for which reason it requires experience and time), while moral virtue comes about as a result of habit, whence also its name *ethike* is one that is formed by a slight variation from the word *ethos* (habit). From this it is also plain that none of the moral virtues arises in us by nature; for nothing that exists by nature can form a habit contrary to its nature. For instance, the stone which by nature moves downwards cannot be habituated to

move upwards, not even if one tries to train it by throwing it up ten thousand times; nor can fire be habituated to move downwards, nor can anything else that by nature behaves in one way be trained to behave in another. Neither by nature, then, nor contrary to nature do the virtues arise in us; rather we are adapted by nature to receive them, and are made perfect by habit.

Again, of all the things that come to us by nature, we first acquire the potentiality and later exhibit the activity (this is plain in the case of the senses; for it was not by often seeing or often hearing that we got these senses, but on the contrary we had them before we used them, and did not come to have them by using them); but the virtues we get by first exercising them, as also happens in the case of the arts as well. For the things we have to learn before we can do them, we learn by doing them, e.g., men become builders by building and lyre [1103ᵇ] players by playing the lyre; so too we become just by doing just acts, temperate by doing temperate acts, brave by doing brave acts.

This is confirmed by what happens in states; for legislators make the citizens good by forming habits in them, and this is the wish of every legislator, and those who do not effect it miss their mark, and it is in this that a good constitution differs from a bad one.

Again, it is from the same causes and by the same means that every virtue is both produced and destroyed, and similarly every art; for it is from playing the lyre that both good and bad lyre players are produced. And the corresponding statement is true of builders and of all the rest; men will be good or bad builders as a result of building well or badly. For if this were not so, there would have been no need of a teacher, but all men would have been born good or bad at their craft. This, then, is the case with the virtues also; by doing the acts that we do in our transactions with other men, we become just or unjust, and by doing the acts that we do in the presence of danger, and being habituated to feel fear or confidence, we become brave or cowardly. The same is true of appetites and feelings of anger; some men become temperate and good-tempered, others self-indulgent and irascible, by behaving in one way or the other in the appropriate circumstances.

Thus, in one word, states of character arise out of like activities. This is why the activities we exhibit must be of a certain kind; it is because the states of character correspond to the differences between these. It makes no small difference, then, whether we form habits of one kind or of another from our very youth; it makes a very great difference, or rather *all* the difference.

2. Since, then, the present inquiry does not aim at theoretical knowledge like the others (for we are inquiring not in order to know what virtue is, but in order to become good, since otherwise our inquiry would have been of no use), we must examine the nature of actions, namely how we ought to do them; for these determine also the nature of the states of character that are produced, as we have said.[1] Now, that we must act according to the right rule is a common principle and must be assumed—it will be discussed later,[2] i. e., both what the right rule is, and how it is related to the other virtues. But this must be agreed [1104ᵃ] upon beforehand, that the whole account of matters of conduct must be given in outline and not precisely, as we said at the very beginning[3] that the accounts we demand must be in accordance with the subject matter; matters concerned with conduct and questions of what is good for us have no fixity, any more than matters of health. The general account being of this nature, the account of particular cases is yet more lacking in exactness; for they do not fall under any art or precept but the agents themselves must in each case consider what is appropriate to the occasion, as happens also in the art of medicine or of navigation.

But though our present account is of this nature we must give what help we can. First, then, let us consider this, that it is the nature of such things to be destroyed by defect and excess, as we see in the case of strength and of health (for to gain light on things imperceptible we must use the evidence of sensible things); both excessive and defective exercise destroys the strength, and similarly drink or food which is above or below a certain amount

1 a 31–b 25.
2 vi. 13.
3 1094ᵇ II–27.

destroys the health, while that which is proportionate both produces and increases and preserves it. So too is it, then, in the case of temperance and courage and the other virtues. For the man who flies from and fears everything and does not stand his ground against anything becomes a coward, and the man who fears nothing at all but goes to meet every danger becomes rash; and similarly the man who indulges in every pleasure and abstains from none becomes self-indulgent, while the man who shuns every pleasure, as boors do, becomes in a way insensible; temperance and courage, then, are destroyed by excess and defect, and preserved by the mean.

But not only are the sources and causes of their origination and growth the same as those of their destruction, but also the sphere of their actualization will be the same; for this is also true of the things which are more evident to sense, e.g., of strength; it is produced by taking much food and undergoing much exertion, and it is the strong man that will be most able to do these things. So too is it with the virtues; by abstaining from pleasures we become temperate, and it is when we have become so that we are most able to abstain from them; [1104^b] and similarly too in the case of courage, for by being habituated to despise things that are terrible and to stand our ground against them we become brave, and it is when we have become so that we shall be most able to stand our ground against them.

3. We must take as a sign of states of character the pleasure or pain that ensues on acts; for the man who abstains from bodily pleasures and delights in this very fact is temperate, while the man who is annoyed at it is self-indulgent, and he who stands his ground against things that are terrible and delights in this or at least is not pained is brave, while the man who is pained is a coward. For moral excellence is concerned with pleasures and pains; it is on account of the pleasure that we do bad things, and on account of the pain that we abstain from noble ones. Hence we ought to have been brought up in a particular way from our very youth, as Plato says,[4] so as both to delight in and to be pained by the things that we ought, for this is the right education.

[4] *Laws*, 653A ff., *Republic*, 401E–402A.

Again, if the virtues are concerned with actions and passions, and every passion and every action is accompanied by pleasure and pain, for this reason also virtue will be concerned with pleasures and pains. This is indicated also by the fact that punishment is inflicted by these means; for it is a kind of cure, and it is the nature of cures to be effected by contraries.

.   .   .   .

Book X

.   .   .   .

7. If happiness is activity in accordance with virtue, it is reasonable that it should be in accordance with the highest virtue; and this will be that of the best thing in us. Whether it be reason or something else that is this element which is thought to be our natural ruler and guide and to take thought of things noble and divine, whether it be itself also divine or only the most divine element in us, the activity of this in accordance with its proper virtue will be perfect happiness. That this activity is contemplative we have already said.[14]

Now this would seem to be in agreement both with what we said before[15] and with the truth. For, first, this activity is the best (since not only is reason the best thing in us, but the objects of reason are the best of knowable objects); and, second, it is the most continuous, since we can contemplate truth more continuously than we can *do* anything. And we think happiness has pleasure mingled with it, but the activity of philosophic wisdom is admittedly the pleasantest of virtuous activities; at all events the pursuit of it is thought to offer pleasures marvelous for their purity and their enduringness, and it is to be expected that those who

[14] This has not been said, but cf. 1095^b 14–1096^a 5, 1141^a 18–^{b} 3, 1143^b 33–1144^a 6, 1145^a 6–11.
[15] 1097^a 25–^{b} 21, 1099^a 7–21, 1173^b 15–19, 1174^b 20–23, 1175^b 36–1176^a 3.

know will pass their time more pleasantly than those who inquire. And the self-sufficiency that is spoken of must belong most to the contemplative activity. For while a philosopher, as well as a just man or one possessing any other virtue, needs the necessaries of life, when they are sufficiently equipped with things of that sort the just man needs people toward whom and with whom he shall act justly, and the temperate man, the brave man, and each of the others is in the same case, but the philosopher, even when by himself, can contemplate truth, and the better the wiser he is; he can perhaps do so better if [1177^b] he has fellow workers, but still he is the most self-sufficient. And this activity alone would seem to be loved for its own sake, for nothing arises from it apart from the contemplating, while from practical activities we gain more or less apart from the action. . . .

"NEEDS" IN EDUCATION*

R. F. Dearden

The concept of need is being increasingly widely used in educational discussions nowadays. Frequently the main weight of the writer's argument is borne by it. This is especially the case in discussions about curriculum construction at all levels of education and in certain theories in educational psychology. A few examples may be given to illustrate this.

In the handbook published by the former Ministry of Education called *Primary Education*, there is mentioned "the awareness of the child as a whole with inter-dependent spiritual, emotional, intellectual and physical needs."[1] Concerning secondary education, the Spens Report said that "before everything else *the school should provide for the pre-adolescent and adolescent years a life which answers to their special needs. . . .*"[2] More recently the National Union of Teachers published a report on secondary education in which it was said that "a primary principle in curriculum construction should be to serve individual needs."[3] Again, in *Primary Education in Scotland*, a recent publication of the Scottish Education Department, we find that the first chapter is devoted, not to a discussion of relevant "aims of education," but to "the needs of the child," which turn out to be just five in number.[4] In educational psychology the concept of needs is used in discussions of the motivation of learning.

There is the process called need-reduction, which derives from Hull's learning theory, and there is the kind of need which the

---

* Reprinted from the *British Journal of Educational Studies,* 14 (November, 1966): 5–12. By permission of the author and the *British Journal of Educational Studies.*

[1] H.M.S.O., *Primary Education* (London, 1959), p. 10.

[2] H.M.S.O., *Secondary Education* (London, 1939), p. 149.

[3] N.U.T., *The Curriculum of the Secondary School* (London, 1952), p. 23.

[4] H.M.S.O., *Primary Education in Scotland* (Edinburgh, 1965), Ch. 1.

social psychologists are interested in, such as the need for love or for participation in the group.

Perhaps these indications will suffice to substantiate the statement, which might in any case have been readily conceded, that the concept of need is being heavily worked these days. However, anyone who is unconvinced of this might well turn to the multitude of examples assembled by R. D. Archambault a few years ago in the Harvard Educational Review,[5] showing how "need" is coming to be relied on to settle all sorts of questions. But can any questions be settled by a reference to "need"? Is it simply a matter of carrying out the relevant piece of research to determine what children's needs are, so that problems of the curriculum and of learning, which have been somewhat intractable and centers of dispute in the past, can now be handed over to the sociologist or psychologist for definitive solution? In other words, are questions as to what people need purely empirical? Indeed, in view of the vacuity of some exhortations to have regard to needs, do needs-statements have any empirical basis at all?

·   ·   ·   ·

The Concept of Need

In trying to explicate the logic of the concept of need, it must be pointed out at the start that there are some things one is *not* trying to do. First of all, nothing is being said about the motives which people may have in talking of needs. If I say to a pupil that he needs to work harder for his examination, my motive might be to improve my reputation as a teacher through the results for which I urge him to strive. Just what it is that people have in mind obviously varies greatly and may be commendable or otherwise. Second, nothing is being said about the variety of functions which needs-statements may be used to perform in different contexts. They may be used, for example, to explain, concede, recommend, justify, warn, advise, exhort, and so on, and this

[5] R. D. Archambault, "The Concept of Need and Its Relation to Certain Aspects of Educational Theory," in *Harvard Educational Review* (Winter, 1957).

variety again does not directly concern us. Finally, where the emphasis is placed in statements of need varies considerably also. The stress may be on who it is that is in need, or on the fact that this is a case of *need*, or on what it is that is asserted to be needed. This, too, does not directly concern us. But whatever a person's motive might be in making a needs-statement, whatever function it might be performing and wherever the emphasis might be placed, it may reasonably be supposed, since the same word is used on each occasion, that there are certain criteria which have to be satisfied if the word is to be used at all, or at least advisedly. It is the explication of these criteria that one has in mind in referring to the *concept* of need.

Perhaps the most obvious criterion of need is that a state of affairs conceived of is absent: people are without food, children are without love, or pensioners are without the means of living comfortably. Alternatively, it may be that the state of affairs conceived of is not in fact absent but could well be, so that there is a real contingency that has to be provided against. We may agree that men need food without first enquiring whether anyone is actually without it. But this is not enough. For a *need* to exist, something more is required than that a state of affairs conceived of be absent. A child may lack musical or artistic ability without thereby being placed in need of those talents. A school may lack a swimming pool, tennis courts, or greenhouse without necessarily being in need of them. The absence of a state of affairs does not create a need unless this absence *ought not* to exist, for example, because then a rule would not be complied with, or a standard would not be attained, or a goal would not be achieved. In short, "need" is a normative concept and, as such, needs are not to be determined just by research into what is observably the case. Since this normative aspect of "need" will prove of great importance in seeing how far sociologists or psychologists can settle questions of need, some illustrations to bring out this aspect more clearly will now be given.

The pensioners' need of an increased pension is not established by pointing out facts about their circumstances. By comparison with people in some parts of the world, they live very comfortably indeed. The perception of the *inadequacy* of their circumstances presupposes a certain standard of living being regarded as so desirable that people ought not be allowed to fall below it. In short, social norms are implied in talk about pensioners' needs, norms which vary so much from society to society that what is regarded as a need in one is a luxury in another. This particular type of norm is discussed at length by S. I. Benn and R. S. Peters.[6] Again, very many statements of need presuppose norms of the *proper functioning* of a thing, for example, of an institution such as a school, of a piece of machinery such as a car, of an organism such as a rat, or of a trade or profession, such as being a carpenter or a schoolteacher. This is the case when it is said that a school needs a certain teacher-pupil ratio, a car needs a new engine, a rat needs water, or a carpenter needs a tool allowance. Finally, this normative aspect of "need" may be illustrated by cases where an explicit rule creates a need, as when it is said that owners of dogs need a license for them, or students need at least two A-levels to be considered for a place in a university.

There are, of course, many different types of norms or standards that may be presupposed by needs-statements, and if it were our purpose to classify these statements it would be convenient to do so according to the type of norm presupposed. However, such distinctions as are to be made here will be made only as they become necessary. A fuller discussion of them has been attempted by P. W. Taylor.[7] But there is one sort of case that must briefly be considered, since on the face of it no norm or standard such as is here being insisted on is presupposed. This is the common case in which something is needed, not in order to attain a social standard, properly fulfil a function, or satisfy a rule, but in order to achieve a particular purpose, as when we need a hammer to knock in a nail, a pencil to sketch a picture, or

[6] S. I. Benn and R. S. Peters, *Social Principles and the Democratic State* (London, 1959), Ch. 6, Sec. 3.

[7] P. W. Taylor, " 'Needs' Statements," in *Analysis* (1958–59), pp. 106–11.

a dictionary to find a meaning. Although the emphasis in these cases is on what is needed and away from any standards, nevertheless standards are being presupposed: standards of appropriateness or of efficiency. Why is it a pencil that I need and not a stick of charcoal or a poker? Why is it a hammer that I need and not a shoe, a brick, or a paperweight? Why consult a dictionary when I could inquire of other people? Such questions cannot be answered without making explicit the standard presupposed in this kind of needs-statement. Indeed, the fact that purposive human activity implies standards is of some importance for a proper understanding of activity methods in teaching, but it would be too much of a digression to pursue that particular point in this article.

So far, then, two criteria have emerged for the application of the concept of need. In order of logical priority they are, first, that there should be some kind of norm, for example a standard of living, the "proper functioning" of a thing, an explicit rule or a notion of what it is to do something properly or efficiently. Second, there is the matter of fact that this norm has not been achieved, or could well fail to be maintained. These two criteria seem to be sufficient for saying that someone is "in need." The subsequent discussion will justify the importance of remarking here that being "in need" is not necessarily a state of which the person concerned is aware. He may be or may not. In this respect being "in need" is different from actually wanting something. As Benn and Peters put it: "To say that a man *wants* food is simply to describe his state of mind; to say that he *needs* food is to say that he will not measure up to an understood standard unless he gets it."[8]

It must be admitted that there are, however, some uses of "want" in which it serves the same function as "need."

If we wish to go beyond saying that someone is "in need" to saying what exactly it is that is needed, in order to measure up to the norm or standard implied, then a third criterion must be satisfied, namely that what is said to be needed really must be the

[8] S. I. Benn and R. S. Peters, p. 143.

relevant condition for achieving what the norm prescribes. For example, if I am in poor health then the remedy offered as being what I need really must be the relevant condition of achieving "good health." Again, if it is a certain amount of increased pension which the pensioners are said to need, then this amount really must be the relevant condition of their attaining the standards of living desiderated. The point seems obvious enough not to need further illustration.

To conclude this analysis, it will now be considered to what extent a needs-statement is empirically based, as this will be of importance in the following discussion of how far questions in education can be *settled* by a statement of needs. As was just remarked (second criterion), it is a question of fact whether or not a particular norm is being attained. For example, some sort of social survey is required to establish how the pensioners are faring. Often the diagnosis of the condition associated with a need requires specialized knowledge, for example, as to just how a car's engine is failing to function properly or just what the nature of an illness is. But whether it is common sense or specialized knowledge that is required, so long as the question is only whether a norm is being attained, or in what precise manner it is not being attained, then it can be settled objectively, either by making observations it is open to anyone to make or by the more sophisticated procedures of an appropriate science or research technique. This conclusion holds too if the question concerns the relevant condition for attaining the norm (third criterion). Here too common sense may suffice ("it's a *hammer* that you need"), or a more sophisticated inquiry into cause and effect may be called for ("it's vitamin B_{12} that persons suffering from anemia need"). It can be seen then that needs-statements do at least have an empirical basis. They can, accordingly, be empirically refuted, for example, by pointing out that the norm *is* in fact being attained ("our survey shows that pensioners already receive . . ."), or by showing that what is said to be needed will not in fact do the trick and so cannot be what is really needed ("the increase proposed would not even match the rising cost of living").

But what of the norms? They can neither be "discovered" nor empirically refuted, since they indicate how things ought to be in various ways. Questions as to desirable standards, proper functioning, desirable rules, or what appropriateness and efficiency are cannot be determined by observation or experiment, though this does not mean that they are arbitrary or insusceptible of being reasoned about. It does mean, however, that conflicts of opinion may be expected here, that in some cases the conflict may be very intractable and that since decisions may be involved, not just discoveries, we are bound to ask by what authority sociologists, psychologists, and specialists of other sorts presume to *settle* for us questions of need. Indeed, one of the purposes of this article is to sift out the debatable from the definitive in educational discussions which revolve around need. Needs-statements considered at this level (first criterion) are rebutted, not by adducing certain facts, but by rejecting the norm being presupposed. If you say that in my emaciated condition I need food, I may refuse to attach any importance to the norms of health that you are presupposing, pointing out that I am engaged in a religious exercise; if you say that children need love, I may refuse to attach any importance to the ideal of a cooperative, affectionate, and trusting character you presuppose, pointing out that we of the Mundugumor admire a different sort of character; and if you say that the curriculum must make provision for such needs as those for instruction in petting, party-organizing, dating, budgeting, and driver-training, I may reject the norm of happy social adjustment that you are presupposing. Plainly, then, although questions of need have an empirical basis, they cannot *ultimately* be settled empirically, for the norms presupposed have to be thrashed out by the nonspecialist procedures of argument and debate. Where, however, there already exists a consensus on norms, either as a shared assumption or as a formal declaration of some sort, then specialist researches, resting on a background of common agreement, may well settle questions of need, since in those cases it is only at an empirical level (criteria two and three) that the question is an open one.

Needs and the Curriculum

Many educationists, especially but not only in America, have taken the concept of need as the main guide to curriculum construction. A fairly well-known example would be the book *Exploring the Curriculum* by H. H. Giles and others.[9] A useful condensation of the "adolescent needs" discussed in that book groups them into six main categories, each further subdivided. These main categories are: (i) establishing personal relationships; (ii) establishing independence; (iii) understanding human behavior; (iv) establishing self in society; (v) normality; (vi) understanding the universe.[10] It is not only the Americans, however, who are attracted by the idea of a curriculum built out of needs. The term finds a congenial home in our own official reports and in publications on education generally, as was briefly indicated in the introduction to this article. But the main difficulty with all such approaches to curriculum construction has been pointed out by B. P. Komisar, namely that *every* curriculum is a needs-curriculum[11]; nobody wishes to defend the inclusion in the curriculum of anything that is *not* needed. What, then, is the attraction of the concept of need here?

One of the attractions of "need" seems to be that it is thought that, by basing a curriculum on needs, the problem of motivation will be solved; but this is not necessarily so at all. The statement that "*X needs Y*" carries no implication at all that "*X wants Y*," as has already been pointed out. If people are careless of their interests, or if they dislike what they need, they may need without wanting whatever it is. In curriculum construction one could, by a consideration of what a subsequent stage of education demands, of what the nature of a subject demands, or of what common

[9] H. H. Giles et al., *Exploring the Curriculum* (New York, 1942).

[10] B. O. Smith, W. O. Stanley, J. H. Shores, *Fundamentals of Curriculum Construction,* rev. ed. (New York, 1957), Ch. 15, Sec. 2.

[11] B. P. Komisar, " 'Need' and the Needs-Curriculum," in *Language and Concepts in Education,* eds. B. O. Smith and R. H. Ennis (Chicago, 1961).

employments demand, arrive at all sorts of needs-statements that would carry no implication either of awareness of these needs or of acceptance of them by the children. Indeed, the motivational problem in teaching is a *problem* precisely because children are regarded as needing something which they cannot be brought to want or to be interested in. Needs will solve the motivational problem only if they are felt and accepted by the children. It might accordingly be suggested that the curriculum be formed out of children's *felt* needs, which is in practice much the same thing as to suggest that the curriculum be based on children's interests. Not surprisingly, therefore, *needs* and *interests* are regularly coupled together and treated as synonyms, or near-synonyms. This conflation is facilitated by an ambiguity in the notion of "interest," which must briefly be mentioned.

There is a considerable difference between saying that something is *in* a person's interest and saying that he *feels* an interest in it. Doubtless the activities arranged for children in schools are thought to be *in* their interests, just as they are thought to meet important educational needs, but it is a further question whether children will feel or show any interest in these activities, just as they may not feel or accept the needs pressed upon them. It can easily be seen, therefore, that the two notions of needs and interests offer glorious opportunities for seeming both to have one's cake and eat it, for by sliding about between these ambiguities of meaning, curricular recommendations can be made to seem to satisfy everybody: those who insist that the teacher knows best can take it that the teacher has to settle what children need or what is in their interests, perhaps by reflection upon the nature of a subject, whereas those who insist on "starting from the child" can take it that what the teacher has to do is to inquire what children feel that they need or feel interested in. Thus a crucial problem of the curriculum may be slurred over. If the problem is squarely faced, however, it is plain that no *use* of the concept of need is going to solve it, since the difficulty here is precisely over the norms which create the needs, the norms implicit in any account of what a desirable education is.

It might be said in connection with needs and the curriculum, however, that there are certain general injunctions about needs which do have point in that they lay down something called "broad policy." Reports which urge us to consider "individual needs," or the "special needs" of some group, may serve to draw attention to something that is being neglected, or to get us facing in what the authors consider to be the right direction. Whether this is a valuable thing to do will depend, of course, on the backing which is offered for regarding these to be real needs at all (the normative question), and on what it is we are supposed to see when we face in the right direction, assuming that more than a bare formula for a recommendation is being offered. These are points about "broad policy" which must always be raised in order to determine whether we are being offered mere pap, or something of greater substance. Obviously particular cases must each be considered on their merits, but enough misgivings have been raised to justify automatic suspicion of curricular discussions which revolve around "need". . . .

ON CERTAIN CRITERIA FOR SELECTING AIMS AND CONTENT OF EDUCATION*

Sidney Hook

Aims and the Nature of Man

We have been attempting to justify the ends of education by their consequences in experience. There is another approach which rules out all reference to consequences as irrelevant. This declares that we are dealing with a metaphysical question, which requires an answer based on the true metaphysics. Its chief exponents in America are Robert M. Hutchins, Monsignor Fulton Sheen, and Mortimer Adler. They hold that the appropriate end of education can be *deduced* from the true nature of man. The true nature of man is that which differentiates him from animals, on the one hand, and angels, on the other. It is expressed in the proposition: "Man is a rational animal." From which it is inferred that the end of human education should be the cultivation of reason.

. . . [But] a patent fallacy is involved in the presumed deduction of the ends of education from what uniquely differentiates man from other animals.

First of all . . . from what man *is* we can at best reach conclusions only about what human education is, not what it *should be*. What man should be is undoubtedly related to what he is, for no man should be what he cannot be. Yet a proposition about what he is no more uniquely entails what he should be than the recognition of the nature of an egg necessitates our concluding that the egg should become a chicken rather than an egg sandwich.

A further assumption of the argument is the Aristotelian doctrine that the good of anything is the performance of its specific virtue or the realization of its potentiality. The "good" egg is one that becomes a chicken, the "good" man is one who realizes his

* Reprinted from *Education for Modern Man: A New Perspective* (New York: Alfred A. Knopf, 1963), pp. 68–72, 75–76, 119–25. By permission of the author. Copyright 1946, © 1963 by Sidney Hook.

natural capacity to think. This overlooks the fact that the natural capacities of a thing limit the range of its fulfillments but do not determine any specific fulfillment. Not every natural power of man has only one natural end; and not every power which has one end achieves it by one mode of development. Thinking is no more or no less natural to man than eating and singing. But what, when, and how a man should eat; what, when, and how a man should sing; about what and when he should think—all this depends not so much upon the natural powers of eating, singing, or thinking as upon an ideal of fitness, appropriateness, or goodness, that is *not* given with natural powers but brought to bear *upon* them in social, historical, and personal experience. When we assert that men *should* be rational, we are not talking biology or metaphysics but voicing a social directive that selectively modifies the natural exercise of human powers in the light of preferred consequences among possible alternate uses.

Second, granted for the sake of the argument that animals other than man are incapable of any rationality. The question is an old and difficult one, handled satirically by Plutarch and experimentally by Köhler, both of whom disagree with the airy dogmatism of the neo-Thomists. Nonetheless, rationality is not the only feature which differentiates man from other animals. Man can be defined, and has been by Benjamin Franklin and Karl Marx, as a "tool-making animal." By the same reasoning employed by neo-Thomists, we can "deduce" that man's proper education should be vocational! Man is also the only animal that can will to commit suicide. Does it follow that education should therefore be a preparation for death? Man is also the only animal that ruts all year round. What educational corollary does this unique trait entail?

Third, even if man is a rational animal, he is not only that. He has many other traits—needs, feelings, emotions, desires, whose nobility or ignobility depend upon their social context. An education appropriate to man would not necessarily limit itself to one aspect of his nature even if that aspect were regarded as more valuable than any other. It is a queer view of the nature of any organism that limits itself to a concern only with its differentia. The notion that the education of reason can or should be carried out independently of the education of the emotions has been called by Whitehead "one of the most fatal, erroneous and dangerous conceptions ever introduced into the theory of education."[1] At any rate, what is clear is that we can go from the nature of man to the conclusion that we should educate for reason only because some selective principle has been introduced. The basic educational issues, like the basic ethical issues, pose problems of choice. The nature of man is always relevant; but just as relevant is our decision as to what we want to make of it, what we want men to become. At this point no metaphysical deduction, whether proceeding from materialistic or spiritualistic premises concerning the nature of "reality," can guide us.

. . . .

If education is determined by human nature, may not human nature change, and with it the nature of education? "*We must insist,*" writes Mr. Hutchins, "*that no matter how environments differ human nature is, always has been, and always will be the same everywhere.*"[4]

This is truly a remarkable assertion. Before we inquire on what evidence Mr. Hutchins knows this to be true, let us see what it implies. For one thing, it implies that human nature is completely independent of changes in the world of physical nature with which the human organism is in constant interaction. Now, certainly, Mr. Hutchins cannot know that the world of nature "is, always has been, and always will be the same everywhere." He therefore must believe that no transformation of the physical basis of human life can possibly affect human nature. His assertion further implies that man's nature is completely independent of changes in the human body, particularly the brain and nervous system. At one stroke this calls into question the whole evolu-

---

[1] Alfred North Whitehead, *The Aims of Education and Other Essays* (New York: Macmillan, 1929), p. 9.

[4] Robert M. Hutchins, "Towards a Durable Society," *Fortune*, Vol. 27, No. 6 (June, 1943), p. 158. My italics.

tionary approach to the origin and development of the human species. Finally, it implies that the habitation of man's nature in a human body is unaffected by changes in society and social nurture. The enormous range of variation in social behavior, which testifies to the plasticity of the simplest physiological response under cultural conditioning, leaves the essence of human nature unaltered. In short, human nature is taken out of the world altogether. It is removed from any verifiable context in experience which would permit us to identify it and observe its operations. For anything which operates in the world does so in *interaction* with other things that help shape its character.

There is only one entity that satisfies all these conditions. It is the supernatural soul as conceived by theologians of the orthodox Christian tradition. It is not the Aristotelian concept of the soul because, for Aristotle, the soul was the form of the body, all forms were incarnate in matter, and the nature of man was construed from his behavior. The constancy of human nature in Aristotle was predicated on the notion of the constancy of the natural order as well. Were he, in the light of modern science, to abandon the latter notion, he would have surrendered the belief in the constancy of human nature, since it was integrally related to the behavior of the body in nature and society. . . .

It is important to know what men are in order intelligently to determine what they should become. Educational aims merely restate what we believe men should become insofar as they can be influenced by the processes of learning and teaching. The comparative study of cultures shows how diverse men may become; it also shows certain similarities and identities. The vital physiological sequences are the same in every culture. A social organization, a form of mating, and other institutions are also everywhere observable where men live together. But there are all types and degrees of cultural institutions. And these institutions, in turn, give varied meanings to identical physiological acts. These meanings enter so integrally into the performance of the physiological action that it requires an abstract science like biology to distinguish between what is attributable to the unlearned behavior of the organism and what is learned from the culture. "It would be idle," says Malinowski, "to disregard the fact that the impulse leading to the simplest physiological performance is as highly plastic and determined by tradition as it is ineluctable in the long run because determined by physiological necessities."[7] Depending upon the particular aspect of human behavior we are interested in, we can establish an empirical case for the constancy or mutability of human nature. Provided we keep the distinctions in mind, there is nothing incompatible in asserting that in certain respects human nature is the same, in others different. What is apparent is that those aspects of human nature which appear constant are a set of unconscious processes that are a condition of life. Although these are taken note of in every sensible educational program, they are far from the center of educational concern, which is understanding the dominant cultural problems of the present in relation to the past out of which they have grown, and to the future whose shape depends in part upon that understanding. Whether men remain the same or different, in the sense in which the question is educationally significant, depends upon whether they choose to retain or transform their culture.

. . . .

Relevance and the Content of Education

The easiest answer to the question "What should we teach?" is also the most deceptive. We should teach—so runs this answer—those subjects which embody the great truths of our human tradition, the accumulated knowledge, skills, and wisdom which are the inalienable heritage of every child. This answer is deceptive because it assumes that there are educators, or others for that matter, who assert that we should *not* teach these things. If there are any such, they have never given a sign of their presence. To infer that those who believe that *more* than these things should be taught are therefore opposed to including them is to exhibit

[7] Bronislaw Malinowski, *A Scientific Theory of Culture and Other Essays,* ed. Huntington Cairns (Chapel Hill: University of North Carolina Press, 1944), p. 87.

one of those passionate lapses in thinking which suggest that the issue lies somewhere else. The answer is deceptive because it is an overall truism through which is insinuated the notion that emphasis upon *present-day problems* involves its rejection or denial. Nothing can be taught which does not at one point or another involve the use of some tradition—let it be no more than language. Nothing can be learned which is not continuous with something already known. Instead of an honest confrontation of the issue: What should be the *relative* place of study of the past and present in our education? the issue is lost in the rhetorical flourishes and overtones of what in Aristotle's day was already recognized as a commonplace.

Nor is the issue fairly stated by those who, like Hutchins and Maritain, charge modern educators with the fallacy of "presentism." According to the former, those who would include a study of modern industrial processes in the education of the American student are adherents of "the cult of immediacy." "In this view the way to comprehend the world is to grapple with the reality you find about you. . . . There is no past."[1] One would imagine that grappling with the realities that surround us is precisely the way to begin to understand the world. One would imagine that through such an effort we would discover not only that there is a past, but that it has an inescapable bearing and importance upon the realities surrounding us. To identify the view that the present world is a legitimate object of study for those who are going to live in it, with the view that the present is nothing but a specious bloom of immediacy with no roots in the past and no fruits in the future, is intellectually cheap. It evades considered argument by caricature, and blocks fruitful discussion of the place of the present *and* past in a desirable educational experience.

There is a certain ambiguity in the term "present" which must be clarified before we ask whether our education is to be oriented toward the past or present. In one sense all education is *for* the present. That is to say, the justification for teaching or learning anything must be its observable consequences within our experi-

[1] Robert M. Hutchins, *Education for Freedom* (Baton Rouge: Louisiana State University Press, 1943), p. 32.

ence. Whatever other world an individual will inhabit, his life will be spent in this one. Whatever may be the society of the future, either it will be continuous with the society in which he now lives or it will develop out of its conflicts and problems.

Whatever we teach, whether it be a tale of glory, the procession of the seasons, or the mystery of the atom, we teach ultimately for the sake of the present. We teach our children reading, writing, and arithmetic not because they are skills that were once acquired by man—there have been many skills developed in the past that were better forgotten—but because they have a *continuing function of a desirable nature in the present world.* Reference to the present is inescapable no matter what interests or powers we would awaken, no matter what knowledge we would impart. Whitehead, who is often invoked to justify educational practices he in fact condemns, states the point with unusual eloquence.

> The only use of a knowledge of the past is to equip us for the present. No more deadly harm can be done to young minds than by depreciation of the present. The present contains all that there is. It is holy ground; for it is the past; and it is the future. At the same time it must be observed that an age is no less past if it existed two hundred years ago than if it existed two thousand years ago. Do not be deceived by the pedantry of dates. The ages of Shakespeare and of Molière are no less past than are the ages of Sophocles and of Virgil. The communion of saints is a great and inspiring assemblage, but it has only one possible hall of meeting, and that is, the present; and the mere lapse of time through which any particular group of saints must travel to reach that meeting-place, makes very little difference.[2]

To say that the present is sacred ground does not imply that the problems and materials of present-day life are sacred. For the present in this context designates the locus of educational justification, not the nature of educational subject matter. But at the same time it does suggest a criterion which will enable us to evaluate the respective claims of different subject matters. This is the criterion of *relevance*.

To demand that the content of instruction be relevant to the

[2] Alfred North Whitehead, *The Organization of Thought* (Philadelphia: J. B. Lippincott Co., 1918), pp. 6–7.

present emphatically does not preclude a study of the past. It only prevents us from getting lost in the past. It enables us to make some intelligent *selection* out of the limitless materials inherited from the past.

.　.　.　.

To what in the present should the content of study be relevant? In the broadest sense of the term, to the fundamental *problems* of the age—to the social, political, intellectual, and, if we like, the spiritual questions posed by our time and culture. Here the issue acquires a biting edge. It is these problems, problems which will not be denied even if we refuse to study them, that should serve as the chief subject matters around which to build educational instruction. By "chief" subject matters, I mean not merely that at a certain point in schooling they become the focal problems of study, but that they become the points of departure for *planning* the content of curriculum at other levels, too. Far from unduly narrowing the course of study, we shall see that such orientation expands and enriches it without converting it into an archaic or contemporary miscellany.

The reason this approach enriches the course of study is twofold. First, the past world and the present are so continuous that there are few problems which can be intelligently understood without transcending the immediate context in which they are discovered. Second, the nature of present-day problems is such that they require the mastery of certain subject matters and techniques which are themselves not problematic, and which have no *direct* relation to these problems. The first reason explains why the study of the present must be included in the education of modern man. For it provides the key to what to include and exclude from the past. The second reason explains why the mastery of certain skills and areas of knowledge must be given precedence over that of others in the organization of a curriculum: why, for example, an ability to read critically is more important than an ability to typewrite; why knowledge of the essential elements of statistics should be more generally required than knowledge of the history of astronomy. Together, these reasons explain, as we shall see, what elements in education should be constant and what not; how curriculums may be intelligently changed in content and emphasis; how they may be different and yet equally good at different times.

There is a way of understanding the doctrine of relevance according to which it is the quintessence of an "anti-educational" attitude. "Relevance" here becomes the pretext under which every passing whim, fancy, or predicament in the social scene stakes a claim for inclusion in the curriculum of studies. The attempt to make education relevant is construed by Mr. Wriston, former president of Brown University, as necessitating overnight revisions of the educational curriculum, and roundly condemned. "The doctrine of relevance is valid only in a perfectly stable world where the future is easily predictable. . . ." But such a world is impossible. Therefore it is a fundamental error to organize a course of study whose consequence is "shallow concentration upon transitory environmental circumstances."[3]

Once more, the injection of an over-simple disjunction burkes genuine issues. Either the world is perfectly stable or it travels like mad! Study must either be profound or shallow! Presumably the past is never studied shallowly or the present profoundly! But these are absurd alternatives. The fundamental problems of an age are not born overnight, nor are they ever solved in a fortnight. They are not disasters before which we are helpless, nor are they business opportunities which we must snatch before they disappear. Education relevant to an understanding of the place of war in modern society is not an education relevant specifically to Pearl Harbor or to the next occasion of war. . . . The problem of reconciling social security and political democracy was not created by the New Deal, nor was the problem of racial conflict created by Hitler. To speak intelligently of *fundamental* problems is at the same time to distinguish between them and *ephemeral* problems. The *specific* form a fundamental problem may take will vary from situation to situation. But recognizing that it is a

3 Theodore M. Greene, et. al., *Liberal Education Re-Examined* (New York: Harper & Brothers, 1943), pp. 9–11.

specific form of a *fundamental* problem is a genuine educational discovery. It is a discovery that immediately lifts the problem out of ephemeral detail, and without losing sight of its dramatic significance for the present, uncovers the connections with the past and the possible bearings on the future which are of its very nature.

Let us examine some concrete illustrations of contemporary problems and issues, so despised by traditionalists, in order to see what would be involved in their adequate understanding. Nothing is more contemporary than present-day totalitarianism in its various forms. Can its nature be understood without a social and economic analysis of capitalism and its periodic cycles? Can we come to grips with its rationalizations, and understand our own minds in relation to it, without some study of the ideas of men like Chamberlain, Nietzsche, Hegel, Rousseau, Locke, Hobbes, Aquinas, Aristotle, and Plato? Can theories of race and racial supremacy be exposed without a sound knowledge of biology and some familiarity with the elements of scientific method? . . .

Or take a prosaic theme like taxation. Properly approached, it is an exciting introduction not only to questions of economic theory but to principles of social philosophy and theories of government. The problem of conservation of natural resources opens doorways into almost all the sciences. Whatever we touch that is of great moment in the modern world—whether it be urbanization, population trends and housing, unemployment, social security, civil rights and duties, the growth of administrative law, the control of the air, the role of the state, individual enterprise and trade-unions in industry, the origins and proposed cures of war, the promise and dangers of socialism, the prospects of a world state, the sources of racial and religious conflicts—cannot be adequately grasped without exploring the causal and ideational lines that radiate from them to ideas and events in the past. They cannot be studied as they should be without some knowledge of systematic disciplines. And they cannot be pursued for long without discovering the moral commitments we bring to them, and test in the bringing. To fail to realize any one of these truths is a failure of imagination. To fail in carrying home these truths in the practice of the classroom is a failure of pedagogic verve and skill. It is one thing to recognize this failure of imagination and verve in much of contemporary educational procedure. It is quite another thing to build an educational philosophy on the basis of these defects and turn away from present-day problems. . . .

REFLECTIONS ON EDUCATIONAL RELEVANCE*

Israel Scheffler

J. L. Austin used to query the importance of importance. I want here to question the educational relevance of educational relevance.

To do so may seem paradoxical, even absurd. For if relevance is not relevant, what is? And who, in his right mind, would wish learning to be irrelevant? The air of obviousness about these questions misleads, however. It derives, not from some mythical relevance axiom of the theory of education, but from the characteristic value-laden import of the word in its categorical use. To stand against irrelevance is like opposing sin and to favor relevance is akin to applauding virtue. The theoretical problem, with relevance as with virtue, is to say in what it consists and why, thus specified, it ought to be pursued. Relevance is, in particular, not an absolute property; nothing is either relevant or irrelevant in and of itself. Relevant to what, how, and why?—that is the question. That is, at any rate, the question if the current demand for relevance is to be taken not merely as a fashionable slogan but as a serious educational doctrine.

There being no single official elaboration of such a doctrine, I shall sketch three philosophical interpretations that might plausibly be offered in defense of current emphases on relevance, and I shall organize my comments around each of these interpretations. The first is primarily epistemological, concerning the nature and warrant of knowledge. The second is primarily psychological, having to do with the character of thought. The third is mainly moral, treating of the purposes of schooling.

1. Epistemological Interpretation

According to a venerable tradition, knowing is a state of union of the knower and the known. In apprehension, the knower is at one

* Reprinted from the *Journal of Philosophy*, 66 (1969): 764–73. By permission of the author and the *Journal of Philosophy*.

with the object, contemplation a form of love in which rational man finds his highest consummation. The state of union is of course not physical; to know a thing is not to be in physical proximity to it. Rather, it is to understand it, that is, to apprehend through the mind its essential structure or abstract form. Knowledge is union, then, not with the ordinary things of the world, but with their ideal essences. Such union affords, however, an indirect grasp of ordinary things and processes, inasmuch as the latter are crude approximations or rough embodiments of the pure forms seen by the eye of intellect alone.

For the Platonic tradition just sketched, knowing thus involves a withdrawal from the immediate world as well as an identification of the mind with the abstract forms which alone render this world intelligible. Education is not an immersion in the ordinary world but an approach to a superior abstract reality remote from it. Ideally, education is mathematical and dialectical, and the mind illuminated by abstract forms is best able to deal with the ordinary processes of the physical and human environment when it is once again directed toward them.

The classical conception we have been discussing has been largely abandoned. The doctrine of abstract forms, in particular, has been severely criticized. Not only are there fundamental difficulties in conceiving the nature and interrelations of these forms; as well as their relations to the ordinary world. The rise of scientific modes of thought has made it increasingly implausible to suppose that knowledge consists in contemplation of a world of essences, of superior reality, lying behind the changing phenomena of the common-sense environment. The world of changes is the one real world. Through addressing itself actively to this world, science seeks the provisional experimental truths that dwell amid change.

From this point of view, an education that draws the student away from the phenomena of his environment diverts him from the task of achieving truth. If the notion of a static world of essences is rejected as myth, an education that encourages the mind to dwell in such a world must frustrate the pursuit of truth. Detached and abstract, it is irrelevant to the only reliable processes available to man for establishing true beliefs by which he can guide his conduct. Such epistemological irrelevance is to be shunned if rational conduct is our ideal. Instead of withdrawal, education must encourage immersion in the changing phenomena constituting the live environment of the student. The radical rejection of classical doctrines of knowledge thus leads us to reject equally a detached and remote education.

Now the trouble with this line of thought, as I see it, is not that it rejects classical epistemology, but that it does not sufficiently reject it. Denying the Platonistic assumption of a superior world of essences, it retains the ancient and even more primitive assumption that knowledge consists in a state of union between knower and known. To know is to draw near to, and be one with, the object of knowledge, to eliminate the distance between. Instead of the object of knowledge being thought to consist in an essential and superior reality, it is now conceived simply as the ordinary world of material and historical processes. To know this object is, however, again to be understood as consisting in a state of union with it. This ordinary world must be directly confronted, without conventional or ideological intermediaries. Education is to abolish distance and detachment, bringing the learner into intimate engagement with the environment to be known.

The underlying assumption of knowledge as union is, however, radically false. Glued to the phenomena, the mind can no more attain perspective than can the viewer with eyeballs glued to the painting. Cognition is inextricably dependent upon categorization, analysis, selection, abstraction, and expectation. It is the very antithesis of dumb contact. If the scientist does not seek to contemplate a static world of essences, neither does he immerse himself in the phenomenal changes of his immediate environment in an effort to confront the facts. Facts, in any case, presuppose conceptualization and derive significance through their bearings on theory. The scientist, far from rejecting the mediation of concepts and theoretical construction, seeks ever newer and more comprehensive intellectual schemes for understanding. These schemes bring with them fresh modes of analysis and order; they create novel definitions of fact and bring forth new dimensions of relevance. What the scientist rejects is the rule of the familiar. His job is precisely not to take for granted the customary conceptual apparatus of his environment but, through criticism and invention, to develop more adequate intellectual equipment which will encompass this very environment along with other actual and possible ones.

Such a mission requires that he step back from the material and conceptual surroundings in which he finds himself. He seeks the distance that lends perspective and the critical detachment that facilitates alternative testable visions. There is a world of difference between such withdrawal and the retreat into never-never lands of myth or pedantry. The alternative to such retreat is not a warm bath in immediate phenomena but a search for theoretical comprehension that transcends the merely local and the merely customary. Epistemological relevance, in short, requires us to reject both myth and mystic union. It requires not contact but criticism, not immersion in the phenomenal and conceptual given, but the flexibility of mind capable of transcending, reordering, and expanding the given. An education that fosters criticism and conceptual flexibility will transcend its environment not by erecting a mythical substitute for this world but rather by striving for a systematic and penetrating comprehension of it.

2. Psychological Interpretation

Thought, according to a widely prevalent doctrine, is problem-oriented. It originates in doubt, conflict, and difficulty. Its function is to overcome obstacles to the smooth flow of human activities. When action is coherent and well adapted to its circumstances, human energy is released into overt channels set by habit and custom. The blocking of conduct, either through internal conflict or environmental hindrance, turns its energy inwards, transforming it into thought. Playing out multiple possibilities for future action, thought proceeds until an envisaged feature of some such possibility sparks overt conduct once more, conduct which, by its impact on surrounding conditions, may succeed in overcoming the initial hindrance to the regular outward flow of action. In the evolutionary perspective, thought is an adaptive instrument for overcoming environmental difficulties. Scientific inquiry, the most highly developed form of thought, is the most effective reaction to such difficulties, and the most explicitly problem-directed.

In general, we may say that when thought is genuine and effective it is a response to an objective breakdown in the organization of habit and belief, an answer to the torment of doubt. Controlled by its initiating perplexity, its effectiveness may be gauged by the extent to which it achieves resolution of the difficulty that gave it birth. Thought which is not thus relevant to a problem does not constitute genuine inquiry or deliberation. An education geared to the encouragement of the latter must, then, take its starting point in the doubts and difficulties of the student, originating in his life conflicts and the social issues of his environment. Its relevance to live problems must be evident in its ultimate motivation, which is to solve these problems, and in its evaluation as facilitating or retarding such solutions.

Now it is easy to read this pragmatic doctrine of thought as a merely descriptive account, but such a reading would be mistaken. The doctrine is not designed to embrace all activity that might readily be described as thinking in everyday parlance. In musing, recollecting, or imagining, one is thinking though not necessarily solving problems. The work of painter, writer, or composer, thoughtful and focused as it is, cannot readily be taken as a species of problem solving: Of what problem is *Macbeth* the solution? The artist's activity does not always originate in the breakdown of habit, nor is it plausibly split into internal deliberation and overt unthinking action, rather than taken as a continuous flow in which making and thinking are smoothly meshed. In attending to my words now, you are thinking, but you have not, I hope, experienced an objective breakdown at the outset of my paper.

The fundamental import of the pragmatic doctrine is, I suggest, rather normative than descriptive. It purports to tell us what *genuine* thinking consists in. Taking its cue from evolutionary categories, it stresses the adaptive function of thinking in the organism's struggle to survive in a hostile or indifferent environment. Interpreting science as the most refined and effective development of such adaptive thinking, it urges the ostensible problem-solving pattern of scientific research as the chief paradigm of intellectual activity, to be favored in all phases of education and culture.

To say that the problem theory of thinking is normative in its import does not, however, imply that it rests on no factual assumptions whatever. As we have just noted, it draws particularly upon a special reading of science as the prime example of responsible and effective thinking, growing out of practical problems and issuing in reconstructed modes of conduct. And this reading cannot, I believe, be sustained. It holds at best for simple types of practical thinking and for technological applications, but it does no justice to science as an autonomous theoretical endeavor. Scientific theories do not, generally, grow out of practical conflicts, nor do they, in themselves, serve to guide practical activities; they are embedded in complex intellectual structures linked only indirectly, and as wholes, to contexts of evidence and experiment. Their assessment is intimately dependent upon these intellectual structures, and involves, aside from practical efficacy, theoretical considerations bearing on their relative simplicity, naturalness, comprehensiveness, elegance, and connectibility with associated structures.

The scientist's work may perhaps be plausibly described as problem-oriented, in that much of it is directed toward the answering of certain questions. But these questions cannot be identified with practical breakdowns in the personal life or social environment of the scientist. They typically cannot even be understood outside the historical context of prior theorizing and experimentation, which determines independent canons of intellectual relevance. The scientist's questioning is, moreover, often hypothetical and speculative. Born of a sophisticated curiosity, it may come to torment his waking hours; it does not itself need to originate in personal or social torment. Even Charles Sanders Peirce, the father of pragmatism, who began by insisting on real and active doubt as the first phase of thought, had increasingly to emphasize the significance of feigned doubt in order to account for the autonomous context of scientific problem solving. An educational conception of thinking as directly addressed to the alleviation of conflicts and breakdowns of behavior would, in sum, constitute not the foundation of a scientific attitude of mind but the death knell of scientific thought. By confining thought to the immediacies of practice, it would eliminate its leverage on practice, reducing its characteristic effectiveness in transforming the environment.

Nor does the problem theory of inquiry, even broadly interpreted in terms of questions, tell the whole story. Thought does not subside when doubts are, for the moment, stilled. A scientist without questions is not a happy thoughtless theorist. Problem finding is at least as important to him as problem solving. He does not, in any event, wait upon difficulties that happen to occur to him but strenuously seeks new difficulties of the widest critical significance. An education modeled on scientific thinking could not possibly remain content with the student's initial problems; it would seek to introduce him to new ones and train him to explore further for himself. More generally, it would strive to create wider perception as well as to improve problem-solving capacity, to develop an alertness to unsettled and conflicting elements in experience as well as a drive to organize, unify, and resolve. It would, in short, aim not only to assess ideas by their relevance to given questions, but also to discover new questions by expanding the sense of relevance.

3. Moral Interpretation

If a defense of educational relevance is to be found neither in the notion of knowledge as union nor in the conception of thought as a response to practical difficulty, can we not hope to find such a defense by considering the purposes of schooling? Granted that knowledge presupposes critical perspective and that the life of thought has its own integrity, is there no practical value to be gained by the development of theoretical understanding? Do we not need to make special provision for bringing such understanding to earth, for applying it toward the resolution of the practical problems of men? Indeed, considering the institution of schools, is it not clear that their primary purpose is to foster the employment of knowledge for desirable social ends?

Reflections such as these, by offering a more restricted interpretation of relevance than the preceding two we have considered, seem to gain in persuasiveness. Social relevance is not to be construed as a necessary feature of all knowledge or thought. Rather, it is a consequence of the primary institutional function of the school. The school's job is, after all, not confined to the advancement of knowledge and the fostering of scientific habits of mind. For knowledge and critical thought are themselves valued for their potential contribution to the achievement of social goals. Such contribution requires not merely the advancement but the employment of knowledge; it depends upon developing not only habits of inquiry but also arts of application. Indeed, application is the ultimate end to which inquiry is a means, and, from the standpoint of society, the school must thus be viewed as an instrument for the realization of its goals. The relation between knowledge and application is, furthermore, not an internal or necessary one; without special care, knowledge may very well be pursued without thought of its practical use. All the more reason, then, to build the context of social application into the life of the school as an encompassing emphasis in relation to which training in inquiry may be seen in its proper instrumental light.

Seen in long-term perspective, then, the school is a means for the improvement of society. The ultimate fruit of the knowledge it seeks is its use in life. Schooling must thus be so organized as to bring knowledge to bear on life's problems and, in so doing, to train students in the proper application of what they may know or come to know. Practical problems of the larger community should serve to provide the major framework within which all the school's activities are set. Separate as abstract intellectual specialties, the school's subjects are to be brought together in their common application to shared social problems. Curricular integration is to be accomplished not by some internal structural scheme but by a pervasive view of the content of schooling as an instrument in the service of the larger society. Education is thus to be made relevant by making its instrumental values dominant. A remote education, bringing nothing to the resolution of the problems of society, is a luxury society neither can nor should allow.

There is much in the foregoing interpretation that seems to me compelling. To argue, as I did earlier, that thought is not generally to be conceived as a response to practical difficulty and that theoretical inquiry involves critical distance and autonomous development does not, after all, imply that practical application is to be shunned. There is no warrant for the stark doctrine that schooling is practical only if thought itself is a practical tool, that, conversely, if thought is independent of practice then schooling must itself be divorced from the life of the surrounding community. The root assumption that the scope of schooling is fixed by the limits of thought must itself be rejected as the source of much mischief.

Theoretical inquiry, independently pursued, has the most powerful potential for the analysis and transformation of practice. The bearing of inquiry upon practice is, moreover, of the greatest educational interest. Such interest is not, contrary to recent emphases, exhausted in a concern for inquiry within the structures of the several disciplines. Students should be encouraged to employ the information and techniques of the disciplines in analysis, criticism, and alteration of their practical outlooks. Habits of practical diagnosis, critique, and execution based upon responsible inquiry need to supplement theoretical attitudes and disciplinary proficiencies in the training of the young. Insofar as the doctrine of educational relevance is to be taken as emphasizing this point, I find myself in complete agreement with it. The example of professional education here points the way. Medical education, for example, must embrace not only disciplinary inquiries but also the arts of judgment and application to cases. And what holds for the specialized concerns of the professions seems to me to hold for schooling generally as an institution of society.

Yet reference to professional education suggests also certain respects in which the interpretation we have been considering is overdrawn. To insist that application is essential to professional training does not imply that it must dominate; to acknowledge the contribution of theoretical inquiry in transforming practice is not to argue that theory is to be treated as solely instrumental. Theory is effective insofar as it provides insight into fundamental processes, and the quest for such insight cannot be systematically bent to any external requirement without hampering its development and its consequent effectiveness. Professional education needs to bring the concerns of independent inquiry and the challenge of a specific range of practical problems into communication; it needs to foster mutual respect and understanding between researchers and practitioners. It cannot require research to be pursued in a practical frame of mind nor impose a uniform instrumental framework upon its constituent activities without reducing its own efficacy.

The conclusion is even stronger when we consider not professional education, oriented as it is toward special social functions, but schooling generally. For the potential ramifications of knowledge cannot be determined in advance; to encase all schooling within the framework of specified applications to practice is to hinder severely its unknown developments in other directions as well as its capacity to generate alternative conceptions of application.

Indeed, the notion that education is an instrument for the realization of social goals, no matter how worthy they are thought to be, harbors the greatest conceivable danger to the ideal of a free and rational society. For if these goals are presumed to be fixed in advance, the instrumental doctrine of schooling exempts them from the critical scrutiny that schooling itself may foster. On the other hand, if these goals are themselves to be subject to public criticism and review, schools may be conceived as social instruments only in the broad sense in which they also facilitate independent evaluation of social practice, only if they are, in effect, conceived as instruments of insight and criticism, standing apart from current social conceptions and serving autonomous ideals of inquiry and truth. A society that supports this conception of schooling is one which, rather than setting external limits to its work, is prepared to incorporate the school's loyalties to independent inquiry and free criticism into its own basic structure and ideals. In effect, such a society must view itself as instrumental to the values of schooling quite as much as it takes schools to serve its own goals.

A conception such as this is indeed what one would expect from an instrumentalism inspired by Dewey's notion of the continuity between means and ends, and it is ironic that the main stress in certain passages of his work is on the school as means. When one considers, however, that Dewey takes the end to be not society as it happens to be, but a reformed society, illuminated by an ideal imagination and a critical intelligence that it is the school's office to foster, it becomes clear that any simple-minded doctrine of the school as social instrument is inadequate, both as an expression of Dewey's views and as an independently persuasive educational philosophy. For the fact is that the larger society that the school is said to serve at any given time cannot be taken for granted as providing an ultimate end. It must itself be judged worthwhile by reference to the rational standards and the heritage of critical values to which the school bears witness. If the fruit of knowledge is its use in life, it must be a life itself infused with a respect for knowledge and criticism. It is, in short, one thing to say that the content of schooling should be brought to bear upon practice, that free inquiry and practical concerns are to be put into communication. It is quite another to say that schooling is to be conceived as an instrument for the implementation of designated social values, taken as ultimate.

This point of difference is decisive. To make education relevant by making it instrumental in the latter sense is to destroy its autonomy and to deliver it to the rule of uncriticized social values. To recognize, on the other hand, that the responsibility of education is not only to serve but also to criticize, enlighten, and create —that its job is not only to provide persons with techniques but, more importantly, to provide techniques with critical, informed, and humane persons—is to realize that it has its own dignity and its own direction to follow. Its primary task is not to be relevant but to help form a society in which its ideals of free inquiry and rationality shall themselves have become chief touchstones of relevance.

EDUCATION AS GROWTH*

John Dewey

1. The Conditions of Growth

In directing the activities of the young, society determines its own future in determining that of the young. Since the young at a given time will at some later date compose the society of that period, the latter's nature will largely turn upon the direction children's activities were given at an earlier period. This cumulative movement of action toward a later result is what is meant by growth.

The primary condition of growth is immaturity. This may seem to be a mere truism—saying that a being can develop only in some point in which he is undeveloped. But the prefix "im-" of the word immaturity means something positive, not a mere void or lack. It is noteworthy that the terms "capacity" and "potentiality" have a double meaning, one sense being negative, the other positive. Capacity may denote mere receptivity, like the capacity of a quart measure. We may mean by potentiality a merely dormant or quiescent state—a capacity to become something different under external influences. But we also mean by capacity an ability, a power; and by potentiality potency, force. Now when we say that immaturity means the possibility of growth, we are not referring to absence of powers which may exist at a later time; we express a force positively present—the *ability* to develop.

Our tendency to take immaturity as mere lack, and growth as something which fills up the gap between the immature and the mature is due to regarding childhood *comparatively*, instead of intrinsically. We treat it simply as a privation because we are measuring it by adulthood as a fixed standard. This fixes attention upon what the child has not, and will not have till he becomes a man. This comparative standpoint is legitimate enough for some

* Reprinted from *Democracy and Education,* paperback ed. (New York: Macmillan, 1961), pp. 41–42, 44–52. By permission of the publisher.

purposes, but if we make it final, the question arises whether we are not guilty of an overweening presumption. Children, if they could express themselves articulately and sincerely, would tell a different tale; and there is excellent adult authority for the conviction that for certain moral and intellectual purposes adults must become as little children.

The seriousness of the assumption of the negative quality of the possibilities of immaturity is apparent when we reflect that it sets up as an ideal and standard a static end. The fulfillment of growing is taken to mean an *accomplished* growth: that is to say, an Ungrowth, something which is no longer growing. . . .

.   .   .   .

2. The specific adaptability of an immature creature for growth constitutes his *plasticity*. This is something quite different from the plasticity of putty or wax. It is not a capacity to take on change of form in accord with external pressure. It lies near the pliable elasticity by which some persons take on the color of their surroundings while retaining their own bent. But it is something deeper than this. It is essentially the ability to learn from experience; the power to retain from one experience something which is of avail in coping with the difficulties of a later situation. This means power to modify actions on the basis of the results of prior experiences, the power to *develop dispositions*. Without it, the acquisition of habits is impossible.

It is a familiar fact that the young of the higher animals, and especially the human young, have to *learn* to utilize their instinctive reactions. The human being is born with a greater number of instinctive tendencies than other animals. But the instincts of the lower animals perfect themselves for appropriate action at an early period after birth, while most of those of the human infant are of little account just as they stand. An original specialized power of adjustment secures immediate efficiency, but, like a railway ticket, it is good for one route only. A being who, in order to use his eyes, ears, hands, and legs, has to experiment in making varied combinations of their reactions, achieves a control that is flexible and varied. A chick, for example, pecks accurately at a bit of food in a few hours after hatching. This means that definite coordinations of activities of the eyes in seeing and of the body and head in striking are perfected in a few trials. An infant requires about six months to be able to gauge with approximate accuracy the action in reaching which will coordinate with his visual activities; to be able, that is, to tell whether he can reach a seen object and just how to execute the reaching. As a result, the chick is limited by the relative perfection of its original endowment. The infant has the advantage of the *multitude* of instinctive tentative reactions and of the experiences that accompany them, even though he is at a temporary disadvantage because they cross one another. In learning an action, instead of having it given ready-made, one of necessity learns to vary its factors, to make varied combinations of them, according to change of circumstances. A possibility of continuing progress is opened up by the fact that in learning one act, methods are developed good for use in other situations. Still more important is the fact that the human being acquires a habit of learning. He learns to learn.

. . . .

2. Habits as Expressions of Growth

We have already noted that plasticity is the capacity to retain and carry over from prior experience factors which modify subsequent activities. This signifies the capacity to acquire habits, or develop definite dispositions. We have now to consider the salient features of habits. In the first place, a habit is a form of executive skill, of efficiency in doing. A habit means an ability to use natural conditions as means to ends. It is an active control of the environment through control of the organs of action. We are perhaps apt to emphasize the control of the body at the expense of control of the environment. We think of walking, talking, playing the piano, the specialized skills characteristic of the etcher, the surgeon, the bridge-builder, as if they were simply ease, deftness, and accuracy on the part of the organism. They are that, of course; but the measure of the value of these qualities lies in the economical and effective control of the environment which they secure. To be able to walk is to have certain properties of nature at our disposal—and so with all other habits.

Education is not infrequently defined as consisting in the acquisition of those habits that effect an adjustment of an individual and his environment. The definition expresses an essential phase of growth. But it is essential that adjustment be understood in its active sense of *control* of means for achieving ends. If we think of a habit simply as a change wrought in the organism, ignoring the fact that this change consists in ability to effect subsequent changes in the environment, we shall be led to think of "adjustment" as a conformity to environment as wax conforms to the seal which impresses it. The environment is thought of as something fixed, providing in its fixity the end and standard of changes taking place in the organism; adjustment is just fitting ourselves to this fixity of external conditions.[1] Habit as *habituation* is indeed something *relatively* passive; we get used to our surroundings—to our clothing, our shoes, and gloves; to the atmosphere as long as it is fairly equable; to our daily associates, etc. Conformity to the environment, a change wrought in the organism without reference to ability to modify surroundings, is a marked trait of such habituations.

.   .   .   .

The significance of habit is not exhausted, however, in its executive and motor phase. It means formation of intellectual and emotional disposition as well as an increase in ease, economy, and efficiency of action. Any habit marks an *inclination*—an active preference and choice for the conditions involved in its exercise. A habit does not wait, Micawber-like, for a stimulus to turn up so that it may get busy; it actively seeks for occasions to pass into full operation. If its expression is unduly blocked, in-

[1] This conception is, of course, a logical correlate of the conceptions of the external relation of stimulus and response, considered in the last chapter, and of the negative conceptions of immaturity and plasticity noted in this chapter.

clination shows itself in uneasiness and intense craving. A habit also marks an intellectual disposition. Where there is a habit, there is acquaintance with the materials and equipment to which action is applied. There is a definite way of understanding the situations in which the habit operates. Modes of thought, of observation and reflection, enter as forms of skill and of desire into the habits that make a man an engineer, an architect, a physician, or a merchant. In unskilled forms of labor, the intellectual factors are at minimum precisely because the habits involved are not of a high grade. But there are habits of judging and reasoning as truly as of handling a tool, painting a picture, or conducting an experiment.

Such statements are, however, understatements. The habits of mind involved in habits of the eye and hand supply the latter with their significance. Above all, the intellectual element in a habit fixes the relation of the habit to varied and elastic use, and hence to continued growth. We speak of *fixed* habits. Well, the phrase may mean powers so well established that their possessor always has them as resources when needed. But the phrase is also used to mean ruts, routine ways, with loss of freshness, openmindedness, and originality. Fixity of habit may mean that something has a fixed hold upon us, instead of our having a free hold upon things. This fact explains two points in a common notion about habits: their identification with mechanical and external modes of action to the neglect of mental and moral attitudes, and the tendency to give them a bad meaning, an identification with "bad habits." Many a person would feel surprised to have his aptitude in his chosen profession called a habit, and would naturally think of his use of tobacco, liquor, or profane language as typical of the meaning of habit. A habit is to him something which has a hold on him, something not easily thrown off even though judgment condemn it.

Habits reduce themselves to routine ways of acting, or degenerate into ways of action to which we are enslaved just in the degree in which intelligence is disconnected from them. Routine habits are unthinking habits: "bad" habits are habits so severed from reason that they are opposed to the conclusions of conscious deliberation and decision. As we have seen, the acquiring of habits is due to an original plasticity of our natures: to our ability to vary responses till we find an appropriate and efficient way of acting. Routine habits, and habits that possess us instead of our possessing them, are habits which put an end to plasticity. They mark the close of power to vary. There can be no doubt of the tendency of organic plasticity, of the physiological basis, to lessen with growing years. The instinctively mobile and eagerly varying action of childhood, the love of new stimuli and new developments, too easily passes into a "settling down," which means aversion to change and a resting on past achievements. Only an environment which secures the full use of intelligence in the process of forming habits can counteract this tendency. Of course, the same hardening of the organic conditions affects the physiological structures which are involved in thinking. But this fact only indicates the need of persistent care to see to it that the function of intelligence is invoked to its maximum possibility. The short-sighted method which falls back on mechanical routine and repetition to secure external efficiency of habit, motor skill without accompanying thought, marks a deliberate closing in of surroundings upon growth.

3. The Educational Bearings of the Conception of Development

We have had so far but little to say in this chapter about education. We have been occupied with the conditions and implications of growth. If our conclusions are justified, they carry with them, however, definite educational consequences. When it is said that education is development, everything depends upon *how* development is conceived. Our net conclusion is that life is development, and that developing, growing, is life. Translated into its educational equivalents, that means (i) that the educational process has no end beyond itself; it is its own end; and that (ii) the educational process is one of continual reorganizing, reconstructing, transforming.

1. Development when it is interpreted in *comparative* terms, that is, with respect to the special traits of child and adult life,

means the direction of power into special channels: the formation of habits involving executive skill, definiteness of interest, and specific objects of observation and thought. But the comparative view is not final. The child has specific powers; to ignore that fact is to stunt or distort the organs upon which his growth depends. The adult uses his powers to transform his environment, thereby occasioning new stimuli which redirect his powers and keep them developing. Ignoring this fact means arrested development, a passive accommodation. Normal child and normal adult alike, in other words, are engaged in growing. The difference between them is not the difference between growth and no growth, but between the modes of growth appropriate to different conditions. With respect to the development of powers devoted to coping with specific scientific and economic problems we may say the child should be growing in manhood. With respect to sympathetic curiosity, unbiased responsiveness, and openness of mind, we may say that the adult should be growing in childlikeness. One statement is as true as the other.

Three ideas which have been criticized, namely, the merely private nature of immaturity, static adjustment to a fixed environment, and rigidity of habit, are all connected with a false idea of growth or development—that it is a movement toward a fixed goal. Growth is regarded as *having* an end, instead of *being* an end. The educational counterparts of the three fallacious ideas are first, failure to take account of the instinctive or native powers of the young; second, failure to develop initiative in coping with novel situations; third, an undue emphasis upon drill and other devices which secure automatic skill at the expense of personal perception. In all cases, the adult environment is accepted as a standard for the child. He is to be brought up *to it*.

Natural instincts are either disregarded or treated as nuisances —as obnoxious traits to be suppressed, or at all events to be brought into conformity with external standards. Since conformity is the aim, what is distinctively individual in a young person is brushed aside, or regarded as a source of mischief or anarchy. Conformity is made equivalent to uniformity. Consequently, there are induced lack of interest in the novel, aversion to progress, and dread of the uncertain and the unknown. Since the end of growth is outside of and beyond the process of growing, external agents have to be resorted to to induce movement toward it. Whenever a method of education is stigmatized as mechanical, we may be sure that external pressure is brought to bear to reach an external end.

2. Since in reality there is nothing to which growth is relative save more growth, there is nothing to which education is subordinate save more education. It is a commonplace to say that education should not cease when one leaves school. The point of this commonplace is that the purpose of school education is to insure the continuance of education by organizing the powers that insure growth. The inclination to learn from life itself and to make the conditions of life such that all will learn in the process of living is the finest product of schooling.

When we abandon the attempt to define immaturity by means of fixed comparison with adult accomplishments, we are compelled to give up thinking of it as denoting lack of desired traits. Abandoning this notion, we are also forced to surrender our habit of thinking of instruction as a method of supplying this lack by pouring knowledge into a mental and moral hole which awaits filling. Since life means growth, a living creature lives as truly and positively at one stage as at another, with the same intrinsic fullness and the same absolute claims. Hence education means the enterprise of supplying the conditions which insure growth, or adequacy of life, irrespective of age. We first look with impatience upon immaturity, regarding it as something to be got over as rapidly as possible. Then the adult formed by such educative methods looks back with impatient regret upon childhood and youth as a scene of lost opportunities and wasted powers. This ironical situation will endure till it is recognized that living has its own intrinsic quality and that the business of education is with that quality.

Realization that life is growth protects us from that so-called idealizing of childhood which in effect is nothing but lazy indulgence. Life is not to be identified with every superficial act and interest. Even though it is not always easy to tell whether what appears to be mere surface fooling is a sign of some nascent as yet untrained power, we must remember that manifestations are not to be accepted as ends in themselves. They are signs of possible growth. They are to be turned into means of development, of carrying power forward, not indulged or cultivated for their own sake. Excessive attention to surface phenomena (even in the way of rebuke as well as of encouragement) may lead to their fixation and thus to arrested development. What impulses are moving toward, not what they have been, is the important thing for parent and teacher. . . .

GROWTH NEEDS A GOAL*

Herman H. Horne

Note that the whole process of growth is subsumed under the conception of habit formation. Even the moral, emotional, and intellectual phases of life are treated as effects of the environment on the responsive organism, as cases of habit. This is accomplished by introducing the conception of "active habits"—a conception not consistently held to in other portions of the discussion. . . . Nevertheless there is an implication that observation, deliberation, judgment, and decision mark the distinction between good and bad habits. Why then the subordination of these acts of intelligence to the concept of "active habits"? It is a naturalistic emphasis which hardly does justice to the value of man's higher powers of mind.

Particularly is this evident if we raise the question whether judgment and decision can change a bad habit into a good one. Apparently not, since the choices and decisions are presented as themselves a part of the emotional disposition which is itself in turn made by habit. This is, of course, the question of man's freedom. Dr. Dewey believes, as we shall see later . . . that man should be socially free to express himself in an unrestrained way, but he does not maintain that man has freedom of choice.

This appears also in the view just presented that the environment is to secure that full use of intelligence which prevents men from becoming machines; it is the environment that invokes the function of intelligence to its maximum. But cannot man invoke his own intelligence? And how is this intelligence-invoking en-

* Reprinted from *The Democratic Philosophy of Education* (New York: Macmillan, 1932), pp. 48–49, 52–56. By permission of the publisher.

Horne's entire book is an exposition and criticism of Dewey's *Democracy and Education*. In this selection, Horne assumes that the reader is familiar with Dewey's conception of education as growth, as set forth in the preceding pages, and he addresses himself critically and specifically to these pages.

vironment to be secured? In short, this whole treatment of habit makes the response and not the respondent responsible. . . .

The doctrine of "education as growth" is one of the most popular and influential advocated by our author. It is well to note particularly the original warning given by him against its misinterpretation. We are not to pay too much attention to superficial interests and we are to see that they lead on. This warning, however, has not been taken by all his followers, and Dr. Dewey has had to repeat it. . . .

And naturally so, for the phrase "education as growth" is too vague to be a practical guide, even when the statement is added that growth leads to more growth. The trio of famous statements, "Education is life," "Life is growth," "Education is growth," all sound well and awaken pleasurable emotional states, but they do not tell us what to do next. The trouble is we have growths as well as growth; there is a wrong way to grow as well as a right way; there is abnormal growth as well as normal growth; there are schools of crime in which there is much growth of the wrong kind; much life is perverted growth; some education called "new" is arrested growth (against this Dr. Dewey warned in advance). It is not enough to say "education is growth"; we must add, education is growth *in the right way*. And criteria of right growth must be set up. Teachers must be able to tell when they are directing growth in the right way. Often they cannot tell; they only know that their pupils are growing. The very definition of growth proposed is not clear: "This cumulative movement of action toward a later result is what is meant by growth." Is there any action without a later result? What is the "movement of an action"? Could not any Fagin's or Gradgrind's school claim to have "a cumulative movement of action toward a later result"? The definition is not only vague; it is defective in giving us no clear distinction between good education and bad education. All directed action leads on to later results. But which later results are worthwhile? A headline in the morning paper says, "Pickpocket arrested, giving boy, 16, lesson." Here is growth, to be sure.

But the difficulty lies deeper. Growth aims at more growth, and education is subordinate only to education. This is the theory. Its weakness is, growth needs a goal. There is no need to mince words at all. Children must be directed in their growth toward something worthwhile in personal and social relations. They must grow up to be something admirable by constantly having admirable models and patterns and associations. Growth must be toward an ideal of human character. This ideal is not the objectionable "idealizing of childhood"; it is the unobjectionable idealizing of life itself as the embodiment of worthwhile purposes and patterns. We do not have to be afraid of the word goal. We need a goal to work toward. If it is really valuable, we rarely fully attain it. If we should attain it, another and higher goal should and would straightway take its place. There is no danger of the pursuit of a goal leading to a static life. Let's have a goal for growth, including the admirable features of social and individual living, and omitting the base. This involves having a standard by which to judge growth. We do not lack such a standard.

Really, there is an implicit contradiction in the conception of growth presented in the text. Growth is said to be relative only to growth, and yet the "cumulative movement of action" must be "toward a later result." Now this later result is preconceived, intended, aimed at, anticipated. Otherwise, how could growth be directed toward it at all? And if so, "the later result" is the goal. Then education does have a goal. Why not admit it, declare it, and formulate the goal.

As we shall see later, though it is here claimed that "there is nothing to which education is subordinate save more education," it would appear that education is subordinate to democracy.

The best phrase in the discussion is "adequacy of life". . . . It is proposed as an equivalent of growth. But it is more than an equivalent. It is an equivalent of right growth. "Adequacy of life" involves setting up standards and ends of living. Really, *to live* is *to live for something*.

Another thing. In the discussion, "growth" and "development" are used as synonymous terms. "Growth" is defined, and then "development" is introduced as a synonym. . . . But the two terms are not synonymous, and the discussion unwarrantably profits by using the associations of the term development along with those of growth. At the same time violence is done the equally valuable conception of development. There is a sense in which education is growth directed toward a right end, and there is a sense in which education is properly stimulated development. What is this difference between growth and development?

Growth, strictly regarded, is enlargement of physical organ or mental function; development is marked by the appearance of new functions or powers. By growth the tissue cells multiply; by development they become differentiated and mature. A little oak becomes a large oak by growth; an acorn becomes a little oak by development. A little chick becomes a chicken mainly by growth; an egg becomes a chick by development; it is also true that the appearance of new mental and physical powers as the chick becomes a chicken is by development. A little muscle becomes a large muscle by growth; a muscle appears at all and the possibility of new muscular coördinations, especially of the smaller muscles, comes by development. A little child becomes a big child by growth; a fertilized ovum becomes a child, and a child becomes a physical and mental grown-up by development. To repeat, growth is expansion of living tissue or mental function already present; development is the appearance of new tissue or function. A tennis player grows a larger muscle in one of his arms but develops a new stroke. Adolescence is marked by both growth and development. Wherever mind is present at all, it is likely that the processes of growth and development are never completely sundered from each other. Normally the two processes of growth and development go together, so that full size (growth) and complete differentiation and maturation (development) are both attained at the end of a suitable amount of time. In early life, growth is rapid and development slow; in later stages, development is rapid and growth slow. Prolonged growth and delayed development mean a massive but sluggish individual, soft, and with low powers of resistance. Arrested growth and precocious development means a small body with small organs though finely organized. In a sense mass is the enemy of organization, and organization is the enemy of mass. Growth without development is burdensome; development without growth is weakness. Nature must be helped to secure the proportionate amount of both growth and development.

But what difference does it make whether a child only grows up or both grows and develops? A great deal. A relatively under-developed mind may very well inhabit a grown body, and a relatively developed mind may very well inhabit a poorly grown body. Education is to secure both right growth and right development of both the physical and the mental constituents of experience.

A very significant point in this, that growth is less dependent on internal factors than is development. By and large, growth is from without, development is from within; growth is dependent on external stimulation, development upon internal changes. Thus, by no manner of means can an acorn become a chick, or a chick become a child. Development is in a measure prefigured in the egg as growth is not. Thus development is rather a matter of nature and growth a matter of nurture. And in this sense nature is probably more than nurture. . . .

EDUCATIONAL METAPHORS*

Israel Scheffler

If we compare metaphors with definitions and slogans, some contrasts are immediately apparent. Metaphors are not normally intended to express the meanings of terms used, either in standard or in stipulated ways. Rather, they point to what are conceived to be significant parallels, analogies, similarities within the subject matter of the discourse itself. Metaphorical statements often express significant and surprising truths, unlike stipulations which express no truths at all, and unlike descriptive definitions, which normally fail to surprise. Though frequently, like programmatic definitions, conveying programs, metaphors do so always by suggesting some objective analogy, purporting to state truths discovered in the phenomena before us. Like slogans in being unsystematic and lacking a standard form of expression, they nevertheless have a much more serious theoretical role. They cannot generally be considered as mere fragments crystallizing the key attitudes of some social movement, or symbolizing explicit parent doctrines. Rather, they figure in serious theoretical statements themselves, as fundamental components.

The line, even in science, between serious theory and metaphor, is a thin one if it can be drawn at all. To say, "This table is composed of electrons," is clearly (at least) to invite comparison of the table and aggregates of tiny particles whose behavior is further elaborated in other statements. To be sure, the initial metaphor must lead to refinements in the comparison, expressed literally, and to experimental confirmation of predictions or other inferences derived from them. But the same holds true of theories generally, and there is no obvious point at which we must say, "Here the metaphors stop and the theories begin." In education,

* Reprinted from *The Language of Education* (Springfield, Ill.: Charles C. Thomas, 1960), pp. 47–52. By permission of the publisher and the author.

too, metaphorical statements are frequently found in key theoretical contexts as well as in policy contexts. What do they convey, and how? We shall proceed from some general remarks to a consideration of selected educational metaphors.

Generally, we may regard the metaphorical statement as indicating that there is an important analogy between two things, without saying explicitly in what the analogy consists. Now, every two things are analogous in some respect, but not every such respect is important. Still, the notion of importance varies with the situation: what is important in science may not be important in politics or art, for example. If a given metaphorical statement is to be judged worthwhile or apt, the analogy suggested must be important with respect to criteria relevant to the context of its utterance.

Further, the metaphorical statement does not actually state the analogy, even where a relevantly important one exists. It is rather in the nature of an invitation to search for one, and is in part judged by how well such a search is rewarded. Again, the pattern is similar to that of a theory or, if you like, a theoretical hunch. It is no wonder, then, that metaphors have often been said to organize reflection and explanation in scientific and philosophical contexts. In practical contexts too, metaphors often serve, analogously to programmatic definition, as ways of channelling action, though always by purporting to indicate that some important analogy may be found within the relevant subject matter.

Aside from independent evaluation of programs that may be conveyed by particular metaphorical assertions, metaphors may be criticized in roughly two ways. First, we may reach the conclusion that a given metaphor is trivial or sterile, indicating analogies that are, in context, unimportant. Second, we may determine the limitations of a given metaphor, the points at which the analogies it indicates break down. Every metaphor is limited in this way, giving only a certain perspective on its subject, which may be supplemented by other perspectives. Such limitation is no more reason to reject a metaphor completely than is the fact that alternative theories always exist in itself a reason to reject any given theory in science. Nevertheless, a comparison of alternative metaphors may be as illuminating as a comparison of alternative theories, in indicating the many-faceted character of the subject. Such a comparison may also provide a fresh sense of the uniqueness of the subject, for to know in what ways something is like many different things is to know a good deal about what makes it distinctive, different from each. Last, where a particular metaphor is dominant, comparison helps in determining its limitations and in opening up fresh possibilities of thought and action. In the rest of the chapter, we shall be concerned to make such a comparison of common metaphorical ways of speaking about education.

Max Black suggests that the familiar growth metaphor is one that lends itself to the expression of revolt against educational authoritarianism.[23] How does this happen? There is an obvious analogy between the growing child and the growing plant, between the gardener and the teacher. In both cases, the developing organism goes through phases that are relatively independent of the efforts of gardener or teacher. In both cases, however, the development may be helped or hindered by these efforts. For both, the work of caring for such development would seem to depend on knowledge of the laws regulating the succession of phases. In neither case is the gardener or the teacher indispensable to the development of the organism and, after they leave, the organism continues to mature. They are both concerned to help the organism flourish, to care for its welfare by providing optimum conditions for the operation of laws of nature. The growth metaphor in itself thus embodies a modest conception of the teacher's rôle, which is to study and then indirectly to help the development of the child, rather than to shape him into some preconceived form, a contrary metaphor which we shall presently consider.

Where does the growth metaphor break down? It does seem plausible with respect to certain aspects of the development of children, that is, the biological or constitutional aspects. Regarding these, we can pretty well say, roughly, what sequences of stages may be normally expected, and how the passage from stage

[23] M. Black, "Education as Art and Discipline," *Ethics,* 54 (1944): 290, reprinted in I. Scheffler, *Philosophy and Education* (Boston: Allyn and Bacon, 1966).

to stage may be helped or hindered by deliberate effort on the part of others. Where such knowledge is lacking concerning details, it may presumably be furnished by further investigation. The nature and order of these stages of physical and temperamental development, and of the capacities for behavior they make possible, are, indeed, relatively independent of the action of other individuals, though even here cultural factors make their impact.

If we once ask, however, how these capacities are to be exercised, toward what the temperamental energy of the child is to be directed, what sorts of conduct and what types of sensitivity are to be fostered, we begin to see the limits of the growth metaphor. The sequence of physical and temperamental stages is, in fact, quite compatible with any number of conflicting answers to these questions. For these aspects of development, there are no independent sequences of stages pointing to a single state of maturity. That is why, with regard to these aspects, it makes no literal sense to say, "Let us develop all of the potentialities of every child." They conflict and so cannot all be developed. To develop some is to thwart others. To withdraw is not to allow nature's wisdom full scope, but to decide in one way rather than another, where both are compatible with nature; responsibility for such decision cannot be evaded.

It has often been remarked that to think of history as if it were a plant, whose development through natural stages can only be facilitated or retarded by individuals, is a way of evading responsibility for affecting social events through choice and action.[24] It should be even more obvious that the course of children's social, cultural, and moral development is not divided into natural stages which cannot be fundamentally altered by others. It is clear that adults—parents and teachers—do more than simply facilitate the child's development toward a unique stage of cultural maturity.

It is the latter insight that underlies another familiar educational metaphor—that of shaping, forming, or molding. The child, in one variant of this metaphor, is clay; the teacher imposes a fixed

[24] See, in this connection, K. Popper, *The Open Society and Its Enemies* (London: Routledge & Kegan Paul, 1957), and K. Popper, *The Poverty of Historicism* (London: Routledge & Kegan Paul, 1957).

mold on this clay, shaping it to the specifications of the mold. The teacher's initiative, power, and responsibility are here brought into sharp focus. For the final shape of the clay is wholly a product of his choice of a given mold. There is no independent progression toward any given shape, as there is with respect to the growth of acorns, for example. Nor is there any mold to which the clay will not conform. The clay neither selects nor rejects any sequence of stages or any final shape for itself. The one choosing the mold is wholly responsible for the result.

In the light of our previous remarks on the growth metaphor, it is clear that this molding metaphor does not fit the biological-temperamental development of the child, which is not alterable throughout by adult action. The molding metaphor does, however, seem more appropriate than the growth metaphor as regards cultural, personal, and moral development, which is, to a greater extent, dependent on the character of the adult social environment.

But even here, the molding metaphor has its limitations. In the case of the clay, the final shape is wholly a function of the mold chosen. The clay neither selects nor rejects any given mold. The clay is, further, homogeneous throughout, and thoroughly plastic. The shape of the mold is fixed before the molding process and remains constant throughout. Each of these points represents a dissimilarity with respect to teaching. For, even if there are no laws of cultural, moral, and personal development, there are nevertheless limits imposed by the nature of the pupils upon the range of developments possible. These limits say what *cannot* be done with the material rather than what *will* develop. Human nature does not automatically select, but it rejects some forms that adults may choose for it. Further, these limits vary from student to student and from group to group. The student population is not thoroughly homogeneous nor thoroughly plastic. Thus, if the educator's decisions are not made for him by nature, neither are they unlimited by nature, and a study of these limits may make his decisons wiser. Finally, if the teacher is indeed to pay attention to the nature of his students, he will modify his methods and aims in the course of his teaching and in response to the process itself. His teaching is, then, not comparable to a fixed mold, but rather to a plan modifiable by its own attempted execution.

It is the latter features of teaching that are accentuated in what may be called the art metaphor in any of several forms, for example, that relating to sculpture. The sculptor's statue does not grow of itself out of the rock, requiring only the artist's nurture; the artist exercises real choice in its production, yet his initial block of marble is not wholly receptive to any idea he may wish to impose on it. It rejects some of these by its internal structure. Neither is every block of marble like every other. Each block requires individual study of its individual capacities and limitations. Finally, the artist's initial idea is not one that is fully formed in advance, remaining fixed throughout. It gets the process started, but is ordinarily modified by the process itself, during which the artist is continuously learning as well as creating.

This sculpture metaphor seems particularly apt with respect to the features just described, but it cannot be said that it is perfect, or even better in every way than the ones previously considered. For example, the growth metaphor at least acknowledges the continuing development of the object in question after the departure of the gardener, whereas the sculpture metaphor does not; the statue ceases to grow when the sculptor is finished with it. Nor is the teacher, unlike the sculptor, bound only by aesthetic standards. His aims and his methods are subject to moral and practical criticism as well.

Thus, it seems mistaken to try to find a progressive order of metaphors in education, each metaphor more adequate and comprehensive than the last. Here the comparison of such metaphors with scientific theories itself breaks down. Educational metaphors in general use are of help in reflecting and organizing social thought and practice with respect to schooling, but they are not tied in with processes of experimental confirmation and prediction. They thus do not develop cumulatively as do scientific theoretical frameworks. They are rather to be thought of, perhaps, as ranged around their common subject, whose individual complex of features may be illumined by a comparative examination of the metaphors.

The analogy indicated by a given metaphor may, as suggested earlier, be important in one context but not in another. A good metaphor is thus not generally good in every context. This fact is important for our present discussion, since education, as we have stressed, is the common ground of a variety of contexts. It is thus wise to be critical about accepting metaphors in a given context that have proved illuminating elsewhere, even though it is the same subject that is involved in both cases. . . .

KNOWLEDGE, THE DISCIPLINES, AND EXPERIENCE IN THE CURRICULUM

INTRODUCTION

Connecting threads run through many of the readings in Part Two. But, in brief, selections 12–15 focus on a number of questions about the structure of knowledge, selections 16–18 provide philosophical analyses of several disciplines or areas of study, and selections 19–21 present diverse conceptions of the nature of experience, including educational experience.

The paper by Phenix (12) and the extract from Broudy, Smith, and Burnett (13) explicate something of the meaning of "the structure of a discipline." Their analyses connect this concept with logical and psychological problems involved in classifying, explaining, and defining things. Explicitly and implicitly, their papers suggest criteria for selecting content and organizing the curriculum. Levit (14) argues for a curriculum that stresses interdisciplinary studies and a unified consideration of both the conclusions and the methodology or logic of inquiry. Schwab's paper (15) considers a number of problems and principles involved in demarcating and organizing the disciplines; it also provides an unusually comprehensive analysis of a variety of syntactical (logical-methodological) and substantive structures of the disciplines.

All these selections (12–15), and especially Schwab's paper, note that our knowledge, our basic concepts and assumptions, "organize our experience" and "determine how we see the world." But some of the papers have widely divergent views about criteria of knowing and about the relation of knowledge to the world. For example, Levit and Schwab seem to have different answers to this question: Is there—despite disciplinary differences in specific techniques and tools of inquiry—a unitary way of knowing, a logic of inquiry essentially common to all truth-seeking disciplines? Turning to another matter, we note that Phenix regards knowledge as, in some sense, a copy or disclosure of the real nature of things as they exist independently of man. In this view, a good act of inquiry reveals, as knowledge, that which exists prior to the act. On the other hand, for Levit and in some ways for Schwab, a fact is more like an artifact. It is not "subjective"; nor is it something that refers to what exists independently of the act and art of construction. In this view, to understand knowledge requires an understanding of modes and criteria of inquiry and an awareness of the interplay between substantive and logical matters.

The next three selections (16–18) constitute a necessarily small sample of the great variety of available philosophical analyses of basic disciplines or broad fields of study. The extract from Cohen and Nagel explains, for people who are not mathematicians, some of the fundamental features of a mathematical or logical system and, indeed, of any scientific theory. In many ways, the extract may be regarded as a more detailed exposition of some statements in selections 12, 14, and 15 on the structures of the disciplines. Frankel argues that values and interests do enter into historical inquiry, but, nevertheless, that it is possible to have objective historical knowledge. His discussion suggests various principles for evaluating historical explanations and interpretations. It may be interesting to compare Frankel's conception of the place of man's interests and purposes in inquiry with the views of Phenix (12), Schwab (15), and Arnstine (18). Arnstine maintains that aesthetic qualities may be characteristic of almost any kind of experience and that aesthetic appreciation need not be confined to special kinds of "art" objects studied in special courses. His philosophy of art is based on more general philosophical views that can be compared or contrasted with those of Phenix (12), Levit (14), and Childs (19).

It need not be argued that in discussions about the curriculum, "experience" is a key term. Unfortunately, it is often used in vague and ambiguous ways. The term is a kind of "melting pot," a meeting place for usually ill-defined, frequently shifting notions about mind, self, thoughts, acts, feelings, motive, attitudes, perceptions, interpretations, reality, meaning, value, and so on. The last three selections (19–21) provide quite diverse conceptions of experience (even when the word "experience" does not happen to be used). Analysis of these selections—plus some comparison with relevant part of selections 12–15—should disclose just a few of the important constellations of ideas that enter into discussions of educational experiences.

Suggested Reading

Alston, William P., *Philosophy of Language* (Englewood Cliffs, N.J.: Prentice-Hall, Inc., 1964).

Fox, June T., "Epistemology, Psychology and Their Relevance for Education in Bruner and Dewey," *Educational Theory,* 19 (1969): 58–75.

Lloyd, A. C., "How Concepts Contain Beliefs," *Proceedings of the Aristotelian Society,* New Series, 58 (1957–58).

Martin, Jane R., "The Disciplines and the Curriculum," *Educational Philosophy and Theory,* 1 (1969): 23–40.

Nagel, Ernest, *The Structure of Science* (New York: Harcourt, Brace and World, Inc., 1961), Chs. 1–2, 12–15.

Stadt, Ronald W., "Intelligence, Categorical Systems, and Content Organizations," *Educational Theory,* 15 (1965): 121–29.

THE USE OF THE DISCIPLINES*

In 1956 I published a paper entitled "Key Concepts and the Crisis in Learning," in which I developed the thesis that economy and efficiency in learning, in a time of vast proliferation of knowledge, can best be achieved by attending to the "key concepts" in the several fields of learning. Since that time many important develop- ments in curriculum studies have taken place along somewhat similar lines.

In recent years various study commissions have been at work reorganizing the subject matter of some of the major fields of learning, the T.E.P.S. commissions have worked for rapproch- ment between academic scholars and specialists in education, and leading investigators like Jerome Bruner have dealt with the im- portance of structure for the mastery of knowledge. The present paper seeks to develop some of these same themes, with special reference to the idea of the disciplines.

I

My thesis, briefly, is that *all* curriculum content should be drawn from the disciplines, or, to put it another way, that *only* knowl- edge contained in the disciplines is appropriate to the curriculum.

Exposition of this position requires first that we consider what is meant by a "discipline." The word "discipline" is derived from the Latin word *discipulus,* which means a disciple, that is, origi- nally, one who receives instruction from another. *Discipulus* in turn stems from the verb *discere,* to learn. Etymologically, then, a discipline may be construed as knowledge the special property

* Reprinted from "The Use of the Disciplines as Curriculum Content," *Educational Forum,* 26 (1962): 273-80. By permission of the author and of Kappa Delta Pi, an Honor Society in Education, publisher of *Educational Forum.*

of which is its appropriateness for teaching and its availability for learning. A discipline is knowledge organized for instruction.

Basic to my theme is this affirmation: the distinguishing mark of any discipline is that the knowledge which comprises it is instructive—that it is peculiarly suited for teaching and learning. Implicit in this assertion is the recognition that there are kinds of knowledge which are not found within a discipline. Such nondisciplined knowledge is unsuitable for teaching and learning. It is not instructive. Given this understanding of what a discipline is, it follows at once that all teaching should be disciplined, that it is undesirable to have any instruction in matters which fall beyond the disciplines. This means that psychological needs, social problems, and any of a variety of patterns of material based on other than discipline content are not appropriate to the determination of what is taught—though obviously such nondisciplinary considerations *are* essential to decision about the *distribution* of discipline knowledge within the curriculum as a whole.

I hardly need to remind you that the position here taken is quite at odds with the one taken by many people both in the field of education and in the several disciplines. The common assumption of these people is that the disciplines are in the realm of pure knowledge—of specialized professional scholarship and research—and that ordinary education is quite a different sort of enterprise. The disciplines have a life of their own, it is held, and knowledge in them is not directly available for the purposes of instruction, but to be suitable for education must be translated and transformed so as to become useful and meaningful to ordinary learners. Thus, the argument goes, for the curriculum we should draw upon life situations, problems, projects, and the like, for the primary *content* of instruction, using the knowledge supplied by the disciplines as auxiliary material to be employed as required by the basic instructional process. The person is supposed to learn primarily from experience as it comes naturally and not as it is artificially conceptualized and organized in the academic fields.

Correspondingly, under this customary view, there are two disparate realms of method: there are methods of professional scholarship and research, and there are quite different methods of instruction. There is a specialized logic of the disciplines and there is a largely unrelated psycho-logic of teaching and learning. From this division arises the well-known bifurcation between the academic scholars and the professional educators. The former pride themselves on their erudition and despise or neglect pedagogy, while the latter busily pursue the problems of teaching and learning, often with little understanding or concern for the standards of rigorous scholarship.

This common dualism is destructive both to scholarship and to education. It presupposes a concept of the academic disciplines which has no relation to the instructiveness of the knowledge contained therein and a concept of teaching and learning disconnected from the essential structure of the products of disciplined inquiry. We need to recover the essential meaning of a discipline as a body of instructive knowledge. So understood, the disciplines will be seen as the clue to good teaching and learning, and instructiveness will be seen as the mark of a good discipline. Furthermore, scholars will learn once more to measure their success by their ability to teach, and teachers will again be judged by the depth of their understanding, and the academics and the educationists will dwell together in peace, if indeed any such distinction will any longer be required!

It is wrong to suppose that the more profound scholarly inquiry is the further removed it is from suitability for teaching purposes. On the contrary, profundity is in proportion to illuminative quality. The esoteric knowledge that is often described as profound is more aptly termed obscure. The characteristic feature of disciplined intelligence is that difficulties and confusions are overcome and understanding of the subject is thereby facilitated. In short, the test for quality in knowledge is its communicability. Knowledge which is hard to teach is for that reason inferior. Knowledge which readily enlightens the learner's understanding is superior.

Now what is it that makes knowledge instructive? How does undisciplined differ from disciplined understanding? There are three fundamental features, all of which contribute to the availability of knowledge for instruction and thus provide measures for degree and quality of discipline. These three are (1) analytic simplification, (2) synthetic coordination, and (3) dynamism. Let us consider each criterion in turn.

II

First, analytic simplification. The primal essential for effective teaching is simplification. All intelligibility rests upon a radical reduction in the multiplicity of impressions which impinge upon the senses and the imagination. The infant begins life with the booming, buzzing confusion of which James spoke, and his learning consists in the growing ability to sort and select, that is, to simplify. The lower animals have built-in simplifiers in the instinctive mechanisms. Human beings have a much more interesting and powerful apparatus of simplification, through intelligence. The index of intelligence is of course, the power of symbolization. Symbols—preeminently but not exclusively those of language—are means of marking out useful and memorable features of experience for special notice. All significant words are such markers. Thus, the word "hand" designates a *kind* of object, to which an indefinite member of particular objects (hands) correspond. The point for emphasis is that a symbol—for example, a word—allows human beings drastically to reduce the complexity of their experience by subsuming an indefinite wealth of particulars under a single concept.

The secret of human learning is in generalization, that is, in transcending the multifariousness of raw experience. All thinking requires conceptualization. Concepts are classes of particulars. They are selections from the inchoate mass of impressions of certain features of things which enable them to be treated as a class rather than one by one. Thought proceeds by a process of rigorous selection, emphasis, and suppression of data. A person is intelligent to the degree that he actively discriminates in his entertainment of stimuli. In our pursuit of the full, rich life we may forget that the key to felicity and wisdom lies as much or more in our power of excluding as in receiving impressions. Our humanness rests upon a wise asceticism, not upon indiscriminate hospitality to every message impinging upon us from the world about us.

This simplification of experience through the use of symbols may be called analytic. The sorting out of classes of things is the process of analysis. It proceeds by the discrimination of similarities and differences, whereby entities may be divided and arranged in orderly fashion. Analysis is possible only because the human mind is able to *abstract*, that is, to discern properties, qualities, or forms of things. Every concept is an abstraction—a drawing out of certain features of a class of things for purposes of generalization and grouping. The function of abstraction is to simplify—to reduce the complexity of unanalyzed experience by selecting certain shared properties of kinds of things and neglecting their other features.

It is commonly assumed that abstract thinking is difficult and complicated. This assumption betrays a misunderstanding of what abstraction is. Analytic abstraction is a way of thinking which aims at ease of comprehension and reduction of complexity. For this reason all learning—all growth in understanding—takes place through the use of simplifying concepts. It is the key to effectiveness of instruction.

All of this bears directly on the question of the place of the disciplines in teaching and learning. A discipline is essentially nothing more than an extension of ordinary conceptualization. It is a conceptual system whose office is to gather a large group of cognitive elements into a common framework of ideas. That is, its goal is the simplification of understanding. This is the function of the techniques, models, and theories which are characteristic of any discipline. They economize thought by showing how diverse and apparently disparate elements of experience can be subsumed under common interpretive and explanatory schemes.

Thus, contrary to the popular assumption, knowledge does not become more and more complicated as one goes deeper into a discipline. If it is a real discipline and not merely a field for the display of erudition, the further one goes in it the more pervasive are the simplicities which analysis reveals. For example, how grand

and liberating is the simplicity afforded by the atomic theory of matter as one seeks to comprehend the endless complexity of the world of material substances! Again, how much simpler Copernicus made the understanding of the apparent motions of the stars and planets, and how much easier Darwin made the comprehension of the varieties of living things!

The test of a good discipline is whether or not it simplifies understanding. When a field of study only adds new burdens and multiplies complexities, it is not properly called a discipline. Likewise, when a real discipline in certain directions begins to spawn concepts and theories which on balance are a burden and hindrance to insight, in those areas it degenerates into undisciplined thinking.

One of the greatest barriers to progress in learning is the failure to catch the vision of simplicity which the disciplines promise. When students (and their teachers) consider the movement from elementary to advanced stages in a subject as requiring the taking on of more and more burdens of knowledge, of ever increasing complexity, just as physically one becomes with exercise capable of carrying increasingly heavy loads, it is little wonder that they so often resist instruction and postpone learning as long as possible. If, on the other hand, it can be made clear that, like Christian in Bunyan's allegory, the academic pilgrimage aims at release from the burdens of merely accumulated experience and leads to intellectual salvation through the insightful and revelatory concepts and theories contained in the traditions of the disciplines, how eager students become to learn and how ready to exchange their hampering ignorance for liberating understanding!

III

Let us now turn, more briefly, to the second feature of a discipline which makes knowledge in it instructive, namely, synthetic coordination. A discipline is a conceptual structure whose function is not only to simplify understanding but also to reveal significant patterns and relationships. Analysis is not an end in itself; it is the basis of synthesis. By synthesis is meant the construction of new wholes, the coordination of elements into significant coherent structures. Disciplined thinking is *organized* thinking. Differences and distinctions are recognized within an ordered framework which permits synoptic vision.

Such synthetic coordination is not opposed in tendency to analytic simplifications; both are aspects of a common process of intelligible ordering. The perception of meaningful differences is possible only against some common measure. Thus, the notion of parts within an ordered whole involves both the differentiation which is presupposed by the idea of parts and the unity which is implied by the idea of a whole. A discipline is a synthetic structure of concepts made possible by the discrimination of similarities through analysis. It is a hierarchy of ideas ordered as a unity-in-difference.

It is only in this sense that disciplined knowledge can be called complex. The simplifications of abstraction make possible the construction of cognitive complexes—i.e., the weaving together of ideas into coherent wholes. Concepts are no longer entertained in isolation, but are seen in their interconnections and relationships.

What occurs in disciplined thinking is a reconstruction of experience. The brute multiplicity of primordial experience is simplified by conceptual abstraction, and these abstractions are then synthesized into more and more comprehensive patterns of coordination. In this way naive experience is transformed from a meaningless hodge-podge of impressions into a relatively meaningful pattern of understanding.

Herein lies the great pedagogical virtue of a discipline. Whatever is taught within a discipline framework draws strength and interest from its membership within a family of ideas. Each new idea is illuminated by ideas previously acquired. A discipline is a community of concepts. Just as human beings cannot thrive in isolation, but require the support of other persons in mutual association, so do isolated ideas wither and die, while ideas comprehended within the unity of a discipline tend to remain vivid and powerful within the understanding.

IV

The third quality of knowledge in a discipline I have called its dynamism. By this is meant the power of leading on to further understanding. A discipline is a *living* body of knowledge, containing within itself a principle of growth. Its concepts do not merely simplify and coordinate; they also invite further analysis and synthesis. A discipline contains a *lure to discovery*. Its ideas excite the imagination to further exploration. Its concepts suggest new constructs which provide larger generalizations and reconstituted modes of coordination.

James B. Conant has pointed to this dynamism as a distinguishing feature of scientific knowledge. Science is an enterprise in which fruitfulness is the mark of a good conceptual scheme. Theories which merely coordinate and organize a given body of data but do not stimulate further experimentation and inquiry are scientifically unimportant. This principle may also be taken as definitive for any discipline. Instructiveness is proportionate to fruitfulness. Knowledge which only organizes the data of experience but does not excite further questions and inquiries is relatively undisciplined knowledge. Disciplined ideas not only constitute families of concepts, but these families beget progeny. They have generative power. This is why they are instructive. They lead on and out: they educate.

There is, of course, no sharp dividing line between disciplined and nondisciplined knowledge. There are on the one extreme isolated bits of information which are not within any organized discipline, and on the other extreme there are precisely articulated theoretical structures which are readily recognized as disciplined according to the meaning developed above. In between are bodies of knowledge which have all degrees of discipline. Perhaps it would be well also to speak of weak disciplines and strong disciplines, the difference being in the degree to which their contents satisfy the three criteria for instructiveness earlier stated. Thus, mathematics, with powerful analytic tools and the dynamic for endless fruitful elaborations, by the present criteria would appear to be a stronger discipline than most present-day political science, which (from my limited knowledge of it) seems to have relatively few unifying concepts and theoretical schemes permitting wide synthesis and creative expansion. Again, I would rate comparative linguistics, which seems to possess a powerful and productive set of concepts, as a stronger discipline than esthetics, which still operates largely in terms of individual subjective judgments about particular objects, one by one.

A distinction may also be useful between a discipline and an area of study. Not all areas of study are disciplines, since not all of them display analytic, synthetic, and dynamic qualities. Thus, it seems to me that "education" is an area of study rather than a discipline. Within this area disciplined learning is possible. For example, I think a good case can be made for a discipline of curriculum, or of educational psychology, or of educational philosophy—though I would not wish to rate these disciplines as to strength. Similarly, "business" and "social studies" appear to be areas of study rather than disciplines. Not everyone that cries "discipline, discipline" shall enter the kingdom of learning, but only those who can show analytic simplification, synthetic coordination, and dynamism in their knowledge schemes.

My theme has been that the curriculum should consist entirely of knowledge which comes from the disciplines, for the reason that the disciplines reveal knowledge in its teachable forms. We should not try to teach anything which has not been found actually instructive through the labors of hosts of dedicated inquirers. Education should be conceived as a *guided recapitulation of the processes of inquiry which gave rise to the fruitful bodies of organized knowledge comprising the established disciplines.*

In this brief analysis there has been no time to consider the problem of levels. I do not intend to suggest that the whole conceptual apparatus of a discipline should be brought to bear on teaching at every level of education. There are elementary and advanced stages of disciplined inquiry. The great simplicities, the comprehensive syntheses, and the powerful dynamisms usually belong to the more advanced stages. Nevertheless, from the very earliest years on up, it is only discipline knowledge which should be taught in the curriculum. Every discipline has in it beginning concepts and more developed concepts, all of which belong to the discipline authentically and properly. There is no place in the curriculum for ideas which are regarded as suitable for teaching because of the supposed nature, needs, and interests of the learner, but which do not belong within the regular structure of the disciplines, for the disciplines are in their essential nature bodies of knowledge organized for the most effective instruction.

This view asserts the identity of the psycho-logic of teaching and learning with the logic of the disciplines, contrary to many of the current theories of the teaching-learning process. Or it might be more generally acceptable among educators to say that the view measures the logic (and the authenticity) of a discipline by its instructiveness.

V

In closing, one further point can only be indicated here, without development or detailed defense. The priority and primacy of the disciplines in education are greatly buttressed by a realistic view of knowledge, as opposed to a nominalistic one. In realism it is asserted that concepts and theories disclose the real nature of things, while in nominalism it is affirmed that the structure of thought is a matter of human convention. Academic and educational nominalists believe that experience can be categorized and concepts organized in endless ways, according to the inclination and decision and for the convenience of individuals and societies. Furthermore, it is held, scholars can choose their own special ways of organizing knowledge and educators can choose other ways, the differences corresponding to the disparity in purposes in the two groups. Thus arise the supposed contrasts between the logic of the disciplines and the psycho-logic of the educative process.

Such nominalism is rejected in the realistic view here proposed. From a realistic standpoint, nominalism is epistemologically impious and pedagogically disastrous, a source of internecine strife and intellectual estrangement. There is a logos of being which it is the office of reason to discover. The structure of things is revealed, not invented, and it is the business of inquiry to open that structure to general understanding through the formation of appropriate concepts and theories. Truth is rich and varied, but it is not arbitrary. The nature of things is *given*, not chosen, and if man is to gain insight he must employ the right concepts and methods. Only by obedience to the truth thus discovered can he learn or teach.

In short, authentic disciplines are at one and the same time approximations to the given orders of reality and disclosures of the paths by which persons may come to realize truth in their own being, which is simply to say that the disciplines are the sole proper source of the curriculum.

I think it is the special province of people in the schools of education to see clearly the relationship between discipline knowledge on the one hand and the tasks of teaching and learning on the other, and the interrelations between the fields of knowledge within the curriculum as a whole. In the light of these visions, educators can help the disciplines to be more true to their own essential nature and instruction to find once again its proper resource.

CONCEPTS AND PRINCIPLES: STRUCTURE AND SELECTION AS CURRICULUM CONTENT*

Harry S. Broudy, B. Othanel Smith, and Joe R. Burnett

Intelligent behavior is prefigured by the individual's scheme of concepts and their relationships. An effective curriculum therefore includes concepts and principles which are basic to intelligent behavior. It also takes into account both the logic and psychology of concept formation and the relation of concepts to principles and their use.

From a psychological standpoint, a concept can be defined as consisting of the abstracted characteristics common to a group of objects, events, and the like. It is also defined by some psychologists as a common way of behaving toward a group of objects. But these two views overlook the role of concepts as nodes in the development of cognitive networks. Concepts are foci of organization in the mental make-up of the individual, focal points in the organization of experience. In this sense, they are to be thought of as intervening conditions lying between stimulus and response. Concepts are, therefore, not linguistic; they are not symbolic, nor are they operations. But they can be expressed either symbolically or operationally. When expressed in either of these two ways, they are called definitions.

Strictly speaking, the curriculum does not contain concepts, but rather their symbolic and operational expressions. Nor does the teacher work with concepts as such. Instead, he deals with definitions and other verbal formulations, together with materials and instruments which build concepts into the student's experience. But for convenience in this discussion, the terms "concept" and "definition" are ordinarily used interchangeably.

* Reprinted from *Democracy and Excellence in American Secondary Schools* (Chicago: Rand McNally and Company, 1964), pp. 115–18, 121–34. © 1964 by Rand McNally and Company. By permission of Rand McNally and the authors.

Kinds of Concepts

Concepts may be classified in various ways. For the purposes of curriculum development, perhaps the most basic classification is that which distinguishes descriptive from valuative concepts.

Descriptive concepts are neutral with respect to our preferences or our picture of the world as we would have it. For example, our concept of a meter is free of preferential elements. Of course, it can be argued that no concept is ever completely devoid of affective tones of pleasantness or unpleasantness. But at least we have concepts in science and often in common experience which, if they do embody preferences, embody those which are so uniformly held that they give rise to no controversy and give us no concern.

Valuative concepts by their very nature embody preferences. We ordinarily include in our concept of democracy whatever we think a society ought to be and have. The liberal concept of democracy embodies preferences not to be found in the conservative concept, and the preferential aspect of the Communist concept of democracy differs radically from that of either the American liberal or the conservative view. We often engage in similar preferential loading when we entertain such concepts as those indicated by the terms "patriotism," "nationalism," "conservatism," "liberalism," and any number of ideas which we use in the social studies, literature, and in common parlance.

In this chapter the discussion is confined to descriptive concepts and principles, reserving the exploration of valuative concepts for the next chapter.

Three types of descriptive concepts are especially important in curriculum theory and practice—classificatory, relational, and operational concepts.

A classificatory concept is based upon a group of objects or events having certain features selected as characteristic of the group in common. For example, when a whale is classified as a mammal rather than a fish, it is because we select the fact that it gives birth to and suckles its young as its defining characteristics rather than the fact that it swims and lives in water.

A relational concept is one which includes reference to a relationship between two or more attributes. The relationship may be expressed either as a ratio or a product. For example, the concept of speed may be expressed as a ratio between distance traversed and the amount of time required to negotiate the distance, and force is expressed as the product of mass and acceleration.

An operational concept consists in a way of doing something—a "know-how." It is an idea consisting of an awareness of an order of operations that when performed lead to a particular result. For example, our concept of weight may consist in a set of ideas which prefer to a set of operations leading to the reading of a number on a scale, a number thus designating the weight. Hence, we may take a spring balance, place an object on the hook of the balance, and read the scale. We then say this is what we mean by weight. At a more naive level, we could say, "Lift this object. Do you feel the resistance? Well, that is what we mean by weight." These concepts may also refer to various forms of order, such that we can say of a given attribute that a is greater, less than, or equal to b with respect to it. For instance, "harder than" may be defined as "x scratches y, but y does not scratch x."

The Logical Structure of Concepts

Although the psychological version of a concept is essential to curriculum development, it is not sufficient. For one thing, it does not reveal the structure of concepts in such a way as to indicate the materials and operations which must be used in teaching, except perhaps at the perceptual level of experience. For another thing, the teacher, as already pointed out, does not work with concepts but with operations and linguistic expressions through which concepts are built. Therefore, a way of looking at concepts more nearly in line with pedagogical requirements is needed. This way is to be found in the logic of concepts, and the discussion begins by considering the classificatory concept.

The logical counterpart of such a concept is a classificatory definition. This type of definition is made up of a class term and a further statement of characteristics which distinguish the group of things to be defined from other members of the class. In other words, if we look at the logical structure of a generic concept, we see that it is made up of two parts, a class of objects and a set of criteria by which to decide which objects are to be included in the class and which are to be excluded. Consider the term "tax" as a word which stands for a concept. A tax is defined in the *Dictionary of American Politics* as follows: "A tax is a compulsory payment made to a government for its support or for the regulation or promotion of certain social purposes and levied according to law uniformly upon all taxpayers of a given class." The logical structure of this concept may be illustrated as in Figure 2.

Category   **Criteria**

1. Payment made to government
2. Levied according to law
3. Levied uniformly upon all payers of a given class
4. Purpose is to support the government or
5. to regulate social purposes or
6. to promote social purposes

Figure 2.

In the structure of this concept, "payment" is the class term, and a tax is classifiable as a member of a certain subclass of payments. The criteria specify the characteristics which a payment must have in order to be called a tax. To tell whether or not a given payment is a tax, the criteria must be applied to the payment. If the given payment meets all of the criteria, it is a tax. If it does not, the payment is not a tax, even though it may be made to the government. For example, an installment on a debt is a payment, but it meets none of the criteria and hence is not a tax. But what about fines, fees, and tariffs? These are all payments to government. Are they to be called taxes? It depends upon whether or not they satisfy the remaining criteria. And of course they do not.

A fine is exacted as punishment for violation of the law and is not a tax. A tariff is designed to protect domestic industry and agriculture, and a fee is paid in return for services rendered directly to the individual. Neither meets the criteria and hence is not a tax.

Note that criteria in a classificatory definition may be conjunctive, that is, they may constitute a set all of which must be satisfied by an exemplar of the class. For instance, an acid is a compound which tastes sour, turns blue litmus paper red, and produces free hydrogen ions. Any acid satisfies all of these criteria. Criteria may also be disjunctive. In this case, the criteria are alternatives, and it is sufficient that the exemplar satisfy any one of them. For example, a citizen of the United States is defined by disjunctive criteria. An individual may be a citizen if he is born in the United States, or if he is born in a foreign country of parents who are citizens of the United States, or if he is born of foreign parentage and in a foreign country, provided he lives in the United States for a specified time and his application for citizenship is accepted. If an individual meets any one of these criteria, he is a citizen. The criteria for deciding whether or not a payment is a tax are both conjunctive and disjunctive. The first three criteria above are conjunctive, the last three disjunctive.

Classificatory definitions are used extensively in biological sciences, where they are basic to the whole system of classification. They are used also in the social sciences, where the disjunctive form is found in abundance, and in grammar and geometry. Of course, classificatory definitions are found in all subjects. But in the natural sciences they are being supplemented and often replaced by operational definitions.

In a relational definition, the characteristics are usually compared and expressed quantitatively. And, as pointed out above, these characteristics are then related to one another as a ratio. Density in physics is defined as a ratio of mass to volume, mass being one characteristic of a substance and volume another. Mass is described by a set of operations, usually those involved in the ordinary measurement of weight, and volume is determined by measuring special dimensions and performing the usual calculations. The ratio of the measured weight to the calculated volume is taken to be the density of the substance. It is so much mass per unit of volume.

It should be noted, however, that the concept is not the actual quotient in any given case, but rather results from the insight into the relationship between the mass of a sample and its volume, as in physics; or between the new and the familiar words per page, as in vocabulary density; or between area and number of persons, as in population studies. If we were to say that the density of water is one, thinking that we had thereby fully conveyed the idea of density, we should be in error. . . .

Relational definitions yield constants which are extremely useful in science. The intelligence quotient—the ratio of mental age and chronological age—is repeatedly used in educational research. These sorts of definitions are found in all fields that have achieved the level of quantitative studies—physics, chemistry, psychology, economics, to mention a few.

It is often thought that clarity is gained if a concept is expressed in words that refer to observable things wherever possible. Terms such as "mass," "force," "elasticity," and "conductivity," as used in physics, and "nationalism," "national income," and "democracy," as used in social science, represent neither observable processes nor entities. If we define the term "force" as meaning the same as "a cause of motion," our definition is couched in terms as abstract as the word "force" itself. For the expression "cause of motion" is just as far removed from what can be observed as is the term "force." This need for concreteness is satisfied by operational definitions.

To see how a concept may be treated operationally, consider the concept of force as it is used in physics. Begin with the anthropomorphic formulation of the concept. Force is, in this view, a push or a pull. It relates kinesthetic sensations to objects. The teacher can say to a student, "Push or pull this table. Now what you exerted when you pushed or pulled is what we mean by force." This way of defining the term "force" leaves the definition at a very low operational level. One can take another step toward a more sophisticated definition by defining the term through the use of devices such as a spring balance. He pulls the spring and says that it exerts a force in proportion to its extension. He can also place a scale over the spring, and by providing the spring with a pointer, he can describe the force quantitatively. A more sophisticated approach defines "force" by reference to the relationship between two variables, namely, mass and acceleration. In this definition, he enters into the process of determining the mass of an object and its acceleration in quantitative terms. He would then use the formula, force = mass $\times$ acceleration, and by calculation arrive at a value which he would call the amount of the force. These operations and calculations would constitute the meaning of the concept of force. The foregoing description represents steps leading from a rather naive to a rather sophisticated operational definition.

Although there are certain criticisms of operational definitions, they are nevertheless extremely useful when the purpose is to reduce concepts to as concrete a form as possible, that is, to operations that can be observed. They are used extensively in the natural sciences, in economics, and in psychology and related fields.

In their more sophisticated form, operational definitions tend to be similar to relational definitions. The difference appears to be the amount of stress placed upon the performance of operations with actual materials. There is less reference to concrete manipulation of materials in a relational definition than in an operational one.

Special Cases and Problems of Defining

Although they present no departure from the logical patterns discussed above, some concepts nevertheless present special problems. These are concepts which are difficult, if not impossible, to define, such as those for which criteria tend to be vague or ambiguous or for which data are difficult to obtain, and those which are "open ended."

Some concepts, such as the notion of importance, cannot be formulated, at least not in a strict or complete sense. Yet terms representing them mean something to us. When someone says,

"This is important," we know we are expected to give it special attention. Ordinary discourse is filled with such terms—specific, general, individual, concrete, to mention only a few examples. And it is ordinarily useless to try to reach a level of clarity beyond our common-sense understanding of them.

Some concepts cannot be clarified except very arbitrarily. For example, most of us use the term "rain," and we ordinarily understand what it means. But if we are to issue rain insurance or purchase such insurance, we want to know more specifically what we are talking about. Does one drop make a rain? How many drops make a rain? We can know what is to count as a rain only by stating precisely what is to be meant by the term "rain," and this requires that we state precisely the criteria for using the term. In this case, an insurance company specifies that the fall of moisture must amount to such and such a quantity in a specified time, if it is to be called "rain." Such definitions are sometimes called *stipulative* definitions. But their logical structure may often be found to be similar to one or another of the definitions discussed above.

There are other sorts of definitions which are unclear, even though we may know the criteria for deciding what is covered by the concept and what is not. Such cases as this arise when the criteria themselves are unclear, or when it is difficult to decide whether or not the given instances satisfy the criteria. Suppose we define "society" as "a group of individuals united by common interests, possessing a sense of corporate unity and discipline, and organized to promote common aims." The criteria—"common interest," "sense of corporate unity," "sense of discipline," and "organized to promote common aims"—are vague. If we were given a large number of social groups and were asked to decide whether these aggregates were societies or not, it would be almost impossible to know whether or not the given aggregates satisfied these criteria. If a number of persons were attempting to decide independently whether these aggregates of individuals were to be called societies or not, the amount of agreement among them would probably be very low. The small amount of agreement would indicate either lack of clarity about the criteria or inability to determine whether or not the criteria apply in particular cases.

By the same token, were we to try to decide which among the nations of the world are imperialistic and which are not, it might turn out to be extremely difficult to do so, even if we had clear-cut criteria. This would be the case for the simple reason that the data suggested by the criteria might not be available to us. Nevertheless, we would understand what we were talking about if our concept of imperialism were identified by clear-cut criteria. Many social-science concepts are unclear in this sense.

Finally, some concepts are undefinable in a complete sense because all of the criteria can never be specified. Definitions of this type of concept are "open ended." Although they present no new problems of logical structure, they do present a unique problem in discussion.

The social sciences appear to have an abundance of these open-ended definitions. For example, "democracy" may be defined with reference to a particular set of criteria, but it is easily possible to add additional criteria and thus to open the question of whether or not a given society heretofore excluded from the category of democracies is to be admitted. . . .

Uses of Concepts

It has already been noted that concepts organize our experience. To say that concepts are centers of organization in our cognitive structure is to say that they are used in identifying and classifying the objects, events, and the like, of our environment. They determine how we see the world. As Kant noted long ago, we depend as much for our understanding upon our concepts as upon our percepts.

There are many things which we experience through our senses and for which we seek interpretations and explanations. Concepts and conceptual systems enable us to understand these features of our environment. In common sense, we assume that we explain that which is strange and new by reference to that which is familiar; the abstract is explained by the concrete. But to understand the role of concepts in helping us explain the features of our environment is to see this whole process in reverse. For when we use concepts in this fashion, we explain the more familiar things of the world by reference to the things that we know least about. We account for what is observed by reference to that which is unseen, that is, explain the concrete by the abstract. For example, we observe that a child resembles its parents. We explain this similarity by saying that it has been inherited. We then go on to explain inheritance by reference to the genes and to other aspects of genetic structure not immediately visible to us. In like manner, we explain the hotness of an object by reference to molecular motion; the greater the speed of the molecules, the higher the temperature. Similarily, we interpret the world of social behavior, the story of man's doings, and the world of art with the concepts we bring to those domains. Concepts are the media not only for bringing the world to us, but also the instruments for sorting out and giving meaning to our experience.

We also use concepts, as has already been indicated, in the formulation of principles. The principle or law of gravity says that any two bodies will be attracted to one another by a force directly proportional to their masses and inversely proportional to the square of the distance between them. The concepts in this statement are given by the terms "body," "mass," "distance," "directly proportional" and "inversely proportional," and "square of the distance." The law in this case is simply a statement relating these concepts.

A law, as someone has said, is an inference ticket. It tells us that if such and such conditions are present, then such and such consequences may be safely inferred. If we know that an actual state of affairs corresponds to what the law prescribes, we know from the law what to expect. The law also suggests what condition must be brought into existence if we want a given result. A basic science such as physics or chemistry is not primarily concerned with the task of bringing about the state of affairs essential to a practical result. It is the business of a technology or of an applied science to work out the ways by which the conditions specified in scientific laws may be realized in a practical situation. Back of all of this—laws and their application—is the conceptual system which comprises the basic elements in the intellectual organization of scientists and technologists, and, in verbal form, makes up a large part of the content of the curriculum.

Criteria for Selecting Concepts [and Principles]

. . . Other things being equal, basic concepts should be emphasized. But how is the basic character of concepts to be ascertained? There are two criteria which may be given in answer to this question. The first of these is that those concepts which are most widely instrumental are basic to the behavior of an individual. There are concepts used by the individual no matter what content he deals with. Such concepts as these are usually acquired in the fields of mathematics and languages—the symbols of information—although other subjects do contribute to their development. One or two examples are appropriate. Direct and indirect proportion are concepts which are used repeatedly by the individual in a great variety of fields. A rudimentary concept of direct proportion is acquired from daily experience. An individual learns that if he buys one apple for ten cents and another at the same price, the amount which he pays for apples is directly proportional to the number of apples he purchases. He may not articulate the concept, but it is implicit in his behavior. The concept of direct proportion is used over and over again in the sciences as well as in everyday life.

The concept of inverse proportion, although encountered in everyday experience, is more difficult for the student to grasp. It is difficult for him to see that there are some relationships such that the more of one thing he has, the less he has of something else. He can see clearly that if he spends money for amusement, say, his money decreases as his time in recreation increases. But when this concept is brought into problems involving data in the natural and social sciences, the student has difficulty in understanding it. When he is told that the volume of a gas varies inversely with its pressure, and especially when this idea is expressed in mathematical terms, the idea often seems strange and unfamiliar to him. Partly for this reason, this concept is often dealt with explicitly and at considerable length in beginning sciences.

These two concepts, as already indicated, are useful in any field where variables are related to one another. They are in a sense without content; that is to say, they can be used in dealing with almost any sort of content. They are modes of operation generalized from a broad base of experience.

The concept of truth is another idea which has general instrumental value. In ordinary experience everyone knows what truth means. But in the domain of history, physics, or mathematics, for example, the individual is very often unable to give the grounds for believing what is claimed or asserted to be true. There are several different ways of defining the term "truth." It may be defined one way in religion, another way in mathematics, and still another way in science. And since the student's thought, at least a great deal of it, presupposes some conception of what it means for a statement to be true, we can say that the various concepts of truth have wide utility and should perhaps be dealt with explicitly in the educational program.

The concept of equilibrium is another case in point. It is used in chemistry, physics, psychology, social sciences, and in ordinary experience. To be sure, there is a difference in meaning from one of these fields to another, but still there is a root meaning of the term "equilibrium" that holds roughly from domain to domain. In all of its uses, the term means a balance of forces. In the final analysis, it reduces to the simple notion that the resultant of all the forces, whatever be their character, is zero.

The second criterion by which to decide upon key concepts is that the concept be logically basic to a given field of study. These concepts do not cut across subject fields but are restricted to a particular domain. In physics, the concepts of time and motion are basic ideas, and it is important that they be thoroughly understood, if the student is to grasp even the elementary aspects of physics. The concept of valence in chemistry is likewise a basic notion. . . .

While logical relationships are to be found in almost every

field of knowledge, the logical structure of knowledge is most clearly illustrated in those fields which are highly developed, such as the disciplines of physics, chemistry, and mathematics. In these domains the most fundamental elements are definitions and postulates based upon the definitions. These are the most fundamental because all other propositions making up the field of knowledge are derivable from these more primitive elements. A classic model of this type of organization is, of course, plane geometry; the physical sciences evidence greater complexity, but it is still fair to consider them as being roughly of the same general type.

Within such a system of organized knowledge, some ideas are more important than others. This is the case for the simple reason that some ideas include other ideas. If this were not the case, deduction would be impossible, because logically one cannot draw a conclusion when its elements are not in the premises. It is not useful, therefore, in a logically organized field of knowledge to think of all ideas as being on the same plane of logical importance. Some ideas have greater explanatory power than others, that is to say, a larger number of events, objects, and other ideas are subsumed by those having the greater power. For example, the molecular theory of matter is more fundamental than Boyle's Law or any of the other gas laws. It is more fundamental in the sense that the molecular theory includes the elements of knowledge from which the gas laws may themselves be derived. Suppose we wish to explain how it is that an inflated tire is able to support the weight of an automobile. We may attempt to do this by appealing to the gas laws, but if we wish to explain the gas laws themselves, we show that they represent special cases of the molecular theory of matter. The molecular theory of matter is more inclusive than the gas laws, not only because the theory explains the gas laws, but also because it accounts for the behavior of solids and liquids as well as gases. The late Boyd Bode used to illustrate this point dramatically by putting the following questions to his classes: "The earth is round and Italy is shaped like a boot. Which idea is more important and why?" Obviously, if we are aiming at general education, the answer is that, it is more important to know that the earth is round than that Italy is shaped like a boot, because more commonly important facts can be interpreted by the idea of the earth's roundness than by the concept of Italy's shape.

The notion that some ideas, because of their logical scope, are more important than others is fundamental in curriculum development. Of course, we have always held that ideas are not equally important, and we have attempted to use this notion in selecting content. But it is only recently that we have come to see that the importance of an idea can best be determined by a logical criterion. In the recent past, we have tended to decide the importance of the content of the curriculum in terms of its practical utility as measured by the frequency of its use, however trivially. Thus, for a Mediterranean fisherman it might be as important to know that Italy is shaped like a boot as that the earth is round. When we have not resorted to the criterion of frequency or immediacy of use, we have appealed to the social significance of ideas. Although these criteria cannot be completely dismissed in curriculum-building, as is evidenced in Chapters X and XI, they do fail to take account of the relational aspects of knowledge and hence of the structural features of the disciplines. The criterion of logical significance takes the curriculum-builder into the intellectual disciplines themselves, and requires of him that he understand the logical structure of these fields. He must know not only the facts and ideas, but also the logical relations among these elements of knowledge. Within the basic concepts of the disciplines, it becomes appropriate to impose the criterion of what is most generally and significantly useful. There is more on this subject in later chapters.

The emphasis being placed upon logical relations among the elements of content, and upon the strategic importance of certain ideas within various fields of knowledge, represents one of the distinguishing features of the new curriculum programs now being encouraged in various subjects, such as Max Beberman's work in mathematics and other work to be mentioned later. These programs tend to emphasize the general concepts which enable the individual to handle a wide range of data. Since they also stress the logical relations within a field of knowledge, they in consequence emphasize inquiry in depth. The student comes to see that ideas can be fruitfully arranged in a hierarchy, and that the further he goes into the hierarchy the deeper he gets into the field of knowledge.

The individual's personal organization of knowledge can be similar to the logical organization of knowledge within the various fields of learning. With proper instruction, the individual builds guiding ideas. These ideas function in his thought as schemata, that is to say, they bring together in one comprehensive view many otherwise disparate and completely unrelated elements in the experience of the learner. These ideas give a sense of direction to the student's activities in the process of learning; they help him to organize the facts and ideas that come to him; and they confer meaning upon those aspects of his experience which he finds difficult to grasp. When these guiding ideas are clear and well understood by the student, he is better able to learn new and unfamiliar ideas and to retain them for further use. These are the ideas of greater logical inclusiveness discussed above, and they are the basic constituents of the cognitive frames or maps typical of persons who have a good general education.

It therefore makes a difference what materials we choose to teach. The curriculum has to include materials that exemplify the major ways in which experience can be ordered and has been ordered. It is insufficient to prescribe a few solid subjects or a rich variety of interesting topics.

INTERDISCIPLINARY EDUCATION AND UNDERSTANDING THE DISCIPLINES*

Martin Levit

In recent decades, hot and cold wars and the pressures for power and productivity have been promoting specialism, subdivision of knowledge, and the virtues of applicatory skills and efficiency. There is a surging enthusiasm for specialization, even in the upper grades of the elementary schools. While here and there an experimental program, school, or college may appear, it is clear, for example, that on the national scene the proportion of integrated courses and programs (from junior high schools to college undergraduate programs) is decreasing. By and large, the call to "teach the structure of a subject," a call often heard in recent years, has not been the slogan of those who seek to integrate the structures of various subjects.

Whether advocating increasing teacher specialization in elementary education or advocating departmental courses as the means of providing a liberal education in college, the proponents of specialism often claim that integrated or interdisciplinary courses must necessarily be intellectually diluted. Terms and phrases like "mushy," "superficial," "hasty survey," "popularization," and "not *real* or *solid*" have been used to describe and evaluate integrated courses. On the other hand, departmental offerings are, of course, "real," and they are "solid"; they are "rigorous," and they provide "the generalizations, so far as we have them, of tested knowledge."

Now behind these "snarl" and "purr" words there often lie arguments which may rest on a variety of philosophical beliefs. I want to argue rather indirectly against a few general beliefs which are shared by many opponents of integration in education. I will do so by arguing that certain aims and assumptions of interdisciplinary education are much more in accord with reliable prin-

* I want to thank Professors Mary Lee Marksberry, Arlene Payne, and Gilbert Rees for their helpful comments on this paper.

ciples for verifying, understanding, and expanding knowledge than are aims and assumptions that characterize many subject-centered, departmental courses. Attention will be focused on certain essential interdependencies that exist both among the disciplines and between the content of subjects and methods or criteria of sound inquiry. It may be that much of what is said is applicable to many aspects of vocational or professional education. However, the aim here is to provide certain arguments for stressing an integrated general education at any level of education.

I will be discussing a few theoretical matters and not performances or labels. Thus I do not hesitate to say that students sometimes can get an excellent general education in departmental courses taught by exceptional specialists. The kinds of integration considered here—and there are many other kinds—*can* be carried on under labels which suggest that attention will be focused on *a* discipline, or on principles that cut across a number of disciplines, on social issues, problem-solving activities, or a variety of other organizing centers. In any event, I will not be considering any particular plan for organizing the curriculum.

There are many important grounds—ranging from aesthetic and psychological to citizenship and technological—on which an integrated general education could be defended. I want to deal with a few problems in epistemology, the theory of knowledge, because exploring the grounds of our beliefs can be a freeing enterprise and because cognitive prizes have too often been awarded to the specialized subjects even by some who defend an integrated education on other grounds.

The argument I wish to sketch rests, for one thing, on the fact that over many centuries of human existence, extremely varied relations among things—including men and other organisms—have been found or established. In general, it has been increasingly noted that new properties or objects—be they species of organisms, attitudes of men, material inventions, chemical elements, or religious beliefs—often developed out of new relations among original materials. Again and again, reputedly unconditioned states of affairs and absolute starting or terminal points were dissolved as developmental histories, dependencies, and possibilities became manifest in new relations and inquiries. Atomic fission—which means division of the indivisible—may be a striking example. But, for present purposes, it is no more important than, for instance, the studies of man which indicate that his "common sense" and his deepest emotional allegiances, his manifestations of egoism and altruism, his uses and abuses of reason are functions of history and culture, and of sociological, psychological, and biological conditions.

From the sun to food, from technological level to the traits of character a society values, from social values to acceptance, rejection or modifications of material inventions, from religion to sex, the energies and things of the world are interdependent, continuous with each other. Of course, there are discontinuities; not everything is related to everything else in every possible way. But there is no property that is possessed or explained by just *a* thing; there is no thing which is self-sufficient, self-explanatory. Qualities and entities derive from interactions of yet other qualities and entities.

The physical, biological, and social studies which lie behind this rough sketch have been variously interpreted. However, for an increasing number of interpreters since the latter part of the nineteenth century, terms denoting relations, change, and context have become basic; terms denoting entities, qualities, and momentary states have become derivative.

Stated in terms of subject matter, these developments have been reflected in the revolutionizing of those disciplines which are open to inquiry in extensions, modifications, and intertwinings of their concepts, procedures, and objects of study. Even in the generally weak domain of social inquiry, the so-called behavioral sciences illustrate (sometimes with unseemly posturing) these tendencies. For example, "information theory," widely applicable in areas ranging from the study of enzymes to sociology and international relations, uses concepts and procedures from psychology, sociology, linguistics, mathematics, engineering, biology, and other disciplines. To take another example: the phenomena and principles of physiology continue to be reinterpreted as they are brought into expanding theoretical and practical relations with the materials and principles of physics and biophysics, chemistry and biochemistry, anatomy, embryology, genetics, ecology, psychology, and many other areas of inquiry. Thus one cannot successfully argue that intensive study of the objects and procedures of physiology at any given time constitutes the best way to understand things in physiology and to advance knowledge in physiology.

The openness of science is the counterpart of a pluralistic world wherein regularities, whether in physics or psychology, are contingent; no finalities in the natural or man-aided production of things and qualities are discernible; there is no reason to believe that there are overarching, all-embracive patterns of development which can be known through the study of *a* subject—say, economics, biology, philosophy, or anthropology. And, to approach the same general notion from another direction, history does not seem to be reducible to economics, psychology, biology, or any set of factors studied in a limited set of subjects. Aesthetic expressions do not seem to be reducible to individual impulse and genius, or technological and sociological conditions, or any set of limited, self-sufficient factors.

Since qualities and things occur only in associations, since traits emerge and are known only in interactions, knowledge must be regarded in terms of related objects and interactions. One of the pervasive and most significant interactions is that of observer and observed, knower and known, process of inquiry and product of inquiry. For present purposes, one point is basic. When we speak of logic and scientific method, research design and statistics, theory construction, criteria of verification, and thousands of detailed acts and concepts of intellectually controlled inquiry, then we are speaking of a wide range of matters that do not "belong" to any one discipline but are or may be relevant to evaluating conclusions of inquiry in any disciplined study.

Psychologists and physiologists should use the same basic rules of logic. While opportunities, specific techniques, and instruments will differ, historians, physicists, and educational researchers should use the same basic principles of sampling. Yet, while these experts use principles of reasoning and sampling, they themselves are rarely authorities in the areas of logic and sampling.

Not all principles or criteria of inquiry have equal bearing in all kinds of studies, areas, and times. Too, there will be some techniques and principles of inquiry that are relatively unique to a field. Moreover, many formal or general procedures and criteria (as logical evaluation of arguments, criteria of sampling, etc.) must be meshed with the specific, material propositions of a field. Still, no field of inquiry can validate its conclusions by procedures or criteria that are limited to that field, or are the unique objects of study of that field.

Theoretical systems which have generated cumulative power and agreement on principles have sought expanding connections among formerly isolated islands of data and ideas. Promotion of extensive relations has maximized the ability to understand and control things, to transform an object into other kinds of objects— mass into energy, apathy into concern, the unconscious into the conscious.

In general, the more powerful the science, the greater will be the variety and interdependence of the criteria used to validate propositions. Agreement of hypothesis with observed results and, especially, precision of prediction of hitherto unobserved events are weighty criteria. But they are far from being enough. For one thing, it is possible to deduce some identical conclusions from sets of premises which, taken as a whole, are dissimilar. And since the conclusions of any theory rest on assumptions which relate to matters studied in a wide variety of disciplines, it becomes true (almost by definition) that it is impossible for a narrow specialist to even know what are some of the available alternative assumptions, and combinations of assumptions, that may be involved in an inquiry. Moreover, the consequences, the deductions, of an argument may be correct, but the theory or premises may be more or less incorrect. It frequently happens that correct predictions are made on the basis of wrong reasons. The logical fallacy of affirming the consequent is a constant and useful reminder of the complex, contextual nature of causality.

If we attempt to evaluate the fertility of a theory or generalization, its ability to work fruitfully with other propositions in a variety of domains, then we must have some knowledge of these fields of inquiry. Again, if we test for economy and simplicity and the avoidance of ad hoc hypotheses in our theory, we must know the varied data which the premises are presumed to explain in a neat, thrifty, and complete fashion.

Support for propositions which are parts of comprehensive systems can be obtained more rapidly and securely than for relatively isolated propositions, since evidence may be provided not only by fairly direct confirmatory instances but also by more or less indirect confirmatory instances supplied through the systemic connections of propositions at varying levels of generality.

As only a partial illustration of a few of these notions, we can recall that the kinetic molecular theory of matter ties together hundreds of kinds of statements about liquids, gases, and solids, about expansion, vaporization, and freezing, about temperature, pressure, and volume, and so on. Again, we can recall that the theory of evolution helps to explain and, in turn, depends on numerous findings or concepts in many biological, physical, and social sciences.

But cognate fields in science (*or* the delimited domains that can be considered *a* discipline) are not just naturally given. Wide or narrow systems of thought and practice are established by man; theoretical and operational connections among phenomena are instituted. If no attempt is made to establish connections among diverse sets of observations and postulates, then the fertility, comprehensiveness, external consistency, and falsifiability of a theory cannot be checked. Yet, for example, I am not aware of many educational psychologists who, studying the influence of variations in social background on motivation and learning, attempt to connect their views and data with the work of sociologists, anthropologists, and other students of human behavior who are studying apparently similar or related phenomena in a variety of contexts.

In general, we are intellectually weakest where we need the greatest theoretical strength—in social, humanistic, moral areas.

We have a relatively meager tradition of critical, intellectually controlled inquiry in these matters. We have a host of social pressures and intellectually weak yet very popular beliefs that protect core values and institutions from concerted critical analysis. Just imagine what would happen if we subjected the school tales we usually pass off as our national history to appropriate doses of materials and concepts from logic, mythology, sociology of knowledge, cultural anthropology, the historical perspectives of other nations, and other areas of study. Surely there would be many investigations of such un-American activities.

In sum, I have suggested that the overall objective of comprehensive, critical, and competent inquiry can be usefully regarded as one which embraces many sub-aims within a unified, directive whole. It includes wide and deep knowledge—but the kind that stimulates inquiry and the integration of ideas into consistent and comprehensive views, rather than the kind consisting of sets of relatively isolated conclusions that close inquiry. It includes a wide range of interests and sensitivities, for without depth and liberality of concern, thought is likely to be absent, superficial, or narrowly focused. It includes an intimate connection between theoretical and practical matters so that words and deeds, means and ends, may confront and illuminate each other.

Here, however, I had better end, for I begin to introduce explicitly kinds of interdependencies which, while intimately related to the few kinds I have discussed, can lead us far beyond the intended limits of this paper.

STRUCTURES AND DYNAMICS OF KNOWLEDGE*

Joseph J. Schwab

... I have no doubt that many professional educators would dearly love a clear, uncomplicated, and definitive description of some univocal "structure" for each of the disciplines normally involved in the school curriculum. They wish, quite naturally, to be about their business of reconstructing the school curriculum and would like a firm foundation for doing so. Nothing, however, could be more unfortunate at this stage of the game than such an easy settlement. In the first place, American education has suffered too much in the past thirty years from the adoption of most recent doctrines about other commonplaces (e.g., learning theories). In the second place, problems about the structures of the disciplines have only recently been reraised. What is wanted, then, is inquiry, not dogma.

· · · ·

Three Basic Problem Areas

The Organization of the Disciplines

Is mathematical knowledge significantly different from knowledge obtained in physics and chemistry? That is, do mathematicals "exist" in a fashion radically different from the existence of the objects of physical inquiry? If so, how can we account for the extraordinary usefulness of mathematics to the physical sciences? If not, how can we account for the air of complete certainty which seems to distinguish mathematical knowledge from the knowledges obtained in the physical sciences through vexed and uncertain weighing of evidence?

* Reprinted from "Problems, Topics, and Issues," in *Education and the Structure of Knowledge,* ed. Stanley Elam (Chicago: Rand McNally and Company, 1964), pp. 6–42. Copyright 1964 by Rand McNally and Company. By permission of Rand McNally and Company and the author.

Is practical knowledge merely the application of scientific knowledge? Or does science take hold of idealizations extrapolated from experience of things in such fashion that practical knowledge must supply an additional bridge for return from scientific ideals to the actual and practicable?

Are living organisms and nonliving organizations of matter so radically different from one another as to require different conceptual frames and different methods for their investigation? If so, what is the relation between biological and physical sciences? If not, how must we account for the largely independent development of these two sciences until recently?

Is "social science" a nomer or misnomer? That is, can there be reasonably certain and general knowledge about the collective behavior of men? Is the behavior of men in groups no more than an expression of their character as individuals? Or, conversely, is an individual personality no more than the outcome of membership in a social group? Or do individual behavior and the behavior of groups pose distinct problems? In short, are psychology and sociology parts of one science or separate sciences?

Such questions illustrate the problem of determining the membership and organization of the disciplines, of identifying the significantly different disciplines (for purposes of instruction), and of locating their relations to one another. I shall call this set of problems "problems of the *organization* of the disciplines."

The significance of this set of problems to education is obvious enough. To identify the disciplines which constitute contemporary knowledge is to identify the various materials which constitute the resources of education and its obligations. To locate the relation of those disciplines to one another is to locate one important factor which determines what may be joined together for purposes of instruction, what should be held apart, and in what sequence they may best be taught.

The Substantive Structures of Each Discipline

The classic experiments of Gregor Mendel on inheritance were dictated by a conception of unit genetic particles which behaved as do the terms in the expansion of a binomial. This conception dictated that the traits for original study should be "discontinuous traits" such as the presence or absence of wrinkles. The same conception required that the objects of inquiry be the offspring of "pure breeding" parents rather than the mixed populations studied earlier by Galton.

The Pavlovian study of animal behavior was regulated by a conception of the congeries of behavioral patterns as consisting of no more than combinations or modulations of a relatively small number of behavioral *elements,* the unlearned reflexes. Later studies of animal behavior were modified considerably by introducing the conception of "goal-direction."

Some historical study is regulated by the notion that human behavior tends to cluster around certain time points or epochs, each of which has its distinctive cast and flavor. Other historical studies proceed on the premise that human affairs run in cycles or mounting spirals. Still other historical studies seek only to determine who did what and when.

Harry Stack Sullivan initiated a new pattern of study of human personality by conceiving it as the relatively labile consequence of relationships established with others. Sullivan's predecessor, Freud, pursued much of his study of personality as if it were the outcome of the interplay of three interrelated psychic organs possessed by all men.

Much research in physiology was controlled by the Aristotelian notions of organ and function. In this view, the organism could be characterized by certain defining behavioral properties and consisted essentially of anatomically distinguishable parts. Each such part was to be understood in terms of the contribution it made to one or another of the behavioral properties characteristic of the organism. Physiological knowledge was enriched in the late nineteenth century by research dictated by a quite different conception, one in which the central "wholeness" of the Aristotelian organism was displaced by a conception of a whole constituted of both organism and environment. Research controlled by this conception sought knowledge of anatomical parts in terms of the role they play in regulating exchanges between organism and environment, together with the role they play in maintaining the boundary between the two parts of this larger whole.

In general, then, inquiry has its origin in a conceptual structure. This structure determines what questions we shall ask in our inquiry; the questions determine what data we wish; our wishes in this respect determine what experiments we perform. Further, the data, once assembled, are given their meaning and interpretation in the light of the conception which initiated the inquiry. Thus we may discover and formulate some of our physiological knowledge in terms of organ and function, our knowledge of atomic structure in terms of particle and wave, our knowledge of personality in terms of the relative strengths and hierarchical relations among its organs.

The second problem of the structure of the disciplines is the problem of identifying these structures and of understanding their powers and limitations as *reflected in the knowledge they produce*. I shall call this set of problems "the problem of the *substantive* structures of each discipline."

There are at least two significant aspects of the problem of the substantive structures of the disciplines as far as education is concerned. In the first place, to know what structure underlies a given body of knowledge is to know what problem we may face in imparting that knowledge. The structure may be as simple as that of a classificatory scheme based on a single visible quality, and firmly embedded in the commonsense experience of the learning child. It may, on the other hand, be as complex as the wavelike particle of modern physics and alien (indeed, contrary to) commonsense experience. In this respect, the significance of substantive structures concerns curricular planning.

The second educational significance of substantive structures involves the desirability of including them as *constituents* of the curriculum, as part of the content to be understood by students. A given body of knowledge, arising under the aegis of a given substantive structure, contains only as much of the richness and complexity of the subject matter as the structure admits. Consequently, no body of knowledge is other than incomplete. Further, substantive structures succeed one another as the knowledge acquired through the use of one structure permits the conceiving and use of another which is presumably more nearly adequate to the complexity of the subject matter. In some sciences, different substantive structures control different inquiries concurrently, resulting in the coexistence of two or more relatively independent bodies of knowledge about the same apparent subject matter. Then it follows that it is desirable, if not necessary, that we so teach that students understand that the knowledge we impart may be incomplete, is relatively ephemeral, and is not mere literal, "factual" truth. This means that we need to clarify for students the role of substantive structures in making knowledge possible and limiting its validity and impart to students some idea of the particular structures which underlie the major bodies of present knowledge, together with the reasons for the appropriateness of these structures and some hint of their limitations.

The Syntactical Structures of the Disciplines

If different disciplines pursue knowledge of their respective subject fields by means of different substantive structures, it follows that there may be major differences between one discipline and another in the manner and the extent to which each can verify its knowledge. The warrant for asserting the desiderata which determined Franklin Roosevelt's decisions at Yalta would differ markedly in kind from the evidence required to assert with confidence where Roosevelt was on the last Monday of his life. More generally, the warranty for historically reliable statements would differ radically from the warranty of scientific statements. Further, the kind of evidence, and the degree to which it is evidential, required by different kinds of research within the natural sciences differ markedly from field to field (biology as against physics, for example) and even between kinds of research within a field. There is, then, the problem of determining for each discipline what it does by way of discovery and proof, what criteria it uses for measuring the quality of its data, how strictly it can apply its canons of evidence, and, in general, to determine the pathway by which the discipline moves from its raw data to its conclusion. This cluster of problems I shall call the problem of the *syntactical structure* of each discipline.

Again, certain obvious significances to education exist. Unless we intend to impart all knowledge as true dogma we shall need to impart to our students some idea of the degrees and kinds of validations which exist.

.   .   .   .

The Problem of the Organization of the Disciplines

Inquiry into the organization of the disciplines is no more exempt from the need for guiding substantive structures than is any other inquiry. Further, since the disciplines are collectively complex and changing, the variety of structures devised for the investigation of their organization has been great. In the following paragraphs I shall review a few of the doctrines which have emerged. Let it be held in mind that the problem of the organization of the disciplines is a problem of classification primarily. The diversity and variety of available modes of classification is great. Consequently, nothing could be more foolish than to suppose that the problem posed to us by this variety of doctrines is the problem of determining which one is "right." With very few exceptions, each of them is, in its own way, "right." What is important about each one is not so much the list of disciplines and definitions which it may provide but rather: (*a*) the distinctions it uses to distinguish disciplines; and (*b*) the educational problems and issues which these distinctions raise to visibility.

Hierarchical Organizations of the Disciplines

The hierarchy of the positive sciences. Let us begin with a relatively modern hierarchical organization, that of Auguste Comte.[1]

---

[1] Auguste Comte, *Cours de Philosophie Positive,* 4th ed. (Paris: J. B. Bailliere et Fils, 1877).

This scheme is based on the view that subject matter, and only subject matter, should provide the basis for classifying disciplines. (This subject matter emphasis, together with a syntactical structure consisting mainly of description, constitutes the "positiveness" of Comte's positivism.) The scheme (which should be read, for the moment, from the bottom up) runs as follows:

Sociology
Biology
Chemistry
Physics
Mathematics.

Ignoring mathematics for the moment, each of these disciplines concerns itself with a given "order" of phenomena, each order consisting of members of the next lower order organized into more complex structures. Thus Comte locates physical things as the simplest of all. Chemicals come next as consisting of physicals organized in a new way. Then come biologicals as still higher organizations of chemicals. Finally come socials as organizations of biologicals. Note that though we might be tempted to insert psychology between biology and sociology, Comte would not, since psychicals would not be amenable to positive investigation.

The educational significance of this arrangement arises mainly from the increasing *dependency* which is alleged to hold as one reads the list upward. Sociology, it is supposed, cannot develop until biology is fully known. Biology, in turn, rests upon chemistry, chemistry upon physics, and physics upon mathematics. A corrupted version of this dependency, uncritically accepted, underlies, I fear, a very high percentage of all the decisions about sequence and order of the curriculum at the high school and college level in this country. The biologist demands chemistry as a prerequisite for his science. The chemist requires physics and the physicist requires mathematics. There is some justice in this view, and Comte recognized it in his recommendations concerning a "dogmatic order" of instruction. Comte recognized, however, that other readings of the hierarchy were possible. One such is worth noting for its educational significance.

The principle of dependency enunciated by Comte asserts that each science in the hierarchy shall be well developed before the one above it can be developed well. Thus an adequate sociology must wait on a thoroughly adequate biology, and so on. This seems to suggest the ordering of prerequisites in the curriculum outlined above. However, if we look closely at the Comtian principles, we realize that a complete positive knowledge of, say, physicals can be developed only if we have sought out and identified all the behaviors of which physicals are capable. At this point, a corollary can be seen which raises serious doubts about the soundness of the scheme which would put physics before chemistry in the curriculum. For, clearly, if chemicals are organizations of physicals, then chemicals constitute the one place in which some large array of physical potentialities become accessible to a positive investigation. It follows, then, that investigation of chemicals must precede any completion of physics. In the same way, a study of biology must precede any completion of chemistry, and a study of sociology must precede any completion of biology. Organic chemistry has, indeed, developed only as we have studied the complex chemistry of the living organism; and the behavior of the human individual has become better understood as we studied human culture and society.

It is, then, just as plausible to read the Comtian hierarchy downward as upward, as far as basing curriculum practices are concerned. For example, we might argue that physics is well taught by examining the obvious behaviors of physical things, up to the point where it becomes clear to student and teacher alike that further progress in physics requires mastery of certain mathematical conceptions or operations. Only at this point would we ask students to turn to mastery of the mathematics required. In the same way, only as we examine the macroscopic behavior of, say, muscle fibers and recognize the need for knowledge of their finer structure would we turn to the chemistry of the muscle cell.

Mathematics, of course, occupies a peculiar place in the Comtian scheme. When the list is read in the "objective" order (from the bottom up), mathematics takes on the character of "queen of the sciences," something prior to all the other sciences on which they depend. The ordering can, however, be read in such a way that" mathematics takes on much more the character of Dewey's mathematics.[2] It becomes much more the hand-maiden than the queen of the other sciences. It becomes, partly, the discipline which abstracts and codifies the substantive structures which other sciences have invented *ad hoc* and have tested in their inquiries. It becomes, too, the discipline which accepts responsibility for the invention of new substantive structures for possible use in later inquiries by other sciences. This matter will assume curriculum importance later when we discuss the long-term syntax of the sciences.

In line with our decision to emphasize terms and distinctions rather than the doctrines generated by them, note the principles which are involved here. In the first place, the organization rests exclusively on subject matter. The subject matters treated are restricted from the start to those capable of "positive" investigation, i.e., those capable of description based on sense experience. Within this limited range of subject matters, different orders of phenomena are recognized by reference to their constituents and their organization. Note the terms which are ignored or obscured. There is no concern for a diversity of intellectual competencies, of different abilities required by different sciences. There is no diversity of aims among the several disciplines: All of them seek knowledge, and all of them seek knowledge of the same kind. Finally, there are no differences of method except technical methods appropriate to subject matters of increasing complexity.

The Platonic organization of the disciplines. The Platonic organization of the disciplines can be seen in the imagery of the Divided Line, with important supplements from the imagery of The Cave.[3] A summary diagram of this structure follows.

Where subject matter was the operative term in the case of Comte's construction, it plays no part at all in the Platonic. There are objects of inquiry (represented on the right-hand side of the

[2] John Dewey, *Logic* (New York: Holt, 1938), Chs. 1, 6, 19, 20; Joseph J. Schwab, "The 'Impossible' Role of the Teacher in Progressive Education," *The School Review,* 67 (1959): 139–59.

[3] John Davies and David Vaughan, trans., Plato's *The Republic* (London: Macmillan, 1950), Bks. 6, 7.

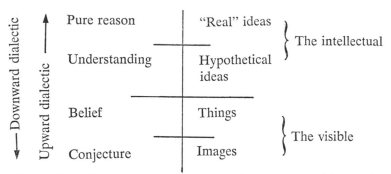

diagram), but in three important senses these are not subject matters. In the first place, any sort of natural thing, such as one of Comte's orders of phenomena, will have its images. In turn, a diversity of such things will lead us to some smaller number of hypothetical ideas; these, in turn, will be representations of some still smaller number and more inclusive group of real ideas. Thus any and all subject matters in the Comtian sense will be represented by the four sorts of objects in the Platonic scheme. Chemistry could be learned as images, as in a vast number of elementary textbooks. It could also be studied in the laboratory at the level of things with the aid of images. It could be studied more "understandingly" by moving through its images and things to its theories. Chemistry would not, itself, be studied at the level of real ideas, but a study of chemistry could lead to the grasp of such real ideas, and they could be turned downward to illuminate and correct chemical theories, our understanding of chemical things, and our understanding of other things as well. In the same way, any discriminated body of subject matter, such as living organisms, moving bodies, or human behavior, could be studied at the same three levels and be illuminated by the fourth.

Our use, earlier, of discriminated subject areas, such as physicals, chemicals, and biologicals, is forced upon us by modern habits and nomenclature. These discriminations have no real meaning in the Platonic scheme. Indeed, whatever the "thing" with which we begin the upward dialectic, we are quickly brought into touch with consideration of other and different things. At a low level of hypotheticals, we may be concerned with hypotheses which embrace only biologicals or physicals or chemicals; higher on the third level, we may be concerned with hypotheticals which take account of all three as one. In the Platonic view, such a move toward unity is a proper aim of the dialectic and reaches its limit at the top of the Divided Line, where it provides us with a single science of all things. It is this move toward unity which is the second sense in which the objects of the Platonic Divided Line are not subject matters in the Comtian sense.

The objects of Platonic inquiry are not subject matters in still a third sense—in that they are not mere patients (subjects) to be heard, seen, and remembered. Rather, they are object matters in the sense that confrontations by them can lead to some degree of opinion or knowledge only insofar as the objects do something to the "learner" which moves him to do something to or with them: compare them, contrast them with one another, oppose one opinion about them with another, seek exceptions to apparently general rules concerning them, and so on. This is the process called the upward dialectic. Its effective use at one or another level of the Divided Line leads to one or another of the states of mind given the names: conjecture, belief, understanding, and pure reason.

The dialectical process is in one sense the same, regardless of the level of the line at which it takes place; i.e., any of the objects can serve as goads and stimuli to the process. However, insofar as the dialectic is directed at different times to different kinds of objects, the process differs. The search for ambiguities and alternative meanings of words (images) is not the same as the search for different systems of similarities and differences among objects. The search for similarities and differences among objects is not the same as the effort to find new conceptions which will bind together two or more hypothetical ideas. Since the process does differ with different objects, we may suppose, with or without Plato, that different men will differ with respect to how far up the Divided Line they are capable of going. In this sense, then, we find that the Platonic construction adds an important term excluded by Comte: the learner, different kinds or degrees of competencies, individual differences with respect to the possession of these competencies. When this factor (learner, mental abilities, etc.) is coupled with the object side of the line, still a third factor emerges—the different resultant states of mind. In more modern terms, these states of mind could be equated, as Plato equates them, to "kinds" of knowledge, differing with respect to degree of clarity and embracingness.

The Platonic scheme and its modern analogues have educational significance in two major directions. On the one hand, such schemes refer directly to such current interests as "problem-solving," "concept formation," and "teaching and learning through inquiry." On the other hand, the scheme has bearing on all efforts at integration of the curriculum: unified science, unified social studies, integration courses generally, and so on.

With respect to "problem-solving," the scheme illuminates certain crucial problems which we must solve before supposing that we have in hand a mode of problem-solving which can be taught in lieu of varieties of solutions. Have we, for example, deluded ourselves into believing we have a universal method by the simple trick of forcing any and every sort of problem into a single pattern, a pattern which does not, in fact, apply as universally as its inventors suppose? Is the method sufficiently rich and flexible to permit adaptation to diversities of problems? Conversely, have we covertly or openly imported diverse classes of problems and a similar diversity of problem-solving methods? If so, have we provided an $n + 1$th method for relating solutions to one kind of problem to solutions to another kind?

With respect to concept formation, the Platonic construction tempts us, at first, to accept the notion that concepts are formed by working with and through things (i.e., the upward dialectic moves from things upward to ideas). Closer scrutiny reveals, however, the possibility that (a) images (culturally determined ways of looking) may be an important part of the process of seeing what we look at, and therefore an important part of concept formation. Closer scrutiny reveals that (b) the movement upward on the Divided Line is not smooth and unjointed. There is not only a radical break between the level of belief (things) and the level of understanding (hypothetical ideas); there is another between the level of understanding and the level of pure reason. The possibility suggested by the latter leap should remind us that, in the order of inquiry, many conceptions have arisen in which hypotheticals or things were only the occasions for thought and in no way the sources of the thought. That is, conceptions may arise not only from scrutiny of things and from the attempt to interrelate previously grasped conceptions but also "creatively," *de novo,* as genuine dialectical inventions. Certainly some conceptions, though arising in connection with some restricted subject matter, have found meaning and application in a much wider area. It follows, then, that any act which consists of leading a youngster to form a concept via some restricted and chosen body of materials may be a mistake in either of two ways: it may corrupt the conception (as in those cases where numbers are taught as the outcome of counting things), or it may artificially and undesirably circumscribe the youngster's understanding of the extension of the conception, the domain to which it may be applicable.

With respect to teaching and learning as inquiry, the Platonic construction should remind us that Plato may be wrong as well as right. There may be one mode of inquiry appropriate to all kinds of things and problems; it may be, however, that there are real diversities of problems and subject matters requiring a similar diversity of modes of inquiry.

In general, then, the Platonic construction throws light on and raises problems of unity and diversity with respect to all versions of "instrumental" learning, whether in the guise of the ancient liberal arts or more modern ones.

Problems of unity and diversity are similarly raised with respect to questions of the wisdom or unwisdom of unification in the curriculum of matters which are not yet unified by inquiry. Most of the sciences, including physics as well as biology, are today pretty much at the same level of the Divided Line as Plato saw them—the hypothetical. Inquiries in different sciences are pursued with the aid of different substantive structures and therefore yield bodies of knowledge which are distinctly plural—stated in different terms and often in terms so different that little connection of meaning may exist between one such set of terms and another.

For example, we may be quite sure that economic, social, and psychological acts are closely interrelated, yet have little knowledge of them as one interconnected body of phenomena because workers in the field have yet to develop a substantive structure to embrace them. Given such a state of knowledge, curriculum efforts at integration inevitably yield a number of unfortunate outcomes. They may injudiciously and indefensibly assimilate one or more of the "integrated" sciences to another. They may protect the integrity of the several sciences by merely juxtaposing them, in which case one wonders why they should be said to be integrated. Or "integration" may be achieved by moving to such high levels of generality that the meaningfulness of the body of ideas when applied to things is lost.

A far more defensible integration could be achieved if we took from Plato his major lesson: that integration is achieved—by the scholar and investigator as well as the student—only as we master and use the overarching disciplines which stand apart from those peculiar to any bounded science or subject-matter, the intellectual-linguistic disciplines, arts, or skills by which distinctions and relations are made and their force and effect examined.

Finally, the fact that the modern sciences remain at the third level of the Divided Line reminds us once again of the extent to which their methods remain heuristic. That is, their inquiries move forward under the guidance of conceptions which are subject to change and improvement. Consequently the body of knowledge extant at any given time is subject not only to addition but to revision, sometimes radical revision. This should in turn remind us of the desirability of finding some way of imparting these bodies of knowledge while at the same time indicating their transient character.

The Aristotelian Organization of the Disciplines[4]

By means of the classic "four causes," Aristotle discriminates three classes of disciplines: the theoretical, the practical, and the

---

[4] See especially Aristotle, *Metaphysics,* Bk. 10, Chs. 1, 2; Bk. E, Ch. 1; Bk. K, Ch. 7; and *Ethics,* Bk. 6, Chs. 3–8.

productive. The theoretical disciplines are those whose aim is to know. They are concerned, consequently, with subject matters capable of being known, i.e., possessing the requisite stability. Commensurate with this aid and this sort of subject matter, the theoretical disciplines require certain specialized competencies in the investigator: the developed capacity to reason logically, the capacity to carry out an induction, the capacity to deal with matters of high abstraction. Aristotle identifies three such theoretical disciplines—metaphysics, mathematics, and the natural sciences. We would include the natural sciences, a substantial portion of most of the social sciences (excluding the normative portions), mathematics, and would probably have our doubts about metaphysics.

The Aristotelian practical disciplines include those concerned with deliberate choice, decision, and action. Because their aim is to do, to alter the course of events, the subject matter of the practical disciplines must be matter possessing precisely the contrary of the property required for the theoretical sciences. The subject matters of the practical sciences must not be inexorable in their behavior but capable of alteration, not fixed and stable but changeable. The most crucial of these changeables is, of course, human character—the leanings, the propensities toward action, and the competences of each individual person. (It is important to note, of course, that the deliberate actions with which the practical disciplines are concerned are those undertaken for their *own sakes*, the actions which in themselves constitute a good life.) The practical sciences were and are, therefore, ethics and politics together, with the education carried out by the latter and yielding the former.

The productive disciplines are those concerned with *making*: the fine arts, the applied arts, engineering. Again, the appropriate subject matter must be malleable and, again, certain specialized competences are required of the practitioners.

The great educative significance of this organization of the disciplines for us derives from the extent to which our schools have tended to treat all disciplines as if they were theoretical. In the case of the practical disciplines, we manage this by ignoring them. No public school and few private schools expend any substantial part of their resources on character development. We pretend that the home and the church are still the appropriate institutions for this purpose; or we postpone efforts indefinitely on the pretense that a consensus about goods is a necessary prerequisite to character education; or we fail to find out how far the behavioral sciences are able to give us means and methods for character development in an institutional, urban setting.

In the case of the productive disciplines our failure is not as great but is great enough as far as the fine arts are concerned. Music appreciation is too often taught as if the purpose of the game were merely to remember identifying themes of symphonies, etc. Performing music is taught as if the aim were merely to follow the notes and obey the teacher's instructions about the score. Literature is taught as if drama and the novel were windows looking out on life or, worse, as if they were windows looking inward on the character, the life, or the times of the author. Art, similarly, is taught as if its aim were to provide a true, faithful photograph of life.

We will do well if we use the Aristotelian organization of the disciplines as a goad toward determining the desirability and feasibility of *(a)* character development and *(b)* development of abilities both to create and to enjoy created objects.

Efforts to Discriminate Unique Disciplines

Three disciplines have been perennially puzzling: mathematics, logic, and history. The reason in each case is obvious enough. Logic, because it allegedly gives canons to all other disciplines, raises a question as to what its own canons are. Mathematics, because of its apparently absolutely right or wrong character (as against the merely probable character of knowledge in other disciplines), raises the question of what its objects are and what sort of knowledge it is. History, because it is alleged to deal with the ultimate particular, raises questions as to what such knowledge is for or whether such knowledge is possible at all. And because history often lays claim to being the supreme integrative discipline, it raises questions about the legitimacy of such integrations.

The matter of logic assumes importance for us where it is proposed to reintroduce it into the curriculum on the bland assumption that it is the indubitable queen of the sciences. It is important, in such a case, to keep in mind that the question of the ultimate subject matter and character of logic remains unsettled. It may, indeed, be a codification of the laws governing movements of the mind or of language. It may, on the other hand, be only a handmaiden of the sciences, a codification of modes of inquiry developed and tested by other disciplines. (See, for example, Comte's conception of a "natural" logic and Dewey's theory of inquiry.)

Were it not for the efforts in recent years of the School Mathematics Study Group, the matter of mathematics would also be of considerable importance. It is still the case that much mathematics is taught as if number and figure were indubitably abstractions from experience of physical things. Such curriculum practice ignores the live possibility that mathematics derives from exploration of the furniture of the human intellect or from the invention of logical forms or from the exhaustion of a more or less arbitrarily chosen set of rules and starting points. Real differences accrue to the content of the curriculum and the understandings of mathematics from adoption of one or another of these views. They should, therefore, be kept in mind.

The issue concerning the nature of history is a live one, not because we have espoused a single doctrine in the schools but because we have, on the whole, left the whole matter alone. Should school history be a series of Platonic myths for regulating the attitudes of the young, or exposition of the ideas, controversies, decisions, and doctrines which have shaped our present, or what?

One other matter deserves attention here. Consider the series: inanimate, animate, human, ethical human. Are all of these equally and absolutely determinate? Almost every possible answer has been satisfactory to someone at some time. As late as 1880, it could be seriously asserted in a medical society meeting in London that the kind of generalizations appropriate to physics and chemistry were impossible in biology. Human affairs have perennially been supposed to enjoy a degree of freedom greater than that possessed by physicals or biologicals. The Kantian discrimination of nature and morals accorded freedom to the latter and fatedness to the former. Some positivists would assert the entirely fated character of all of them.

It is probably no longer viable to consider the possible drawing of the line between fate and freedom lower than that which discriminates ethical behavior from the rest. This discrimination, however, remains moot and important. The importance may be summarized thus: Shall we capitulate to a Skinnerian conception of character as wholly a matter of operant conditioning, or shall we give some thought to the possibility that early character may be so shaped as, in fact, to confer on the individual some competence at controlling his own further character development? A similar question can be raised about the manner in which we should teach some parts of history and the social sciences.

Practical-Theoretical

In view of the many different social-political-economic services which the American school performs, the question of the nature of practical knowledge, of theoretical knowledge, and of the relations between them is of paramount importance. Yet no other issue is treated quite so cavalierly. Typically, the school administrator takes the position that practical and theoretical knowledge are noncommunicating species, and that only the practical matters; "theoretical" becomes an epithet. Still other schoolmen uncritically assume that any and all items of scientific knowledge are immediately applicable to concrete and particular situations. These persons would be very much surprised to be told that the Newtonian equation, $F = MA$, will not predict the outcome of a child's push of a heavy automobile unless recourse is had to sophistries about friction or complications involving the kinetic molecular theory. It would be well, therefore, to examine a few of the different ways of treating the problem of the relation of theoretical and practical.

We can adapt the Aristotelian position to yield the following conception: Scientific investigation seeks to discover and formulate the *regularities* characteristic of a group of similar things. In so doing, it abstracts a general or ideal case from the variabilities exhibited by numerous particular instances. The resulting knowledge applies, therefore, only approximately to any given particular, whether it be one of the sample from which the knowledge was drawn or another. Medicine, for example, will have its classic description of typhoid fever. The description will be a description of a type, however, and no particular case of typhoid fever will correspond to the type. Yet it is the particular case of typhoid fever and the particular person who has it which constitute the problem of the "practical." It is this case of typhoid which must be cured and this patient who must be treated. Consequently, in this view, there is need for a special kind of practical competence which takes over where theoretical knowledge leaves off to permit reasonably sound judgment about the individual case. Aristotle called the developed competence to exercise this judgment *practical wisdom*. He (and we) considered it a competence which accrues from experience and which is more or less incapable of being formulated or taught. The view that practical wisdom cannot be taught is memorialized in our continued use of apprenticeship and internship, and, since both of these practices are extremely costly educational endeavors, it would be exceedingly helpful if someone were to challenge this Aristotelian view. However, let it be noted that, ironically, the challenge, to be meaningful, must be practical.

The Baconian variant of the Platonic Divided Line throws a different helpful light on the question of theory and practice.[5] Bacon erects a pyramid of theoretical sciences. Its broad base consists of "natural history," a catalogue and description of the variety of things to be seen in the world. The middle science, physic, is concerned with immediate physical causes and effects, e.g., that heat hardens eggs, that heat softens wax, what sub-

[5] Francis Bacon, The Advancement of Learning, *British Philosophers of the 18th Century* (New York: Random House, 1939), Bk. 7, 1–5; Bk. 8, 3.

stances will bleach red colors, what other substances will render dyes fast. The apical science of this trio, metaphysic, seeks to discover the inner nature of those qualities (such as heat, hardness, gravity, motion) which, taken together, would be the constituent terms of all things. Metaphysical knowledge in this sense would correspond to the most encompassing and therefore economical theories of modern science.

It is Bacon's point that this, the most theoretical of theoretical knowledges, is at the same time of the greatest practical significance. As Bacon himself remarks,[6] "It doth enfranchise the power of man under the greatest liberty and possibility of works and effects. For physic carryeth man in narrow and restrained ways, give light to new inventions in *like* manner. But whosoever knoweth any form knoweth the utmost possibility of super-inducing that nature upon any variety of matter." We have only to remember the connection between the Einstein energy-mass equation and the atomic bomb as a case in point.

The Platonic original of this scheme would also affirm the notion that the most theoretical states are the most practical. That is, it is the man who has reached the top of the Divided Line, who has emerged from the cave and looks straight at the sun, who is most competent to return to the cave to teach and rule. However, the return to the cave, the descent of the Divided Line, the downward dialectic, poses its own difficulties. "Now consider what would happen if such a man were to descend again and seat himself on his old seat? Coming so suddenly out of the sun would he not find his eyes blinded with the gloom of the place"[7] Thus Plato takes note, as Bacon does not, of the need for a special adjustment to the problems of material instances presumably embraced by grand ideas.

In Bacon and Plato, then, the highest reaches of theoretical knowledge are the sources of most effective practice (with or without some added competence required to bring the theoretical knowledge to bear). In Aristotle the separate competences of practice and theory each reigns supreme in its own bailiwick. That

[6] *Ibid.*
[7] Davies and Vaughan, Bk. 7, 516.

is, politics, the major practical science, is called the architectonic science in the volume devoted to discussion of politics. In volumes devoted to the theoretical sciences, on the other hand (*Physics, Metaphysics*), we are told that one or another of these theoretical sciences is supreme. "Evidently, then, there are three kinds of theoretical sciences—physics, mathematics, theology. The class of theoretical sciences is the best, and of these themselves the last named is best; for it deals with the highest of existing things."[8]

If we emphasize the increasingly formal and metaphorical character of scientific knowledge as it grows more and more theoretically embracing, we are forced to still a third relation between theory and practice. Practice (prediction and control) becomes the only test of the goodness of the theoretical construction.

Finally, we should take note of the pragmatic-dialectical view in which practice and theory, though different from one another, interpenetrate and interact in such a way that they are interdependent. Thus it is the practical (felt, organismic needs) which instigates inquiries which may become theoretical. Conversely, the outcomes of theoretical investigations then lead to such modifications of both the organism and the environment as to enrich or otherwise modify organismic needs. That is, science arises as the codification and outgrowth of the accumulation of practical know-how. Science in turn gives birth to technology. Technology alters ourselves and the face of our world, thus creating new problems, calling for new know-how, and therefore leading to new theoretical inquiries and new bodies of science.[9]

We have not exhausted the possible relations between theory and practice. There is still the radically empiricist view that scientific knowledge should be limited to the report of phenomena, in which case theoretical and practical knowledge become one. There is the positive view in which theoretical knowledge will be the sole source of guided practice but will require the development of special skills or rules for its application (engineering).

What all this boils down to, as far as the curricular preservation

[8] Aristotle, Bk. K, 7.
[9] John Dewey, *Experience and Education* (New York: Macmillan, 1944), Preface; John Dewey, *Logic* (New York: Holt, 1938), Chs. 4, 9.

of practicality is concerned, is this: Different items of scientific knowledge, because of differences in the syntactical and substantive structures leading to their production, differ with respect to their relation to practicality. Some bodies of knowledge (e.g., Freudian personality theory) are so highly metaphorical that it is only in practice (therapy) that they find their meaning and warrant. In the case of such items of knowledge, the important thing is to make sure that the learner knows how metaphorical they are; this means that teaching must not only interpret the results of practice in terms of the theory but reinterpret the theory in the light of disclosures through practice. Other items of scientific knowledge, such as disease taxonomy, have been developed at the expense of much of the richness of detail of the particulars involved. In such cases, theoretical instruction must be supplemented by (practical) experience of the range and character of the individual variability involved, and of ways in which this variability may be taken into account in actual practice. In still other cases, the gulf between theoretical knowledge and practice is so great, as in the present primitive state of administration theory, that teaching must proceed mainly by doing. The theory must be seen as a first, tentative effort to encompass practice.

Meanwhile, as far as the preservation of the theoretical is concerned, we need only take note of the Baconian emphasis: theory contains the quintessence of practice.

The Syntactical Structure of the Disciplines

What a Syntax Is

As earlier indicated . . . the syntactical structure of a discipline is not to be equated to "method," at least not to method as a highly schematized and abstract exposition. Rather, syntactical structure concerns itself with concrete descriptions of the *kinds* of evidences required by the discipline, how far the kinds of data required are actually obtainable, what sorts of second-best substitutes may be employed, what problems of interpretation are posed, and how these problems are overcome.

The syntax of Aristotelian structure-function physiology[10] as adapted by William Harvey[11] will serve as an example. Recall, if you please, that the substantive structure (the conception of organism) determining this syntax required that we terminate each inquiry by asserting with some warrant the function, the contribution, of each organ to the economy of the whole organism.

The first necessity in such an inquiry is an estimate of the character or nature of the whole organism involved, usually expressed in a catalogue of the capacities and activities characteristic of it. This estimate is obtained by means of a classical induction complete with all the doubts that accompany the inductive leap from the enumeration of instances with their individual variability to the terminal pronouncement concerning the nature of organism as such.

Given this estimate of the whole, the next step is the discrimination of "parts," e.g., organs. At this point in an adequate formulation of the syntax of such inquiries, it is important to point out that the notion of "part" is flexible. In the case of the living organism, parts may be taken at one time as such gross parts as the entire circulatory system, digestive tract, and so on. At another point in the investigation, we may focus down, treating each such system as a "whole" and discriminating its parts, e.g., heart, arteries, veins, capillaries. Such organs, in turn, may be treated as wholes while we investigate their tissues or their cells.

Once parts have been discriminated and one part focused upon as the object of the present inquiry, the next step in the syntax is the attempt to determine the role or function of the part. Here, the task of an adequately formulated syntax of the inquiry, as distinct from an abstract schematism of method, consists in pointing out the concrete kinds of data which are taken as indicative of function and what principle warrants the use of such data and controls their interpretation. In the Aristotelian pattern, the principle, the crucial commitment, is this: The *structure* of each part,

[10] Aristotle, *Generation of Animals,* Bk. 1, 2; *Parts of Animals,* Bk. 1, 1; *Posterior Analytics,* Bk. 2, 19.
[11] Robert Willis, trans., William Harvey's *An Anatomical Desquisition on the Motions of the Heart and Blood* (London, 1847).

the *location* of each part, and observable *actions* of or in each part are appropriate to, fitted for, the role the part plays in the whole. This commitment permits a syntax through which the role may be inferred from knowledge of structure, locations, and actions. (Thus Harvey locates the chambers of the heart, the moveable flaps which guard entry into each chamber, the arrangement of the fibers which compose its walls. He identifies the fibers as muscular and traces the consequences of their contraction. He takes note of the consequences of the constriction of the heart's inner space which results and notes the impulsion of blood from heart to arteries. Harvey then turns to the question of the local relations of the heart vis-à-vis its neighbors and the visible actions seen among these neighboring parts following the action of the heart.)

An adequate formulation of the syntax of this pattern of inquiry would, of course, also include comment on its weaknesses and strengths. For example, it would point out that numerous "motions" (spatial, chemical, physical changes) may be seen in the neighborhood of a part, only some of which may be essential "actions." The syntax would remark on the fact that there is no infallible sign by which the important action may be distinguished from the nonevidential motions and that, in consequence, the inference of function from such evidence is always doubtful. The syntax would go on to point out the self-correcting feature of the pattern, that related organs are each treated in the same way and that error would be revealed by incoherencies among the conclusions reached about each such organ. The syntax would similarly point out the doubtfulness of the crucial commitment that locates the appropriate data of the inquiry ("fitness" of each part); it would indicate the extent to which heuristic adoption of the commitment permits test of the commitment itself. The syntax might end by pointing once again to the inherent doubtfulness of the original, inductive estimate of the character of the whole organism and show (again, a self-correcting feature) how inferences about organ-functions pursued under the aegis of this estimate could be used reflexively to test the estimate.

This example clarifies, I hope, the great difference between an abstract schematism of method and what is here conceived to be the syntax of a discipline. Of greatest importance, perhaps, in view of the present state of education in this regard, is that *syntax* effectively does away with the embarrassing divorce of "method" and "content." A syntax cannot be described except through reference to the concrete subject matter involved in concrete inquiries. It is equally clear, I hope, that adequate syntactical descriptions for purposes of instruction are almost wholly lacking in the available school literature. They are most wanting and most needed in history and in science.

Syntax of Discovery—Syntax of Proof

With respect to effective formulation of good syntaxes for the sciences, a special problem is created by the tyranny of the ubiquitous description of science as a series of steps by which hypotheses are "verified." Two matters cast grave doubt on the wisdom of this description of science. The logical factor involved is now familiar enough; experimental verification of the existence of the logical consequences of an hypothesis does not, by itself, constitute verification of the hypothesis. And failure to find these logical consequences does not constitute disverification. Only if it is possible to assert that the consequent in question is not only a consequence of the hypothesis under test, but also that it is *not* the consequence of any other conceivable hypothesis, does experimental verification of the existence of the consequent constitute verification of the hypothesis. Similarly, failure to discover consequents experimentally may mean that they do not exist but also may mean that we have looked in the wrong place or in the wrong way. Yet much science proceeds by precisely this "illogical" method.

The improbability of obtaining definitive proof or disproof in science suggests that it might be wise, for purposes of instruction at least, to treat science not only as a process of proof or verification but as a process of discovery, a process of disclosing events in nature and of discovering ways of relating these events to one another in such fashion that our understanding is enhanced. It would be exceedingly helpful if our formulation of syntaxes emphasized science as a process of constructing bodies of tentative knowledge, of discovering different ways of making data coherent and "telling." In such formulations, the burden of "proof" would shift from the logical to the pragmatic. A body of tentative knowledge would be judged by its usefulness—its usefulness in practice, its usefulness in satisfying our demand for a coherent account, its usefulness in leading to further inquiry.

. . . .

The Long-Term Syntax of the Sciences

What was described [in the section "What a Syntax Is"] I have called the short-term syntax of the sciences or the syntax of stable inquiry. Such inquiries are stable in the sense that their authors think they know exactly what they are doing. There is no wavering about what questions to ask or what substantive structures to employ. If the current principles of physiology are organ and function, the stable researcher in physiology treats organ and function as brute facts: organs obviously exist; equally obviously, each organ has a function. There is no asking whether the organism is well understood in terms of organ and function or better understood in some other way. The substantive structure guides the inquiry but is never itself the subject of an inquiry. I have called such inquiry short-term in the sense that separate problems can be pursued separately; each such problem, such as the function of the heart, can be settled in a relatively short time.

The syntax of fluid inquiry or the long-term syntax of the sciences arises when what the short-term inquirer assumes to be true is treated as a problem. The moving force back of fluid inquiry is the demand for increasing validity of substantive structures, i.e., that they shall reflect as much as possible of the richness and complexity of the subject matter to which they are applied.

The aims of fluid inquiry are four in number. They are, first, to detect among stable inquiries the incoherencies of data, the failures of subject matter to respond to the questions put under the aegis of the extant structures, the conflict of conclusions, which indicate inadequacies of the substantive structure used. The second problem of fluid inquiry is to obtain clues from current stable inquiries as to the specific weakness or inadequacy which characterizes the principle in question. The third problem of fluid inquiry is, of course, to devise a modification of the existing structure or a wholly new structure to replace it. The fourth problem of fluid inquiry is to test proposed new structures by submitting them to the community of the discipline for debate, defense, and attack.

I call such inquiries "fluid" for two reasons. They mark a period of fluidity in the science; its underpinnings, its basic principles, are called into question. The inquiries are themselves fluid in the sense that there is practically no limit to the flexibility with which the fluid inquirer may work, or much chance of describing a fixed, generic pattern of fluid inquiry. The detection of inadequacies in current structures and the interpretation of diagnostic clues, as well as the invention of new or modified structures, are acts of creative "insight" and imagination. Nevertheless, a few guides for the formulation of fluid syntaxes can be suggested.

The existence of fluid inquiry, the replacement of one substantive structure by another as science enlarges its grasp of its subject matter, means that the existing body of knowledge is relatively ephemeral, subject to revision. It follows, then . . . that we convey to students: (*a*) the revisionary character of bodies of scientific knowledge; (*b*) the extent to which knowledge is yet knowledge, though provisional; (*c*) some idea of the enhancement of knowledge which accrues from the reflexive testing and replacement of principles. No such schematic presentation of these matters as is used here would be appropriate to the curriculum unless we are willing to commit, in the case of long-term syntax, the sin of grandiose abstractness characteristic of methodical talk about the short-term syntax. In short, I see no better way to convey viable understanding of the points numerated than by treatment of long-term syntaxes in the context of the inquiries which gave rise to them and profited from them.

Such a syntax would draw from selected stable inquiries the

signs of weakness or exhaustion which they exhibited in their principles. It would relate the fluid inquirer's judgment about these weaknesses. It would quote, paraphrase, or summarize the replacements proposed. It would exhibit the arguments about the new principle with an eye to the exercise of four criteria as follows: their adequacy, their interconnectingness, their continuity, and their feasibility. The meanings of the four words are outlined briefly below.[12]

Adequacy. The apparent capacity of the proposed new structure to establish such interconnections *within* the subject matter that the incoherencies and inconsistencies exhibited by the use of earlier principles will be repaired.

Continuity. The extent to which the proposed new structure retains such connections of meanings with the old one that the work of reformulating existing bodies of knowledge and of maintaining communication between past and future researches is minimally onerous.

Interconnectingness. Principles vary in the extent and richness of connection which they promise to establish *between* subject matters formerly held separate (e.g., between terrestrial and celestial mechanics; between literary criticism and psychology; between psychology and economics).

Feasibility. The ease, cost, precision, and reliability with which the data required by the proposed new principle can be collected and analyzed.

The Substantive Structures of the Disciplines

Substantive structures underlie short-term inquiries and are the focus of long-term inquiries. Hence, much which needs to be said about substantive structures has already been said. . . . There remains only the task of enlarging upon one or two matters and adding one new item—some idea of the variety of substantive structures used in the sciences.

[12] For a more complete description of them and their use in the scientific community, see Joseph J. Schwab, "What Do Scientists Do?" *Behavioral Science*, 5 (1960): 1–27.

Structure and Meaning

We remarked . . . that a body of knowledge arising under the aegis of a given substantive structure contains only as much of the richness and complexity of the subject matter as the structure admits. We remarked further that different substantive structures succeed one another, leading to a distinctly revisionary character of scientific knowledge. We suggested that the revisionary character of scientific knowledge made it desirable if not necessary that a given body of scientific knowledge be taught in terms of the substantive structures and syntax which produce it. Only by such means can we convey to students the fact of revision of scientific knowledge, the significance of revision, and the real but limited validity of any given body of scientific knowledge. There remains the task of indicating another reason for the inclusion of substantive and syntactical structures in the teaching of a body of content.

The additional reason is simply this: The state of inquiry in most modern sciences is now such that there is hardly a single proposition from the corpus of one of these sciences whose meaning is clear when it stands alone. On the contrary, the body of knowledge which emerges from use of an effectively valid substantive structure is itself structured. The parts of this structure, like the organs of Aristotelian physiology, take their meaning and significance from one another and from the whole of which they are parts. Thus it is virtually impossible to discuss energy in classical mechanics without discussing work. It is impossible to discuss work without discussing force, and force cannot be discussed without concern for momentum. Further, not one of these can be defined by mere pointing. Pushing, pulling, or lifting are ways of applying force but do not correspond to "force" as this conception appears in classical mechanics. In short, if scientific subject matter is not to be un-understood or misunderstood, it must be conveyed by a narrative of inquiry, thus rendering it visible to students as the structure it is, a structure whose cornerstones are the terms of the substantive structure which made the science possible.

It need hardly be added that if meaning is lost by the absence of the structure appropriate to a body of knowledge, that meaning is seriously distorted by replacing the appropriate structure by some other structure. Yet, in the past twenty years, we have warped and revised any number of subject matters in order to fit them to the bed of views about how and when and under what circumstances this or that is most readily learned. It would be well if, in the future, we thought twice before we modified an item of knowledge in order to fit it to a psychological structure alien to it.

• • • •

The Forms of Substantive Structures in Inquiry

It need hardly be remarked that the number and variety of substantive structures used in the sciences are indefinitely large. Newton's "hard glassy particles," the *element* of nineteenth-century chemistry, the Pavlovian reflex, the goal-gradient of late behaviorism, Freud's psychic organs, Sullivan's interpersonal relations, Bernard's homeostatic mechanism, Aristotelian organ-function, the wave-particle of modern physics, the free market, and Hobbes's social organism are all cases in point.

In an earlier paper,[13] I reported an effort to impose some order on this chaos. The ordering consists of a scheme of *forms* of structure consisting of five main kinds: reductive, rational, holistic, anti-principled, and primitive. Reductive, holistic, and anti-principled principles are each represented by subspecies. A brief sketch follows.

Reductive Principles. Reductive principles instruct the inquirer to treat his subject matter as something which takes on its important properties from elements or parts of which it is constituted. Thus the properties of the larger whole are accounted for by the summations, combinations, and interactions of the constitutive parts. The constituents in most such cases go unexplained. They are treated as irreducible elements which simply "are."

[13] Joseph Schwab, "What Do Scientists Do?" *Behavioral Science,* 5 (1960): 1–27.

The nineteenth-century chemical element is a typical instance. Chemical substances are reduced to the elements or simples and to the connections which exist between them (affinities or valences). Early atomic physics, with its irreducible electron and proton, is another case in point.

For obvious reasons, I have called this subspecies of reductive principles *atomic* reductions. There are also "molecular" reductives. A molecular reduction is the effort to find the irreducible minimum of the subject matter under investigation without denying to this molecule the existence of knowable parts, but insisting that further reduction to the irreducible knowable parts constitutes a movement *out* of the subject area under investigation into another. Thus we have the *family* of early political science, the cell of nineteenth-century physiology, the "dyadic group" of some recent sociology.

Molecular reductions are peculiar in that they are incomplete as principles of inquiry. Given, for example, the stimulus-response reflex, the inquirer must still decide what to observe or measure about the molecule and how to interpret his data. Hence he must add further principles.

Holistic Principles. Holistic principles are superficially the opposite of reductive ones. Where reductive principles instruct us to find our explanation of wholes in their constituent parts, holistic principles require us to treat the larger whole as itself simply "being" (i.e., describable but not explained) and demands an account of discernible parts in terms of the unexplained whole. The procedure dictated by such principles requires, first, that the whole of interest be identified, bounded, and described (via genus and differentia). Then various parts of this whole are discriminated and "explained" in terms of the contribution they make to the bounded whole.

Such principles are so numerous as to require no examples. They underlie all investigations which terminate in a classificatory scheme, such as that of biological taxonomy and geology. They give rise, also, to bodies of knowledge such as the Aristotelian physiology of organ and function.

Here, too, two subspecies can be identified. One of these,

which I call formal-material, is almost precisely the original Aristotelian conception and is, by far, the most usual. This subspecies is characterized by hanging on to both formal properties and to material constituents as operative terms. In biology, for example, structure (anatomy) and the doing-undergoing relations among parts are treated as coordinate and complementary. The merely formal holistic principle is rarer. It treats the subject of interest as capable of embodiment in a *variety* of materials or sets of parts. The principle may use material parts as evidence of the character of the whole it deals with but the stable focus of inquiry is the pattern, the organization, or form exhibited via the material. It is a case of insisting that relations are of such efficacy that the relata are of little consequence. (Occasionally, indeed, the relata are made to take such a subordinate role that all their important characteristics are seen as determined by relations. This is the case, for example, in exaggerated versions of interpersonal psychiatric theory.)

Rational Principles. Principles of this kind require that the subject of interest be seen as given its character by its place in some larger determinative whole or by some *ratio* imposed from without. Again, a psychiatric theory is a case in point, one in which the human organism is treated as mere prime matter on which society (taken as a formal pattern and not as people in their severalty) imposes some character.

It will be noted that rational principles appear to overlap the formal holistic. The difference lies in the fact that formal holistic principles seek explanations of parts in terms of the formal whole, where both whole and part are conceived as the proper subjects under investigation (e.g., the human organism and its parts); the rational principle, on the other hand, attempts to account for what it treats as its legitimate subject matter in terms of a larger, pervasive formal pattern which is *not* its proper subject of study. Thus the psychiatric example cited earlier is concerned with accounting for individual, human personality and cites the determinative efficacy of the pervasive society without pretending to be competent to investigate this society.

Rational principles have a distinctly Platonic cast, which leads to the fact that many (but not all) bodies of knowledge generated by rational principles tend to be mathematical. The obvious example is the relativity field of Einstein, the Keplerian conic sections, and so on. A good example of a rational structure which cries for mathematical formulation but lacks it is the psychological field of Kurt Lewin.

Anti-Principled Principles. Anti-principled principles embody the familiar view that science ought to avoid principles and stick to the "facts." There are two common forms of such anti-principles. On the one hand, the "facts" take the form of algebraic or verbal equations whose terms are supposed to be in one-to-one correspondence with objective, discrete, measurable quantities. This sort of anti-principle is commonest in physics.

Elsewhere, and especially in the biological sciences, the "facts" take the form of chains of Millsian antecedent-consequent relations. The antecedent and consequent events are treated as objectively given, and no rash statements about "cause" are made. There is only the affirmation of invariant antecedent-consequent relation.

Some anti-principled investigations are carried on *on principle*. Their authors accept as prescriptive such positivistic notions as those of Mach and Karl Pearson. Such proposed anti-principled investigations, though numerous, are usually abortive. Most anti-principled investigations occur as preliminary skirmishes in a new field of inquiry and generate enough knowledge to permit their own retirement.

Primitive Principles. Occasionally, a science may exhaust its current principles and find no effective replacements at hand. In such cases, inquiry may be refreshed temporarily by return to problems couched in common sense or practical terms. One conspicuous recent example is the large-scale search for a cure for cancer by discarding all available knowledge in favor of ad hoc empirical tests of an army of chemical materials chosen pretty much at random. Thus science, for the moment, becomes trial-and-error biological engineering, the search for a "cure." The strife and confusion of principles which currently characterize political science have also generated occasional returns to primitive principles. A few studies of political science return to such questions as who voted for whom and what economic, social, or ideological class the voters belong to. Some studies of the self-government of small groups proceed by asking what variations in self-government increase efficiency or loyalty to employer or task.

THE NATURE OF A LOGICAL OR MATHEMATICAL SYSTEM*

Morris R. Cohen and Ernest Nagel

1. The Function of Axioms

Although the Babylonians and Egyptians had much information about the eclipses of the sun and the moon, the measurement of land and the construction of buildings, the disposition of geometric figures in order to form symmetrical designs, and computation with integers and fractions, it is generally recognized that they had no *science* of these matters. The idea of a science was a contribution of the Greeks.

Information, no matter how reliable or extensive, which consists of a set of isolated propositions is not science. A telephone book, a dictionary, a cookbook, or a well-ordered catalogue of goods sold in a general store may contain accurate knowledge, organized in some convenient order, but we do not regard these as works of science. Science requires that our propositions form a logical *system,* that is, that they stand to each other in some one or other of the relations of equivalence and opposition already discussed. Therefore in the present chapter we continue our study of the nature of proof, in order to make clearer some of the generic characteristics of deductive systems. Such a study, we shall find, is identical with the study of the nature of mathematics.

Let us remember that no proposition can be *demonstrated* by any experimental method. The reader is doubtless familiar with the Pythagorean theorem that in a right triangle the square of the hypotenuse is equal to the sum of the squares of the arms. He has, no doubt, "proved" or "demonstrated" it in his school days. Nevertheless every gathering of college-trained men is likely to contain at least one member who, when asked how the theorem

* Abridged from *An Introduction to Logic and Scientific Method,* pp. 129–42, by Morris R. Cohen and Ernest Nagel, copyright 1934 by Harcourt Brace Jovanovich, Inc.; renewed 1962 by Ernest Nagel and Leonora Cohen Rosenfield. Reprinted by permission of the publishers.

may be proved, will suggest protractors, carefully drawn triangles, and finely graduated rulers. In this respect, such an individual has made no essential advance upon the methods of the ancient Egyptian surveyors.

Suppose, for instance, we were to attempt to prove the Pythagorean theorem by actually drawing the squares on the three sides of a right triangle on some uniformly dense tinfoil, then cutting them out and by weighing them seeing whether the square on the hypotenuse does actually balance the other two squares. Would this constitute a proof? Obviously not, for we can never know that the tinfoil is in fact absolutely uniform in density, or that the pieces cut out are perfect squares. Hence, if in a number of experiments we should fail to find a perfect balance in the weights, we should not consider that as evidence against the view that there *would* be a perfect equilibrium *if* our lines were perfectly straight, the angles of the square were perfect right angles, and the mass of the tinfoil were absolutely uniform. A logical proof or demonstration consists, as we have seen, in exhibiting a proposition as the necessary consequence of other propositions. The demonstration asserts nothing about the factual truth of either the premises or their logical consequences.

"But look here!" the reader may protest. "Don't we prove that the theorems in geometry are *really* true? Isn't mathematics supposed to be the most certain of the sciences, in which some property is shown to hold for all objects of a definite type, once and for all? If you examine any statement of a theorem, for example the Pythagorean, you find something asserted about 'all' triangles. Now, if you admit that something is in fact proved true of all triangles, why do you refuse to admit that we are establishing the 'material' truth of such a theorem? Doesn't 'all' really mean 'all'?"

This protest, however, simply ignores that fact already noted that a logical proof is a "pointing-out" or "showing" of the implications between a set of propositions called axioms and a set called theorems, and that the axioms themselves are not demonstrated.

The reader may reply: "The axioms are not proved, because they need no proof. *Their truth is self-evident.* Everybody can recognize that propositions like *The whole is greater than any one of its parts* or *Through two points only one straight line may be drawn* are obviously true. They are therefore a satisfactory basis for geometry, because by their means we can establish the truth of propositions not so obvious or self-evident."

Such a reply represents a traditional view. Up to the end of the nineteenth century it was generally believed that the axioms are materially true of the physical world, and that the cogency of the demonstrations depends upon their being thus materially true. Nevertheless, this view of the axioms confuses three different issues:

1. How is the material truth of the axioms established?
2. Are the axioms materially true?
3. Are the theorems the logical consequences of the explicitly stated axioms?

We must consider these separately.

1. The answer generally given to the first question is that the axioms are self-evident truths. But this view is a rather complacent way of ignoring real difficulties. In the first place, if by "self-evidence" is meant psychological obviousness, or an irresistible impulse to assert, or the psychological unconceivability of any contrary propositions, the history of human thought has shown how unreliable it is as a criterion of truth. Many propositions formerly regarded as self-evident (for example: *Nature abhors a vacuum; At the antipodes men walk with their heads beneath their feet; Every surface has two sides*) are now known to be false. Indeed, contradictory propositions about every variety of subject matter, thus including most debatable propositions, have each, at different times, been declared to be fundamental intuitions and therefore self-evidently true. But whether a proposition is obvious or not depends on cultural conditions and individual training, so that a proposition which is "self-evidently true" to one person or group is not so to another.

This view assumes a capacity on the part of human beings to establish universal or general propositions dealing with matter of fact simply by examining the *meaning* of a proposition. But, once more, the history of human thought, as well as the analysis of the nature of meaning, has shown that there is an enormous difference between *understanding the meaning* of a proposition and *knowing its truth*. The truth of general propositions about an indefinite number of empirical facts can never be absolutely established. The fundamental reason, therefore, for denying that the axioms of geometry or of any other branch of mathematics, are self-evidently true is that each of the axioms has at least one significant contrary.

"But doesn't the mathematician discover his axioms by observation on the behavior of matter in space and time?" the reader may ask. "And aren't they in fact more certain than the theorems?"

In order to reply, we must resort to the ancient Aristotelian distinction between the *temporal order* in which the logical dependence of propositions is discovered and the *logical order* of implications between propositions. There is no doubt that many of the axioms of mathematics are an expression of what we believe to be the truth concerning selected parts of nature, and that many advances in mathematics have been made because of the suggestions of the natural sciences. But there is also no doubt that mathematics as an *inquiry* did not historically begin with a number of axioms from which subsequently the theorems were derived. We know that many of the propositions of Euclid were known hundreds of years before he lived; they were doubtless believed to be materially true. Euclid's chief contribution did not consist in discovering additional theorems, but in exhibiting them as part of a system of connected truths. The kind of question Euclid must have asked himself was: Given the theorems about the angle sum of a triangle, about similar triangles, the Pythagorean theorem, and the rest, what are the minimum number of assumptions or axioms from which these can be inferred? As a result of his work, instead of having what were believed to be independent propositions, geometry became the first known example of a deductive system. The axioms were thus in fact *discovered later* than the theorems, although the former are *logically prior* to the latter.

It is a common prejudice to assume that the logically prior

propositions are "better known" or "more certain" than the theorems, and that in general the logical priority of some propositions to others is connected in some way with their being true. Axioms are simply assumptions or hypotheses, used for the purpose of systematizing and sometimes discovering the theorems they imply. It follows that axioms *need not* be known to be true before the theorems are known, and in general the axioms of a science are much less evident psychologically than the theorems. In most sciences, as we shall see, the material truth of the theorems is not established by means of first showing the material truth of the axioms. On the contrary, the material truth of axioms is made *probable* by establishing empirically the truth or the probability of the theorems.

2. We must acknowledge, therefore, that an answer to the question, "Are the axioms materially true?" cannot be given on grounds of logic alone, and that it must be determined by the special natural science which empirically investigates the subject matter of such axioms. But it must also be admitted that the material truth or falsity of the axioms is of no concern to the logician or mathematician, who is interested only in the fact that theorems are or are not implied by the axioms. It is essential, therefore, to distinguish between *pure mathematics,* which is interested only in the facts of implication, and *applied mathematics,* or natural science, which is interested also in questions of material truth.

3. Whether the theorems are logical consequences of the axioms must, therefore, be determined by logical methods alone. This is not, however, always as easy as it appears. For many centuries Euclid's proofs were accepted as valid, although they made use of other assumptions than those he explicitly stated. There has been a steady growth in the logical rigor demanded of mathematical demonstrations, and today considerable logical maturity, as well as special technical competence, is a prerequisite for deciding questions of validity. Indeed, in certain branches of mathematics the cogency of some demonstrations has not yet been established.

We may now state summarily our first results concerning the nature of a logical system. Propositions can be demonstrated by exhibiting the relations of implication between them and other propositions. But not all propositions in the system can be demonstrated, for otherwise we would be arguing in a circle. It should, however, be noted that propositions which are axiomatic in one system may be demonstrated in another system. Also, terms that are undefined in one system may be definable in another. What we have called pure mathematics is, therefore, a *hypothetico-deductive system*. Its axioms serve as hypotheses or assumptions, which are entertained or considered for the propositions they imply. In general, the logical relation of axioms and theorems is that of a principal to its subaltern. If the whole of geometry is condensed into one proposition, the axioms are the antecedents in the hypothetical proposition so obtained. But they also characterize, as we shall see presently, the formal structure of the system in which the theorems are the elements.

2. Pure Mathematics—An Illustration

The reader is probably familiar with some examples of logical systems from his study of mathematics. . . . It will be valuable, however, to start anew. Consider the following propositions, which are the axioms for a special kind of geometry.

Axiom 1. If *A* and *B* are distinct points on a plane, there is at least one line containing both A and B.

Axiom 2. If *A* and *B* are distinct points on a plane, there is not more than one line containing both *A* and *B*.

Axiom 3. Any two lines on a plane have at least one point of the plane in common.

Axiom 4. There is at least one line on a plane.

Axiom 5. Every line contains at least three points of the plane.

Axiom 6. All the points of a plane do not belong to the same line.

Axiom 7. No line contains more than three points of the plane.

These axioms seem clearly to be about points and lines on a plane. In fact, if we omit the seventh one, they are the assumptions made by Veblen and Young for "projective geometry" on a plane in their standard treatise on that subject. It is unnecessary for the reader to know anything about projective geometry in order to understand the discussion that follows. But what are points, lines, and planes? The reader may think he "knows" what they are. He may "draw" points and lines with pencil and ruler, and perhaps convince himself that the axioms state truly the properties and relations of these geometric things. This is extremely doubtful, for the properties of marks on paper may diverge noticeably from those postulated. But in any case the question whether these actual marks do or do not conform is one of *applied* and not of *pure* mathematics. The axioms themselves, it should be noted, do not indicate what points, lines, and so on "really" are. For the purpose of discovering the implications of these axioms, it is unessential to know what we shall understand by points, lines, and planes. These axioms imply several theorems, not in virtue of the visual representation which the reader may give them, but in virtue of their logical form. Points, lines, and planes may be any entities whatsoever, undetermined in every way except by the relations stated in the axioms.

Let us, therefore, suppress every explicit reference to points, lines, and planes, and thereby eliminate all appeal to spatial intuition in deriving several theorems from the axioms. Suppose, then, that instead of the word "plane," we employ the letter S; and instead of the word "point," we use the phrase "element of S." Obviously, if the plane (S) is viewed as a collection of points (elements of S), a line may be viewed as a class of points (elements) which is a subclass of the points of the plane (S). We shall therefore substitute for the word "line" the expression "l-class." Our original set of axioms then reads as follows:

Axiom 1'. If A and B are distinct elements of S, there is at least one *l-class* containing both A and B.

Axiom 2'. If A and B are distinct elements of S, there is not more than one *l-class* containing both A and B.

Axiom 3'. Any two *l-classes* have at least one element of S in common.

Axiom 4'. There exists at least one *l-class* in S.

Axiom 5′. Every *l-class* contains at least three elements of *S*.

Axiom 6′. All the elements of *S* do not belong to the same *l-class*.

Axiom 7′. No *l-class* contains more than three elements of *S*.

In this set of assumptions, no explicit reference is made to any specific subject matter. The only notions we require to state them are of a completely general character. The ideas of a "class," "subclass," "elements of a class," the relation of "belonging to a class" and the converse relation of a "class containing elements," the notion of "number," are part of the fundamental equipment of logic. If, therefore, we succeed in discovering the implications of these axioms, it cannot be because of the properties of space as such. As a matter of fact, none of these axioms can be regarded as propositions; none of them is in itself either true or false. For the symbols, *S*, *l-class*, *A*, *B*, and so on are *variables*. Each of the variables denotes any one of a class of possible entities, the only restriction placed upon it being that it must "satisfy," or conform to, the formal relations stated in the axioms. But until the symbols are assigned specific values the axioms are *propositional functions,* and not propositions.[1]

Our "assumptions," therefore, consist in relations considered to hold between undefined terms. But the reader will note that although no terms are *explicitly* defined, an *implicit* definition of them is made. They may denote anything whatsoever, provided that what they denote conforms to the stated relations between themselves. This procedure characterizes modern mathematical technique. In Euclid, for example, *explicit* definitions are given of points, lines, angles, and so on. In a modern treatment of geometry, these elements are defined *implicitly* through the axioms. As

---

[1] The statement in the text is concerned with forms such as *"X is a man,"* which does not assert anything until some definite value is assigned to the variable *X*. In this case, the truth of the proposition asserted by the sentence (obtained by substituting a determinate value of *X*) depends upon the value assigned to *X*. Propositions, however, of the form *X is a man implies X is mortal, for all values of X* do assert something which is true no matter what value is assigned to *X*. In this case, *X* is said to be an apparent variable, since the truth of the proposition does not depend upon the value given to *X*.

we shall see, this latter procedure makes it possible to give a variety of interpretations to the undefined elements, and so to exhibit an identity of structure in different concrete settings.

We shall now demonstrate six theorems, some of which may be regarded as trite consequences of our assumptions.

Theorem I. If A and B are distinct elements of S, there is one and only one *l-class* containing both A and B. It will be called the *l-class* AB.

This follows at once from Axioms 1' and 2'.

Theorem II. Any two distinct *l-classes* have one and only one element of S in common.

This follows from Axioms 2' and 3'.

Theorem III. There exist three elements of S which are not all in the same *l-class*.

This is an immediate consequence of Axioms 4', 5', and 6'.

Theorem IV. Every *l-class* in S contains just three elements of S.

This follows from Axioms 5' and 7'.

Theorem V. Any class S which is subject to Axioms 1' to 6' inclusively contains at least seven elements.

Proof. For let A, B, C be three elements of S not in the same *l-class*. This is possible by Theorem III. Then there must be three distinct *l-classes*, containing AB, BC, and CA, by Theorem I. Furthermore, each of these *l-classes* must have an additional element, by Axiom 5'. And these additional elements must be distinct from each other, and from A, B, C, by Axiom 2'.

Let these additional elements be designated by D, E, and G, so that ABD, BCE, and CAG form the three distinct *l-classes* mentioned. Now AE and BG also determine *l-classes*, which must be distinct from any *l-classes* yet mentioned, by Axiom 1'. And they must have an element of S in common, by Axiom 4', which is distinct from any element so far enumerated, by Axiom 2'. Let us call it F, so that AEF and BFG are *l-classes*.

Consequently, there are at least seven elements in S.

Theorem VI. The class S, subject to all seven assumptions, contains no more than seven elements.

Proof. Suppose there were an eighth element *T*. Then the *l-class* determined by *AT* and *BFG* would have to have an element in common, by Axiom 3′. But this element cannot be *B*, for the elements *AB* determine the *l-class* whose elements are *ABD,* so that *ABTD* would need to belong to this very same *l-class*; which is impossible by Axiom 7′. Nor can this element be *F*, for then *AFTE* would have to belong to the *l-class AEF*; nor *G*, for then *AGTC* would need to belong to the *l-class AGC*; these results are impossible for the same reason (Axiom 7′).

Consequently, since the existence of an eighth element would contradict Axiom 7′, such an element cannot exist.

We have now exhibited a miniature mathematical system as a hypothetico-deductive science. The deduction makes no appeal whatsoever to experiment or observation, to any sensory elements. The reader has had a taste of pure mathematics. Whether anything in the world of existence conforms to this system requires empirical knowledge. If this be the case, that portion of the actual world must have the systematic character indicated formally in our symbolic representation. That the world does exemplify such a structure can be verified only within the limits of the errors of our experimental procedure.

3. Structural Identity or Isomorphism

We want to show now that an abstract set such as the one discussed in the previous section may have more than one concrete representation, and that these different representations, though extremely unlike in material content, will be identical in logical structure.

Let us suppose there is a banking firm with seven partners. In order to assure themselves of expert information concerning various securities, they decide to form seven committees, each of which will study a special field. They agree, moreover, that each partner will act as chairman of one committee, and that every partner will serve on three and only three committees. The following is the schedule of committees and their members, the first member being chairman:

Domestic railroads	Adams	Brown	Smith
Municipal bonds	Brown	Murphy	Ellis
Federal bonds	Murphy	Smith	Jones
South American securities	Smith	Ellis	Gordon
Domestic steel industry	Ellis	Jones	Adams
Continental securities	Jones	Gordon	Brown
Public utilities	Gordon	Adams	Murphy

An examination of this schedule shows that it "satisfies" the seven axioms if the class S is interpreted as the banking firm, its elements as the partners, and the *l-classes* as the various committees.

We exhibit one further interpretation, which at first sight may seem to have nothing in common with those already given. In the following figure there are seven points lying by threes on seven lines, one of which is "bent." Let each point represent an element of S, and each set of three points lying on a line an *l-class*. Then all the seven assumptions are satisfied. This geometric pattern exemplifies the *same formal relations* as does the array of numbers and the schedule of the banker's committees we have already given. . . .

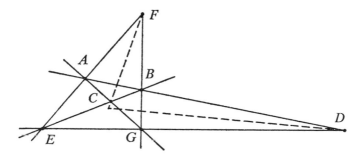

Let us examine these three representations. We find, in the first place, that we can make correspond in a one-to-one manner every element of one interpretation with elements of the other two. And in the second place, every relation between the elements in one representation corresponds to a relation with the same logical properties between the *corresponding* elements in the other two. Thus, as an illustration, the element 0 in the numerical interpretation given below, can be placed in one-to-one correspondence with the point A in the geometrical interpretation, and also with Mr. Adams in the banking firm; the element 1 corresponds to point B, and also to Mr. Brown, and so on. . . .

Two or more systems which are related in this manner are said to be *isomorphic* or to have an *identical structure* or *form*. We may now give a general definition of *isomorphism*. Given two classes S, with elements a, b, c . . . and S', with elements a', b', c' . . . ; suppose the elements of S can be placed in one-to-one correspondence with those of S', so that, say, a corresponds to a', b to b', and so on. Then, if for every relation R between elements of S (so that, for example, aRb) there is a relation R' between the corresponding elements of S' ($a'R'b'$), the two classes are *isomorphic*.

We are now prepared to understand the great importance of the mathematical method as a tool in the natural sciences. In the first place, a hypothesis or set of assumptions may be studied for its implications without raising questions of material truth or falsity. This is essential if we are to understand to *what* a given hypothesis commits us. In the second place, a hypothesis when abstractly stated is capable of more than one concrete representation. Consequently, when we are studying pure mathematics we are studying the possible structures of many concrete situations. In this way we discover the constant or invariable factor in situations sensibly different and undergoing change. Science has been characterized as a search for system (order, constancy) amidst diversity and change. The idea of isomorphism is the clearest expression of what such a system means.

Some examples of isomorphism are well known. An ordinary map is a useful device because the relations between the points on it have a structure identical with the relations between the places in the countryside to which the map points correspond. In physics, we can see how the formula of inverse squares applies to electrical attraction and repulsion as well as to the force of gravitation. This is possible because these different subject matters have an identical formal structure with respect to the properties studied. Physics also discovers that the same set of principles is applicable to the motion of planets, the dropping of a tear, and the swinging of a pendulum. It is the isomorphism found in diverse subject matter which makes possible theoretical science as we know it today. . . .

It should be noted that two systems may not be identical in structure *throughout* and yet share many common properties. Euclidean and non-Euclidean geometries have many theorems in common, while at the same time some theorems in one system are formally incompatible with some theorems in the other. This suggests the possibility that two systems may be incompatible with each other in their totality and yet possess a common subsystem. We may illustrate this as follows. Consider the system determined by Axioms 1' to 7'. Consider also the system obtained by replacing 7' with the assumption 7'': *No* l-class *contains more than four elements of S*. These two systems are not isomorphic. . . . Nevertheless, all the theorems in both systems which follow from the first six axioms will be the same. The system determined by Axioms 1' to 6' is therefore a common subsystem of the incompatible systems determined by 1' to 7' on the one hand and by 1'' to 7'' on the other.

This is a very important observation. Research in the natural sciences often tempts us to believe that a theory is true because some consequence of the theory has been verified. Nevertheless, an identical consequence may be drawn from an alternative and incompatible theory. We cannot, therefore, validly affirm either theory. With care, however, we may discover those common assumptions of both theories upon which the identical consequence depends. It may then be possible to ascertain *which* of the assumptions in virtue of which the theories are *different* theories are in disagreement with experimental findings.

One further remark needs to be made about deductive systems. Every system is of necessity *abstract:* it is the structure of certain *selected* relations, and must consequently omit the structure of other relations. Thus the systems studied in physics do not include the systems explored in biology. Furthermore, as we have seen, a system is deductive not in virtue of the special meanings of its term, but in virtue of the universal relations between them. The specific quality of the things which the terms donate do not, as such, play any part in the system. Thus the theory of heat takes no account of the unique sensory qualities which heat phenomena display. A deductive system is therefore doubly abstract: it abstracts from the specific qualities of a subject matter, and it selects some relations and neglects others. It follows that there is a *plurality* of systems, each of which may be explored in isolation from the others. Such a plurality of systems may, indeed, constitute a set of subsystems of a single, comprehensive system, but we have no evidence for such a state of affairs. In any case, it is not necessary to know this comprehensive system in order to explore adequately any one of the many less inclusive systems. It appears that human knowledge of the natural world is possible only because it is capable of being studied as a set of relatively autonomous systems. . . .

EXPLANATION AND INTERPRETATION IN HISTORY*

Charles Frankel

Historians, philosophers, and men of affairs frequently raise questions about the "meaning" of history, or of selected segments of history, and frequently disagree about the relative merits of competing interpretations of specific historical periods or of the historical process as a whole. Such discussions are anything but idle. They affect what historians and others say about the past, and, in doing so, they influence the construction of social policies in the present. Indeed, they affect the very quality of a culture. For the view that a group of people hold toward their past is one of the controlling factors in their morals, religion, art, and intellectual pursuits, to say nothing of the sights, sounds, and actual feel of their daily experience.

. . . .

In this paper I wish to consider some questions relating to the general nature of explanation and interpretation in history. What is the relationship between an "interpretation" of an historical event, in which we try to state its meaning or value, and an "explanation" of that event, in which we try to say how it was connected with other events and why it happened as it did? What sort of issue is raised when we speak of the "meaning" of historical events, and what sort of evidence can we give to support such statements when we make them? What, if any, are the standards by which we can appraise the relative merits of competing interpretations of history? Finally, does it make any sense to speak of being objective with respect to interpretations of history?

* Reprinted from *Philosophy of Science,* 24 (1957): 137–55. By permission of the Williams and Wilkins Company, Baltimore.

I

It will be useful first to review briefly certain basic considerations about the nature of historical explanation.

Although books on history usually contain at least a few explicit generalizations about human behavior or the relations of social institutions to one another, they contain for the most part singular statements asserting the occurrence of unique events at specific places and times.[1] No matter how much a historian may give in to his itch to generalize, we should all be surprised if the basic currency of his work were not names, dates, and places, and if he did not in the main give an account of individual events that have occurred once and only once.

Nevertheless, despite the fact that the historian is primarily concerned with making singular statements, it is misleading to believe that explanation in history is radically different from explanation in other fields. In the first place, there are many natural sciences such as geology, for example, which are also predominantly concerned with discovering individual occurrences that have taken place at some particular place and time; and even generalizing sciences like physics have, after all, an inescapable reference to *this* world, as it happens contingently to shape up, and not to any possible world. In the second place, beliefs that are general in character and refer to recurrent properties of events have to be taken into account on at least two levels within history itself. To begin with, general beliefs about the physical world, human nature, and social structure have to be invoked to justify the inferences we draw about the past from the skimpy traces that the past leaves in the present. The historian has to make use of such beliefs when he determines the authenticity of the documents, traditions, reports, and the like with which his work begins, and draws the inference that the existence of such

---

[1] Needless to say, the "unique events" whose occurrence is asserted may range from complex institutional structures (such as European feudalism) through styles in art (such as the Gothic) to individual personalities (such as Napoleon).

and such an item in the present implies the occurrence of such and such an event in the past. Thus generalizations taken over from chemistry, for example, are now regularly employed in determining the age and authenticity of manuscripts. And when the historian goes on to the second level and tries to construct a connected story out of his materials, he has equally to depend on beliefs about the ways in which the *types* of events he is reporting are generally related to one another. These and other considerations, such as the obvious one that history has to be written in a language, and that any language must contain general terms, would seem to suggest that historical explanation, like causal explanations in other fields, involves an at least implicit appeal to regularities and recurrences and is similar in its fundamental logic to explanations anywhere else.

However there are certain distinctive features of historical inquiry which create difficulties in applying this general picture of explanation to what the historian actually does. And it is in part because these special problems arise in the writing of history that the view exists that historical explanation is radically different from other kinds of explanation, and that an incorrigibly subjective element of "interpretation" creeps into all historical explanations. These problems must be taken into account, I think, in any view of historical explanation lest, on the one side, we overestimate the actual accomplishments of historians, or, on the other side, dismiss these accomplishments out of hand because they fail to meet wholly unrealistic standards. It is questionable, however, that these distinctive features of historical inquiry justify the view that historical explanation is something whose logic is special or discontinuous from the logic of disciplined inquiry elsewhere.

1. Consider, first, the fairly obvious fact that historical explanations, more than is the case in many fields, neither offer nor clearly presuppose precise, finished generalizations from which the actual events recorded can in fact be inferred. As Professor Hempel has pointed out, they offer rather "explanation sketches" whose details would have to be filled in before they actually permitted us to deduce the events in question; and the

filling in of these details is not usually in the power of the historian.[2] Similarly, it is usually harder in history than it is in other domains to justify the counter-factual statements that are involved in making causal imputations in any field. Would the French Revolution have been different if Rousseau had not written *The Social Contract*? Would the Reconstruction period after the Civil War have been different if Booth, like most would-be assassins, had been a poor shot? Plainly, when we impute causal influences of a certain type to Rousseau or Lincoln, we assume that these questions would be answered in the affirmative. But it is not easy to marshal evidence that convincingly supports these assumptions. Accordingly, it must be said that the proofs which historians can actually provide for the explanations they offer is frequently of a comparatively low order, and that a dose of skepticism is in place with respect to many of the explanations historians give.

However, it is of equal importance to see that what these features of historical explanation point to is a contingent fact about the state of the historian's knowledge, and not a necessary or unavoidable limitation on what he can do. They do not show that there is a firm line between history and sciences in which generally accepted, objective explanations can be attained. They point to the need for filling in the details of sketchy generalizations, or to the historian's ignorance of many facts; more generally, they point to our present poverty with respect to firm and reliable generalizations about human affairs, and to the manifest difficulties of getting at past facts about the human scene by way of the skimpy, and often distorted, traces they leave in the present. But with respect to any specific historical occurrence, these are empirical and contingent states of affairs; they are not unalterable logical necessities.

2. Even more striking, however, is the fact that historical

[2] Carl Hempel, "The Function of General Laws in History," *The Journal of Philosophy*, 39 (1942). It should be made clear, of course, that Professor Hempel introduces the concept of "explanation sketches" as part of an argument showing the essential continuity, rather than the discontinuity, of historical explanation with explanation in other sciences.

explanations, even apart from the sketchiness of the generalizations employed, usually do not have a predictive (or retrodictive) value. They state essential conditions for the occurrence of an event, but not the sufficient conditions. Thus if we ask why the Estates General was convened in France in 1789 and are told that the King was bankrupt, or if we ask why there was agitation for the repeal of the Corn Laws in nineteenth-century Britain and are told that the price of bread was too high, we regard these as explanations of the events in question and as answers to the questions we have asked. But each of these answers, at best, only states conditions without which the events in question would not have taken place. They do not state conditions from which it is possible to deduce exactly what did take place. For example, we might infer from the bankruptcy of the French King that some sort of drastic measure would be taken. But we cannot infer solely from the fact that the King of France was bankrupt that he would convene the Estates General, or solely from the fact that the price of bread was high in Victorian England that industrial capitalists and workers would agitate for repeal of the Corn Laws.

It is true, of course, that the notion of finding the full set of essential and sufficient conditions for an event states an ideal which is not fully attained in many domains. Nevertheless, the fact that historical explanations often do not have a predictive power does significantly differentiate historical explanations from other explanations. Indeed, what is interesting is not that historical explanation fails to meet an ideal of full explanation, but rather that, on many occasions, it seems fully to satisfy our demand for an explanation. It seems to be the case sometimes that when we ask for an explanation of a given phenomenon, what we want, and are satisfied to get, is an account of the stages of a process, the last stage of which is the phenomenon in the shape in which it exhibits those traits about which we have asked our question. This is one of the stable and accepted meanings of "explanation" in ordinary usage. The fact that historical explanations frequently, and perhaps characteristically, state only the essential but not the sufficient conditions of events, and that they are regarded all the same as satisfactory explanations, suggests, in other words, that not all satisfactory explanations supply us with exactly the same type of information, and that not all requests to have something explained are unequivocal requests for a single kind of answer.

However, this point, while it may keep us from imposing irrelevant standards on the work of historians, does not destroy the conclusion that historical explanation is a normal type of causal explanation. For in the first place, this sort of distinctively "historical" explanation occurs in other domains—e.g., embryology —as well as in that study of the sequence of human affairs over the last six thousand years which is normally called "history." And in the second place, the statement of the stages of a process, or of essential conditions for the occurrence of an event, rests as much as does a fully predictive explanation on tacit or expressed generalizations. Otherwise we could not distinguish between a mere succession of events and a series of connected events. For it is only in terms of generalizations to the effect that events of a given type do not take place unless they are conjoined with other events of a given type that we are able to say what we mean by an "historical process," or separate one historical process from another—in short, that we are able to make the basic sort of statement that is inescapable in writing history.

3. Similar conclusions apply to another kind of statement that is frequent in writing history. Many historical explanations do not actually seem to be attempts to state even the essential conditions that have determined an event. Frequently, they are much more limited attempts to state only what was "primary" or "most important" in bringing about the event in question. Such statements are frequently vague or ambiguous. But one reason for this is that there seem to be a number of meanings of "primary" or "most important," and that historians frequently oscillate from one to another in the course of giving a single explanation. The exact character of what they are asserting, therefore, and the evidence for it, cannot be easily specified. Furthermore, even when the nature of their assertions can be definitely determined, the actual evidence they have at their disposal for supporting these claims is frequently, and perhaps usually, dis-

couragingly inadequate. Again, however, this does not show that
vagueness and confusion are inevitable in what historians say, or
that it is impossible for them to be clear about what they mean
to assert.[3]

4. However, it has sometimes been said, and it is probably
much more frequently believed, that there is something both
unrealistic and irrelevant in demanding that the historian avoid
ambiguity and vagueness in what he is saying. It is pointed out
(for example, by Isaiah Berlin in his *Historical Inevitability*)
that the language of the historian is the language of ordinary
speech, and that his statements are not embedded in a conceptual
system which has definite and precise rules for applying and testing it. Moreover, it is said that we do not in fact want or expect
the historian to speak a specialized scientific language; on the
contrary, it is his specific contribution to speak about the bewildering complexity of human affairs in the ordinary, loose,
accommodating, practical language in which they are actually
carried on. Thus, in his illuminating book, *The Nature of Historical Explanation*, Patrick Gardiner has written:

> There is something fishy about asking the historian questions of
> a type we should feel justified in asking a theoretical or practical
> scientist. . . . [The historian's] aim is to talk about what hap-
> pened on particular occasions in all its variety, all its richness,
> and his terminology is adapted to this object. That is the reason
> why terms like 'revolution' are left so vague and so open. They
> are accommodating terms, able to cover a vast number of events
> falling within an indefinitely circumscribed range. . . . General-
> izations about revolutions, class-struggles, civilizations, must *in-
> evitably* be vague, open to a multitude of exceptions and saving
> clauses, because of the looseness of the terms they employ. . . .
> But this is not to criticize such generalizations provided that they
> are not expected to do more work than they are fitted for. The
> scientific model of precise correlation is misleading in any at-
> tempt to comprehend the role of these generalizations in history,
> where they function frequently as *guides to understanding*.[4]

[3] Five meanings of "primary" or "most important" have been analyzed
by Ernest Nagel, "The Logic of Historical Analysis," *The Scientific Monthly*, 74 (1952).

[4] Patrick Gardiner, *The Nature of Historical Explanation* (Oxford,
1952), pp. 53, 60–61.

There is some substance to this point of view. The usual historian, it may be said, uses generalizations in precisely the unexpressed and porous way in which practical men do so; and just as we do not judge the performance of the practical man by the generalizations he utters (and may even have our suspicions of his practicality aroused by such generalizations), but rather by the specific decisions he makes, so we judge the performance of the historian, not by the rigor of his theories, but by the account he gives of concrete affairs. Thus it is frequently misleading to take statements such as "Power corrupts, and absolute power corrupts absolutely," when historians use them, as attempts to give an exact statement of a universal law. For the first part of this statement is clearly false if taken strictly as a universal statement (e.g., Lincoln); and the second part asserts the existence of something—absolute power—which in fact never does exist. But such remarks may be taken as statements of strategy, rules to which it is best to conform in the absence of very strong countervailing considerations. They represent "common sense" or "wisdom" rather than "science," and in many circumstances it is perhaps preferable to be guided by such principles in judgments about the practical affairs of men rather than by principles which possess a higher order of generality and exactness but which are also more rigid, remote, and abstract. It is both important and true to say, therefore, that we may wish to apply standards to the work of historians over and above the standards that follow the model of the theoretical sciences. We may properly admire a history even though its conceptual framework is vague or banal; and we may consider it unsatisfactory even though the generalizations it employs are all precise, profound, and true. Indeed, over and above the explanations an historian gives, whether "commonsensical" or "scientific," we want him to tell a story well and to make it come to life.

However, this does not seem to me to mean that "generalizations about revolutions, class struggles, civilizations, must *inevitably* be vague," or that history stops being history, or doing the only thing we want it to do, when it forsakes the vague language of common sense for the tighter and more refined vocabulary of science. For if the looseness of terms like "revolution" or "feudalism" is a function of their use apart from a firm theoretical framework, then it is not *inevitable* that statements employing such terms be vague. And if it be said that precise theoretical explanations of what has happened in human affairs are not properly called history but something else, then the question arises as to how to classify what it is that Marx or Max Weber, however unsuccessful they may have been, were trying to do. Most important, what can or cannot be said in ordinary language depends on the state of that language, and this is a shifting thing. Ordinary language has in fact been repeatedly influenced by developments in theoretical science, and what it has thereby gained in precision it has not invariably lost in flexibility. There are important distinctions between the logic of theoretical judgements and the logic of practical judgements; but the separation between the two is not as firm as Mr. Gardiner's statement appears to make it. And the consequence of establishing such a firm separation may well be the erection of an additional and unnecessary barrier to the application of theory to practice, and to the illumination and improved control of practice that might thereby result.[5]

[5] Of course, if we ever did achieve a body of solid theory adequate for explaining human behavior, this theory might be formulated in a special language remote from ordinary language and from the language that is now regarded as the language of historiography. Accordingly, we might not be inclined to regard the explanations that such a theory provided as cases of what is now called "historical explanation." In this sense, it is clearly true to say that it *may* be impossible to write history in terms of rigorous and exact statements of laws, if by "history" is meant a discipline whose results are expressed in what is now ordinary language. However, this is at least in part a terminological issue. Whether or not we used the term "historical" to characterize the explanations derived from such high-level theories, they would in fact provide explanations of the same events that are now putatively explained by historians. And since we are usually willing to call an explanation a "better" explanation when the generalizations it invokes are more exact, systematic, and embracing, such explanations would be "better" explanations, in at least one sense of the term, than those which historians can now provide. It should be added immediately, however, that a history written in such a specialized language as is here envisaged, if "history" it be called, could hardly be expected to replace history as it is now understood. We would still wish *also* to talk about what has happened in human affairs in the everyday

5. This point touches, however, on another issue of importance. Many or most of the generalizations historians employ seem to enjoy a very curious status. On the one hand, it always seems possible to find counter-instances to them; on the other hand, the historian seems to cling to a given generalization and to continue to use it for the specific case at issue even in the face of these counter-instances. And in defending his generalization, he does so, not by showing that it derives from a more embracing scheme of generalizations, but rather by filling in the actual details of the concrete situation to which he is applying it. Thus a historian may say, for example, that the cause of Louis XIV's unpopularity at his death was his severe tax policies. But if we produce counter-instances against the generalization that severe tax policies cause unpopularity, the historian does not ordinarily relinquish this explanation. Rather, he tells us more and more about the actual story of Louis XIV's reign, in the apparent conviction that if we knew all the relevant details we should become convinced of the truth of his explanation.

For this reason, many historians and philosophers of history are inclined to believe that the generalizations that seem to be operative in the writing of history are in fact specious generalizations. When all the restrictions and qualifications are in, they suggest, these generalizations are in reality disguised singular statements. For example, what exactly is the generalization that lies behind a statement of historical causation such as "Cleopatra's beauty caused Mark Antony to linger in Egypt"? Are all generals susceptible to beauty? On the record, it is doubtful. Did Cleopatra's beauty cause all visiting dignitaries to linger in Egypt? The evidence is negative. Was Mark Antony always so affected by the sight of beauty as he was by Cleopatra's? It seems unlikely that he could have had the career he did have if this were so. And is it always for reasons of love that generals

---

language in which those affairs are actually conducted. To keep only a high-level theoretical explanation of human affairs and to dispense with history written in ordinary language would be like having only a micro-physics and no macro-physics. (The specific analogy has been suggested to me by Ernest Nagel.)

fail to move their armies in time? Unhappily, they frequently have less admirable reasons. And so it seems that we must progressively introduce more and more restrictions, until in the end our "generalization" is merely the statement, "If a man exactly like Mark Antony falls in love with a woman exactly like Cleopatra, and in exactly the same circumstances and at just the same time that Mark Antony actually did fall in love with Cleopatra, then this man will linger in Egypt." And so it is sometimes argued that the causal relations which are asserted by historians really involve no appeal to generalizations. The relation involved is one between two unique events, and unlike causal imputations in other fields, nothing is presupposed about invariant or even statistically frequent relations between events of given types.

The facts, however, do not necessitate this interpretation. (1) To begin with, historians in fact do sometimes change the explanations they offer when counter-instances are produced, or when embracing psychological theories like Freud's or sociological theories like Marx's are produced. (2) Further, most historical generalizations do not seem attempts to state invariant relations, but only correlations of a significant frequency. Hence the historian feels free to cling to his generalization, even though counter-instances may be produced. The difficulty in refuting such generalizations does not lie in the fact that they are disguised singular statements. It lies in the fact that the imputed frequency of the relation in question is left highly indeterminate. (3) Again, the historian's continued commitment to his generalization in the face of apparent negative evidence seems frequently to be a case of his supplying hitherto missing restrictive clauses, so that the apparent counter-instances are shown not really to apply to the class of events in question. This is one reason why the historian fills out the details when called upon to defend his explanation of an event. And the difficulty again is not that these restrictions must inevitably lead in the end to a mere singular statement, but rather that they are usually understood only vaguely at the beginning, and come to be progressively sharpened as we go along. (4) One particular subclass of the "missing restrictive clause" type of statement is worth noting by itself. Difficulties sometimes arise involving the specification of so-called "essential conditions" for an event. There is a sense in which we sometimes speak of "essential conditions" such that, given an event E which does not occur unless *either* condition X *or* condition Y are present, we may speak of X as being an "essential condition" for E. This sort of issue arises in many fields, but is particularly frequent in historiography. (Thus, to take a simple example, the essential, though not the sufficient, conditions for the desegregation of schools in the United States include a Supreme Court decision *or* joint action on the part of state legislatures. In fact, a Supreme Court decision was the essential condition for the present process of desegregation; but such a process could in principle occur without a Supreme Court decision.) Accordingly, the statement that X was "essential" for E is not necessarily falsified by producing evidence that E sometimes occurs without X. Under such circumstances, however, an historian may well give the impression that he is persisting in an explanation in the face of apparently negative evidence, and that the generalization to which he is appealing is only a spurious one. And this impression is frequently heightened by the fact that the generalization is expressed in loose terms, and that the historian may not have indicated, or even be aware, that there are alternative "essential conditions" for the occurrence of the event in question. Nevertheless, the explanation he offers may in fact be a sound one, involving a genuine generalization.[6] (5) Finally, at least some of the generalizations that historians employ, and particularly those involving expressions like "the Puritan mind," "the Prussian officer," "the Victorian business man," seem to have the status of methodological rules for organizing specific materials under inquiry. Such rules exist in other domains when inquiry has reached a certain stage of development, and the inquirer retains them for use in a specific, delimited area even though they do not apply

[6] This point has been put, of course, in an intentionally simplified way. The case is strengthened when we consider that usually the historian is confronted by more than two alternatives, and that these alternatives are not precisely defined *legal* conditions (as in the example above) but elements in complex empirical states of affairs.

outside that area. What seems to distinguish history in this respect from other sorts of inquiry is only that the boundaries within which such regulative principles apply are not clearly set. Indeed, the existence and usefulness of such principles in history is worth stressing, since many historians are in the habit of saying that the major intellectual contribution of history lies in exposing such "abstractions."

II

It would appear, therefore, that wholesale skepticism about historical explanations is not justified, at any rate by any of the considerations examined above; nor does the view seem to be justified that historical explanation is something whose logic is special and distinctive. Despite certain special features of historical inquiry, such inquiry seems to be similar at bottom to other kinds of empirical inquiry and does not fit into a distinct category of its own. Nevertheless, such considerations as those that have been raised do not apparently succeed in arriving at one of the principal issues affecting the claims of history to be an objective and impersonal discipline. It is frequently said that "even the most scrupulous honesty on the part of the historian cannot prevent his viewpoint from coloring the historical picture."[7] It is held, that is to say, that over and above the "explanations" the historian gives, he cannot help providing an overall "interpretation" of events as well, that this "interpretation" affects even the actual "explanations" he gives, and that objectivity in history, accordingly, is a will-o'-the-wisp.

What are the reasons for this widely held point of view? Leaving aside a variety of assumptions attached to general philosophic positions (such as notions about the relations of parts to wholes, the alleged necessity for "ontological" premises to any inquiry, and the claim that a unique logic is involved in any scrutiny of human affairs), there is one significant and inescapable fact about historical explanations which must be recognized by any scrupulous observer, whatever his philosophy, and which seems to sup-

[7] Reinhold Niebuhr, *Faith and History* (New York, 1949), pp. 117–18.

port this point of view. It seems to be the case that an element of "interpretation," a judgment about events that is governed by the historian's values, frequently controls his writing of history—not simply in his choosing and delimiting the story he tells, nor even in the moral judgement he passes on it, but *in the actual imputation of causal connections*.

How, in fact, may a historian's moral or social commitments, even assuming that he succeeds as far as it is possible in divesting himself of bias, affect the actual causal explanations he gives? In imputing causes in history, the term "cause" is employed perhaps most frequently in the way in which we use it in commonsense or practical affairs, where we are trying to control a specific situation. In these affairs we normally use the term "cause" to designate that factor in a situation which, if it can be manipulated, will produce a desired or adequate result. The "cause" of forest fires, we say for example, is human carelessness, though forest fires would not take place if forests were always damp; or again, the cause of traffic accidents is bad roads or human negligence, though traffic accidents would not take place if there were no automobiles. Similarly, in history an historian may say that the German invasion of Belgium was "the cause" of Great Britain's entrance into World War I, although Great Britain would not have entered World War I if she had had no interest in Belgium or any treaty with that country. As such examples indicate, when causal imputations between an event C and another event E are made in this way, they are made by tacitly setting aside factors which are necessary for the occurrence of that event, but which are regarded as fixed or unmanipulable, from another set of factors which are or were allegedly subject to change or control, and which are designated as the "*causes*" of that event. Accordingly, the assertion of a causal relation in practical affairs or in history frequently rests either on an assumption of fact or a stipulation of value. Either certain variables are assumed, in fact, to have been unmanipulable; or it is tacitly stipulated that certain variables *should* not be manipulated. And when this latter sort of stipulation enters, an element of interpretation seems to be present in the actual content of the historian's causal explanations.

Thus, where Englishmen were inclined to say that the cause of Britain's entry into World War I was the German invasion of Belgium, because this seemed to them the manipulable factor, the German foreign minister expressed his shocked incredulity that Britain should set a general war loose merely on account of a scrap of paper, because the British treaty with Belgium seemed to him manipulable while the conditions which German military strategy had to face did not. And when larger issues arise, for example, as to the causes of war, and one group of historians puts it down to an imbalance of power and another group to the prevailing property-system, similar issues are usually involved concerning what should be regarded as fixed and what as variable in a given state of affairs. Thus the conclusion seems to follow that explanation and interpretation in history are inextricably intertwined, and that even the most impassive historian cannot wholly succeed in keeping his values from affecting the actual account he gives of events.

We come, therefore, to the general question of the nature and logic of the sort of thing that is called "interpreting" history. What is it we are doing when we interpret history, and how does it relate to historical explanation?

Examples of interpretations of history are abundant:

(1) The history of all hitherto existing society is the history of class struggles [The Communist Manifesto].

(2) Civilizations are nothing but . . . efforts to move on from . . . the accomplished fact of Human Nature to another nature, super-human or divine, which is the unattained goal of human endeavors [Arnold Toynbee].

(3) In History . . . I can see only one emergency following upon another as wave follows upon wave; only one great fact with respect to which, since it is unique, there can be no generalizations; only one safe rule for the historian: that he should recognize in the development of human destinies the play of the contingent and the unforeseen [H. A. L. Fisher].

(4) As I see it, the function of the nineteenth century was to disengage the disinterested intelligence, to release it from the entanglements of party and sect—one might almost add of sex—and to set it operating over the whole range of human life and circumstance [G. M. Young].

These examples illustrate three characteristic ways in which we speak of an "interpretation of history." (1) An interpretation of history may assert that some variable or group of variables—e.g., economics, geography, technology—are the most important causal agencies in history. (2) An interpretation of history may state the meaning or purpose of history as a whole, showing that all historical occurrences subserve some final goal or ideal. Usually this sort of interpretation of history also offers an interpretation of history in the first sense as well; but it goes farther than such interpretations by providing a moral justification of what has happened in history. (3) An interpretation of history may tell us what the "meaning" or "function" of a given historical sequence or set of institutions is. Thus, historians frequently argue about the meaning of Greek civilization, or of the Enlightenment, or of the Bolshevik Revolution. Let us consider each of these kinds of "interpretation" in turn.

1. So far as I can see, the first kind of interpretation of history presents no general difficulties, but only the specific, though usually overwhelming, difficulty of actually marshalling evidence for any specific interpretation that may be offered. At their most ambitious, such interpretations of history are attempts to offer a comprehensive theory as a framework for explaining what has happened in human affairs. In the formulation of this theory, a specific variable (e.g., property systems, geographical location, climate) plays a fundamental role. Since such theories, if they were adequately warranted, would obviously rest on embracing considerations about human psychology or sociology, the force of the explanations they offered would be greater than that provided by ideas of a lower order of generality. To put this in other terms, the "necessity" of the specific causal relations that were asserted by histories written in terms of such theories would be greater because they would be logically related, in terms of the laws embodied in the theory, to a wider range of other events.

When they are less ambitious, such interpretations of history need not be regarded as attempts to formulate a finished theory, but only as attempts to provide guides to research. They offer the advice that if the historian looks into the relation of events to a variable of a given kind, his research is more likely to yield fruitful results; and the test of such advice, obviously, is whether this is so. In this more modest, but not unimportant, sense, the idea of the economic interpretation of history, for example, is clearly one of the seminal ideas of the nineteenth century.

It should be noted, incidentally, that such interpretations of history, whether taken strictly or loosely, need by no means be monistic or "one-cause" explanations. They may help explain a given event only in connection with other, independent variables; but while these other variables may differ from situation to situation, the key variable in question, if the interpretation of history that is offered is sound, must be invoked in all or most situations. Thus, in saying that an economic interpretation of history is truer than an interpretation of history in terms of men's moral values, a man may merely be saying that one must specify the economic institutions under which men live much more often than the moral values they profess in order to explain their behavior. One is not necessarily saying that men's moral values never have anything to do with the way men behave.

2. The second kind of interpretation of history, however, is a very different sort of thing; and it is due to its frequent association with interpretations of the first kind, probably, that there is so much suspicion of the first. This second kind of interpretation of history proposes an interpretation of *the historical process as a whole*, and usually tries to show that in history nothing is wasted and everything serves a single design. But a law directly predicting the overall direction in which a system as a whole must move can only apply to an isolated system, and it should be plain that historical sequences do not fall into this class. Brooks Adams to the contrary notwithstanding, the kind of system to which the second law of thermodynamics, for example, applies is not the kind of system with which one is dealing in history. More generally, interpretations of history of this second type must be able to show that all the events that have taken place or will take place in history—and, in the end, in the natural world as well—must comprise a single, integrated system, each of whose parts is necessarily related to every other part. That ordinary empirical methods can

yield no such conclusion is evident; and, in fact, this notion can only be maintained on the basis of some such questionable philosophic idea as the doctrine of internal relations.

Finally, such interpretations of history run afoul of the simple problem of justifying the values they present as the exclusive measure of human achievement. That men have measured their success and failure by a variety of standards is a plain fact of human history; and that they should all relinquish their different standards and accept a common one can be plain only to those who regard moral standards as commands imposed from outside the human scene, and as ultimately independent of what human beings actually are or want. There is not, to my knowledge, a single interpretation of history of this sort which does not turn history into the scene for the crucifixion of man in the name of some transcendent and occult purpose. This is true whether we think of Saint Augustine, Hegel, Mr. Toynbee, or Marxism in its more Stalinoid variations.

3. It is when we come to the third kind of interpretation of history that the most interesting issues arise. Broadly, when an historian provides an "interpretation" of an age or a culture or an institution, he is doing something like the following. He is telling a story of a sequence of causally related events that have consequences of value or dis-value: in other words, he is showing that certain events are causally related to what I shall call "terminal consequences." To state the "meaning" of an historical process is to state these terminal consequences. And it is the question of the choice of terminal consequences that raises most of the issues concerning the possibility of objectivity in history. For it is plain that no historian, insofar as he wishes merely to delimit his problem, let alone pass judgement on the events he is recording, can avoid selecting certain terminal consequences as the frame of his story.

Now, in considering the problems raised by the historian's selection of terminal consequences, it is important to keep certain fairly obvious distinctions firmly in mind. To begin with, the question of whether a given sequence of events did or did not have certain results is an objective, a factual question. Accordingly, while two historians may legitimately choose different terminal consequences in interpreting the same general period of history, this does not mean that any terminal consequences at all may be chosen. Further, two interpretations of a given period may in fact not be offering two accounts of the same facts, but accounts of different facts. The first begins with an event, E, and traces its consequences, $C_1, C_2, C_3 \ldots$ to terminal consequence T_1. The second begins with the same event E, but it traces *other* consequences, $C_x, C_y, C_z \ldots$ to terminal consequence T_2. Thus, a sixteenth-century American Indian's interpretation of the meaning of Columbus's discovery of America would be different from a sixteenth-century Spaniard's, and this difference reflects a real and tragic clash of interests. But both can be equally true and objective. Interpretations of history sometimes *seem* to clash because they are employed as instruments in a practical conflict of interests; but from the point of view of the facts, they may not be in conflict at all, since they talk about different facts.

The failure to see this elementary point is the source of much of the wholesale skepticism that arises concerning the possibility of being objective in the writing of history. It is also responsible for many attempts to subject history to purely pragmatic standards. For although it is obvious that historians with different social habitats will view the stream of events from different perspectives, it does not follow that the past, or our beliefs about the past, must necessarily be recreated in each generation. Sometimes new evidence about what has happened turns up, or new and more reliable theories of human nature or social structure. When this happens, the historians of later ages really do rewrite the histories of their predecessors: they disagree about the facts. But when the historians of a later age write history in terms of terminal consequences that are different from those with which their predecessors were concerned, they are not rewriting history: they are writing another history. The old history can also be true, and true not only for the earlier age in which it was written but for the later age as well. The writing of history is the major way in which the social memory of any fairly complicated group is refined and corrected, and it is of considerable significance to the life of such a group when its social memory is accurate and when it has certain stable features that persist through emergencies and shifting currents of opinion and sentiment. It is not only false to say that the histories written in each generation must necessarily disagree with those written in the past, or that histories written in any particular age can be true only for that age and not for any other; more than this, such statements lend sanction, wittingly or unwittingly, to a way of writing history that prevents history from achieving one of its most important social values.

III

These considerations, however, merely bring us to the main issue. It may be granted that more than one interpretation of a historical period can be true and legitimate, provided they do not give incompatible accounts of exactly the same facts. But there nevertheless seems to be a difference of better and worse between interpretations that are offered. It is true to say, for example, that the "meaning" of modern science is an increase in creature comforts; it is also true to say that its "meaning" lies in the rise of a culture with new standards of intellectual and moral authority and a new view of human excellence. Yet even though men might agree that two quite distinct, though intersecting, chains of events were being recounted in these two interpretations, the first seems somehow skimpier than the second and inferior to it. What, then, are the considerations that enter into the choice of terminal consequences, and what are the standards, if any, by which we may make comparative judgments among such choices?

The selection of terminal consequences by the historian seems to be governed by four distinct, though not wholly separate, considerations.

1. The first, and most obvious, is the simple element of "interestingness." The historian obviously writes his story and exhibits its meaning in terms of terminal consequences in which he happens to be interested. Equally obviously, therefore, there is room for choice here. However, this does not necessarily imply that history must be "violently personal," or that historical events

"can be correlated only within a framework of meaning to which the viewpoint of an age, a class, or a nation contributes as much as the facts themselves."[8] For in the first place, there is a clear difference between the historian whose interests are shifting or capricious, or who chooses terminal consequences that interest him or a small coterie alone, and the historian who makes his selection in terms of stable interests that are more widely shared. And since the writing of history is a public activity and is normally the attempt to give an account of publicly significant events, it is natural to prefer the latter sort of historian to the former. Indeed, instead of having values that are evanescent, expressing some local prejudice or passing fashion, an historian may have values of a more durable sort which express the deeper, longstanding commitments of a larger civilization. Such values, to be sure, are still the values of some particular place and time. But myopia in human affairs is measured in decades, not in millennia, and when the place whose values are expressed is an entire civilization and the span of time involved some twenty-five hundred or three thousand years, surely the charge of parochialism loses some of its sting.

Even more important, however, is the fact that an interpretation of history is not usually offered solely on the grounds that the values on which it turns happen to fall within the present interests of the historian or his audience. When a chain of events is said to have a "meaning" of a certain sort, something more is intended and something more is expected than only that the values involved are values that some men hold. The values involved, an interpretation of history seems to suggest, are values that men ought to hold, and which it is peculiarly right to employ as the measures of historical events. So while it is true that no interpretation of history can pass muster which does not turn on values that some men somewhere might in fact find interesting, other elements as well as the criterion of "interestingness" usually enter into interpretations of history.

2. A second consideration which frequently enters into the choice of terminal consequences is a concern with those which

[8] Ibid.

have the greatest explanatory value—which are, that is to say, most pregnant in still further consequences. In selecting terminal consequences for this reason, the historian is tacitly treating these consequences as themselves causes of other events, as the beginnings of other histories; he is asserting that they are points of intersection from which the greatest number of lines radiate. Such an assertion plainly depends on general beliefs of a factual character about the weight of various sorts of causal factors in history. When governed by this consideration, therefore, an interpretation of history involves an ordinary form of causal assertion and falls ultimately within the class of interpretations of history that are attempts to formulate theoretical frameworks for the explanation of the procession of human affairs.

3. A third element that may enter into the selection of terminal consequences is related to the second but is not identical with it. Certain consequences may be selected because they are held, tacitly or explicitly, to be the key variables in the formulation and implementation of an effective social policy—the variables that can and should be manipulated. Thus, the so-called "new historians" turned away from military and narrowly political history and made the rise of science their central concern; they did so because they were convinced that science was the key social instrument that had to be understood and employed if modern societies were to solve their problems. Similarly, Marx made the emergence of an industrial proletariat the great event of the nineteenth century because he believed that only this class had the power and interest to do what needed to be done to organize an industrial society effectively. Of course, such interpretations of history are more or less disguised instances of advocating a cause and are not only descriptions. Nevertheless, the worth of an interpretation of history, judged from this point of view, is not independent of factual considerations. It depends on the soundness of the social program it implicitly offers and is to be judged as we judge social programs—in terms of the generalizations and specific predictions they make, the feasibility of their proposals, and the objective consequences of following them. Choice and

personal preference may of course enter; but it might be said that the function of such interpretations of history, and of the factual investigations into which they lead, is to make such choices more responsible by showing the limited number of alternatives that are possible and by clarifying their objective implications.

4. This brings us to a fourth element that may enter into interpretations of history. It has to do not simply with the explanatory or practical value that selected terminal consequences may have, but with their importance, actual or potential, with respect to some scheme of human good. An interpretation of history, in short, may rest on an implicit theory of human progress. No such theory, of course, can be absolute or exclusive. Nevertheless, this does not seem to me to mean that objective and impersonal considerations do not also enter, and that they cannot logically govern our choice of one interpretation of an historical sequence over another. For a scheme of human good represents an attempt to find some equilibrium among a variety of not always compatible human drives and interests. Its worth depends on its relation to the facts and on how much it can make out of the limited opportunities with which, at any moment in history, we are confronted. There is an important and objectively identifiable difference between an historian whose interpretation of history is governed by unrealistic or impossible standards and one whose standards are realistic and possible; there is an even more important difference between an historian whose image of human excellence is provincial and niggardly and one whose image is full and generous. The employment of such distinctions in our judgment of the work of historians is both relevant and inescapable. For we go to history not simply to find out what has happened in human affairs, but also what is possible. And not only is it difficult for an historian to mask his beliefs about what is possible and desirable, but that history which is lit by some clear and circumspect idea of what human life can be is generally preferred to the history that is impassive, that never commits itself, and that lacks a guiding ideal or the irony or tears that go with applying such an ideal to the record of human affairs.

IV

In view of these considerations, it does not seem to me that there is never an impersonal way of choosing between competing "schemes of meaning" in history. Despite the fact that interpretations of history frequently enter into the actual explanations that are offered by historians, the writing of history is not condemned to be a battleground for irreconcilable points of view. Nor do we have to remain content with an uncritical pluralism which simply asserts that history may be read from many points of view and that each man may choose his own. It is certainly improbable that any single point of view can ever claim an exclusive sovereignty; but it is equally improbable that all points of view are equally legitimate, even when they are all in the hands of scrupulous historians who do not falsify the facts.

These considerations apply in particular to a final way in which the term "interpretation" is sometimes used in connection with history. It is sometimes said that statements about the "true" or "primary" cause of a historical event or sequence of events are all "matters of interpretation"—matters that depend, that is to say, simply on the level on which we choose to describe a sequence of events or the kind of interest we have in these events. According to this point of view, therefore, disagreements about the "true cause" of an historical sequence are actually not genuine disagreements at all (at any rate, when there is no disagreement about what specifically happened), but are only the expression of different, and equally legitimate, interests or perspectives. This view has been expressed by Mr. Gardiner with lucidity and force:

> It is . . . a mistake to imagine that the historian is contradicting the journalist when he says that the Sarejevo assassination was not the true cause of the outbreak of the First World War. He is merely regarding the outbreak of war from a different point of view, talking about it upon a different level. The question 'why did the First World War occur?' is answerable in various ways: it is answerable upon the level of individual human purposes, desires, weaknesses, and abilities; it is answerable upon

the level of national policies, traditions of diplomacy, plans; it is answerable upon the level of political alignments, treaties, the international structure of Europe in 1914; it is answerable upon the level of economic trends, social organization, political doctrine, ideology, and the rest.[9]

This position as it stands, it seems to me, is true only if so many qualifications are added that it no longer actually says what it seems to be saying. It is of course undeniable that a term like "World War I" covers such a vast congeries of events that two men who seem nominally to be talking about the war may in fact be talking about quite different sequences of events, or about sequences that intersect each other at only limited points. As I have tried to suggest above, historians may of course ask a number of different questions quite legitimately about a given "event," and from a number of different points of view. Arguments among historians about the "true cause" of a given event are frequently only pseudo-arguments and not the assertion of incompatible statements about the facts.

But this is not necessarily the case always. For there are a considerable number of cases where historians (or a historian and a journalist) seem to have exactly the same event, or the same aspects of an event, in mind, and where they still disagree about the "true cause" of the event. And at least some of these disputes appear to be disagreements about what was "primary" or "most important" in producing the event in question. Frequently such disputes arise, to be sure, because people have different notions of what is meant by "primary" or "most important," or only vague or ambiguous notions. However, the notion of "primary" or "most important" is capable of being given one or another specific and definite meaning in a given context,[10] such that disagreements about what in fact was primary or most important (or what was the "true cause") are in principle capable of being resolved by appeal to a common body of evidence. Frequently, of course, the evidence available is not enough to give a positive answer one way or the other. But this is because it is

[9] Patrick Gardiner, p. 105.
[10] Cf. Nagel.

difficult to get at the facts, and not because the issue is not a factual one.

More specifically, a historian may in fact sometimes be genuinely contradicting the journalist, and rightly, when he says that the Sarajevo assassination was not the "true cause" of the outbreak of the First World War. He may be saying, for example, that while World War I needed a trigger to set it going, other triggers were available and would probably have been pulled; and as a result the particular trigger that happened to set the conflagration going is largely "accidental." This does not make the journalist's account of what happened either false or unnecessary, but it calls very definitely into question the journalist's allegation (or, more probably, the reader's belief) that he has stated the "true cause" of what happened. Suppose, for example, there was a factory in which it was the careless practice to leave explosives here, there, and elsewhere; suppose, further, that it was the practice for visitors and workers in the factory to throw lighted matches around. When the factory blew up, would we be satisfied with nothing but an account of the event which merely stated that a certain match had been thrown by a certain person on a certain day, and left out the above facts? And would we regard this account as providing as good an explanation as one that included these facts?

Indeed, it is ordinarily not just a question of different perspectives, between which we may take our choice, when one historian asserts that World War I can be explained on the level of "individual human purposes, desires, weaknesses, and abilities," and a second asserts that it ought rather to be explained on the level of "economic trends, social organization, political doctrine, ideology, and the rest." An historian who prefers the second kind of explanation to the first may believe (whether rightly or wrongly is not the question) that the deliberate purposes, desires, etc., of individuals are not so important in determining what happens as are the unintended consequences that come about when individuals interact within definite institutional structures. He may, that is to say, hold an "institutional" interpretation of history rather than, say, a "biographical" interpretation. Thus, with respect to the outbreak of World War I, he may believe that the institutional structure prevailing in 1914 was such that it gave individuals in power no choice but war, and that even if other individuals had been in power, the result would have been the same; or he may believe that individuals with quite the same purposes, desires, weaknesses, and abilities as those who held power would have succeeded in avoiding war in 1914 if the institutional structure had been different. All this may or may not be easy to prove. But surely it is not just a different way of looking at things, another answer to what is really another question. It is another and competing answer to the same question as that which the man who explains the war on the level of "individual human purposes, desires, weaknesses, and abilities" is trying to answer.[11]

Different approaches to history thus seem to represent, at least some times, substantive disagreements about the actual ways in which events are connected with one another, disagreements that are of the highest significance and cannot be dissolved simply by regarding them as the expressions of different and equally legitimate perspectives. Sometimes two interpretations of history are in fact recounting different sequences of events; sometimes they are recounting the same sequence of events, and explaining them in the same way, but in two different languages; but sometimes they are disagreeing about what were the most important causes or the most important consequences of a given sequence of events—about what, in other words, should or should not be

[11] Of course, it is possible to write individual biography institutionally and to describe institutions in terms of the careers of individuals. Frequently the "difference" between one approach and the other may be only a difference between two mutually inter-translatable languages, both of which are saying the same thing. But if this is the case, then the accounts of events that are given by the two languages are not simply not in disagreement; they are not even really different, and cannot be described as being on different "levels" any more than two identical descriptions of a dog, one in English and one in German, can be described as being on different "levels." One language or the other may be more convenient for the job in question, but this is the only issue. At least sometimes, in other words, there seems to be no objective reason for choosing between "two" approaches to history only because, in fact, there is no real difference between them.

included in the historian's story to make that story an adequate answer to the question that has been raised. Arguments about the proper interpretation of a historical sequence, or about its "true" or "basic" causes, it would thus appear, are at least sometimes genuine and important arguments that are factual in character. And given a willingness to be clear and a good deal more information than we now normally possess, they are capable of being resolved.

THE AESTHETIC AS A CONTEXT FOR GENERAL EDUCATION*

Donald Arnstine

The term "aesthetic education" will be used very broadly here to indicate whatever conditions might increase sensitivity to the artistic features of the world and to the aesthetic qualities of experience and whatever might increase the understanding, appreciation, and enjoyment of those features and qualities. Aesthetic education (in the visual arts) is currently promoted in schools by setting aside a specific time of day for the study of works of art and for practice in a variety of art media and techniques. This arrangement makes it clear to the student that what is pursued in the art course is a quite different sort of affair from what is pursued in other school courses. I will try to show that art courses so organized are not likely to contribute very much to aesthetic education. The reasons why this is so stem from certain untenable assumptions about art and the aesthetic which are usually implicit in art courses. I will first make these assumptions explicit, then expose some of the difficulties one encounters in trying to maintain them, and finally, by suggesting some alternative conceptions about art and the aesthetic, show what the results might be for instruction throughout the school curriculum.

I

The curriculum is usually made up of a number of courses, one of which focuses on the practice and study of art. The very existence of an art course is predicated on certain beliefs assumed to be true. First, it is assumed that works of art have a special significance not possessed by other sorts of things. This significance is often called aesthetic quality, and it is thought to be valuable for

* Reprinted from "The Aesthetic as a Context for General Education," *Studies in Art Education*, 8 (1966): 13–22. By permission of the author and the editor of *Studies in Art Education*.

students to become sensitive to it. Second, since it is assumed that aesthetic quality is to be found in works of art, it is also assumed that the other subjects of school study—e.g., science and history, language and mathematics—do not possess this quality. And third, since aesthetic quality is not a feature of what is studied elsewhere in school, it is assumed that an understanding and appreciation of such quality can be developed by exposing students to works of art and by affording them some practice in creating works of art.

Taken together, these assumptions provide a sort of justification for courses in the arts. In the visual arts they are variously called art, survey of art, art history, and art appreciation. What has been the result of sending students to these courses? It is not easy to tell, but one might suppose that when it rains on Sundays, well-intentioned parents take their children to the art museum instead of to the zoo. But if the arts of the mass media or of public architecture are indicators of the sensitivity of the public to aesthetic qualities, then great success could not be claimed for art education in schools. If art courses have not been very effective in fostering aesthetic education, the mischief can probably be traced to the assumptions on which those courses are based. How well do they stand up under investigation? We will examine each of them in turn.

1. The first assumption is that works of art have a special significance, usually called aesthetic quality, which is not possessed by other sorts of things. Experts disagree about what aesthetic quality might be,[1] but whatever it is, difficulties appear when we try to conceive it as uniquely the property of works of art. If it were such a property, we would be at a loss to tell how it came to reside in works of art alone. Art is created by men, but no one who watched an artist at work ever saw him put the aesthetic quality into his painting. How did it get there, then? Claims about the intervention of divine inspiration guiding the hand of the

---

[1] A broad sampling of such opinions may be found in Melvin Rader, ed., *A Modern Book of Esthetics* (New York: Holt, 1952). Analyses of many of these opinions may be found in William Elton, ed., *Aesthetics and Language* (Oxford: Basil Blackwell, 1959).

creator[2] only offer a mystery to explain a riddle. On the other hand, the notion that it is the viewer who *finds* aesthetic quality in art simply gives the viewer license to find aesthetic quality in anything at all he chooses.

The problems that appear whenever aesthetic qualities are treated as properties of particular things only recall earlier failures in assigning properties to objects. Whether a body possesses aesthetic quality is a far less determinable question than whether it possesses color or weight. Yet the fact that a body may under certain conditions appear to be any color at all or even weightless suggests that, far from being properties possessed by objects, color and weight are functions of the manner in which observers situated in a certain way relate to certain events. If color and weight are not permanent properties of objects, it is even less likely that something so diffuse as aesthetic quality is a property possessed by objects.

Before scales and spectroscopes are brought into the picture, let us admit that weight and color are most assuredly experienced by people. That a thing is heavy or of a certain color is immediately felt by someone who tries to lift it or distinguish it from other things. Weight and color, we might say, are qualities of the experience of people when they come into contact with certain features of the world. Only the need to be specific about weight and color and the consequent need to check our experience against the experience of others called forth the use of measuring instruments. The common use of those instruments probably gave rise to the usually harmless error of thinking that somehow the instruments "found" certain properties "within" the things being measured.[3]

---

[2] An analysis of this particular range of opinions may be found in Milton C. Nahm, *The Artist as Creator* (Baltimore: Johns Hopkins Press, 1956).

[3] To assign a weight of five pounds to a package for the purpose of mailing it is harmless enough. But to assign a certain numerical score to a person for the purpose of teaching him has many dangers, for the person is then labeled as "having" just so much "creativity" or "intelligence." The expectations and teaching procedures respecting that person are then adjusted to his score, and attention is unduly drawn away from consider-

The point is that if weight and color are qualities of experience, it makes at least as much sense to say that the aesthetic is a quality of experience, too. It is not, then, something possessed by objects—much less by certain objects called works of art. But while experience is attended by the quality of weight when we try to lift something, it is not so easy to specify the conditions under which experience is marked by aesthetic quality. Since aesthetic education must remain a will-o'-the-wisp unless we have some understanding of the conditions for the appearance of aesthetic quality, I will make a rather sketchy attempt to indicate those conditions.

If the way people typically describe their reactions to art and to other things is any indication, we might hypothesize that aesthetic quality pervades experience when people find some intrinsic interest in the way in which perceptible elements of the world are related to one another. The term "perceptible elements" refers to what can be felt or heard or seen. To speak of the relations of perceptible elements to one another is to refer to what artists and critics sometimes call form. And to speak of intrinsic interest in this regard is to refer to the way in which the perception of form can call forth and hold attention on its own account. All this amounts to saying is that when one's attention or interest is attracted and held by his having perceived the relations of, for example, colored shapes to one another, then his experience is aesthetic in quality. This is not all that may occur when experience is aesthetic in quality, but it is minimally what must occur.

We are, of course, surrounded by sights and sounds, but we are not lovers of them all. Why is aesthetic quality relatively uncommon in our experience? An answer to this will further clarify some instructional implications for aesthetic education.

Our most common orientation to the world is a practical or an intellectual one. We are concerned about what it will do to us, or what we can do to it, or about what it really is, or how it got to be that way. Thus what we see or hear or feel is most usually

ing and adjusting the conditions under which the individual's performance resulted in that score.

related not to other perceptible things, but rather to these interests and concerns. Practical and intellectual concerns, then, often render us insensitive to form and block the appearance of aesthetic quality in experience.[4]

Yet experience is not always aesthetic in quality, even when we deliberately attend to the formal relations of perceptible elements. This is simply because we do not always find those elements interesting in their own right. What may account for this is the fact that what is seen or heard may be perceived as regular or, on the other hand, as complex and disorganized. Perceived regularity is felt as monotony or boredom; perceived disorganization is felt as confusion. And what is boring and confusing seldom holds interest for very long. The appearance of aesthetic quality in experience, then, depends both on the posture taken by the perceiver and on the perceived features of what is before him.

With this in mind, we may consider again works of art. Without making any claim about their "possessing" aesthetic quality, we may grant their special significance. For they are usually made in such a way that the relations among their perceptible elements are neither oppressively regular nor confusingly chaotic. That is, works of art are organized in such a way as to facilitate the perception of form for a viewer who is willing to attend to the relations among the things he perceives. While this sort of facilitation is intended by artists, it is also true that a great many other man-made things are also intended by their makers to facilitate the perception of form. And it is equally true that a multitude of natural objects and events may be such as to make possible the perception of form. Aesthetic quality, then, may characterize virtually any sort of experience at all and is in no reasonable sense limited to confrontations with what are traditionally called works of art. The special significance that works of art do have lies in their capacity to emphasize and heighten the qualities of experience that we meet only accidentally when confronting other

---

[4] The intrusion of these practical and intellectual concerns is what Edward Bullough called a loss of psychical distance. See "Psychical Distance as a Factor in Art and an Aesthetic Principle," *British Journal of Psychology,* 5 (1912–13): 87–118.

things and events in the world.[5] Aesthetic education which ignored works of art would thus lose a valuable resource. But aesthetic education which ignored examining the rest of the world in its artistic dimensions could only result in a sharp distortion of both art and the world. I shall return to this point later, but it is now time to examine the second assumption underlying art courses.

2. The existence of art courses is also predicated on the assumption that aesthetic qualities cannot be felt and enjoyed in connection with the other offerings in the curriculum. Put more concretely, it is assumed that science is science, and history is history, and neither one is art. But on the basis of what has been said, this is an oversimplification so gross that it distorts the truth of what is relevant. The world is full of many things and happenings, but none of these things is in itself "science" or "history." So far from denoting things *found* in the world, science and history rather connote particular *ways of dealing* with those things. A flower or the topic of yesterday's headlines are not *in themselves* science or history. They *are* just what they are. We may, of course, attend to them in different ways. Thus our experience of them may be dominantly practical or cognitive or aesthetic in quality. And depending on how we attend to flowers or to yesterday's events, we may treat them as agriculture or politics, as botany or history, or as art or drama.

Thus it makes no sense to say that the matters treated in the so-called academic courses are themselves *without* aesthetic quality. It is simply that aesthetic quality may not always characterize experience when things become matters of cognitive concern. And it is equally true that the things and events which are examined scientifically and historically may also figure in experience that is aesthetic in quality. It would never occur to scientists and historians to treat cognitively their respective subject matters *unless* they were found to be, at least initially, of interest on

[5] A systematic exposition of these views is to be found in John Dewey's *Art as Experience* (New York: Minton, Balch, 1934), especially in Chs. 1 and 5.

their own account.[6] And this is simply to say that the experience from which inquiry grows is itself not without some minimal aesthetic quality.

One could not attach too much importance to the implications of this for instruction in science and history. Some people find certain events in the world interesting and fascinating. When they become curious about the spatial and temporal connections of those events with other events, they may conduct inquiries that result in what is called science and history. Scientists and historians have good reasons for being interested in their disciplines, but do children in schools? Boredom and confusion are not uncommon reactions for students of science and history, but this should only be expected to result when students are required to pursue cognitively events that are neither interesting nor fascinating *to them*. To present the materials of scientific and historical study in ways that afford aesthetic quality to students' experience is simply to act on the obvious truth that people are likely to attend to matters that they find interesting. There are, of course, many ways to initiate learning. But to assume on a priori grounds that the materials of scientific and historical study are somehow *without* aesthetic quality or artistic worth is prematurely to abandon an effective resource for learning.

3. The third assumption underlying most art courses is that an understanding and appreciation of aesthetic qualities is to be developed by exposing students to works of art and by affording them some practice in creating works of art. As far as it goes, this assumption is justifiable, for we have seen that works of art can heighten and make more explicit the artistic features that are easily overlooked elsewhere in the world. But this assumption does not go far enough, for its exclusive emphasis on works of

[6] What is initially found as attractive or interesting may be pursued in respect to its artistic features, wherein the quality of experience is dominantly aesthetic. Or it may be pursued cognitively, in which case, the initial attraction stimulates curiosity that may eventuate in scientific or historical investigation. See Donald Arnstine, "Curiosity," *Teacher's College Record,* 67 (1966): 595–602.

art may be as inimical to aesthetic education as it would be to ignore art works altogether.

Art, like science and history, is made by men. Like science and history, art is the result of treating things and events in the world in a certain way. And, as in the case of a scientific explanation and an historical generalization, it is a long way from the world, just as we perceive it, to a work of art. To cover this distance and thereby to find meaning in art (or in science or history) requires much time and effort at learning. It follows, then, that school children—who may respond with interest and enjoyment to much of what they find in the world—are as far removed from meaning in art as they are from meaning in science.

The instructional consequences of the need for deliberate education in order to understand art parallel those that follow from the need to educate people to understand science and history. We may present to students a table of atomic weights or a chronology of English kings. But if the tables and the chronologies have no immediate appeal, and if students have neither familiarity with nor an interest in the events of which the tables and the chronologies are the cognitive formulations, then they have no recourse but to memorize them. In a similar manner, we may confront students with a still life or a reproduction of the Parthenon. And if students neither find them immediately appealing nor have much familiarity with or interest in the things or events of which the still life and the Parthenon are artistic expressions, then they can be treated only as things to be recognized. This is, of course, the outcome of much art teaching, but recognition is no more closely related to the appearance of aesthetic quality in experience than memorization is related to understanding or inquiry.

The upshot of all this is that works of art can forward the aims of aesthetic education only insofar as they facilitate the appearance of aesthetic quality in the experience of students. Such works are more likely to do this the more they are artistic expressions of what school children already, and on other grounds, find interesting or personally significant. The same conclusion follows in the case of the creative activity assigned to students. The aims of aesthetic education are more likely to be forwarded the more possible it is for students to make things that embody what they think and feel about what is of interest and concern to them. The other side of this coin is equally important for aesthetic education. There are things in the world in which students are interested, but which themselves could not be called works of art. Yet those things, whether they be cars or clothing, can both become invested with greater meaning and serve as vehicles for the development of aesthetic sensitivity if they become the focus, in schools, of aesthetic analysis.

II

I have tried to show how a critical examination of some of the assumptions which underlie art teaching can result in the adoption of a quite different approach to aesthetic education. In light of this approach, we might briefly consider some of the directions aesthetic education might take.

As already indicated, formal instruction in art must be so organized as to make possible the appearance of aesthetic quality in students' experience. If students do not experience such qualities, they cannot have the slightest idea why they are enjoined to "take" art. In a utilitarian culture like ours, it is hard enough to arouse interest and support for art which is allegedly nonutilitarian. And, if the art presented to students and the art activities they pursue fail even to be interesting or enjoyable on their own account, students can only draw the conclusion that art is wholly without value.

The chances of making an aesthetic impact on students through the presentation of works of art will be greatly increased if those works render into artistic terms that in which students have an interest. In many cases this will reduce the emphasis put on classic exemplars of art and focus attention on more contemporary and even popular arts. These latter arts treat of an enormously wide range of topics, many of which are within the range of students' experience. Little damage is risked by having a class consider a work which is not, and may never be, universally acclaimed as great. But to be drawn into the analysis of a work which throws a highlight on what already concerns students may not only broaden that concern but may increase sensitivity to aesthetic qualities as well. If the art of the connoisseurs is ever to be appreciated and enjoyed, this may be the only way to bring it about.[7]

For the same reasons, works of art need not be the sole focus of the art course. The common objects of daily experience—from bathtubs to cooking pots to apartment houses—can serve as a focus of aesthetic analysis and creative activity. In considering such things, both artistic qualities and practical meanings come under investigation when the question is asked, "Does the thing *look* like the way it is intended to be *used?*"[8] Such a question put to a student who is, for example, designing a garment focuses critical attention both on artistic qualities and on social conventions which may be elaborated by those qualities. A question about the relation of form to function in the consideration of an apartment house may eventually reveal the intimate connection of aesthetic with political, sociological, and economic considerations.

The same considerations that hold for the kinds of art to which students are exposed also hold for the creative experiences in which students might engage. The isolated practice of skills may be appropriate for professionals, but public school students are not yet professionals, and most of them never will be. Greater sensitivity to the problems and satisfactions of creative artwork can result only from the opportunity to try putting into artistic terms what one feels about what is important to him. This is to suggest that having students dutifully and interminably render in pen and ink the teacher's still-life set-up may be just the wrong way to develop aesthetic sensitivity or enjoyment of art. If it be noted that Van Dyck may not have been very interested in his

[7] Expressing his distrust of the "classics" and the traditional liberal arts as means of developing taste and sensitivity in students, Bernard Mehl writes, ". . . it may well be that high culture á la Swinburne is not the saviour of taste but, rather like *Kitsch,* the sure way to make taste meaningless and phony." See "Come Back to High School, Huck, Sir," *Teachers College Record,* 67 (1966): 449.

[8] The import of this question is pursued with great insight in Rudolf Arnheim's "From Function to Expression," *Journal of Aesthetics and Art Criticism,* 23 (1964): 29–41.

portrait subjects, it should also be remembered that Van Dyck, unlike public school students, was already a professional.

Aside from considerations about instruction in art courses, this conception of aesthetic education bears important implications for instruction throughout the school curriculum. The aesthetic is a quality of experience and may be cued by any sort of thing or event, and it is for this quality that experience is prized on its own account. It follows, then, that an artistically organized presentation of any subject matter in school becomes one important way of helping students find an interest in subjects of study and become sensitized to the reasons for the cognitive examination of those subjects. A thing or event presented in a dramatic or in an aesthetically problematic context is directly perceived as a topic of thought and inquiry. Seen the other way around, the cognitive development of what first appears in artistic form makes more meaningful subsequent confrontations with those forms and with other forms of art. A consideration of the paintings of Orozco, for example, may give point and meaning to a study of certain social and political problems. But at the same time, the study of those problems affords greater meaning to the paintings of Orozco.

· · · ·

Objections have frequently been made to the integration of art with the rest of the school curriculum. It is said that art will be swallowed up and made a mere handmaiden of science and history.[9] But the objection either underestimates the impact of art or presupposes a poor choice of artistic materials. If the creation of an aesthetic context assists in the pursuit of cognitive studies, much has been gained. If that initial context was one of genuine artistic merit and one which was experienced aesthetically by students, then they can be depended upon to return to it again. If they do not, and the interest of students in the aesthetic disappears, it might be suspected that what initially aroused that interest did not

[9] See, for example, Thomas Munro's "Modern Art and Social Problems," *Art Education Today* (New York: Bureau of Publications, Teachers College, Columbia University, 1938), pp. 49–64.

merit further attention. Art presented as mere decoration and plastered incidentally onto a subject matter deserves all the contempt it has won.

So long as art and the sciences are competitors with each other, neither will compete very successfully with the arts of the juke box and the box office or the sciences of public relations, war, and space shots. These latter arts and sciences, however shallow or destructive they may often be, at least have appeal. But art studied in school that is disconnected from the natural and social events which are its chief source of meaning and significance is, at best, an esoteric amusement and, at worst, a bore. And history and sciences that are presented in isolation from the aspects of immediate aesthetic appeal which constitute the very motivation for their cognitive study are, at best, mere rituals to perform and, at worst, a form of persecution. What I am proposing is a conception of aesthetic education in which all studies are initiated and carried forward by what is of immediate appeal and in which sensitivity to artistic presentations themselves is maintained and developed, because what is presented is perceptibly significant to the world in which students live.

THE MORALITY OF PRIMARY EXPERIENCE*

John L. Childs

. . . .

Experience and Meaning

For those who accept the evolutionary account of the genesis of
man, it is evident that man must have been a creature of action
and feeling long before he achieved the capacity for reflective
thought. Nor can an empirical thinker today seek to explain the
development of mind by resort to the historic mind-body dualism.
The evolutionary conception, for example, has bred an outlook
and a mode of interpreting human personality which has dissolved
the very foundations of the dualistic presupposition inherent in the
following account by T. H. Green:

> It will be found, we believe, that this apparent state of the case
> can only be explained by supposing that in the growth of our ex-
> perience, in the process of our learning to know the world, an
> animal organism, which has its history in time, gradually be-
> comes the vehicle of an eternally complete consciousness. What
> we call our mental history is not a history of this consciousness,
> which in itself can have no history, but a history of the process
> by which the animal organism becomes its vehicle.[2]

For the evolutionist, "the history of the process by which the
animal organism becomes the vehicle of mind" is not the story
of "an eternally complete consciousness" descending from some
transcendental realm in order to make its abode in a human organism; it is rather the record of the manner in which the sentient
organism becomes progressively aware of its own interests, and of

* Reprinted from *Education and Morals* (New York: Appleton-
Century-Crofts, Inc., 1950), pp. 140–53. By permission of Appleton-
Century-Crofts, Educational Division, Meredith Corporation.
[2] T. H. Green, *Prolegomena to Ethics*, 5th ed. (Oxford: Oxford University Press, 1907), pp. 77–78.

the principles implicit in the habits which regulate its interactions with its surroundings. The transformation of the habit patterns of the living creature into the consciously purposeful activities of the human person is a great transformation, and we properly celebrate the role of symbols in making possible this transformation, for it is this evolutionary development which marks the emergence of mind. But the world of symbols is not an independent, self-sufficient world; nor is the realm of mind a realm of rational principles and concepts unrelated to the doings and the undergoings of ordinary experience. On the contrary, symbols have intellectual significance precisely because they do represent—symbolize—the values of things and organic acts in the world of natural existences. It is only as these verbal forms preserve for a human group that which it has learned about the way in which things are actually involved in one another, that they become charged with meaning. Symbols are important in the development of mind because they convey to man the import of things that are other than symbols. Words—oral or written—have no intellectual significance whatsoever apart from these life contexts.

Thus, if we accept the evolutionary point of view, we must recognize that *things* are prior to *symbols* or *words,* and that *activities* are prior to *meanings.* Nor is the priority merely chronological in nature; behavioral adjustments to surroundings not only come earlier than language and thought, they also constitute the matrix from within which all conceptions of relationships, or meanings, are developed. Conscious or cognitive experience is a derived mode of experiencing; it is sourced in the doings, the undergoings, the sufferings, and the enjoyments of primary experience, and its ultimate controls and tests are also provided by the events of primary experience. No matter how deep our respect for the life of reason, we do not serve the ends of reason when we attempt to make it a thing in and of itself. The life of reason has its vital continuities with the life of action and feeling, and although there is a sound basis for our high regard for the transformations wrought in experience by the development in man of the capacity for reflective thought, we should never assume that reason can become the source of its own subject matter. The

process of human thought is indeed a distinctive kind of functioning, but it is nevertheless a form of human functioning, and like all other functionings of the living creature it is carried on by means of an environment. Apart from some context of ordinary human experience, the activity we designate as mind or reason does not occur.

This nondualistic, functional theory of mind has important consequences for the work of education. Indeed, the evolutionary interpretation cuts the ground from beneath all of those educational practices that assume mind is an inborn essence that unfolds according to its own pre-formed and rational principles. The empirical evidence has never corroborated this doctrine of a universal, inborn mind; it has always supported the view that minds are the kind of affairs that are conditioned by particular cultures, and that they reflect the actual life experiences of the individuals who live in these different cultures. And with the development of an evolutionary, functional view of mind, we are rapidly growing in the ability to provide an empirical explanation for those mental phenomena which were long supposed to demand a dualistic theory to account for them. Educators concerned to develop a program of education in harmony with modern thought and knowledge will not continue to ground their activity in a view which assumes that mind is an inborn latency that unfolds in its own predetermined way irrespective of the life history of the individual human being. Fortunately, there is a growing tendency in education to recognize that we can understand the life and the mind of a child only as we understand the character of the surroundings in which he lives.

Nor does the faculty theory of mind, with its reliance on formal discipline as the preferred mode of educational preparation, rest on more defensible foundations. The experimental data do not justify the educational claims made for this theory, and its basic assumption that mind is a substance is obviously an inheritance from the transcendental, dualistic conception of an earlier philosophical outlook. Neither the findings of science nor everyday human experience support these preconceptions. Our modes of thinking and intellectual mastery are conditioned by our modes of experiencing: the sailor is at home on the sea, the farmer on his land, the artisan with his tools and materials, the research scientist with his techniques and his special subject-matter of inquiry, the statesman with the affairs of the world of politics, and the artist with his paints and brushes. There is no universal subject matter and no single form of training that can develop competency in all of these different fields apart from actual experience in them. What we know about the conditions for the "transfer" or "spread" of training would seem to indicate that a process of exclusive concentration on the manipulation of symbols would be one of the least promising of all possible educational practices for the development of the intellectually mature and resourceful human being.

Experiment and Meaning

These evolutionary interpretations of the nature of experience and of the significance and patterns of intellectual activity are confirmed and enriched by an analysis of the procedures of experimental science. We owe much to the pioneer studies of Charles Sanders Peirce in the nature of the pattern of thought implicit in the procedures of modern science. In his discussion of the characteristics of the mind that has been molded by scientific practice, Peirce declares that whenever you have discourse with a typical experimentalist, "you will find that whatever assertion you make to him, he will understand as meaning that if a given prescription for an experiment ever can be and ever is carried out in an act, an experience of a given description will result, or else he will see no sense at all in what you say."[3]

In this statement, Peirce contends that a significant idea is always an "assertion" or a "proposition" about some determinate situation or subject-matter. He holds that an assertion, an hypothesis, a proposition, or an idea, has a dual function. On the one hand, it *prescribes* an experiment or an act to be tried out;

[3] Charles Hartshorne and Paul Weiss, *Collected Papers of Charles Sanders Peirce*, 5 (Cambridge: Harvard University Press, 1934): 272–73.

on the other, it *describes* an experience or a condition that will follow when the idea—the meaning—is put to the test of action. Thus an idea or a meaning is at one and the same time a plan for an action to be performed and a prediction of a result.

An idea is therefore intrinsically prospective in character: it asserts that if these definite things are done, these definite results will follow. The having of an idea, or the making of an assertion, also involves the making of inferences—that is, present and given things are taken as the signs of future and absent things. In other words, thinking is a process in which given things are taken as the ground, the evidence, or the sign, of future things, or occurrences. Without the use of things as signs, no mind, for mind denotes the ability to use present and given things as reliable indicators of future and possible things.

But these conceived or projected possibilities can be tested and turned into actualities only by the means of action. An idea is therefore not only an expectation of a result; it is also a defined plan of treating or acting on certain materials or conditions in order to bring an anticipated result, or consequence, into existence. Hence our statements make sense—they are possessed of significant meaning—only as we are aware of what they signify for action. Without this reference to behavior, or experience, a statement is a verbalism; it is void of genuine intellectual significance.

In his article, Peirce generalizes this insight into what has come to be known as the *operational* theory of concepts. He contends that for a mind disciplined in the practices of experimental inquiry, the meaning of a concept—the rational purport of any term or proposition—lies exactly in its "bearing upon the conduct of life." He states:

> Endeavoring, as a man of that type naturally would, to formulate what he so approved, he framed the theory that a *conception*, that is, the rational purport of a word or other expression, lies exclusively in its conceivable bearing upon the conduct of life; so that, since obviously nothing that might not result from experiment can have any direct bearing upon conduct, if one can define accurately all the conceivable experimental phenom-

ena which the denial or the affirmation of a concept could imply, one would have therein a complete definition of the concept, and *there is absolutely nothing more in it.*[4]

The great merit of this operational theory of the nature of a concept is that it brings together into a cooperative partnership two factors—"sensory experience" and "reason"—that our rival traditions of empiricism and a priori rationalism have tended to separate and to oppose to each other. In the operations of experimental inquiry, the subject matters of ordinary experience and the world of meaning, made possible by the development of concepts, are shown to have dynamic continuity. Experiment is action within the context of some empirical subject matter, but it is also action that is guided by an idea. The idea, or hypothesis, is the product of both knowledge and observation. It originates as a possible response to the observed characteristics of the problematic or doubtful situation; it is elaborated and refined in imagination by the utilization of concepts and meanings developed in previous experience; and it is ultimately either rejected, or put to the test of overt behavior.

Experimental activity is thus not mere random physical manipulation of things; neither is it a self-enclosed process of ratiocination. It is reflective activity—a controlled procedure in which inferences are made by the disciplined use of observation and reason—by use of the companion processes of induction and deduction. We think, only as we think experimentally, that is, in terms of actions to be performed. Meanings or concepts are functional in nature. They are primarily properties of behavior, and, by extension, they become properties of things that have become known through having been subjected to experimental treatment. We may be said to know things when we can predict the manner in which they will behave—that is, the effects or consequences they will produce when brought into specified connections with other things. All meanings are meanings *of*— we have the meaning of a thing or a situation, not when we have simply memorized the name by which it is designated, but when

[4] Ibid, p. 273.

we know what to expect of it, how to behave with reference to it, and what can be done with it.

The educational implications of this functional, or operational, interpretation of meaning are fundamental. In order to communicate a meaning to a child, it is necessary to do more than to put a sound into his ear, or to get him to learn how to spell or pronounce a word, or to read a sentence. Words are not ideas or meanings. These verbal forms or terms have their referents in the behavior of things and persons; we grasp their intellectual significance only as we acquire an appreciation of the concrete conditions and behaviors for which they stand.

Unless we are to burden the young with meaningless catch-phrases—sheer verbalisms—that may deaden their intellectual perceptions and weaken their capacity for thought, we must provide them with the experiences that will communicate the life significance of that which they are expected to learn from oral and printed sources. As the modes of living and making a living in our present-day industrial civilization tend to lessen the opportunity of the young for direct participation in the life activities of their society, the obligation of the school to provide a program of rich and varied primary experience becomes ever more urgent.

These primary activities of observing, manipulating, doing, exploring, and making, as well as the opportunity for pupils to cooperate in significant life projects, are not made a part of the work of the school because educators want to relieve children of the rigorous demands and disciplines of the life of intelligence. On the contrary, these experiences are now provided in the curriculum of the school, because in contemporary industrial society they have been so largely subtracted from the life the young now lead outside the school. The crucial point is that without this body of primary experiences, we simply do not have the conditions essential to the growth of meanings—of mind. Nothing is deeper in the life of the person than his characteristic ways of responding to conditions and people, and no education meets the moral test which fails to provide for this medium of primary experience in and through which immature human beings achieve the modes of their personhood. Experience is the ultimate source of human competence and intellectual authority; a school that fails to provide these primary conditions for the growth of mind is immoral—it fails to treat children as ends in themselves.

Dewey's View of Activity and The Nature of Mind

Respect for the child and concern for his present happiness and welfare were undoubtedly important considerations in the minds of those who led in the development of the experience, or activity, curriculum. Scientific study of child behavior had demonstrated that children, with their restless and abundant energy, have a more satisfying experience when they are engaged in purposeful group activities than when they are isolated, confined to fixed seats, and subjected to endless routines of drill and memorization in a formal school situation in which study and learning are measured by the ability of the child to recite assigned lessons in prescribed textbooks and the good pupil is defined as the docile child who adjusts to the fixed regimen of the classroom without making trouble for the teacher. But deep as was their concern for the present happiness and welfare of the child, the pioneers in the activity curriculum were fully aware that these more immediately satisfying experiences would be gained at too dear a cost if they were attained by the sacrifice of his deeper intellectual needs and potentialities. Nor did the emphasis on the all-around growth of the child—emotional, social, and moral, as well as intellectual—imply that the development of the intellectual powers were not primary in the new education. This emphasis on the primacy of thought in the nurture of the young has been expressed by Dr. Dewey:

> The sole direct path to enduring improvement in the methods of instruction and learning consists in centering upon the conditions which exact, promote, and test thinking. Thinking *is* the method of intelligent learning, of learning that employs and rewards mind. . . . Processes of instruction are unified in the degree in which they center in the production of good habits of thinking. While we may speak, without error, of the method of thought, the important thing is that thinking is the method of an

educative experience. The essentials of method are therefore identical with the essentials of reflection.[5]

The moral insistence of the new education that we cease viewing childhood as a mere preparation for a remote future and seek instead a school that would increase the meaning of present experience was not the product of indifference to the demands of adult life; it was rather a product of the insight that the best possible preparation for the future is found in the most significant living in the present. This conviction, of course, is the correlative of the faith that a satisfying and rich experience in the present necessarily involves growth in meaning—in mind.

Nor were the educational views of the founders of the activity curriculum the result of a lack of appreciation of the intellectual and moral worth of the social heritage. Their conception of the social genesis of human personality necessarily points in another direction. The pioneers in the philosophy and psychology of the new education believe that the child literally learns his distinctively human attributes by virtue of his membership in a human society. It was Dewey, not a traditionalist in education, who wrote:

> It is of grace not of ourselves that we lead civilized lives. There is sound sense in the old pagan notion that gratitude is the root of all virtue. Loyalty to whatever in the established environment makes a life of excellence possible is the beginning of all progress. The best we can accomplish for posterity is to transmit unimpaired and with some increment of meaning the environment that makes it possible to maintain the habits of decent and refined life.[6]

No one with this regard for the role of culture in the nurture of human beings could have been uncertain about the importance of providing opportunity in the life of the school for the young to learn that which man has achieved through all that he has undergone, suffered, and enjoyed. As a matter of fact, it was concern for cultural and intellectual values, not indifference to

[5] John Dewey, *Democracy and Education* (New York: Macmillan, 1916), pp. 179–80.
[6] John Dewey, *Human Nature and Conduct* (New York: Henry Holt and Co., 1922), p. 21.

them, that led Dewey to experiment with an activity, or experience, curriculum. He was searching for a theory and practice of education that would take account of revolutionary developments in the intellectual and moral outlook of modern man.

He perceived, first, that any thorough-going adoption of the evolutionary point of view involved a reconstruction of the classical view of the nature of human experience and the nature of man. When human experience is viewed as "certain modes of interaction, of correlation, of natural objects among which the organism happens, so to say, to be one," it has no place for the earlier dualistic assumption "that experience centers in, or gathers about, or proceeds from a center or subject which is outside the course of natural existence, and set over against it: it being of no importance, for present purposes, whether this antithetical subject is termed soul, or spirit, or mind, or ego, or consciousness, or just knower or knowing subject."[7]

Once this dualistic view of human experience and mind is abandoned, the conception of knowledge as the view of a "spectator" must also be discarded. We gain knowledge not by making a photograph, or a copy, of an external object. If meanings, as Peirce had affirmed, are intrinsically operational in nature, Dewey perceived that the assumption that there can be knowledge by immediate acquaintance, by a mere process of beholding, or by sheer intuition, was untenable. We gain knowledge not by gazing at things, but by having interactions with them, and by discovering the connections they sustain to other things. Knowledge is acquired through experience, and experience is not a process in which a subjective mind beholds or intuits an external world; it is, as Dewey has emphasized, an active process of doing and undergoing—a process in which we do things to the environment and the environment reacts on us, and we make connections between that which we do and that which we undergo. In other words, we get knowledge in and through activity, and without activity there is no acquisition of knowledge.

Dewey also recognized that a dynamic conception of learning

[7] John Dewey, *Creative Intelligence* (New York: Henry Holt and Co., 1917), pp. 30, 37.

was involved in this functional view of experience and meaning. We learn as we experience—as we have interactions or transactions with our environment. Habits and attitudes are inevitably developed as we experience and adjust to the qualities of the diversified affairs that constitute the environment. But although learning is involved in all experiencing, not all learning is of the kind that results in the apprehension of meaning and in the growth of mind. Activity becomes meaningful—intellectually significant—only as we consciously apprehend and retain the connections between that which we do and that which happens as a result of what we do.

> If it be true that the self or subject of experience is part and parcel of the course of events, it follows that the self *becomes* a knower. It becomes a mind in virtue of the distinctive way of partaking in the course of events. The significant distinction is no longer between the knower *and* the world; it is between different ways of being in and of the movement of things, between a brute physical way and a purposive, intelligent way.[8]

The meaning of freedom resides in this distinction between experience as brute, physical involvement in "the movement of things," and experience as a purposive, intelligent way of interacting with the course of events. Obviously this distinction is foundational in Dewey's conception of the relation of thought to activity. Our acts are *free,* not simply because they are not under constraint from others, but because they are becoming *intelligent.* They become intelligent as they grow in their grasp of meanings. We become free as we *learn* to *think.* And the heart of thinking is the capacity to make inferences that enlarge our ability to control events in the interests of human well-being. There can be no growth of freedom without activity, because there can be no growth of mind without activity. But there can be a type of activity that does not result in the significant enrichment of meaning. We grow in the knowledge that means power to do—freedom—only as we use our experiences, our activities, to form reasonable expectations. We grow in our capacity to form reasonable expectations as we grow in our ability to use given condi-

[8] Ibid, p. 59.

tions as signs of future consequences and to control our behavior in accordance with these forecasts of future occurrences.

Utilizing these conceptions of the nature of experience and of the relation of knowing—cognitive experience—to the doings and the undergoings, the sufferings and the enjoyments, the attractions and the aversions, the loves and the hates of primary experience, Dewey undertook the development of a theory of the nature and pattern of reflective thinking. For Dewey, the long search of man for a dependable method to control the course of his own intellectual activity has culminated in the logic of discovery and testing inherent in experimental inquiry. In his logical studies, he has distinguished the five phases or aspects of this process of experimental inquiry, and in his theory of education he has sought to develop an educational practice that is grounded in this analysis of the pattern of reflective thinking. He describes the essentials of this educational practice as follows:

> First, that the pupil have a genuine situation of experience—that there be a continuous activity in which he is interested for its own sake;
> Secondly, that a genuine problem develop within this situation as a stimulus to thought;
> Third, that he possess the information and make the observations needed to deal with it;
> Fourth, that suggested solutions occur to him which he shall be responsible for developing in an orderly way;
> Fifth, that he have opportunity and occasion to test his ideas by application to make their meaning clear and to discover for himself their validity.[9]

Thus for Dewey, the cultivation of thinking is central in his view of both the ends and the means of education. His demand for an activity curriculum was a demand for a school program better designed to foster the intellectual powers of the young. He perceived that thought was inquiry, and that inquiry could be real for the child only as it was grounded in problems of felt significance, and that the school therefore should provide the conditions for the purposeful pursuit of ends as well as the oppor-

[9] John Dewey, *Democracy and Education,* p. 192.

tunity for the exploration, the utilization, and the ordering of means for the attainment of these ends.

Nor was this emphasis on *inquiring* something that was hostile to *acquiring*. On the contrary, *inquiring* was approved because it was believed to be the essential method of *acquiring,* particularly of the acquiring of the kind of knowledge that means power. Meanings that signify increased power to function—to predict and to control—cannot be poured into children as water is poured into empty containers; neither are meanings acquired by a process of mechanical addition; they are, rather, developed in the process by which present experience is purposefully reconstructed. It was the insight of the founders of the activity curriculum that this kind of reconstruction cannot be carried on by adults for the young; without the purposeful participation of the young in the program of the school, this meaningful reconstruction of experience does not take place. The problem and the art of education, therefore, is to provide the conditions in which the young will be encouraged to engage in those complete acts of inquiry—of reflection—by which new meanings and new powers of control are developed.

It is this form of purposeful reconstruction of experience that signifies the growth of mind. And this kind of reconstruction finds both its stimulus and its test in the varied affairs of primary experience. An educational program therefore that is concerned to treat individuals as ends, will also be a program that is concerned to provide all of those conditions which are essential to the nurture of their minds, that is, the conditions through which individuals develop the capacity to learn from their own first-hand experiences. A primary moral responsibility of the school is to provide opportunity for those complete acts of thought in which knowledge is gained as a result of that which the children do and undergo. The deepest discipline of mind results when the young *acquire* because they are encouraged to *inquire.* To be most fully educative, the realms open to inquiry should be co-extensive with the life affairs of a human group. Whenever we block inquiry, we block the means through which minds are developed in the young.

EDUCATION AS DIALOGUE*

Martin Buber

The release of powers can be only a presupposition of education, nothing more. Put more generally, it is the nature of freedom to provide the place, but not the foundation as well, on which true life is raised. That is true both of inner, "moral" freedom and of outer freedom (which consists in not being hindered or limited). As the higher freedom, the soul's freedom of decision, signifies perhaps our highest moments but not a fraction of our substance, so the lower freedom, the freedom of development, signifies our capacity for growth but by no means our growth itself. This latter freedom is charged with importance as the actuality from which the work of education begins, but as its fundamental task it becomes absurd.

There is a tendency to understand this freedom, which may be termed evolutionary freedom, as at the opposite pole from compulsion, from being under a compulsion. But at the opposite pole from compulsion there stands not freedom but communion. Compulsion is a negative reality; communion is the positive reality; freedom is a possibility, possibility regained. At the opposite pole of being compelled by destiny or nature or men there does not stand being free of destiny or nature or men but to commune and to covenant with them. To do this, it is true that one must first have become independent; but this independence is a footbridge, not a dwelling place. Freedom is the vibrating needle, the fruitful zero. Compulsion in education means disunion, it means humiliation and rebelliousness. Communion in education is just communion; it means being opened up and drawn in. Freedom in education is the possibility of communion; it cannot be dispensed with, and it cannot be made use of in itself. Without

* Reprinted from *Between Man and Man* (New York: Macmillan, 1967), pp. 90–102. Copyright 1965 by The Macmillan Company. By permission of The Macmillan Company.

it nothing succeeds, but neither does anything succeed by means of it; it is the run before the jump, the tuning of the violin, the confirmation of that primal and mighty potentiality which it cannot even begin to actualize.

Freedom—I love its flashing face: it flashes forth from the darkness and dies away, but it has made the heart invulnerable. I am devoted to it; I am always ready to join in the fight for it, for the appearance of the flash, which lasts no longer than the eye is able to endure it, for the vibrating of the needle that was held down too long and was stiff. I give my left hand to the rebel and my right to the heretic: forward! But I do not trust them. They know how to die, but that is not enough. I love freedom, but I do not believe in it. How could one believe in it after looking in its face? It is the flash of a significance comprising all meanings, of a possibility comprising all potentiality. For it we fight, again and again, from of old, victorious and in vain.

It is easy to understand that in a time when the deterioration of all traditional bonds has made their legitimacy questionable, the tendency to freedom is exalted, the springboard is treated as the goal and a functional good as substantial good. Moreover, it is idle sentimentality to lament at great length that freedom is made the subject of experiments. Perhaps it is fitting for this time which has no compass that people should throw out their lives like a plummet to discover our bearings and the course we should set. But truly *their* lives. . . . Let us realize the true meaning of being free of a bond: it means that a quite personal responsibility takes the place of one shared with many generations. Life lived in freedom is personal responsibility, or it is a pathetic farce.

I have pointed out the power which alone can give a content to empty freedom and a direction to swaying and spinning freedom. I believe in it, I trust those devoted to it.

This fragile life between birth and death can nevertheless be a fulfillment—if it is a dialogue. In our life and experience we are addressed; by thought and speech and action, by producing and by influencing, we are able to answer. For the most part we do not listen to the address, or we break into it with chatter. But if the word comes to us and the answer proceeds from us, then human life exists, though brokenly, in the world. The kindling of the response in that "spark" of the soul, the blazing up of the response, which occurs time and again, to the unexpectedly approaching speech, we term responsibility. We practice responsibility for that realm of life allotted and entrusted to us for which we are able to respond, that is, for which we have a relation of deeds which may count—in all our inadequacy—as a proper response. The extent to which a man, in the strength of the reality of the spark, can keep a traditional bond, a law, a direction, is the extent to which he is permitted to lean his responsibility on something (more than this is not vouchsafed to us, responsibility is not taken off our shoulders). As we "become free," this leaning on something is more and more denied to us, and our responsibility must become personal and solitary.

From this point of view, education and its transformation in the hour of the crumbling of bonds are to be understood.

It is usual to contrast the principle of the "new" education as "Eros" with that of the "old" education as the "will to power."

In fact the one is as little a principle of education as the other. A principle of education, in a sense still to be clarified, can only be a basic relation which is fulfilled in education. But Eros and the will to power are alike passions of the soul for whose real elaboration a place is prepared elsewhere. Education can supply for them only an incidental realm and, moreover, one which sets a limit to their elaboration; nor can this limit be infringed without the realm itself being destroyed. The one can as little as the other constitute the educational attitude.

The "old" educator, insofar as he was an educator, was not "the man with a will to power," but he was the bearer of assured values which were strong in tradition. If the educator represents the world to the pupil, the "old" educator represented particularly the historical world, the past. He was the ambassador of history to this intruder, the "child"; he carried to him, as the Pope in the legend did to the prince of the Huns, the magic of the spiritual forces of history; he instilled values into the child or he drew the child into the values. . . .

This situation of the old type of education is, however, easily used, or misused, by the individual's will to power, for this will is inflated by the authority of history. The will to power becomes convulsive and passes into fury when the authority begins to decay, that is, when the magical validity of tradition disappears. Then the moment comes near when the teacher no longer faces the pupil as an ambassador but only as an individual, as a static atom to the whirling atom. Then no matter how much he imagines he is acting from the fullness of the objective spirit, in the reality of his life he is thrown back on himself, cast on his own resources, and hence filled with longing. Eros appears. And Eros finds employment in the new situation of education as the will to power did in the old situation. But Eros is not a bearer or the ground or the principle any more than the will to power was. He only claims to be that, in order not to be recognized as longing, as the stranger given refuge. And many believe it.

Nietzsche did not succeed in glorifying the will to power as much as Plato glorified Eros. But in our concern for the creature in this great time of concern, for both alike we have not to consider the myths of the philosophers but the actuality of present life. In entire opposition to any glorification we have to see that Eros—that is, not "love," but Eros the male and magnificent— whatever else may belong to him, necessarily includes this one thing, that he desires to enjoy men; and education, the peculiar essence bearing this name which is composed of no others, excludes precisely this desire. However mightily an educator is possessed and inspired by Eros, if he obeys him in the course of his educating then he stifles the growth of his blessings. It must be one or the other: either he takes on himself the tragedy of the person and offers an unblemished daily sacrifice, or the fire enters his work and consumes it.

Eros is choice, choice made from an inclination. This is precisely what education is not. The man who is loving in Eros chooses the beloved, the modern educator finds his pupil there before him. From this unerotic situation the *greatness* of the modern educator is to be seen—and most clearly when he is a teacher. He enters the schoolroom for the first time; he sees them crouching at the desks, indiscriminately flung together, the misshapen and the well-proportioned, animal faces, empty faces, and noble faces in indiscriminate confusion, like the presence of the created universe; the glance of the educator accepts and receives them all. He is assuredly no descendant of the Greek gods who kidnapped those they loved. But he seems to me to be a representative of the true God. For if God "forms the light and creates darkness," man is able to love both—to love light in itself, and darkness toward the light.

If this educator should ever believe that for the sake of education he has to practice selection and arrangement, then he will be guided by another criterion than that of inclination, however legitimate this may be in its own sphere; he will be guided by the recognition of values which is in his glance as an educator. But even then his selection remains suspended, under constant correction by the special humility of the educator for whom the life and particular being of all his pupils is the decisive factor to which his "hierarchic" recognition is subordinated. For in the manifold variety of the children the variety of creation is placed before him.

In education, then, there is a lofty asceticism: an asceticism which rejoices in the world, for the sake of the responsibility for a realm of life which is entrusted to us for our influence but not our interference—either by the will to power or by Eros. The spirit's service of life can be truly carried out only in the system of a reliable counterpoint—regulated by the laws of the different forms of relation—of giving and withholding oneself, intimacy and distance, which of course must not be controlled by reflection but must arise from the living tact of the natural and spiritual man. Every form of relation in which the spirit's service of life is realized has its special objectivity, its structure of proportions and limits which in no way resists the fervor of personal comprehension and penetration, though it does resist any confusion with the person's own spheres. If this structure and its resistance are not respected, then a dilettantism will prevail which claims to be aristocratic, though in reality it is unsteady and feverish; to provide it with the most sacred names and attitudes will not help it past its inevitable consequence of disintegration. Consider, for example, the relation of doctor and patient. It is essential that this should be a real human relation experienced with the spirit by the one who is addressed; but as soon as the helper is touched by the desire—in however subtle a form—to dominate or to enjoy his patient, or to treat the latter's wish to be dominated or enjoyed by him other than as a wrong condition needing to be cured, the danger of a falsification arises, beside which all quackery appears peripheral.

The objectively ascetic character of the sphere of education must not, however, be misunderstood as being so separated from the instinct to power and from Eros that no bridge can be flung from them to it. I have already pointed out how very significant Eros can be to the educator without corroding his work. What matters here is the threshold and the transformation which takes place on it. . . . A reversal of the single instinct takes place, which does not eliminate it but reverses its system of direction. Such a reversal can be effected by the elemental experience with which the real process of education begins and on which it is based. I call it experiencing the other side.

A man belabors another who remains quite still. Then let us assume that the striker suddenly receives in his soul the blow which he strikes: the same blow; that he receives it as the other who remains still. For the space of a moment, he experiences the situation from the other side. Reality imposes itself on him. What will he do? Either he will overwhelm the voice of the soul, or his impulse will be reversed.

A man caresses a woman, who lets herself be caressed. Then let us assume that he feels the contact from two sides—with the palm of his hand still, and also with the woman's skin. The twofold nature of the gesture, as one that takes place between two persons, thrills through the depth of enjoyment in his heart and stirs it. If he does not deafen his heart he will have—not to renounce the enjoyment but—to love.

I do not in the least mean that the man who has had such an experience would from then on have this two-sided sensation in every such meeting—that would perhaps destroy his instinct. But the one extreme experience makes the other person present to him for all time. A transfusion has taken place after which a mere elaboration of subjectivity is never again possible or tolerable to him.

Only an inclusive power is able to take the lead; only an inclusive Eros is love. Inclusiveness is the complete realization of the submissive person, the desired person, the "partner," not by the fancy but by the actuality of the being.

It would be wrong to identify what is meant here with the familiar but not very significant term "empathy." Empathy means, if anything, to glide with one's own feeling into the dynamic structure of an object, a pillar or a crystal or the branch of a tree, or even of an animal or a man, and as it were to trace it from within, understanding the formation and motoriality of the object with the perceptions of one's own muscles; it means to "transpose" oneself over there and in there. Thus it means the exclusion of one's own concreteness, the extinguishing of the actual situation of life, the absorption in pure aestheticism of the reality in which one participates. Inclusion is the opposite of this. It is the extension of one's own concreteness, the fulfillment of the actual situation of life, the complete presence of the reality in which one participates. Its elements are, first, a relation, of no matter what kind, between two persons; second, an event experienced by them in common, in which at least one of them actively participates; and, third, the fact that this one person, without forfeiting anything of the felt reality of his activity, at the same time lives through the common event from the standpoint of the other.

A relation between persons that is characterized in more or less degree by the element of inclusion may be termed a dialogical relation.

A dialogical relation will show itself also in genuine conversation, but it is not composed of this. Not only is the shared silence of two such persons a dialogue, but also their dialogical life continues, even when they are separated in space, as the continual potential presence of the one to the other, as an unexpressed intercourse. On the other hand, all conversation derives its genuine-

ness only from the consciousness of the element of inclusion—
even if this appears only abstractly as an "acknowledgement" of
the actual being of the partner in the conversation; but this acknowledgement can be real and effective only when it springs
from an experience of inclusion of the other side.

The reversal of the will to power and of Eros means that relations characterized by these are made dialogical. For that very
reason, it means that the instinct enters into communion with the
fellow man and into responsibility for him as an allotted and entrusted realm of life.

The element of inclusion, with whose recognition this clarification begins, is the same as that which constitutes the relation in
education.

The relation in education is one of pure dialogue.

I have referred to the child lying with half-closed eyes waiting
for his mother to speak to him. But many children do not need
to wait, for they know that they are unceasingly addressed in a
dialogue which never breaks off. In face of the lonely night which
threatens to invade, they lie preserved and guarded, invulnerable,
clad in the silver mail of trust.

Trust, trust in the world, because this human being exists—
that is the most inward achievement of the relation in education.
Because this human being exists, meaninglessness, however hard
pressed you are by it, cannot be the real truth. Because this human being exists, in the darkness the light lies hidden, in fear
salvation, and in the callousness of one's fellow men the great
Love.

Because this human being exists: therefore he must be really
there, really facing the child, not merely there in spirit. He may
not let himself be represented by a phantom: the death of the
phantom would be a catastrophe for the child's pristine soul.
He need possess none of the perfections which the child may
dream he possesses; but he must be really there. In order to be
and to remain truly present to the child, he must have gathered
the child's presence into his own store as one of the bearers of
his communion with the world, one of the focuses of his respon-

sibilities for the world. Of course he cannot be continually concerned with the child, either in thought or in deed, nor ought he to be. But if he has really gathered the child into his life, then that subterranean dialogic, that steady potential presence of the one to the other, is established and endures. Then there is reality *between* them, there is mutuality.

But this mutuality—that is what constitutes the peculiar nature of the relation in education—cannot be one of inclusion, although the true relation of the educator to the pupil is based on inclusion. No other relation draws its inner life like this one from the element of inclusion, but no other is in that regard like this, completely directed to one-sidedness, so that if it loses one-sidedness it loses essence.

We may distinguish three chief forms of the dialogical relation. The first rests on an abstract but mutual experience of inclusion.

The clearest example of this is a disputation between two men, thoroughly different in nature and outlook and calling, where in an instant—as by the action of a messenger as anonymous as he is invisible—it happens that each is aware of the other's full legitimacy, wearing the insignia of necessity and of meaning. What an illumination! The truth, the strength of conviction, the "standpoint," or rather the circle of movement, of each of them, is in no way reduced by this. There is no "relativizing," but we may say that, in the sign of the limit, the essence of mortal recognition, fraught with primal destiny, is manifested to us. To recognize means for us creatures the fulfillment by each of us, in truth and responsibility, of his own relation to the Present Being, through our receiving all that is manifested of it and incorporating it into our own being, with all our force, faithfully, and open to the world and the spirit. In this way living truth arises and endures. We have become aware that it is with the other as with ourselves, and that what rules over us both is not a truth of recognition, but the truth-of-existence and the existence-of-truth of the Present Being. In this way we have become able *to acknowledge*.

I have called this form abstract, not as though its basic experience lacked immediacy, but because it is related to man only as a spiritual person and is bound to leave out the full reality of his being and life. The other two forms proceed from the inclusion of this full reality.

Of these the first, the relation of education, is based on a concrete but one-sided experience of inclusion.

If education means to let a selection of the world affect a person through the medium of another person, then the one through whom this takes place, rather, who makes it take place through himself, is caught in a strange paradox. What is otherwise found only as grace, inlaid in the folds of life—the influencing of the lives of others with one's own life—becomes here a function and a law. But since the educator has to such an extent replaced the master, the danger has arisen that the new phenomenon, the will to educate, may degenerate into arbitrariness, and that the educator may carry out his selection and his influence from himself and his idea of the pupil, not from the pupil's own reality. One only needs to read, say, the accounts of Pestalozzi's teaching method to see how easily, even with the noblest teachers, arbitrary self-will is mixed up with will. This is almost always due to an interruption or a temporary flagging of the act of inclusion, which is not merely regulative for the realm of education, as for other realms, but is actually constitutive; so that the realm of education acquires its true and proper force from the constant return of this act and the constantly renewed connection with it. The man whose calling it is to influence the being of persons that can be determined must experience this action of his (however much it may have assumed the form of nonaction) ever anew from the other side. Without the action of his spirit being in any way weakened, he must at the same time be over there, on the surface of that other spirit which is being acted upon—and not of some conceptual, contrived spirit, but all the time the wholly concrete spirit of this individual and unique being who is living and confronting him, and who stands with him in the common situation of "educating" and "being educated" (which is indeed one situation, only the other is at the other end of it). It is not enough for him to imagine the child's individuality, nor to experience him directly as a spiritual person and then to acknowledge him. Only when he catches himself "from over there," and feels how it affects one, how it affects this other human being, does he recognize the real limit, baptize his self-will in Reality and make it true will, and renew his paradoxical legitimacy. He is of all men the one for whom inclusion may and should change from an alarming and edifying event into an atmosphere.

But however intense the mutuality of giving and taking with which he is bound to his pupil, inclusion cannot be mutual in this case. He experiences the pupil's being educated, but the pupil cannot experience the educating of the educator. The educator stands at both ends of the common situation; the pupil, only at one end. In the moment when the pupil is able to throw himself across and experience from over there, the educative relation would be burst asunder or change into friendship.

We call friendship the third form of the dialogical relation, which is based on a concrete and mutual experience of inclusion. It is the true inclusion of one another by human souls.

The educator who practices the experience of the other side, and stands firm in it, experiences two things together; first, that he is limited by otherness, and, second, that he receives grace by being bound to the other. He feels from "over there" the acceptance and the rejection of what is approaching (that is, approaching from himself, the educator)—of course, often only in a fugitive mood or an uncertain feeling; but this discloses the real need and absence of need in the soul. In the same way the foods a child likes and dislikes is a fact which does not, indeed, procure for the experienced person but certainly helps him to gain an insight into what substances the child's body needs. In learning from time to time what this human being needs and does not need at the moment, the educator is led to an ever deeper recognition of what the human being needs in order to grow. But he is also led to the recognition of what he, the "educator," is able and what he is unable to give of what is needed—and what he can give now, and what not yet. So the responsibility for this realm of life allotted and entrusted to him, the constant responsibility for this living soul, points him to that which seems impossible and yet is somehow granted to us—to self-education. But self-education, here as everywhere, cannot take place through one's being concerned with oneself but only through one's being concerned, knowing what it means, with the world. The forces of the world which the child needs for the building up of his substance must be chosen by the educator from the world and drawn into himself.

The education of men by men means the selection of the effective world by a person and in him. The educator gathers in the constructive forces of the world. He distinguishes, rejects, and confirms in himself, in his self which is filled with the world. The constructive forces are eternally the same; they are the world bound up in community, turned to God. The educator educates himself to be their vehicle.

Then is this the "principle" of education, its normal and fixed maxim?

No; it is only the *principium* of its reality, the beginning of its reality—wherever it begins.

There is not and never has been a norm and fixed maxim of education. What is called so was always only the norm of a culture, of a society, a church, an epoch, to which education too, like all stirring and action of the spirit, was submissive, and which education translated into its language. In a formed age there is in truth no autonomy of education, but only in an age which is losing form. Only in it, in the disintegration of traditional bonds, in the spinning whirl of freedom, does personal responsibility arise which in the end can no longer lean with its burden of decision on any church or society or culture, but is lonely in face of Present Being.

In an age which is losing form, the highly praised "personalities," who know how to serve its fictitious forms and in their name to dominate the age, count in the truth of what is happening no more than those who lament the genuine forms of the past and are diligent to restore them. The ones who count are those persons who—though they may be of little renown—respond to and are responsible for the continuation of the living spirit, each in the active stillness of his sphere of work.

The question which is always being brought forward—"To

where, to what, must we educate?"—misunderstands the situation. Only times which know a figure of general validity—the
Christian, the gentleman, the citizen—know an answer to that
question, not necessarily in words, but by pointing with the finger
to the figure which rises clear in the air, out-topping all. The
forming of this figure in all individuals, out of all materials, is
the formation of a "culture." But when all figures are shattered,
when no figure is able any more to dominate and shape the present human material, what is there left to form?

Nothing but the image of God.

.   .   .   .

KNOWLEDGE IS SOMETHING DIFFERENT FROM PERCEPTION*

Plato

Soc. Then now, Theaetetus, take another view of the subject: you answered that knowledge is perception?

Theaet. I did.

Soc. And if any one were to ask you: With what does a man see black and white colors? and with what does he hear high and low sounds?—you would say, if I am not mistaken, "With the eyes and with the ears."

Theaet. I should.

Soc. The free use of words and phrases, rather than minute precision, is generally characteristic of a liberal education, and the opposite is pedantic; but sometimes precision is necessary, and I believe that the answer which you have just given is open to the charge of incorrectness; for which is more correct, to say that we see or hear with the eyes and with the ears, or through the eyes and through the ears.

Theaet. I should say "through," Socrates, rather than "with."

Soc. Yes, my boy, for no one can suppose that in each of us, as in a sort of Trojan horse, there are perched a number of unconnected senses, which do not all meet in some one nature, the soul or whatever we please to call it, of which they are the instruments, and with which through them we perceive objects of sense.

Theaet. I agree with you in that opinion.

Soc. The reason why I am thus precise is because I want to know whether, when we perceive black and white through the eyes, and again, other qualities through other organs, we do not perceive them with one and the same part of ourselves; and whether, if you were asked, you could refer all such perceptions

* Reprinted from Benjamin Jowett, trans., *The Dialogues of Plato,* 4th ed., 3 (Oxford: Clarendon Press, 1953): 285–88. By permission of the Clarendon Press, Oxford. Socrates and Theaetetus (the name, also, of the dialogue) here discuss some points about the nature of knowledge.

to the body. Perhaps, however, I had better allow you to answer for yourself and not interfere. Tell me, then, are not the organs through which you perceive warm and hard and light and sweet, organs of the body?

Theaet. Of the body, certainly.

Soc. And you would admit that what you perceive through one faculty you cannot perceive through another; the objects of hearing, for example, cannot be perceived through sight, or the objects of sight through hearing?

Theaet. Of course not.

Soc. If you have any thought about both of them, this common perception cannot come to you, either through the one or the other organ?

Theaet. It cannot.

Soc. How about sounds and colors: in the first place you may reflect that they both *exist*?

Theaet. Yes.

Soc. And that either of them is different from the other, and the same with itself?

Theaet. Certainly.

Soc. And that both are two and each of them one?

Theaet. Yes.

Soc. You can further observe whether they are like or unlike one another?

Theaet. I dare say.

Soc. But through what do you perceive all this about them? for neither through hearing nor yet through seeing can you apprehend that which they have in common. Let me give you an illustration of the point at issue: If there were any meaning in asking whether sounds and colors are saline or not, you would be able to tell me what faculty would consider the question. It would not be sight or hearing, but some other.

Theaet. Certainly; the faculty of taste.

Soc. Very good; and now tell me what is the power which discerns, not only in sensible objects, but in all things, universal properties, such as those which are called being and not-being, and those others about which we were just asking—what organs will you assign for the perception of these by the appropriate power in us?

Theaet. You are thinking of being and not-being, likeness and unlikeness, sameness and difference, and also of unity and any other number which occurs in our judgment of objects. And evidently your question applies to odd and even numbers and other arithmetical conceptions—through what bodily organ the soul perceives them.

Soc. You follow me excellently, Theaetetus; that is precisely what I am asking.

Theaet. Indeed, Socrates, I cannot answer; my only notion is that these, unlike objects of sense, have no separate organ, but that the mind, by a power of her own, contemplates such common properties in all things.

Soc. You are a beauty, Theaetetus, and not ugly, as Theodorus was saying; for he who utters the beautiful is himself beautiful and good. And besides being beautiful, you have done me a kindness in releasing me from a very long discussion if you believe that the soul views some things by herself and others through the bodily organs. For that was my own opinion, and I wanted you to agree with me.

Theaet. Indeed, I do believe it.

Soc. And to which class would you refer being or essence; for this, of all our notions, is the most universal?

Theaet. I should say, to that class which the soul aspires to know of herself.

Soc. And would you say this also of like and unlike, same and other?

Theaet. Yes.

Soc. And would you say the same of the noble and base, and of good and evil?

Theaet. These also I conceive to be among the chief instances of those relative terms whose nature the soul perceives by comparing in herself things past and present with the future.

Soc. Hold! does she not perceive the hardness of that which is hard by the touch, and the softness of that which is soft equally by the touch?

Theaet. Yes.

Soc. But their *being,* I mean the fact that they are, and their opposition to one another, and the being (to repeat that term) of this opposition, the soul herself endeavours to decide for us by the review and comparison of them?

Theaet. Certainly.

Soc. The simple sensations which reach the soul through the body are given at birth to men and animals by nature, but their reflections on the being and use of them are slowly and hardly gained, if they are ever gained, by education and long experience.

Theaet. Assuredly.

Soc. And can a man attain truth who fails of attaining being?

Theaet. Impossible.

Soc. And can he who misses the truth of anything have a knowledge of that thing?

Theaet. He cannot.

Soc. Then knowledge does not consist in impressions of sense, but in reasoning about them; in that only, and not in the mere impression, truth and being can be attained?

Theaet. Apparently.

Soc. And would you call the two processes by the same name, when there is so great a difference between them?

Theaet. That would certainly not be right.

Soc. And what name would you give to seeing, hearing, smelling, being cold, and being hot.

Theaet. I should call all of them perceiving—what other name could be given to them?

Soc. Perception would be the collective name of them?

Theaet. Certainly.

Soc. Which, as we say, has no part in the attainment of truth, since it does not attain to being?

Theaet. Certainly not.

Soc. And therefore not in knowledge?

Theaet. No.

Soc. Then perception, Theaetetus, can never be the same as knowledge?

Theaet. Apparently not, Socrates; and knowledge has now been most distinctly proved to be different from perception.

Soc. But the original aim of our discussion was to find out rather what knowledge is than what it is not; at the same time we have made some progress, for we no longer seek for knowledge in perception at all, but in that other process, however called, in which the mind is alone and engaged with being.

Theaet. And that, Socrates, if I am not mistaken, is called thinking or opining.

Soc. You conceive truly. . . .

PART THREE

CURRICULUM AS A FIELD OF STUDY

INTRODUCTION

Let us take it for granted that improving inquiry into curricular problems depends in good measure on our ability to "let go"—to question what we usually take for granted and to move beyond established resources and habits. The selections in this part were brought together because they question various elements of our curricular conventional wisdom or suggest somewhat novel approaches.

None of the papers provides a blueprint for action. In this area we must grope. Indeed, if Schwab (22) and Hirst (23) are correct, there is no possibility of developing anything like a blueprint in the foreseeable future. From somewhat different bases, both authors argue, explicitly or in effect, that current schemata serving as educational or curricular theory grossly misconceive the nature and function of a theory developed to guide practical activities. Both authors point to a variety of narrow, overly simple conceptions that render us unable to appreciate, let alone manage, the complexity of the problems involved in improving curricular theory and practice.

Schwab and Hirst both sharply distinguish scientific theories, which are organized to further the pursuit of knowledge, from practical theories, which may include scientific theories but are developed to guide some practical activities, like curricular activities. Both of these noted theoreticians, and Schwab in particular, press the need for improving the neglected arts of making practical decisions in concrete circumstances. The arts of the practical are not viewed as being antitheoretical or atheoretical, but as including more than the theoretical. At this stage, the "more than" cannot be set out in detail, but some indications are given of new orientations or emphases in the training and organization of curriculum specialists, in research and communication, in policy formation, and in other activities. The papers by Schwab and Hirst are comprehensive and can serve to raise numerous questions, including questions about the time-honored distinction between theory and practice.

Heslep (24) has some doubts about the customary practice and principle of defining objectives in behavioral terms. He proposes the possibility that the concept of action is an improvement over the concept of behavior in the study of educational problems. Comparison of the concepts of behavior and action may stimulate questions about the relations of freedom and intelligence to "rule-conforming behavior" and the relations of individual purpose to social or objective values.

In curricular activities we are often concerned about such matters as distinguishing means from ends and causes from effects, giving "proofs" or reasons for conclusions, classifying our objects of study and organizing them from the "simple" to the "complex," giving due consideration to both "individual" and "social" factors in a problem. Are there philosophical principles which unify and illuminate such diverse activities? Cohen's thesis of systematic relativism (25) may be seen as one touchstone for consistent and comprehensive thought in such matters, providing we agree with it. There are, of course, many other possible touchstones.

However, Jaspers (26) argues not only against the just-mentioned ideal of consistency but against the view that any criteria of rationality can justify our actions and decisions. Assuming that rationality involves the use of ultimately unsupported reasons, Jaspers contends that commitment to rationality should be replaced by commitment to other values.

Somerville's paper (27) raises the problem of defining significant problems to investigate. He offers some criteria for assessing the worthiness of proposed problems. With his paper we seem to have come full circle, for surely the question he raises, when applied to curricular matters, will lead us at least to problems and proposals considered in preceding sections of this reader.

Suggested Reading

Barnett, George, ed., *Philosophy and Educational Development* (Boston: Houghton Mifflin Company, 1966), Chs. 3–4, 6.

Kaplan, Abraham, *The Conduct of Inquiry* (San Francisco: Chandler Publishing Company, 1964).

Rudner, Richard S., *Philosophy of Social Science* (Englewood Cliffs, N.J.: Prentice-Hall, Inc., 1966).

Scheffler, Israel, *Science and Subjectivity* (Indianapolis: Bobbs-Merrill Co., Inc., 1967).

Tykociner, Joseph T., "Zetetics and Areas of Knowledge," in Stanley Elam, ed., *Education and the Structure of Knowledge* (Chicago: Rand McNally and Co., 1964), pp. 120–47.

Wallia, C. S., ed., *Toward Century 21: Technology, Society and Human Values* (New York: Basic Books, Inc., 1970).

THE PRACTICAL: A LANGUAGE
FOR CURRICULUM*

Joseph J. Schwab

I shall have three points. The first is this: that the field of curriculum is moribund, unable by its present methods and principles
to continue its work and desperately in search of new and more
effective principles and methods.

The second point: the curriclm field has reached this unhappy
state by inveterate and unexamined reliance on theory in an area
where theory is partly inappropriate in the first place and where
the theories extant, even where appropriate, are inadequate to the
tasks which the curriculum field sets them. There are honorable
exceptions to this rule, but too few (and too little honored) to
alter the state of affairs.

The third point, which constitutes my thesis: there will be a
renaissance of the field of curriculum, a renewed capacity to contribute to the quality of American education, only if the bulk of
curriculum energies are diverted from the theoretic to the practical, to the quasipractical, and to the eclectic. By "eclectic" I
mean the arts by which unsystematic, uneasy, but usable focus
on a body of problems is effected among diverse theories, each
relevant to the problems in a different way. By the "practical" I
do *not* mean the curbstone practicality of the mediocre administrator and the man on the street for whom the practical means
the easily achieved, familiar goals which can be reached by familiar means. I refer, rather, to a complex discipline, relatively
unfamiliar to the academic and differing radically from the disciplines of the theoretic. It is the discipline concerned with choice
and action, in contrast with the theoretic, which is concerned with
knowledge. Its methods lead to defensible decisions, where the
methods of the theoretic lead to warranted conclusions, and
differ radically from the methods and competences entailed in

* Reprinted from *School Review*, 78 (1969): 1–23, by permission of
the author. Copyright 1969 by Joseph J. Schwab.

the theoretic. I shall sketch some of the defining aspects of practical discipline at the appropriate time.

A Crisis of Principle

The frustrated state of the field of curriculum is not an idiopathology and not a condition which warrants guilt or shame on the part of its practitioners. All fields of systematic intellectual activity are liable to such crises. They are so because any intellectual discipline must begin its endeavors with untested principles. In its beginnings, its subject matter is relatively unknown, its problems unsolved, indeed, unidentified. It does not know what questions to ask, what other knowledge to rest upon, what data to seek or what to make of them once they are elicited. It requires a preliminary and necessarily untested guide to its inquiries. It finds this guide by borrowing, by invention, or by analogy, in the shape of a hazardous commitment to the character of its problems or its subject matter and a commitment to untried canons of evidence and rules of inquiry. What follows these commitments is years of their application, pursuit of the mode of inquiry demanded by the principles to which the field has committed itself. To the majority of practitioners of any field, these years of inquiry appear only as pursuit of knowledge of its subject matter or solution of its problems. They take the guiding principles of the inquiry as givens. These years of inquiry, however, are something more than pursuit of knowledge or solution of problems. They are also tests, reflexive and pragmatic, of the principles which guide the inquiries. They determine whether, in fact, the data demanded by the principles can be elicited and whether, if elicited, they can be made to constitute knowledge adequate to the complexity of the subject matter, or solutions which, in fact, do solve the problems with which the inquiry began.

In the nature of the case, these reflexive tests of the principles of inquiry are, more often than not, partially or wholly negative, for, after all, the commitment to these principles was made before there was well-tested fruit of inquiry by which to guide the commitment. The inadequacies of principles begin to show, in the case of theoretical inquires, by failures of the subject matter to respond to the questions put to it, by incoherencies and contradictions in data and in conclusions which cannot be resolved, or by clear disparities between the knowledge yielded by the inquiries and the behaviors of the subject matter which the knowledge purports to represent. In the case of practical inquires, inadequacies begin to show by incapacity to arrive at solutions to the problems, by inability to realize the solutions proposed, by mutual frustrations and cancelings out as solutions are put into effect.

Although these exhaustions and failures of principles may go unnoted by practitioners in the field, at least at the conscious level, what may not be represented in consciousness is nevertheless evidenced by behavior and appears in the literature and the activities of the field as signs of the onset of a crisis of principle. These signs consist of a large increase in the frequency of published papers and colloquia marked by a *flight from the subject of the field*. There are usually six signs of this flight or directions in which the flight occurs.

Signs of Crisis

The first and most important, though often least conspicuous, sign is a flight of the field itself, a translocation of its problems and the solving of them from the nominal practitioners of the field to other men. Thus one crucial frustration of the science of genetics was resolved by a single contribution from an insurance actuary. The recent desuetude of academic physiology has been marked by a conspicuous increase in the frequency of published solutions to physiological problems by medical researchers. In similar fashion, the increasing depletion of psychoanalytic principles and methods in recent years was marked by the onset of contributions to its lore by internists, biochemists, and anthropologists.

A second flight is a flight upward, from discourse about the subject of the field to discourse about the discourse of the field, from *use* of principles and methods to *talk* about them, from grounded conclusions to the construction of models, from theory to metatheory and from metatheory to metametatheory.

A third flight is downward, an attempt by practitioners to return to the subject matter in a state of innocence, shorn not only of current principles but of all principles, in an effort to take a new, a pristine and unmediated look at the subject matter. For example, one conspicuous reaction to the warfare of numerous inadequate principles in experimental psychology has been the resurgence of ethology, which begins as an attempt to return to a pure natural history of behavior, to intensive observation and recording of the behavior of animals undisturbed in their natural habitat, by observers, equally undisturbed by mediating conceptions, attempting to record anything and everything they see before them.

A fourth flight is to the sidelines, to the role of observer, commentator, historian, and critic of the contributions of others to the field.

A fifth sign consists of marked perseveration, a repetition of old and familiar knowledge in new languages which add little or nothing to the old meanings as embodied in the older and familiar language, or repetition of old and familiar formulations by way of criticisms or minor additions and modifications.

The sixth is a marked increase in eristic, contentious, and ad hominem debate.

I hasten to remark that these signs of crisis are not all or equally reprehensible. There is little excuse for the increase in contentiousness nor much value in the flight to the sidelines or in perseveration; but the others, in one way or another, can contribute to resolution of the crisis. The flight of the field itself is one of the more fruitful ways by which analogical principles are disclosed, modified, and adapted to the field in crisis. The flight upward, to models and metatheory, if done responsibly, which means with a steady eye on the actual problems and conditions of the field for which the models are ostensibly constructed, becomes, in fact, the proposal and test of possible new principles for the field. The flight backward, to a state of innocence, is at least an effort to break the grip of old habits of thought and thus leave space for needed new ones, though it is clear that in the matter of inquiry, as elsewhere, virginity, once lost, cannot be regained.

In the present context, however, the virtue or vice of these various flights is beside the point. We are concerned with them as signs of collapse of principles in a field, and it is my contention, based on a study not yet complete, that most of these signs may now be seen in the field of curriculum. I shall only suggest, not cite, my evidence.

The Case of Curriculum

With respect to flight of the field itself, there can be little doubt. Of the five substantial high school science curricula, four of them—PSSC, BSCS, Chems, and CBA—were instituted and managed by subject matter specialists; the contribution of educators was small, and that of curriculum specialists near vanishing point. Only Harvard Project Physics, at this writing not yet available, appears to be an exception. To one of two elementary science projects, a psychologist appears to have made a substantial contribution but curriculum specialists very little. The other—the Elementary Science Study—appears to have been substantially affected (to its advantage) by educators with one or both feet in curriculum. The efforts of the Commission on Undergraduate Education in the Biological Sciences have been carried on almost entirely by subject matter specialists. The English Curriculum Study Centers appear to be in much the same state as the high school science curricula: overwhelmingly centered on subject specialists. Educators contribute expertise only in the area of test construction and evaluation, with here and there a contribution by a psychologist. Educators, including curriculum specialists, were massively unprepared to cope with the problem of integrated education and only by little, and late, and by trial and error, put together the halting solutions currently known as Head Start. The problems posed by the current drives toward ethnicity in education find curriculum specialists even more massively oblivious and unprepared. And I so far find myself very much alone with respect to the curriculum problems immanent in the phenomena of student protest and student revolt. (Of the social studies curriculum efforts, I shall say nothing at this time.)

On the second flight—upward—I need hardly comment. The models, the metatheory, and the metametatheory are all over the place. Many of them, moreover, are irresponsible—concerned less with the barriers to continued productivity in the field of curriculum than with exploitation of the exotic and the fashionable among forms and models of theory and metatheory: systems theory, symbolic logic, language analysis. Many others, including responsible ones, are irreversible flights upward or sideways. That is, they are models or metatheories concerned not with the judgment, the reasoned construction, or reconstruction of curriculums but with other matters—for example, how curriculum changes occur or how changes can be managed.

The flight downward, the attempt at return to a pristine, unmediated look at the subject matter, is, for some reason, a missing symptom in the case of curriculum. There are returns—to the classroom, if not to other levels or aspects of curriculum—with a measure of effort to avoid preconceptions (e.g., Smith, Bellack, and studies of communication nets and lines), but the frequency of such studies has not markedly increased. The absence of this symptom may have significance. In general, however, it is characteristic of diseases that the whole syndrome does not appear in all cases. Hence, pending further study and thought, I do not count this negative instance as weakening the diagnosis of a crisis of principle.

The fourth flight—to the sidelines—is again a marked symptom of the field of curriculum. Histories, anthologies, commentaries, criticisms, and proposals of curriculums multiply.

Perseveration is also marked. I recoil from counting the persons and books whose lives are made possible by continuing restatement of the Tyler rationale, of the character and case for behavioral objectives, of the virtues and vices of John Dewey.

The rise in frequency and intensity of the eristic and ad hominem is also marked. Thus one author climaxes a series of petulances by the remark that what he takes to be his own forte "has always been rare—and shows up in proper perspective the happy breed of educational reformer who can concoct a brand new, rabble-rousing theory of educational reform while waiting for the water to fill the bathtub."

There is little doubt, in short, that the field of curriculum is in a crisis of principle.

A crisis of principle arises, as I have suggested, when principles are exhausted—when the questions they permit have all been asked and answered—or when the efforts at inquiry instigated by the principles have at last exhibited their inadequacy to the subject matter and the problems which they were designed to attack. My second point is that the latter holds in the case of curriculum: the curriculum movement has been inveterately theoretic, and its theoretic bent has let it down. A brief conspectus of instances will suggest the extent of this theoretic bent and what is meant by "theoretic."

Characteristics of Theory

Consider first the early, allegedly Herbartian efforts (recently revived by Bruner). These efforts took the view that ideas were formed by children out of received notions and experiences of things, and that these ideas functioned thereafter as discriminators and organizers of what was later learned. Given this view, the aim of curriculum was to discriminate the right ideas (by way of analysis of extant bodies of knowledge), determine the order in which they could be learned by children as they developed, and thereafter present these ideas at the right times with clarity, associations, organization, and application. A theory of mind and knowledge thus solves by one mighty coup the problem of what to teach, when, and how; and what is fatally theoretic here is not the presence of a theory of mind and a theory of knowledge, though their presence is part of the story, but the dispatch, the sweeping appearance of success, the vast simplicity which grounds this purported solution to the problem of curriculum. And lest we think that this faith in the possibility of successful neatness, dispatch, and sweeping generality is a mark of the past, consider the concern of the National Science Teachers Association only four years ago "with identifying the broad principles that can apply to any and all curriculum development efforts in science," a concern crystallized in just seven "conceptual schemes" held to underlie all science. With less ambitious sweepingness but with the same steadfast concern for a single factor —in this case, a supposed fixed structure of knowledge—one finds similar efforts arising from the Association of College Teachers of Education, from historians, even from teachers of literature.

Consider, now, some of the numerous efforts to ground curriculum in derived objectives. One effort seeks the ground of its objectives in social need and finds its social needs in just those facts about its culture which are sought and found under the aegis of a single conception of culture. Another grounds its objectives in the social needs identified by a single theory of history and of political evolution.

A third group of searches for objectives are grounded in theories of personality. The persuasive coherence and plausibility of Freudianism persuaded its followers to aim to supply children with adequate channels of sublimation of surplus libido, appropriate objects and occasions for aggressions, a properly undemanding ego ideal, and an intelligent minimum of taboos. Interpersonal theories direct their adherents to aim for development of abilities to relate to peers, "infeers," and "supeers," in relations nurturant and receiving, adaptive, vying, approving, and disapproving. Theories of actualization instruct their adherents to determine the salient potentialities of each child and to see individually to the development of each.

Still other searches for objectives seek their aims in the knowledge needed to "live in the modern world," in the attitudes and habits which minimize dissonance with the prevailing mores of one's community or social class, in the skills required for success in a trade or vocation, in the ability to participate effectively as a member of a group. Still others are grounded in some quasi-ethics; some view of the array of goods which are good for man.

Three features of these typical efforts at curriculum making are significant here, each of which has its own lesson to teach us. First, each is grounded in a theory as such. We shall return to this point in a moment. Second, each is grounded in a theory from the social or behavioral sciences: psychology, psychiatry, politics, sociology, history. Even the ethical bases and theories of "mind" are behavioral. To this point, too, we shall return in a moment. Third, they are theories concerning *different* subject matters. One curriculum effort is grounded in concern for the individual, another in concern for groups, others in concern for cultures, communities, societies, minds, or the extant bodies of knowledge.[1]

Need for an Eclectic

The significance of this third feature is patent to the point of embarrassment: no curriculum grounded in but one of these subjects can possibly be adequate, defensible. A curriculum based on theory about individual personality which thrusts society, its demands, and its structure far into the background or ignores them entirely can be nothing but incomplete and doctrinaire; for the individuals in question are in fact members of a society and must meet its demands to some minimum degree since their existence and prosperity as individuals depend on the functioning of their society. In the same way, a curriculum grounded only in a view of social need or social change must be equally doctrinaire and incomplete, for societies do not exist only for their own sakes but for the prosperity of their members as individuals as well. In the same way, learners are not only minds or knowers but bundles of affects, individuals, personalities, earners of livings. They are not only group interactors but possessors of private lives.

---

[1] It should be clear by now that "theory" as used in this paper does *not* refer only to grand schemes such as the general theory of relativity, kinetic-molecular theory, the Bohr atom, the Freudian construction of a tripartite psyche. The attempt to give an account of human maturation by the discrimination of definite states (e.g., oral, anal, genital), an effort to aggregate human competences into a small number of primary mental abilities—these, too, are theoretic. So also are efforts to discriminate a few large classes of persons and to attribute to them defining behaviors: e.g., the socially mobile, the culturally deprived, the creative.

It is clear, I submit, that a defensible curriculum or plan of curriculum must be one which somehow takes account of all these sub-subjects which pertain to man. It cannot take only one and ignore the others; it cannot even take account of many of them and ignore one. Not only is each of them a constituent and a condition for decent human existence, but each interpenetrates the others. That is, the character of human personalities is a determiner of human society and the behavior of human groups. Conversely, the conditions of group behavior and the character of societies determine in some large part the personalities which their members develop, the way their minds work, and what they can learn and use by way of knowledge and competence. These various "things" (individuals, societies, cultures, patterns of inquiry, "structures" of knowledge or of inquiries, apperceptive masses, problem solving), though discriminable as separate subjects of differing modes of inquiry, are nevertheless parts or affectors of one another, or coactors. (Their very separation for purposes of inquiry is what marks the outcomes of such inquires as "theoretic" and consequently incomplete.) In practice, they constitute one complex, organic agency. Hence, a focus on only one not only ignores the others but vitiates the quality and completeness with which the selected one is viewed.

It is equally clear, however, that there is not, and will not be in the foreseeable future, one theory of this complex whole which is other than a collection of unusable generalities. Nor is it true that the lack of a theory of the whole is due to the narrowness, stubbornness, or merely habitual specialism of social and behavioral scientists. Rather, their specialism and the restricted purview of their theories are functions of their subject, its enormous complexity, its vast capacity for difference and change. Man's competence at the construction of theoretical knowledge is so far most inadequate when applied to the subject of man. There have been efforts to conceive principles of inquiry which would encompass the whole variety and complexity of humanity, but they have fallen far short of adequacy to the subject matter or have demanded the acquisition of data and modes of interpretation of data beyond our capabilities. There *are* continuing efforts to find bridging terms which would relate the principles of inquiry of one subfield of the social sciences to another and thus begin to effect connections among our knowledges of each, but successful bridges are so far few and narrow and permit but a trickle of connection. As far, then, as theoretical knowledge is concerned, we must wrestle as best we can with numerous, largely unconnected, separate theories of these many, artificially discriminated sub-subjects of man.

I remarked in the beginning that renewal of the field of curriculum would require diversion of the bulk of its energies from theory to the practical, the quasi-practical, and the eclectic. The state of affairs just described, the existence and the necessarily continuing existence of separate theories of separate sub-subjects distributed among the social sciences, constitutes the case for one of these modes, the necessity of an eclectic, of arts by which a usable focus on a common body of problems is effected among theories which lack theoretical connection. The argument can be simply summarized. A curriculum grounded in but one or a few sub-subjects of the social sciences is indefensible; contributions from all are required. There is no foreseeable hope of a unified theory in the immediate or middle future, nor of a meta-theory which will tell us how to put those sub-subjects together or order them in a fixed hierarchy of importance to the problems of curriculum. What remains as a viable alternative is the unsystematic, uneasy, pragmatic, and uncertain unions and connections which can be affected in an eclectic. And I must add, anticipating our discussion of the practical, that *changing* connections and *differing* orderings at different times of these separate theories, will characterize a sound eclectic.

The character of eclectic arts and procedures must be left for discussion on another occasion. Let it suffice for the moment that witness of the high effectiveness of eclectic methods and of their accessibility is borne by at least one field familiar to us all—Western medicine. It has been enormously effective, and the growth of its competence dates from its disavowal of a single doctrine and its turn to eclecticism.

The Place of the Practical

I turn now from the fact that the theories which ground curriculum plans pertain to different sub-subjects of a common field, to the second of the three features which characterize our typical instances of curriculum planning—the fact that the ground of each plan is a theory, a theory as such.

The significance of the existence of theory as such at the base of curricular planning consists of what it is that theory does not and cannot encompass. All theories, even the best of them in the simplest sciences, necessarily neglect some aspects and facets of the facts of the case. A theory covers and formulates the *regularities* among the things and events it subsumes. It abstracts a general or ideal case. It leaves behind the nonuniformities, the particularities, which characterize each concrete instance of the facts subsumed. Moreover, in the process of idealization, theoretical inquiry may often leave out of consideration conspicuous facets of *all* cases because its substantive principles of inquiry or its methods cannot handle them. Thus the constantly accelerating body of classical mechanics was the acceleration of a body in "free" fall, in a perfect vacuum, and the general or theoretical rule formulated in classical mechanics is far from describing the fall of actual bodies in actual mediums—the only kinds of fall then known. The force equation of classical dynamics applied to bodies of visible magnitudes ignores friction. The rule that light varies inversely as the square of the distance holds exactly only for an imaginary point source of light. For real light sources of increasing expanse, the so-called law holds more and more approximately, and for very large sources it affords little or no usable information. And what is true of the best of theories in the simplest sciences is true a fortiori in the social sciences. Their subject matters are apparently so much more variable, and clearly so much more complex, that their theories encompass much less of their subjects than do the theories of the physical and biological sciences.

Yet curriculum is brought to bear not on ideal or abstract representatives but on the real thing, on the concrete case in all its completeness and with all its differences from all other concrete cases on which the theoretic abstraction is silent. The materials of a concrete curriculum will not consist merely of portions of "science," of "literature," of "process." On the contrary, their constituents will be particular assertions about selected matters couched in a particular vocabulary, syntax, and rhetoric. They will be particular novels, short stories, or lyric poems, each, for better or for worse, with its own flavor. They will be particular acts upon particular matters in a given sequence. The curriculum will be brought to bear not in some archetypical classroom but in a particular locus in time and space with smells, shadows, seats, and conditions outside its walls which may have much to do with what is achieved inside. Above all, the supposed beneficiary is not the generic child, not even a class or kind of child out of the psychological or sociological literature pertaining to the child. The beneficiaries will consist of very local kinds of children and, within the local kinds, individual children. The same diversity holds with respect to teachers and what they do. The generalities about science, about literature, about children in general, about children or teachers of some specified class or kind, may be true. But they attain this status in virtue of what they leave out, and the omissions affect what remains. A Guernsey cow is not only something more than cow, having specific features omitted from description of the genus; it is also cowy in ways differing from the cowiness of a Texas longhorn. The specific not only adds to the generic; it also modulates it.

These ineluctable characteristics of theory and the consequent ineluctable disparities between real things and their representation in theory constitute one argument for my thesis, that a large bulk of curriculum energies must be diverted from the theoretic, not only to the eclectic but to the practical and the quasi-practical. The argument, again, can be briefly summarized. The stuff of theory is abstract or idealized representations of real things. But curriculum in action treats real things: real acts, real teachers, real children, things richer and different from their theoretical representations. Curriculum will deal badly with its real things if it treats them merely as replicas of their theoretic representations. If, then, theory is to be used well in the determination of curricular practice, it requires a supplement. It requires arts which bring a theory to its application: first, arts which identify the disparities between real thing and theoretic representation; second, arts which modify the theory in the course of its application, in the light of the discrepancies; and, third, arts which devise ways of taking account of the many aspects of the real thing which the theory does not take into account. These are some of the arts of the practical.

Theories from Social Sciences

The significance of the third feature of our typical instances of curriculum work—that their theories are mainly theories from the social and behavioral sciences—will carry us to the remainder of the argument for the practical. Nearly all theories in all the behavioral sciences are marked by the coexistence of competing theories. There is not one theory of personality but twenty, representing at least six radically different choices of what is relevant and important in human behavior. There is not one theory of groups but several. There is not one theory of learning but half a dozen. All the social and behavioral sciences are marked by "schools," each distinguished by a different choice of principle of inquiry, each of which selects from the intimidating complexities of the subject matter the small fraction of the whole with which it can deal.

The theories which arise from inquiries so directed are, then, radically incomplete, each of them incomplete to the extent that competing theories take hold of different aspects of the subject of inquiry and treat it in a different way. Further, there is perennial invention of new principles which bring to light new facets of the subject matter, new relations among the facets and new ways of treating them. In short, there is every reason to suppose that any one of the extant theories of behavior is a pale and incomplete representation of actual behavior. There is similar reason to suppose that if all the diversities of fact, the different aspects of behavior treated in each theory, were somehow to be brought within the bounds of a single theory, that theory would still fall short of comprehending the whole of human behavior—in two respects. In the first place, it would not comprehend what there may be of human behavior which we do not see by virtue of the restricted light by which we examine behavior. In the second place, such a single theory will necessarily interpret its data in the light of its one set of principles, assigning to these data only one set of significances and establishing among them only one set of relations. It will remain the case, then, that a diversity of theories may tell us more than a single one, even though the "factual" scope of the many and the one are the same.

It follows, then, that such theories are not, and will not be, adequate by themselves to tell us what to do with human beings or how to do it. What they variously suggest and the contrary guidances they afford to choice and action must be mediated and combined by eclectic arts and must be massively supplemented, as well as mediated, by knowledge of some other kind derived from another source.

Some areas of choice and action with respect to human behavior have long since learned this lesson. Government is made possible by a lore of politics derived from immediate experience of the vicissitudes and tangles of legislating and administering. Institution of economic guidances and controls owes as much to unmediated experience of the marketplace as it does to formulas and theories. Even psychotherapy has long since deserted its theories of personality as sole guides to therapy and relies as much or more on the accumulated, explicitly nontheoretic lore accumulated by practitioners, as it does on theory or eclectic combinations of theory. The law has systematized the accumulation of direct experience of actual cases in its machinery for the recording of cases and opinions as precedents which continuously monitor, supplement, and modify the meaning and application of its formal "knowledge," its statutes. It is this recourse to accumulated lore, to experience of actions and their consequences, to action and reaction at the level of the concrete case, which constitutes the heart of the practical. It is high time that curriculum do likewise.

The Practical Arts

The arts of the practical are onerous and complex; hence only a sampling must suffice to indicate the character of this discipline and the changes in educational investigation which would ensue on adoption of the discipline. I shall deal briefly with four aspects of it.

The practical arts begin with the requirement that existing institutions and existing practices be preserved and altered piecemeal, not dismantled and replaced. It is further necessary that changes be so planned and so articulated with what remains unchanged that the functioning of the whole remain coherent and unimpaired. These necessities stem from the very nature of the practical—that it is concerned with the maintenance and improvement of patterns of purposed action, and especially concerned that the effects of the pattern through time shall retain coherence and relevance to one another.

This is well seen in the case of the law. Statutes are repealed or largely rewritten only as a last resort, since to do so creates confusion and diremption between old judgments under the law and judgments to come, confusion which must lead either to weakening of law through disrepute or a painful and costly process of repairing the effects of past judgments so as to bring them into conformity with the new. It is vastly more desirable that changes be instituted in small degrees and in immediate adjustment to the peculiarities of particular new cases which call forth the change.

The consequence, in the case of the law, of these demands of the practical is that the servants of the law must know the law through and through. They must know the statutes themselves, the progression of precedents and interpretations which have effected changes in them, and especially the present state of affairs—the most recent decisions under the law and the calendar of cases which will be most immediately affected by contemplated additions to precedent and interpretation.

The same requirements would hold for a practical program of improvement of education. It, too, would effect its changes in small progressions, in coherence with what remains unchanged, and this would require that we know *what is and has been going on in American schools.*

At present, we do not know. My own incomplete investigations convince me that we have not the faintest reliable knowledge of how literature is taught in the high schools, or what actually goes on in science classrooms. There are a dozen different ways in which the novel can be read. Which ones are used by whom, with whom, and to what effect? What selections from the large accumulation of biological knowledge are made and taught in this school system and that, to what classes and kinds of children, to what effect? To what extent is science taught as verbal formulas, as congeries of unrelated facts, as so-called principles and conceptual structures, as outcomes of inquiry? In what degree and kind of simplification and falsification is scientific inquiry conveyed, if it is conveyed at all?

A count of textbook adoptions will not tell us, for teachers select from textbooks and alter their treatment (often quite properly) and can frustrate and negate the textbook's effort to alter the pattern of instruction. We cannot tell from lists of objectives, since they are usually so vastly ambiguous that almost anything can go on under their aegis or, if they are not ambiguous, reflect pious hopes as much as actual practice. We cannot tell from lists of "principles" and "conceptual structures," since these, in their telegraphic brevity, are also ambiguous and say nothing of the shape in which they are taught or the extent.

What is wanted is a totally new and extensive pattern of *empirical* study of classroom action and reaction; a study, not as basis for theoretical concerns about the nature of the teaching or learning process, but as a basis for beginning to know what we are doing, what we are not doing, and to what effect—what changes are needed, which needed changes can be instituted with what costs or economies, and how they can be effected with minimum tearing of the remaining fabric of educational effort.

This is an effort which will require new mechanisms of empirical investigation, new methods of reportage, a new class of educational researchers, and much money. It is an effort without which we will continue largely incapable of making defensible decisions about curricular changes, largely unable to put them into effect and ignorant of what real consequences, if any, our efforts have had.

A very large part of such a study would, I repeat, be direct and empirical study of action and reaction in the classroom itself, not merely the testing of student change. But one of the most interesting and visible alterations of present practice which might be involved is a radical change in our pattern of testing students. The common pattern tries to determine the extent to which *intended* changes have been brought about. This would be altered to an effort to find out what changes have occurred, to determine side effects as well as mainline consequences, since the distinction between these two is always in the eye of the intender and side effects may be as great in magnitude and as fatal or healthful for students as the intended effects.

A second facet of the practical: its actions are undertaken with respect to identified frictions and failures in the machine and inadequacies evidenced in felt shortcomings of its products. This origin of its actions leads to two marked differences in operation from that of theory. Under the control of theory, curricular changes have their origin in new notions of persons, group or society, mind or knowledge, which give rise to suggestions of new things curriculum might be or do. This is an origin which, by its nature, takes little or no account of the existing effectiveness of the machine or the consequences to this effectiveness of the institution of novelty. If there is concern for what may be displaced by innovation or for the incoherences which may ensue on the insertion of novelty, the concern is gratuitous. It does not arise from the theoretical considerations which commend the novelty. The practical, on the other hand, because it institutes changes to repair frictions and deficiencies, is commanded to determine the whole array of possible effects of proposed change, to determine what new frictions and deficiencies the proposed change may unintentionally produce.

The other effective difference between theoretical and practical origins of deliberate change is patent. Theory, by being concerned with new things to do, is unconcerned with the successes and failures of present doings. Hence present failures, unless they coincide with what is repaired by the proposed innovations, go unnoticed—as do present successes. The practical, on the other hand, is directly and deliberately concerned with the diagnosis of ills of the curriculum.

These concerns of the practical for frictions and failures of the curricular machine would, again, call for a new and extensive pattern of inquiry. The practical requires curriculum study to seek its problems where its problems lie—in the behaviors, misbehaviors, and nonbehaviors of its students as they begin to evince the effects of the training they did and did not get. This means continuing assessment of students as they leave primary grades for the secondary school, leave secondary school for jobs and colleges. It means sensitive and sophisticated assessment by way of impressions, insights, and reactions of the community which sends its children to the school; employers of students, new echelons of teachers of students; the wives, husbands, and cronies of exstudents; the people with whom exstudents work; the people who work under them. Curriculum study will look into the questions of what games exstudents play; what, if anything, they do about politics and crime in the streets; what they read, if they do; what they watch on television and what they make of what they watch, again, if anything. Such studies would be undertaken, furthermore, not as mass study of products of the American school, taken in toto, but as studies of significantly separable schools and school systems—suburban and inner city, Chicago and Los Angeles, South Bend and Michigan City.

I emphasize sensitive and sophisticated assessment because we are concerned here, as in the laying of background knowledge of what goes in schools, not merely with the degree to which avowed objectives are achieved but also with detecting the failures and frictions of the machine: what it has not done or thought of doing, and what side effects its doings have had. Nor are we concerned with successes and failures only as measured in test situations but also as evidenced in life and work. It is this sort of diagnosis which I have tried to exemplify in a recent treatment of curriculum and student protest.[2]

A third facet of the practical I shall call the anticipatory generation of alternatives. Intimate knowledge of the existing state of affairs, early identification of problem situations, and effective formulation of problems are necessary to effective practical decision but not sufficient. It requires also that there be available to practical deliberation the greatest possible number and fresh diversity of alternative solutions to the problem. The reason for this requirement, in one aspect, is obvious enough: the best choice among poor and shopworn alternatives will still be a poor solution to the problem. Another aspect is less obvious. The problems which arise in an institutional structure which has enjoyed good practical management will be novel problems, arising from changes in the times and circumstances and from the consequences of previous solutions to previous problems. Such problems, with their strong tincture of novelty, cannot be solved by familiar solutions. They cannot be well solved by apparently new solutions arising from old habits of mind and old ways of doing things.

A third aspect of the requirement for anticipatory generation of alternatives is still less obvious. It consists of the fact that practical problems do not present themselves wearing their labels around their necks. Problem situations, to use Dewey's old term, present themselves to consciousness, but the character of the problem, its formulation, does not. This depends on the eye of the beholder. And this eye, unilluminated by possible fresh solutions to problems, new modes of attack, new recognitions of degrees of freedom for change among matters formerly taken to be unalterable, is very likely to miss the novel features of new problems or dismiss them as "impractical." Hence the require-

[2] *College Curriculum and Student Protest* (Chicago: University of Chicago Press, 1969).

ment that the generation of problems be anticipatory and not await the emergence of the problem itself.

To some extent, the *theoretical* bases of curricular change—such items as emphasis on inquiry, on discovery learning, and on structure of the disciplines—contribute to this need but not sufficiently or with the breadth which permits effective deliberation. That is, these theoretic proposals tend to arise in single file, out of connection with other proposals which constitute alternatives, or, more important, constitute desiderata or circumstances which affect the choice or rejection of proposals. Consider, in regard to the problem of the "single file," only one relation between the two recent proposals subsumed under "creativity" and "structure of knowledge." If creativity implies some measure of invention, and "structure of knowledge" implies (as it does in one version) the systematic induction of conceptions as soon as children are ready to grasp them, an issue is joined. To the extent that the latter is timely and well done, scope for the former is curtailed. To the extent that children can be identified as more or less creative, "structure of knowledge" would be brought to bear on different children at different times and in different ways.

A single case, taken from possible academic resources of education, will suggest the new kind of inquiry entailed in the need for anticipatory generation of alternatives. Over the years, critical scholarship has generated, as remarked earlier, a dozen different conceptions of the novel, a dozen or more ways in which the novel can be read, each involving its own emphases and its own arts of recovery of meaning in the act of reading. Novels can be read, for example, as bearers of wisdom, insights into vicissitudes of human life and ways of enduring them. Novels can also be read as moral instructors, as sources of vicarious experience, as occasions for aesthetic experience. They can be read as models of human creativity, as displays of social problems, as political propaganda, as revelations of diversities of manners and morals among different cultures and classes of people, or as symptoms of their age.

Now what, in fact, is the full parade of such possible uses of the novel? What is required by each in the way of competences of reading, discussion, and thought? What are the rewards, the desirable outcomes, which are likely to ensue for students from each kind of reading or combinations of them? For what kinds or classes of students is each desirable? There are further problems demanding anticipatory consideration. If novels are chosen and read as displays of social problems and depictions of social classes, what effect will such instruction in literature have on instruction in the social studies? What will teachers need to know and be able to do in order to enable students to discriminate and appropriately connect the *aperçus* of artists, the accounts of historians, and the conclusions of social scientists on such matters? How will the mode of instruction in science (e.g., as verified truths) and in literature (as "deep insights" or artistic constructions or matters of opinion) affect the effects of each?

The same kinds of questions could be addressed to history and to the social studies generally. Yet, nowhere, in the case of literature, have we been able to find cogent and energetic work addressed to them. The journals in the field of English teaching are nearly devoid of treatment of them. College and university courses, in English or education, which address such problems with a modicum of intellectual content are as scarce as hen's teeth. We cannot even find an unbiased conspectus of critical theory more complete than *The Pooh Perplex*, and treatments of problems of the second kind (pertaining to interaction of literature instruction with instruction in other fields) are also invisible.

Under a soundly practical dispensation in curriculum, the address of such questions would be a high priority and require recruitment to education of philosophers and subject matter specialists of a quality and critical sophistication which it has rarely, if ever, sought.

As the last sampling of the practical, consider its method. It falls under neither of the popular platitudes: it is neither deductive nor inductive. It is deliberative. It cannot be inductive because the target of the method is not a generalization or explanation but a decision about action in a concrete situation. It cannot be deductive because it deals with the concrete case, not abstractions from cases, and the concrete case cannot be settled by mere application of a principle. Almost every concrete case falls under two or more principles, and every concrete case will possess some cogent characteristics which are encompassed in no principle. The problem of selecting an appropriate man for an important post is a case in point. It is not a problem of selecting a representative of the appropriate personality type who exhibits the competences officially required for the job. The man we hire is more than a type and a bundle of competences. He is a multitude of probable behaviors which escape the net of personality theories and cognitive scales. He is endowed with prejudices, mannerisms, habits, tics, and relatives. And all of these manifold particulars will affect his work and the work of those who work for him. It is deliberation which operates in such cases to select the appropriate man.

Commitment to Deliberation

Deliberation is complex and arduous. It treats both ends and means and must treat them as mutually determining one another. It must try to identify, with respect to both, what facts may be relevant. It must try to ascertain the relevant facts in the concrete case. It must try to identify the desiderata in the case. It must generate alternative solutions. It must make every effort to trace the branching pathways of consequences which may flow from each alternative and affect desiderata. It must then weigh alternatives and their costs and consequences against one another and choose, not the right alternative, for there *is* no such thing, but the best one.

I shall mention only one of the new kinds of activity which would ensue on commitment to deliberation. It will require the formation of a new public and new means of communication among its constituent members. Deliberation requires consideration of the widest possible variety of alternatives if it is to be most effective. Each alternative must be viewed in the widest variety of lights. Ramifying consequences must be traced to all parts of the curriculum. The desirability of each alternative must be felt out, "rehearsed," by a representative variety of all those who must live with the consequences of the chosen action. And a similar variety must deal with the identification of problems as well as with their solution.

This will require penetration of the curtains which now separate educational psychologist from philosopher, sociologist from test constructor, historian from administrator; it will require new channels connecting the series from teacher, supervisor, and school administrator at one end to research specialists at the other. Above all, it will require renunciation of the specious privileges and hegemonies by which we maintain the fiction that problems of science curriculum, for example, have no bearing on problems of English literature or the social studies. The aim here is *not* a dissolving of specialization and special responsibilities. Quite the contrary: if the variety of lights we need are to be obtained, the variety of specialized interests, competences, and habits of mind which characterize education must be cherished and nurtured. The aim, rather, is to bring the members of this variety to bear on curriculum problems by communication with one another.

Concretely, this means the establishment of new journals, and education of educators so that they can write for them and read them. The journals will be forums where possible problems of curriculum will be broached from many sources and their possible importance debated from many points of view. They will be the stage for display of anticipatory solutions to problems, from a similar variety of sources. They will constitute deliberative assemblies in which problems and alternative solutions will be argued by representatives of all for the consideration of all and for the shaping of intelligent consensus.

Needless to say, such journals are not alone sufficient. They stand as only one concrete model of the kind of forum which is required. Similar forums, operating viva voce and in the midst of curriculum operation and curriculum change, are required: of the teachers, supervisors, and administrators of a school; of the supervisors and administrators of a school system; of representatives of teachers, supervisors, and curriculum makers in subject areas and across subject areas; of the same representatives and specialists in curriculum, psychology, sociology, administration, and the subject-matter fields.[3]

The education of educators to participate in this deliberative process will be neither easy nor quickly achieved. The education of the present generation of specialist researchers to speak to the schools and to one another will doubtless be hardest of all, and on this hardest problem I have no suggestion to make. But we could begin within two years to initiate the preparation of teachers, supervisors, curriculum makers, and graduate students of education in the uses and arts of deliberation—and we should.

For graduate students, this should mean that their future inquiries in educational psychology, philosophy of education, educational sociology, and so on, will find more effective focus on enduring problems of education, as against the attractions of the current foci of the parent disciplines. It will begin to exhibit to graduate students what their duties are to the future schoolmen whom they will teach. For teachers, curriculum makers, and others close to the classroom, such training is of special importance. It will not only bring immediate experience of the classroom effectively to bear on problems of curriculum but enhance the quality of that experience, for almost every classroom episode is a stream of situations requiring discrimination of deliberative problems and decision thereon.

By means of such journals and such an education, the educational research establishment might at last find a means for channeling its discoveries into sustained improvement of the schools instead of into a procession of ephemeral bandwagons.

[3] It will be clear from these remarks that the conception of curricular method proposed here is immanent in the Tyler rationale. This rationale calls for a diversity of talents and insists on the practical and eclectic treatment of a variety of factors. Its effectiveness in practice is vitiated by two circumstances. Its focus on "objectives," with their massive ambiguity and equivocation, provides far too little of the concrete matter required for deliberation and leads only to delusive consensus. Second, those who use it are not trained for the deliberative procedures it requires.

THE ROLES OF PHILOSOPHY AND OTHER DISCIPLINES IN EDUCATIONAL THEORY*

Paul H. Hirst

In the somewhat chaotic historical development of the study and teaching of education . . . it is possible to see two distinct emphases. On the one hand there has been a serious concern for the fundamental aims and values of education, and on the other a marked desire to base educational practice fairly and squarely on the results of scientific investigation. Although the first emphasis has only too often resulted in the production of educational sermons intended to commend certain specific aims and to exhort students and teachers to the ardent pursuit of them, it has also led at times to a critical examination of aims and values in an attempt to find a rationally defensible basis for educational practice. Maybe there is a place for educational preaching, but to exhort or commend is not to rationally justify. The second emphasis, though it has suffered at times from the prevailing fashions in psychology and sociology, has likewise resulted in most valuable efforts to get rid of purely personal opinion and prejudice in settling educational questions. Wherever soundly based empirical knowledge is available about learning, child development, the influences of social factors on educational attainment, and so on, it is by these that we now wish to be guided.

But to recognize both these elements in the development and teaching of educational theory is one thing; to characterize accurately the nature and function of that theory as a whole and as a distinctive pursuit, is quite another matter. . . . It is surely plain that, though educational theory has in many ways made great strides in recent years, it still lacks a clear and precise concept of what the whole enterprise is about. Such questions as:

* Reprinted from *The Study of Education,* ed. J. W. Tibble (London: Routledge and Kegan Paul, 1966), pp. 29–56. By permission of the author and the publisher, and, for the United States and its territories and possessions, by permission of Humanities Press, Inc.

What is educational theory, as a theoretical pursuit, trying to achieve? How does this theory relate to educational practice? What kind of theoretical structure has it got, and how in fact do the various elements that are obviously part of it fit in? These questions have received far too little sustained attention. As a result educational studies have tended to become either a series of unrelated or even competing theoretical pursuits, or a confused discussion of educational problems where philosophical, psychological, sociological, or historical and other issues jostle against one another, none being adequately dealt with. This chapter is therefore concerned with examining the concept of educational theory in the hope that we can move toward a more adequate framework within which research and teaching in this area can develop.

The particular concern of some educationists for the aims and values involved in the enterprise has not infrequently led them to a belief that educational theory is, in the last analysis, philosophical in character. They have taken it as obviously true that from a system of philosophical beliefs there must follow directly and necessarily certain clear explicit implications for educational practice.[1] For after all, if people differ about the nature of ultimate reality, surely they must for instance differ in judging what is important in the school curriculum. Must not a religious person think religious education absolutely essential and an atheist think it thoroughly undesirable? Must not a Western liberal democrat, because he holds different ethical doctrines, necessarily disagree with a communist on at least some issues in moral education? And must it not therefore be true that philosophical beliefs do determine clear educational principles which must be put into practice if obvious inconsistencies are to be avoided?

Certainly few people would wish to deny that a system of metaphysical, epistemological, and ethical beliefs that provides a theory of what is ultimately real and ultimately important in life must have some significant contribution to make to educational

---

[1] For a further statement and criticism of this view, see H. W. Burns, "The Logic of the 'Educational Implication,'" *Educational Theory*, Vol. 12, No. 1 (1962).

ideas and practice. But while it is perhaps obvious that there is here some connection between philosophy and education, the view being discussed takes this to be one of direct implication, assuming that thoroughly valid principles for determining educational practice can be readily inferred straight from philosophical beliefs. Even if the view that philosophy is a body of beliefs of this kind is accepted, what is here said about its connection with education is surely not only far from obvious but in fact quite unacceptable in two important respects.

First, the account is far too simple and as a result gives a seriously misleading picture of what is involved in making judgments on educational issues. It is too simple because it implies that on philosophical grounds alone we can satisfactorily answer the central questions of educational practice. This, however, is not so. By their very nature all such questions are necessarily complex, and any answers based on philosophical beliefs only must therefore be regarded as ill-considered. No matter what one's ethical views may be, to ignore in issues of moral education what is known of the psychological development of moral understanding is bound to result in irresponsible judgments. Similarly, to decide matters of curriculum content without due regard to social and psychological, as well as philosophical considerations, is quite indefensible. Whether we are thinking about particular practical decisions made while teaching or, as here, about the formation of general principles that state what ought to be done in practice, there are many diverse aspects to the issues that must be taken into account. The philosophical alone can never be sufficient for the task. This is not to deny that on the basis of certain philosophical beliefs alone some valuable general statements about education can be made, and that these have an important place in educational discussion. But it is to deny that such statements are adequately formed principles that ought to be allowed to determine our educational practice.

An attempt might be made to avoid this criticism by trying to draw a sharp distinction between the aims of education and the methods or means, arguing that the former are philosophically determined whereas only the latter depend on other considerations. This distinction, however, simply will not do, for, in judging what we are to aim at in education, psychological and social factors for instance are clearly of central importance. If the term "aims" is to be used of what we practically wish to achieve in the conduct of education, then we cannot judge this purely philosophically. What kind of curriculum is appropriate at the sixth-form level, or whether an educational system should be co-educational or comprehensive in pattern, are not in any sense simply philosophical issues. However much one may think that "the aims of life" or "what is good" can be known or justified philosophically, it is a confusion to think that the aims of education as a practical enterprise can be set up in the same way. And surely the function of educational theory is the determination of these practical aims, not the determination of the aims and values of life in general.

The distinction between aims and methods or means can be further criticized as a quite false dichotomy when we are concerned with many educational matters. In developing mathematical understanding, say, what is achieved depends crucially on the methods used. Methods are not simply different routes or different modes of transport that will get us to the same destination. For, while sharing certain goals, they involve developing quite distinct elements of understanding (or misunderstanding) and may convey also quite different notions of what mathematics is. In education the journey is as important as the destination reached—indeed, no two methods can in fact take us to precisely the same place in the development of understanding. Aims and methods are inextricably intertwined, and neither presents us with problems that are essentially either philosophical or empirical in character.

If this is so, it means that responsible educational principles need to be formed by a serious attempt to build together whatever knowledge, values, and beliefs are relevant to the practical issues. And further, it means that, between philosophical beliefs in general and educational practice, we must clearly recognize a domain of theoretical discussion and investigation concerned with forming these principles. To this domain of educational theory, philosophical beliefs make their own distinctive contribution alongside history, social theory, psychological theory, and so on. The view that there is a direct connection between philosophy and educational practice either totally ignores, or heavily underestimates, the real significance of educational theory in this sense. It fails to recognize the important truth that, unless philosophical beliefs are to influence educational practice in a distorting manner, they must influence it indirectly through the medium of educational theory, where they are considered conjointly with many other elements before any particular principles for educational practice are explicitly formulated.

In reply to this it might be argued that, if the term philosophical beliefs is interpreted broadly enough, it will embrace all the considerations that could possibly be relevant to judgments of educational principle. In that case, it would be true to say, after all, that educational principles do follow directly from philosophical beliefs. But this reply simply covers up the problem by a blanketing use of the term "philosophy." If the term is to be used so as to include psychology, sociology, and all else that is significant for education, then by definition the theory is "philosophical." One can then only protest at the refusal to recognize important distinctions and point out that without them we must give up all hope of distinguishing the role of philosophy in educational affairs from that of psychology, sociology, etc. For a purely verbal victory one must pay a very high price. And even if the application of the term "philosophical beliefs" is restricted so as not to cover those psychological, sociological, and other elements that are of immediate importance when it comes to formulating educational principles, there are still serious difficulties about the genuinely philosophical character of the remaining domain. For if philosophy is still thought to be supplying to educational theory a whole area of general beliefs about the nature of man, of reality, of the good life, etc., then one must protest that these general beliefs are the result of no distinctively philosophical enterprise, being derived from much knowledge of diverse kinds about human nature, society, the physical world, etc.

One can only conclude that conceiving educational theory as essentially philosophical in character involves failing to do justice to the complex nature of the problems it has to deal with, seriously underestimating the importance of other forms of knowledge in dealing with these, and conceiving philosophy in so ambiguous a way as to make it the label of no clearly distinctive form of understanding.

In some of its forms this concept of educational theory has associated with it a second feature which is open to serious criticisms of a different kind. Not infrequently it seems to be held that educational principles can be, and ought to be, formally deduced from philosophical beliefs. And even when it is granted that philosophical beliefs are not of themselves adequate to the task, it might still be maintained that, given all the necessary understanding whatever its nature, educational principles ought then to be derived in much the same way as we can derive the theorems in Euclidean geometry from the axioms.

The process of deduction depends entirely on the formal manipulation of statements, and the conclusions to which it leads are therefore based solely on what is actually and literally expressed in the premises. The process must begin with statements that cover quite explicitly all the considerations that are involved in the issues. What is more, all the concepts and terms that are used must be fully related to each other so that no gaps appear in the chains of argument. Deduction can never be used unless we can start with premises equal to the task, covering all the necessary facts and beliefs and relating these so that the conclusions are reached in a purely formal manner.

Can we then set out our beliefs and knowledge in series of statements so that from them we can work out deductively what our educational principles must be? There are several reasons why in general this is impossible. Sometimes when an issue is clear cut and the factors on which it depends are limited, deduction may be used, and small pieces of deduction may well occur too as part of some larger argument. But in general the complexity of practical issues is so great that it is quite impossible to set out explicitly all the facts and beliefs which must be taken into account. Nor is this difficulty simply one of time and space for the job. Many of the terms in which we express the knowledge and beliefs that are vital for educational issues are not exact and precise but vague and ill-defined. Terms expressing personal relations and moral values are notoriously lacking in the quite clear constant meaning that the deductive use of statements assumes. Again, much of our relevant understanding is not expressible in literal terms but depends on metaphor, analogy, and even paradox. Deductive arguments using, or rather misusing, such statements are quite valueless even when they make sense. In addition, to evolve educational principles by deduction certainly means using, among other statements, a set of moral principles; and while these can be used formally in this way, if they are it means that, morally speaking, educational judgments are being produced by rule. Yet moral principles are never once-and-for-all rules whose formal implications should be invariably accepted. If they are used formally to produce educational principles, they are likely to be as destructive of what is good in educational practice as mechanical living is in everyday affairs. Finally, it is difficult to see how conclusions that depend on the putting together of considerations from practical experience, from psychology, social theory, and philosophy, weighing them up, estimating their relative importance, could possibly be reached in an uninterrupted chain of deduction. The process that is employed generally is far removed from the formal manipulation of accepted statements, being rather a form of judgment based on as comprehensive a view of the issues as it is possible to get.

Again, this is not to deny that, from statements of our knowledge and beliefs, we can by a process of deduction come to make some valuable statements for education. It is the adequacy of these as principles for practice that is in question. For the reasons given above deduction seems to be far too limited, and in some respects far too dangerously perverting, a method for us to work by it uncritically in this field. It follows from the nature of adequate educational principles that in general they cannot and ought not to be formed in this way. We need to think in terms of a much looser and much more open process of judgment to which philosophical beliefs, psychological and social theory, historical knowledge, etc., contribute in their appropriate ways. Beliefs, knowledge of facts, and general values provide the grounds on which judgments of educational principle are made, and it is by reference to these that we give the reasons for what we advocate. But this does not mean that there is some logically necessary connection between the knowledge, beliefs, and values on the one hand and the education principles on the other. It is not that we work out formally our conclusions from explicit statements which are the complete and necessary grounds for the resulting principles. It is rather that in the midst of a complex network of understanding which cannot be adequately and formally expressed, we form reasons, drawing attention to the major considerations which have influenced us. This being so, it is not at all surprising that people who agree to certain statements of their beliefs do often in fact advocate quite different educational principles. It is not at all uncommon, for instance, to find Christians who favor a secular school system, and not a few atheists judge there to be good reasons for having universal religious instruction. Contrary to the crude assumption mentioned earlier, it appears on closer inspection that educational principles that are adequate for directing practice do not follow by simple deduction from philosophical beliefs. This is borne out by the fact that philosophical agreement is no guarantee of educational agreement, and fortunately many educational principles are acceptable to the holders of very diverse philosophical views. This does not mean that philosophical beliefs are unimportant for educational theory; it means simply that the part they play is not that of axioms in a deductive system. Their role is highly influential but much more subtle than that some envisage, being part of a broad overall understanding that lies behind all educational judgments. A philosophical system of considerable generality may of course greatly determine a set of educational principles even when other factors have been taken into account. It is then tempting to speak loosely of the principles as derived or even deduced from the system. This is, however, most misleading, and it would be better to describe the principles as constructed so as to be consistent with the system. Consistency between beliefs and principles denotes nothing more than the absence of any contradiction between the two. This there must be, but it by no means follows that there must also be an explicit deductive chain that leads from the one to the other.

In criticizing too philosophical a view of the nature of educational theory, it has nevertheless been taken for granted thus far that philosophy is indeed concerned with establishing certain beliefs and values and that these beliefs and values do have a legitimate and important place in the theory. In his book *An Introduction to the Philosophy of Education,* Professor D. J. O'Connor goes much further and questions even these concessions to philosophical imperialism. Early in this volume, the author makes it clear that in his view, "philosophy is not in the ordinary sense of the phrase a body of knowledge, but rather an activity of criticism or clarification." It is not "a kind of superior science" which can "be expected to answer difficult and important questions about human life, and man's place and prospects in the universe" by using special techniques. Rather it is "an activity of criticism or clarification,"[2] an attempt to answer questions where the meaning of terms and their relations to each other have produced complex and far reaching difficulties in our understanding. Clearly this analytical activity, which can be exercised on any subject matter, can be used to deal with questions in educational theory. Certainly, when trying to formulate educational principles difficulties of this sort arise. On this view, philosophy still has some place in educational debate, but now it no longer seems to contribute significantly to the substance of the theory; it is but an aid, clearing up confusions of meaning wherever these appear. This is not the place for a general discussion of the nature of philosophy. It must, however, be said that, while most contemporary British philosophers would be in considerable agreement with O'Connor's emphasis on the analytical function of philosophy, many would find his treatment of metaphysical beliefs and moral values far too dismissive. And when

[2] D. J. O'Connor, *An Introduction to the Philosophy of Education* (1957), p. 4.

it comes to characterizing educational theory, the significance of these elements in it is crucial. From accepting a markedly analytical view of philosophy therefore, it does not necessarily follow that it has quite the insubstantial function for education that O'Connor seems to think.

But whatever the rights and wrongs in this matter, the specific account of educational theory that O'Conner gives raises quite different issues. Professing to look for the "job an educational theory is supposed to do,"[3] O'Connor first distinguishes four main senses of the word "theory," two of which seem to be important in educational contexts. In one of these, theory is contrasted with practice, and here the word refers to "a set or system of rules or a collection of precepts which guide or control actions of various kinds. . . . Educational theory would then consist of those parts of psychology concerned with perception, learning, concept formation, motivation and so on which directly concern the work of the teacher."[4] In the other, the word "theory" is used as it occurs in the natural sciences where it refers to a single hypothesis or a logically interconnected set of hypotheses that have been confirmed by observation. It is this sense of the word that is said to provide us with "standards by which we can assess the value and use of any claimant to the title of "theory." In particular this sense of the word will enable us to judge the values of the various (and often conflicting) theories that are put forward by writers on education."[5]

Judged by these standards, a great deal of educational theory certainly comes off rather badly. For, as O'Connor himself states, educational discussions are not usually entirely empirical in character but include as well value judgments and appeals to metaphysical beliefs. These other two elements differ quite radically from the first, as his earlier analysis of them has shown. The importance of value judgments in this field is not questioned, and O'Connor's chief concern is that we should recognize them for

[3] Ibid., p. 74.
[4] Ibid., p. 75.
[5] Ibid., p. 76.

what they are so that we do not get into muddles by confusing them with assertions of fact. Of metaphysical statements, however, it is said that we have no way of confirming what they assert and that we cannot even be sure that they have any cognitive meaning at all. Their contribution to educational theory is therefore of very doubtful value. He thus concludes:

> We can summarize this discussion by saying that the word "theory" as it is used in educational contexts is generally a courtesy title. It is justified only where we are applying well established experimental findings in psychology or sociology to the practice of education. And even here we should be aware that the conjectural gap between our theories and the facts on which they rest is sufficiently wide to make our logical consciences uneasy. We can hope that the future development of the social sciences will narrow this gap and this hope gives an incentive for developing these sciences.[6]

The first thing that must be said about this account is that O'Connor has singularly failed to do what he set out to do—to discover the job educational theory performs. If in fact he had begun to discover this, a very different picture of the theory would certainly have emerged. In addition, because of his obsession with scientific theory as a paradigm for all theories, he totally misjudges the importance of the nonscientific elements that he himself diagnoses in educational discussions. In the last analysis, metaphysical statements and value judgments are dismissed as not being elements that fundamentally characterize this field of discourse.

If we accept O'Connor's classification of the two main senses of the word "theory" that are important for education, it is surely the first of these that gives the primary meaning here, not the second as he suggests. Educational theory is in the first place to be understood as the essential background to rational educational practice, not as a limited would-be scientific pursuit. Even when O'Connor momentarily recognizes this, he nevertheless fails to realize the complex kind of theory that is necessary to determine

[6] Ibid., p. 110.

a whole range of practical activities. He therefore falls back on his scientific paradigm, maintaining that the theory must be simply a collection of pieces of psychology.[7]

Yet the theories of science and the theories of practical activities are radically different in character because they perform quite different functions; they are constructed to do different jobs. In the case of the empirical sciences, a theory is a body of statements that have been subjected to empirical tests and which express our understanding of certain aspects of the physical world. Such tested theories are the objects, the end products, of scientific investigation; they are the conclusions of the pursuit of knowledge. Where, however, a practical activity like education is concerned, the place of the theory is totally different. It is not the end product of the pursuit, but rather it is constructed to determine and guide the activity. The function of the theory is to determine precisely what shall and what shall not be done, say, in education. The distinction I am drawing between scientific theory and, say, educational theory is the traditional distinction between knowledge that is organized for the pursuit of knowledge and the understanding of our experience, and knowledge that is organized for determining some practical activity. To try to understand the nature and pattern of some practical discourse in terms of the nature and pattern of some purely theoretical discourse can only result in its being radically misconceived.

O'Connor's important distinctions between different uses of the term "theory" draw attention to the fact that the phrase "educational theory" can have two quite different meanings. It can be used as O'Connor wishes for the body of scientific knowledge on which rational educational judgments rest. It is, however, also used for the whole enterprise of building a body of rational principles for educational practice. In this second sense it is the label for a domain of theory that not only draws on educational theory in the first, scientific sense, but draws on much else besides by way of other forms of knowledge and belief, and results in the formation of practical principles. Neither of these uses can be said to be the correct one, and what matters is not a fight over

[7] See the passage quoted earlier, ibid., p. 75.

the right to a label but the recognition that the two types of theory concerned are radically different in kind. . . .

O'Connor's account of the matter is misleading, not so much because he wishes to restrict the use of a term but because of his tendency to reduce the whole concept of educational theory, in the larger sense, to the narrower scientific concept. It is on the development of the theory in its larger sense that rational educational practice depends, not simply the development of scientific study. Reductionism of this kind, which conceives all educational theory as essentially scientific in character, is as unacceptable as the philosophical reductionism discussed in the first section of this chapter. And that because it again mis-characterizes the theory in two major respects, first as to its content and second as to its logical form. As to its content, the wider theory is necessarily drawing on knowledge other than science; it must, for instance, draw on historical, philosophical, and moral understanding as well. In particular, whatever one may think of the truth claims of metaphysical beliefs and the form of justification of moral values, both these enter into the formation of educational principles and judgments. They cannot be ignored or wished out of the way. As to its form, the wider theory is not concerned simply with producing explanations on the scientific model but with forming rationally justified principles for what ought to be done in an area of practical activity. In the last analysis, therefore, scientific theory and educational theory are as different logically as judgments of what is the case are different from judgments of what ought to be the case.

From the discussion thus far, it would seem clear that an adequate account of educational theory must do justice both to its connection with educational practice and its connection with a vast range of different forms of purely theoretical understanding. Its further characterization, therefore, turns on showing precisely how knowledge of such different kinds is organized into a theoretical structure which culminates in rationally justified principles for educational practice. In order to bring out the features of this logical structure, it is necessary to distinguish it as one of three quite different structures or organizations that knowledge has or can have. In the first place, all knowledge can be seen as necessarily structured into what will be referred to as distinct "forms." Second, knowledge can be organized into what will be called different "fields." And third, it can be organized into a variety of "practical theories."

(1) Forms of Knowledge

All knowledge that man has achieved can be seen to be differentiated into a number of logically distinct domains or forms. That this is so comes from the fact that knowledge is possible only because of the use of patterns of related concepts in terms of which our experience is intelligible. Our understanding, be it in the affairs of everyday or in matters of advanced research, in science or history or morals, is achieved through the development and use of conceptual schemes by means of which we make sense of things. Successive generations acquire these conceptual schemes by learning to use meaningfully the symbolic systems in which they are expressed and in their turn these generations can develop further both the schemes and their use. But knowledge depends on more than the existence of such schemes. For unless in their use we are able to distinguish truth from error, fact from fable, what is valid from what is invalid, what is right from what is wrong, then we are not in a position to claim anything by way of genuine understanding and knowledge as distinct from conjecture and fantasy. Our knowledge is thus dependent on the use both of conceptual schemes and criteria for validity or truth. In public terms, this means that our knowledge is expressed in symbolic statements which have been judged for their validity according to recognized criteria that are appropriate to them.

That there are distinct forms within knowledge can be seen by the logical analysis of the whole domain. These forms can be distinguished from each other in three interrelated ways. First, within the domain there are distinct types of concepts that characterize different types of knowledge. Mathematical concepts (such as number, integral, matrix) generate a different form of understanding because they have a different function in relation to experience from, say, the scientific concepts (hydrogen, atom, magnetic field) or the religious concepts (God, sin, heaven) or the moral concepts (good, ought, virtue). Second, these concepts occur within different networks whose relationships determine what meaningful propositions can be made. Moral terms can only be used meaningfully in certain relations to other concepts that occur in moral discourse. Scientific terms like "atom" can be related to other terms only by strict adherence to a whole network of logical rules for them. One can no more make meaningful statements about the color of atoms than one can about the goodness of right-angled triangles. Third, the domains can be distinguished by the different types of test they involve for the truth or validity of propositions. In science, the tests of observation and experiment are final. In mathematics, the criteria are those of deduction from axioms. Likewise moral and aesthetic judgments are each unique in their forms of justification. In recent philosophical work, even where no really adequate positive account of the logical features of the domains has been achieved, there would seem to be growing agreement that we must recognize as distinct those forms of understanding we have in science, mathematics, history, morals, aesthetics, philosophy, and religion. Whether or not the domain of religion can be regarded as one of knowledge rather than belief is a matter of dispute, and some might question the autonomous character of history. Maybe there are good grounds for thinking that the human sciences are logically distinguishable from the physical sciences. What would certainly seem to be beyond dispute is that the history of the development of knowledge is the story of its progressive differentiation into a number of logically distinct forms, each providing unique understanding because of the uniqueness of its concepts, its conceptual structure, and its criteria for validity. If this is so, then the growth of an individual's knowledge involves the progressive mastery and use of the appropriate conceptual schemes and their criteria. Understanding or knowledge, if it is to be anything other than superficial, cannot be acquired in random fashion; for to understand is in part to appreciate a whole network of ordered conceptual relations and to be aware of the appropriate bases for truth and validity that are involved. Here there is an implicit structuring of knowledge into distinct forms, an organization in no sense optional to understanding, conventional or convenient in its divisions. It is an ordering that is essentially part of knowledge as we have it. These conceptual structures may become further differentiated; they may be extended; they may be applied in new ways; but it would seem logically impossible to conceive of the growth of knowledge either as a public deposit or as a personal development, outside this framework.

If what is being said here is not to be seriously misunderstood, two further points must be made. First, within the forms which have been logically distinguished by their formal structural features, further distinctions can be drawn in terms of their content. The domain of science, for instance, can be subdivided into physics, chemistry, zoology, biochemistry, and so on. These divisions, made according to an interest in a particular selection of empirical phenomena, or the use of particular methods, do not, however, result in domains that are logically distinguishable, for in logical respects the sciences are all strictly similar. All the sciences have the same type of structure and test. These subdivisions are in fact convenient or conventional, being logically coherent selections from the larger domain, subsections which can be developed and taught in relative independence. To a greater or less degree, therefore, each of a multitude of existing and possible sciences is an expression of the same logical form but is different in content.

Second, to say that the forms are each unique in their essential logical features is not to say that they are totally divorced from each other. That would be manifestly false when, for instance, the sciences make such great use of mathematics, history uses the results of scientific investigation, and moral judgments equally depend on much empirical understanding. But, in these interrelations, one form is making use of some other. In each case, one form A accepts the relevant contribution of some other form B entirely as it is, without any right to question, and it employs this knowledge as an instrument to its own ends. As far as form A is concerned, it is simply the achievements or results of form *B* that matter, and these it takes in, formulating its own theories or statements of principles to be tested according to criteria uniquely appropriate for form *A*. A theory in physics may use the results of some vast mathematical system. It is then taking over mathematical knowledge which for the purpose of the theory is assumed to be valid according to mathematical criteria. But the theory itself then stands or falls not by any mathematical tests but by those of empirical experiment and observation appropriate to a science. A theory in physics is not even a starter as a scientific theory if it is based on faulty mathematics. But the mathematical validity of a theory in no way guarantees its scientific truth. One form may indeed employ the findings of one, or several others, but this in no way invalidates the general truth that the forms are unique in kind having their own structures and tests for validity.

(2) Fields of Knowledge

Apart from the forms of knowledge and the subdivisions within them, we do also organize knowledge into artificial units. Round some kind of object, phenomena, abstract entity, or other interest, knowledge from many different forms can be collected. Such "fields of knowledge" are frequently formed as a basis for use in education under such titles as, for instance, "the neighborhood," "power," "the modern European mind." These fields may, of course, be of considerable value in promoting the growth of knowledge in certain areas, and they are not necessarily organizations developed simply for teaching purposes. Though the nature of geography is hotly disputed by professionals, the subject as commonly found would seem to have all the features of a field. Centering round an interest in "place" or "man and his environment," historical knowledge, for instance, rubs shoulders with the results of work in the human as well as the physical sciences. What is more crucial, however, is that all the questions with which geographers deal seem to be intelligible and answerable only within the canons of one of the several forms. Certainly geography has concepts which other areas of knowledge do not use, but that does not make them unique in kind. From a logical point of view, they would all appear to be either, say, scientific or historical in character and geographical solely by virtue of their use for those particular empirical and historical matters which geographers wish to consider. If there are geographical truths which are unique in logical kind, where the tests for truth are not simply of a type used elsewhere in, say, scientific or historical pursuits, it is not clear what these are. Geography may be marked out as a distinctive area because of the subjects with which it deals, but that is not sufficient to distinguish it as a form. There must also be a conceptual structure that leads to propositions with their own unique criteria of validity, and that geography has not been shown to possess.

What is meant by a field here is in fact simply a collection of knowledge from various forms which has unity solely because this knowledge all relates to some object or interest. There is no inherent logical structure which gives unity to the domain. There are no concepts of a kind peculiar to the field. And the field is not concerned with the validation of distinctive statements according to unique criteria. It follows from this that, whereas the advancement of a form of knowledge depends on the development of the relevant conceptual scheme and its wider application according to its own canons, the advancement of a field is a far more complex affair. It consists in the development and application of whatever forms of knowledge are considered valuable and relevant in coming to understand the selected topic. Whereas a professional historian must have mastered the canons and methods of historical thought, being primarily engaged in extending these and their use, the geographer is necessarily involved in employing the canons and methods of several different forms, those of the historian, the economist, the physicist, and so on. And this not because the canons of geography presuppose these other forms in any sense, as the historian may need to draw on scientific knowledge. It is rather that there are no distinctive canons and methods of geography, for all those it employs are in fact those of the relevant forms it uses. To master a field of knowledge is therefore necessarily a complex and difficult matter. To understand "the modern European mind," for instance, involves at least a grasp of the conceptual schemes and criteria of history, science, philosophy, and the arts as applied to the selected cultural phenomena.

(3) Practical Theories

Both the patternings of knowledge considered so far are important if we are to understand the growth of knowledge both publicly and personally. Forms like history or science and fields like geography or the modern European mind are all organizations of knowledge significant primarily because of their importance for the development of cognition, of understanding in itself. We do, however, also have organizations of knowledge, which will be called "practical theories," whose whole *raison d'être* is their practical function. In these it is not a patterning of understanding that is of first importance but the determination of what ought to be done in some range of practical activities. This distinction between practical theories and forms and fields of knowledge is exactly that discussed in Section 2 as a distinction between the theories of practical knowledge and those of theoretical knowledge. It is now, however, possible to pursue further the question of the differences in logical structure that are involved.

In practical theories, knowledge is collected from several different forms because of a particular interest, just as in the various fields mentioned above. The interest now, however, is a particular range of practical activities as, for example, in engineering, medicine, or education. But whereas fields of knowledge are simply collections of knowledge from the forms, practical theories are collections of knowledge used in the formulation of principles for practice. Educational theory, like political theory or engineering, is not concerned simply with collecting knowledge about certain practical affairs. The whole point is the use of the knowledge to determine what should be done in educational practice. In the process the theory draws on all the knowledge within the various forms that is relevant to educational pursuits but proceeds from there to grappling with practical problems. The educationist is not simply interested in, for instance, the nature of historical explanation, the place in it of moral judgments, and the psychological aspects of acquiring historical concepts. He is concerned with using these kinds of knowledge to form rationally defensible principles about the place of history teaching in education, what history should be taught in schools, and how it ought to be done. Thus educational theory, like all other practical theories, has a logical unity that a mere field of knowledge centered on education would not have. The unity of the theory goes beyond that of a collection of knowledge centered on some interest to that of a rational structure where knowledge from the forms provides the basis of justification for a series of educational principles.

From this it might be supposed that a practical theory is in structure more like a form of knowledge than a field. For could it not be argued that just as physics uses mathematics but results in distinctive, validated scientific statements, so educational theory uses philosophy, psychology, sociology, etc., and issues in distinctive, validated educational principles? Just this has been argued by those who have wanted to maintain that education is in some sense an autonomous discipline.[8] On closer examination, however, the parallel cannot be maintained. Whatever the relationship between mathematics and physics, any scientific theory involves distinctive empirical concepts unique in character so that the theory's validity turns on related empirical tests. In educational theory no such concepts exist any more than they do in say geography or any other field. There is nothing logically unique about such educational concepts as, for example, classroom, teacher, subject, comprehensive school. These simply serve to pick out those particular empirical, moral, philosophical, and other elements with which education is concerned. These concepts are used to mark out the area of education and its interests but do not pick out any unique form or awareness of knowledge for,

[8] See F. McMurray, "Preface to an Autonomous Discipline of Education," *Educational Theory*, Vol. 5, No. 3 (1955). This, and many other questions mentioned here, are discussed in J. Walton and J. L. Kuethe, eds., *The Discipline of Education* (1963).

indeed, educational theory has no such function. Because this is so, it follows that there can be no unique form of test for educational principles. However they are validated, it is in no way that is logically parallel to the experiment and observation of the sciences. In spite of the claim to some unique type of test within educational theory and one by which the contributions of philosophers, psychologists, and others can be assessed, no such tests have in fact been produced. And if the analysis here given is correct, by the nature of the case they cannot be.

What is happening in this parallel between educational theory and a form of knowledge is a total mis-characterization of educational principles. This can be seen if the place of mathematics in physics is at all carefully compared with that of philosophy, psychology, etc., in educational theory. For, granted the validity of any mathematics involved, the truth of statements in physics turns on empirical evidence. But granted the validity of the historical, psychological, moral, or other elements involved, the validity of the educational principle rests on nothing further. Granted the mathematics, statements in physics must survive crucial scientific tests. For these, however, educational theory has no parallel, and its principles stand or fall entirely on the validity of the knowledge contributed by the many forms. Of course a statement or theory in physics can be invalidated by faulty mathematics, yet to establish any mathematics used does not begin to validate the theory as a scientific theory. An educational principle, however, while it can likewise be invalidated because it rests on, say, faulty psychology, can only be justified by virtue of the psychological and other knowledge on which the principle rests. In the pattern of justification in science, some statement or theory A is validated because granted the truth of $x, y, z \ldots$, the items of mathematics and other forms of knowledge that may be used, there are crucial scientific reasons $a, b, c, d \ldots$ for its truth that stem from the appropriate empirical observations. In educational theory, some practical principle A is validated simply in terms of $x, y, z \ldots$, where these are items of empirical, philosophical, moral, or other knowledge which are relevant to the educational issue. (There are no strictly educational reasons $a, b, c, d \ldots$

which are not empirical, philosophical, moral, etc., in form.) A principle that all secondary education ought to be given in comprehensive schools must be justified by appealing to all the sound empirical evidence that is available on the effects of selection and nonselection both psychologically and sociologically, on the administrative possibilities and difficulties for institutions of this kind, etc.; the case must be argued in the light of the historical context in which appropriate changes would have to be made; it must rest on certain general value judgments which in their turn can be given justification and so on. In the light of all this, but only this, can the specifically educational judgment be rationally made. Similarly, a principle for compulsory religious instruction in maintained schools must be defended in terms of the philosophical status of claims to religious knowledge, what is known of the psychological development of religious concepts and beliefs, the relationship between morals and religion logically, psychologically, and sociologically, the historical significance of religious beliefs, the guarding of the principle of complete religious liberty, etc.

Educational principles are, therefore, justified simply by producing reasons for them of an empirical, philosophical, moral, or other logical kind. Once it is understood that the validity of the principles turns on nothing "educational" beyond these, it is clear that the only way to attack or defend them is by a critical examination of these reasons. The psychological reasons must be shown to stand according to the strictest canons of that science. Equally the historical, philosophical, or other truths that are appealed to must be judged according to the criteria of the relevant discipline in each case. Any significant debate about educational principles must be about reasons for them, and this immediately turns into the discussion of a series of questions radically different in kind, questions answerable only within the terms of highly developed distinct forms of knowledge and their subdivisions. Far from being an autonomous discipline, educational theory would seem to be rather as complex as any field of knowledge can be, and different from those fields not because some unique form of understanding is involved, but because the elements are used in the making of practical principles. It is but a confusion to regard the formation of practical principles as parallel to the development of an autonomous form of knowledge or thought when those principles stand or fall on nothing but knowledge contributed by other forms.

If educational theory is not, then, in any sense, autonomous, it might well be argued that it (or any other practical theory, for that matter) is a subdivision of what has been referred to as the form of moral knowledge. Though to prevent serious misunderstanding a quite separate classification for practical theories has been argued thus far, there is in fact a great deal to be said for characterizing these theories under moral knowledge. What is distinctive about them is that they issue in practical principles for a particular range of activities. Just as within science the different sciences are distinguishable according to the different topics considered, so practical theories are distinguishable from each other by the range of activities for which they formulate principles. Engineering, medicine, political theory, and educational theory clearly differ from each other because of the activities with which they are concerned. What is perhaps most important in this is that the activities differ widely in kind and that they therefore call for practical principles of varying types. By and large the central problems involved in engineering and medicine can be marked out with little difficulty. With this goes the fact that, in large measure, the aims of engineering and medicine are commonly agreed. In political and educational theory, however, the area of activities being discussed is not so clear and the precise aims of those activities are often matters of serious dispute. Professor R. S. Peters, in his papers "Education as Initiation"[9] and "What is an Educational Process?"[10] has sought to outline the criteria for those activities we label "educational" and therefore to demarcate the territory of educational theory. One thing that is abundantly plain from his analyses is that, certainly in this case, it is a fundamental task of the theory to determine the ends and

[9] R. S. Peters, *Education as Initiation,* 1964; and included in R. D. Archambault, *Philosophical Analysis and Education* (1965).
[10] R. S. Peters, "What is an Educational Process?" in R. S. Peters, *The Concept of Education* (1966).

goals to be pursued as much as the means to be employed. Thus whereas engineering consists almost entirely of the use of scientific knowledge in determining efficient means to agreed ends, educational theory in large measure depends on the making of value judgments about what exactly is to be aimed at in education.

Whatever the character of engineering may be, it is certainly characteristic of educational theory that it formulates principles of a distinctly moral kind. In doing this it, of course, relies on the logic of moral reasoning and therefore rightly falls within the domain of moral knowledge. At the same time, however, the principles formulated are not high-level statements about what is good or what ought to be done in general. They are principles specifically concerned with education, and it is the function of the theory in moral reasoning to use general moral principles and all other relevant knowledge to this end. Insofar, then, as practical theories of this kind are regarded as subdivisions of moral understanding, it must be remembered that the problems they deal with directly are practical. Educational theory as such is not concerned with the justification of such fundamental and basic principles as those of freedom, respect for persons, truth telling, that other things being equal a man has a right to worship as he pleases and a responsibility to provide for his family. It is concerned with establishing what ought to be done in educational activities. The justification needed for the most fundamental moral principles may well be quite different in form from that needed for those at lower levels. The pattern of reasoning for practical principles outlined earlier is that in which knowledge of many kinds, including fundamental and high-level moral principles, is brought to bear on restricted and specific practical issues. This can be considered as a form of moral reasoning, but it is not the only form. It is simply that form appropriate to dealing with practical problems of a moral kind.

From this discussion it emerges that even when a practical theory centrally involves moral questions, its restricted focus limits the level and character of these moral considerations and introduces the need for much specialized knowledge of empirical and other kinds. In these theories, too, by no means all the questions are essentially moral. Educational theory has to deal with many questions about, for instance, teaching techniques and administrative organization, which are purely technical. As has been pointed out previously, there are also practical theories like engineering which are almost entirely of this character. There are thus good reasons for thinking of practical theories as organizations of knowledge distinct in kind. They are the product of interests in groups of related practical activities; they are concerned with forming principles saying what ought to be done; and, to varying degrees, they are not only technical but also moral in character.

Earlier in this section, great emphasis was placed on the fact that educational principles stand or fall entirely on the validity of the relevant knowledge contributed from the various forms. Judgments stating what ought to be done morally or technically are based on nothing beyond the empirical facts, more general value judgments, etc. From this it might be thought that educational principles must somehow follow from a theoretical synthesis of all the contributory elements, that unless some harmony is brought to the relevant philosophy, psychology, history, etc., the principles will lack adequate justification. Not only would this be a task for educational theory that is quite impossible practically, for no one could have mastered all the relevant specialist knowledge; it would be asking for something that might well be logically impossible. It is not at all clear what is meant by synthesizing knowledge achieved through the use of logically quite different conceptual schemes. But such a synthesis is in fact quite unnecessary for the formation of practical principles. The diverse character of the contributions of psychology, philosophy, or history to a discussion of the comprehensive school and equality of opportunity is immaterial. That many of the considerations may pull in different directions, and that they have not been technically harmonized, is not germane. Indeed, it is precisely the function of the theory to form practical principles in the light of diverse and conflicting evidence. Educational theory is not to be thought of as starting with a purely theoretical structure, integrating elements of science with some history and philosophy, etc. It is a theory which formulates principles the reasons for which are radically diverse in kind, a theory which by these principles alone unites knowledge from many different forms.

In this analysis of the nature of educational theory, the following important characteristics have emerged:

(1) It is the theory in which principles, stating what ought to be done in a range of practical activities, are formulated and justified;

(2) The theory is not itself an autonomous "form" of knowledge or an autonomous discipline. It involves no conceptual structure unique in its logical features and no unique tests for validity. Many of its central questions are in fact moral questions of a particular level of generality, questions focused on educational practice.

(3) Educational theory is not a purely theoretical field of knowledge because of the formulation of principles for practice in which it issues. It is, however, composite in character in a way similar to such fields.

(4) Educational principles are justified entirely by direct appeal to knowledge from a variety of forms, scientific, philosophical, historical, etc. Beyond these forms of knowledge, it requires no theoretical synthesis.

It is a necessary consequence of this characterization of the theory that its development depends crucially on the progress of scientific knowledge, philosophical work, etc., which is relevant to questions of educational practice. It is only by rigorous work within these forms, according to their own critical canons, that valid reasons can be brought to the formation of educational principles. If work or study in the theory is to be anything but superficial, it must readily become differentiated out into the serious and systematic treatment of the relevant philosophical, sociological, or historical questions that are raised. Given a particular educational problem, recognizing the philosophical or psychological issues it involves is by no means a simple matter. Nor, given a great deal of philosophical or psychological understanding, is it easy to see its bearing on educational questions. To discern where, and precisely how, a given discipline contributes to the theory demands first a highly specialized knowledge of the discipline and the kind of problems with which it deals. It demands, too, the ability to see beneath the practical problems of education those underlying questions which this discipline alone can hope to answer. Philosophy of education must indeed be philosophy. Educational psychology must indeed be psychology. But as contributing to educational theory, these and other specialisms aim at determining educational practice by providing the basic understanding on which rationally justified principles can be built. . . .

ACTION, BEHAVIOR, AND EDUCATIONAL ENDS AND MEANS*

Robert D. Heslep

I

During much of this century, the concept of behavior has been widely utilized as a guide in understanding social phenomena, and it shows no signs of losing favor among its adherents. In recent years, however, an alternative concept has been gaining currency among those seriously concerned with social affairs, namely, that of action. The concept has been quite notably employed to examine the subject-matters of sociology,[1] economics,[2] and anthropology.[3] There are two reasons, its proponents argue, which make the concept worthy of entertainment: (*a*) the concept is significant of a large segment of social phenomena, and (*b*) the concept, which speaks to the subjective as well as the objective aspect of social affairs, enables a broader comprehension of such affairs than that allowed by the concept of behavior.

The use of the concept of action to investigate the problems of education appears to have been small. Very little pertinent literature seems to exist, and what there is of it is noticeably limited in scope. Regardless, what has been especially disappointing in the literature is that it has failed to provide an explicit view of action. While one portion of the writing makes no pretense at explaining action, the other discusses only some facet of it. The

* Reprinted from "Action and Education," *Philosophy of Education, 1966: Proceedings of the Twenty-Second Annual Meeting of the Philosophy of Education Society,* ed. Francis T. Villemain (Edwardsville, Ill.: Studies in Philosophy and Education, 1966), pp. 129–34. By permission of the author and the editor of the *Proceedings.*

[1] Talcott Parsons, *The Structure of Social Action* (New York: McGraw-Hill, 1937).

[2] Ludwig von Mises, *Human Action: A Treatise on Economics* (New Haven: Yale University Press, 1949).

[3] Douglas Browning, *Act and Agent: An Essay in Philosophical Anthropology* (Coral Gables, Fla.: University of Miami Press, 1964).

outcome is that the writing involves numerous inadequacies. It seems appropriate, then, to clarify the concept of action.

One way to help carry out this task is to present the major commonplaces of action and to employ the view of action constituted by them in an examination of statements about action and education found in educational literature. The statements in the literature which are to be used in this inquiry will be taken from Professor Thomas F. Green's essay, "Teaching, Acting, and Behaving."[4] This article alone has been chosen because it appears to be the only serious piece which has been done on action and education.

II

One commonplace of action is purpose. Action has been commonly recognized as purposive activity, that is, activity wherein the subject, or actor, is pursuing a consciously proposed objective.[5] Furthermore, any case of purposive activity has ordinarily been taken as a case of action. Accordingly, the property of purpose may be used to distinguish action, for example, from motion, blind routine, impulsive activities, and behavior, which includes a subject inasmuch as he strives toward a goal object but excludes him insofar as he proposes the object to himself as a goal. That action involves a subject's conscious aim does not necessarily preclude subconscious factors. They are pertinent insofar as they influence the actor in his formulation and fulfillment of purpose.

[4] *Harvard Educational Review,* 34: 507–24. Much discussion was given to this article in a subsequent issue of the same journal, but it did little to clarify the concept of action. See Jonas F. Soltis, R. S. Peters, James E. McClellan, and Thomas F. Green, "'Teaching, Acting, and Behaving': A Discussion," *Harvard Educational Review,* 35: 191–209.

[5] The remarks in this section are reflected in other investigations of the same subject matter. Cf. von Mises, pp. 11–29; Talcott Parsons and Edward A. Shils, eds., *Toward a General Theory of Action* (New York: Harper & Row, 1951), Harper Torchbooks, pp. 53–109; Carl G. Hempel, "Rational Action," *Proceedings and Addresses of the American Philosophical Association, 1961–1962,* 35: 5–23; Alfred Schutz, *Collected Papers,* ed. Maurice Natanson, 1 (The Hague: Martinus Nijhof, 1962): 3–47.

The status of purpose in action suggests some preconditions of the latter. One of them, of course, is the existence of purpose. To say that action contains purpose is not to say that there is no purpose apart from action. There is a plentitude of ends consciously held but not sought. A purpose becomes ingredient to an action when there is an effort to realize it. A second prior condition is a determination, or willingness, by the subject who has conceived a purpose to try to fulfill it. Otherwise, there will not be an attempt to realize the purpose; there will be only a "wish" or an "intention." A third antecedent condition is a subject's feeling of dissatisfaction with his given situation. If this condition does not obtain, the subject will not have an occasion to want to modify his situation. A fourth precondition is what makes the third possible: an interruption of the subject's given activities. The disruptive factor may have either positive or negative value for the subject.

Another point widely received about action is that it is contextual. In other words, any action takes place within a situation. A situation is the context constituted by a subject and its environment. The environment of a subject is, perforce, subject-oriented; it consists of those objects (and relations among them) which have significant connections with the subject's present activities. Objects may be meaningfully related to a subject's given activities as obstacles, conditions, materials, instruments, and goal objects. Although a subject is affected by his environment, he can alter it, somewhat, by changing given objects in it and by introducing new ones. More generally, he and his environment are interactive. While some objects are connected with a subject's present activities whether or not the subject ignores them ("stubborn and irreducible facts"), others are related because they are viewed by him as important (goal objects and materials, for example). The elements of an environment may be physical and mental, concrete and abstract, and natural and social-cultural. Every situation has the quality of singularity, but by degree. Although some situations are so different from one another that they are said to be, for practical purposes, utterly dissimilar, they do bear some common features. At the other extreme, some situations vary so little from one another that they are said to be virtually identical. A situation does not become related to action until the involved subject formulates a purpose which he seeks to realize. The subject's attainment of his objective does not necessarily imply the transformation of his situation into a harmonious one. It is well known that the fulfillment of some purposes has left some milieux disturbed.

The third major commonplace of action is means. It is universally recognized that one cannot realize a purpose without employing means. The means of an action consist of the materials and instruments utilized and the operations performed by the actor to realize his purpose. The means may be mental and physical, concrete and abstract, and natural and social-cultural. By virtue of his selection and use of means, an actor institutes changes in his environment—by modifying objects in it and by introducing new ones into it. Some of the alterations, of course, may not be within his control. He cannot always anticipate all the alterations in his surroundings to which his operations will lead.

III

In his article, Professor Green does not provide an overall statement of action. The only chief commonplace of action to which he explicitly refers is situation, and it is looked at but briefly and incidentally. What he does, primarily, is to analyze a single (but, perhaps, not an essential) feature of action, viz., that action is rule-obeying, or norm-regarding. He concentrates on this property because, he thinks, it provides an understanding of teaching. His argument makes some important remarks about action; nonetheless, it is somewhat unsatisfactory in its concern with action. It could have averted its inadequacies, perhaps, if it had included a serious consideration of the chief commonplaces of action.

Professor Green starts his discussion by distinguishing between behavior and action. He sums up the differences in this fashion:

> Thus, the contrast between conformity to a law of behavior and obedience to a rule of action is related to a possible contrast be-

tween giving an explanation of one's behavior and giving a reason for acting in a certain way. Similarly, the contrast between conforming to a rule and obeying a rule is the central distinction in a possible contrast between behaving and acting [p. 508].

Then Professor Green proceeds to show what action says about teaching. In his presentation, he indicates some of what is involved in rule-obeying activity. (1) Such activity is the disposition of a person to act in a certain way because the person thinks it to be a correct way (p. 509ff.). (2) To be able to obey a rule, a person does not have to be able to cite the rule; but he must have the attitude of disapproval of violations of the rule (p. 510). (3) Rules take an actor's situation into account: Any rule requires similar action in similar cases but not in dissimilar ones (p. 518). (4) Action is not only rule-obeying but rule-creating. It is what makes rules concrete (p. 519ff.). (5) A rule is taken as binding only when one views it as a rule of an activity in which one somehow participates and when one is faithful to it (p. 521).

Whether or not Professor Green is correct in his claim that giving a reason is impertinent to behavior is immaterial here. But it must be noted that he appears to be correct in contending that providing a reason is appropriate to action. After all, a person pursuing a goal consciously proposed by himself is surely able to attempt a justification of what he is doing. Professor Green's remarks about giving a reason for an action are certainly not definitive and, presumably, are not meant by him to be. Even so, they ignore a question which needs to have been raised, and they indicate no answer to it. The question concerns the sorts of things which count as reasons for an action. Professor Green writes that, when a person takes one of his activities as in obedience to a rule, ". . . the principle or rule of action being 'followed' or 'applied' may be cited as his reason for acting as he did" (p. 507). He also says that a person's giving a reason for acting as he did ". . . involves the citation of a rule of action" (p. 508). What these statements mean is not made clear by Professor Green. What they plainly intend, of course, is that the rule or rules being obeyed in an action may serve as a reason or reasons for the action. But what they cause one to wonder, upon scrutiny, is whether or not the related rule or rules is or are all that may serve as a reason or reasons. Not having brought this question into the open, Professor Green's comments on giving reasons in action might lead the unwary reader to think that rules are all that may be cited as reasons for action, which would be unfortunate.

According to the chief commonplaces of action, any of several matters may count as a reason for an action. When one asks an actor to justify what he is doing, one might intend, among other things, any or all of these three more specific questions: What was the occasion of the action? What is to be accomplished by the materials used and the operations employed? And what is the sense in attaining the purpose at hand? If the first question is meant, the actor may merely refer to his dissatisfaction with the previous state of affairs. If the second is meant, he may simply point out his purpose. If the third is intended, he may merely reveal an ulterior interest or state that the purpose is being achieved for its own sake. Hence, dissatisfaction, purpose, and ulterior interest may be counted as reasons for action. There are significant differences, of course, between these as reasons and rules as reasons. The former are particular reasons, and the latter are general ones. Also, insofar as rules are used to attempt the justification of particular reasons, they may be thought of as basic reasons (and the particular ones may be called "immediate" or "superficial"). It should be mentioned, however, that an "immediate" reason may be supported without the citation of a rule. The actor may endeavor to undergird a "superficial" reason by reference to nothing more than his likes, as in, "I am doing this in order to get a TV set, and I want that because I like TV." Whether or not one's likes are ever sufficient grounds is immaterial here. . . .

[Another] inadequacy concerns the function of rules in action. Professor Green does not take up this question overtly and appears to intimate, at most, an opaque answer to it. By not discussing the question, he overlooks the point that rules, or norms, are tested by action—a point which, as it shall be later shown, has vital importance for teaching. A glimpse of the function may be had when action is quickly viewed within the framework of its major commonplaces. Rules appear to be appropriate at two places in action: where the actor formulates his purpose, and where he determines his means. At only these places is there relevance, in action, for doing what might be believed to be correct. Apparently, then, the job of rules is to help the actor, by general prescriptive guidance, to frame his purpose and select his means. When, therefore, rules, or norms, employed by an actor are found not to be serviceable in defining purposes and means for him, they should, it seems, no longer be used by him.[6] For example, if the rules utilized by an actor were to lead him to choose means which were never effective in fulfilling his purposes, they plainly ought to be abandoned by him. Or, from the other end, if the rules were to lead him to conceive purposes which are not achievable by any available means, they obviously should be discarded by him. Presumably, then, one's faithfulness to rules ought to be circumspect.

IV

Professor Green appears to be correct when he avers that teaching is a form of rule-obeying action. Doubtless, there are no generally accepted rules of teaching; but virtually everyone insists that teaching must follow rules of some sort. Moreover, Professor Green seems to be on safe ground when he posits that at least a part of the aim of teaching is to make students capable of some rule-obeying action. Language, morality, science, and sports—any of them is a rule-obeying action. Consequently, he believes that an analysis of rule-obeying action will do much to clarify teaching (pp. 208–9). Since many conclusions are seem-

---

[6] "What are the traits of helpful rules?" is a question whose answer requires a complex and lengthy discussion, one which cannot be given at this time. One might be tempted to say simply that clarity, consistency, and relevancy are minimum traits; but the meanings and justification of even these seemingly obvious ones are hardly self-evident.

ingly established by his examination, only those will be mentioned which have not been suggested by previous discussion. (1) In some cases, learning to obey a rule is a sufficient condition for learning the rule (the "active" sense of learning a rule); in other instances, learning a rule does not imply learning to obey the rule (the "verbal" sense of learning a rule) (pp. 513–14). (2) Either way of teaching a student to learn a rule—in the active or in the verbal sense—is a satisfactory start in teaching a rule-obeying action (pp. 516ff.). (3) Learning to obey a rule is not simply acquiring a disposition to do the same thing in similar circumstances but includes acquiring the capacity to see what counts as "doing the same thing" and what constitutes "similar circumstances" (p. 518).

On the surface, at least, Professor Green's conclusions are acceptable. Where his investigation fails is where it overlooks certain consequences which the concept of action bears for the teaching of rule-obeying actions. A consideration of the major commonplaces of action could have prevented these oversights.

Since teaching aims, at least partially, at making students capable of rule-obeying action, it should regard the prior conditions of action, some of which were mentioned earlier. One of these was the subject's dissatisfaction with his given situation, which will obtain only if the subject's present activities have been interrupted. Unless a subject dislikes his present situation, he has no occasion to propose a different state of affairs. This condition has obvious importance for any position holding that learning in the classroom should proceed by "doing." If a student is to learn rule-obeying action by participating in such action, then he will have to have occasions on which to propose conscious goals and, therefore, will have to be, at times, in circumstances with which he is unhappy. Accordingly, the teacher in the classroom will have the job of identifying appropriate situations in which students are discontented and, perhaps, of pointing out to them disruptive elements which are in suitable situations of theirs but of which they are not presently cognizant ("appropriate" and "suitable" in the sense of being likely to contribute to the pedagogic purpose at hand). But the precondition of discontent is also important to any view of teaching which assumes that learning in the classroom should proceed mainly by verbal instruction. By pointing out the sorts of occasions which precede the conception of the kinds of purposes and means compatible with the rules of concern, the teacher will enhance the student's understanding of the related rule-obeying action.

Two other antecedent conditions of any action are the existence of a purpose and the willingness to attain the purpose. A distinguishing mark of a purpose is that it is conceived by its subject; it is never simply told to him. This means that he entertains the proposed objective in view of a state of dissatisfaction and decides whether or not he would be happy with the objective if it were had. For those, then, who assume that the classroom learning of rule-obeying actions should be by "doing," the student, at some point, must be permitted to devise his goals. The teacher, at such time, has only the task of helping the student to see what is involved in his entertained aims—including any possible violation of the rules of concern. For those who hold that the classroom learning of rule-obeying actions should be mainly by verbal instruction, the teacher may serve not by telling the student what his goal is but by pointing out to him what possible purposes are compatible with the related rules and what possible ones are incoherent with such rules.

Both views of learning find a hard limitation in the prior condition of willingness. Insofar as a student has no determination to try to realize any purposes which he conceives according to the rules of concern, he cannot be completely taught, by either view, rule-obeying actions. On first appearance, at least, this point suggests that learning by "doing" has an advantage over learning by verbal instructions. The former seems to provide the teacher with a greater opportunity to spot any unwillingness by the student and, thus, a larger opportunity to try to rectify the matter.

Finally, the teaching of rule-obeying action should regard the function of rules in action. This means, quite briefly, that students should be made to see that rules are used inasmuch as they help one to frame purposes and determine means, and that rules failing in their function ought to be replaced with others. Without this precaution, students might very well come to believe that the rules employed by them should be clung to at all times and places, irrespective of their quality of function.

A FABLE OR A CURRICULUM GUIDELINE?*

Felix S. Cohen

The Fable of the Hottentot Hunters and the Systematic Relativist

Once upon a time, two Hottentot hunters came upon a herd of elephants, and each hunter proceeded to systematize the situation by counting the elephants. It so happened that one of the hunters counted from left to right and the other hunter counted from right to left. Despite this important difference in starting point and in the direction of research, the two hunters agreed that there were eleven elephants. But whereas one hunter insisted that Elephant No. 1 was a large male with a bad temper and offered many plausible arguments in support of this thesis, the other hunter insisted that Elephant No. 1 was a small and rather timid young female and offered equally plausible arguments in support of that thesis. From argument the two hunters descended to epithet, and would finally have come to blows but for the fact that a systematic relativist happened along who offered to mediate the quarrel.

When he had listened to both sides, the systematic relativist said: "It is clear that the opposite characteristics which the two of you attribute to Elephant No. 1 cannot, in the nature of elephants, coexist. However, the world is a manifold of systems, and the two of you are talking in two different systems. Elephant No. 1 in one system is identical with Elephant No. 11 in the other system. Speaking generally, if n represents the ordinal number of any elephant in one system and n' represents the ordinal number of the same elephant in the other system, your formula of translation in order to understand each other is: n equals $12 - n'$. So you see, gentlemen, when you ascribe incompatible characteris-

* Reprinted from "The Relativity of Philosophical Systems and the Method of Systematic Relativism," *The Journal of Philosophy,* 36 (1939): 57–58, 65–72. By permission of *The Journal of Philosophy* and Mrs. Lucy K. Cohen.

tics to Elephant No. 1, you are not contradicting each other at all, and there is no dispute between you for me to settle."

This was very confusing to the two Hottentot hunters, so they ate the systematic relativist and called in a nearby witch doctor to settle their dispute. The witch doctor, after donning his judicial robes and examining the entrails of a bull, declared: "Elephants should always be counted from left to right. This follows from the nature of the universe, and also it follows from the nature of elephants. In accordance with this simple and salutary rule, we find that Elephant No. 1 is, in reality, a large male with a bad temper. The hunter who has denied this obvious truth has fallen into error by failing to observe this simple and salutary rule. In fact he has been thinking backwards and standing the universe on its head. For these errors he should make due compensation."

The two hunters were well satisfied with this commonsense decision, which they faithfully observed, and lived happily for ever after.

The Thesis of Systematic Relativism

The thesis which I wish to defend is that the systematic relativist was right in thinking that there was no inconsistency between the viewpoints of the two Hottentot hunters, that each was right in what he was affirming and each was wrong in thinking that he was contradicting his companion, and that the two Hottentot hunters should have eaten the witch doctor instead of the systematic relativist. Put more abstractly, statements which, if made within the same system, would be incompatible propositions, may be both true in two different but compatible systems, and may even be identical within two such systems.

. . . .

The Relativity of System

The method of analysis which we have called systematic relativism is applicable, I believe, not only to systems of philosophy but to all rational systems. It offers, I think, an organon for eliminating unreal questions and false alternatives in the jungles of politics as well as in the Elysian fields of philosophy. Broadly stated, the viewpoint of systematic relativism may be summed up in the thesis that every assertion and every concept depends for its significance upon a systematic context which is not uniquely determined by the assertion or concept itself. Except within a given context, an assertion is neither true nor false, neither probable nor improbable, neither a priori nor derivative. Except within a given context, a concept is neither simple nor complex, neither one nor many. Except within a single context, one assertion cannot be said either to support or to contradict another assertion.[13] Order, causality, proof, analysis, all have significance only within a system. And many systems are possible.

This viewpoint compels a reformulation of significant categories. With some trepidation I offer a few suggestions for this task of reformulation.

1. The Relativity of Simplicity

Any ordered system begins with undefined terms which are used to define other terms. For purposes of the system, the undefined terms are ultimate simples, and all other concepts in the system can be explained, analyzed, or defined in terms of these simples. Different systems, however, may locate simplicity in different parts of the universe. Within the system of chemistry, the physical elements are the base points of analysis; but within the system of physics, each of the elements is a composite structure of forces. For economics, a human want is an ultimate datum. For psychology, the want is something to be analyzed and explained. No significant term is in itself simple or complex. Simplicity and complexity are relative to context.

If this view is sound, the search for first elements or atomic facts, whether carried on by metaphysicians[14] or by antimeta-

[13] Cf. Carnap, *Philosophy and Logical Syntax* (1935), p. 78.

[14] The classic argument for the existence of simple substances is that of Leibniz: "And there must be simple substances, since there are compounds; for a compound is nothing but a collection or *aggregatum* of

physicians,[15] is, like the search for first elephants, doomed to failure, unless the seeker recognizes that things are "first" or "atomic" only within the framework of a given system and that no given system monopolizes reality.

Explanation or analysis involves direction. In any concrete situation, analysis can proceed along alternative lines.[16] You can divide a piece of pie into six equal portions, or into five equal portions, or into fat, protein, and carbohydrates, or into carbon, hydrogen, and various other physical elements. Does the pie now, in reality, consist of sixths, fifths, chemical compounds, or physical elements? I think this question is parallel to the question of whether law is the creature of the state or the state the creature of law, or the question of whether the world in reality consists of material things, ideas, substance, and attributes, things in relations, events, or atomic facts. The viewpoint of systematic relativism suggests that the process of analysis, whether applied to the cosmos, the nature of the state, or apple pie, can begin at different points, proceed in different directions, use different instruments, and still produce equally exhausive results, with no crumbs left over.

2. The Relativity of Proof

The same viewpoint that suggests that the direction of analysis and the location of simplicity and complexity are functions of a

simple things" (*Monadology*, Sec. 2). This argument fails to exclude two logical possibilities: (*a*) that there are no compounds *per se*, but merely entities which are compounds relative to a given system, and which may be simples relative to another system; and (*b*) that compounds are collections or aggregates of other compounds, and that there are no simples.

[15] Wittgenstein echoes Leibniz: "2.021. Objects form the substance of the world. Therefore they cannot be compound" (*Tractatus logico-philosophicus*, 1922, p. 35). And cf. Russell, *Our Knowledge of the External World as a Field for Scientific Method in Philosophy* (1915), pp. 51–55.

[16] Cf. Morris R. Cohen, in "Qualities, Relations, and Things" *Journal of Philosophy* (1914): 617, 622. "The world of existence is thus a network of relations whose intersections are called terms. These termini may be complex or simple, but the simplicity is always relative to the system in which they enter. . . . Even the mathematical point is not absolutely simple. . . . In line geometry a point is a complex formed by the intersection of two lines, and there is no reason for supposing that point geometry is more fundamental than line geometry."

contextual system also suggests that the direction of proof, generalization, and particularization and the location of probabilty and the a priori are functions of such a system.

In the field of deductive proof, systematic relativism asserts only what I think we should all maintain, namely, that propositions or theorems are proved with reference to assumptions or postulates, and that no proof is conclusive if you reject the assumptions, which you can always do, logically, though as a moral human being you may find certain assumptions indispensable.

The viewpoint of relativism is equally applicable, I believe, to so-called inductive proof.

To the absolute pluralist induction is a mystery.[17] If the falling of apple *A* is intrinsically and ineluctably a particular, distinct from the falling of apple *B,* then no sum of these particulars can establish a general proposition about the falling of apples or about gravity in general.

But induction is not a mystery if one accepts the relativistic view that what is particular is also general—in another context. From this standpoint, the physicist does not have to traverse the infinite distance from the particular to the universal, because he does not start with the particular in the first place. He views only those aspects of the universe which are common to apples and other material things, namely, such universals as mass, velocity, acceleration, weight, shape, color. The process of induction is not an addition of particulars but a subtraction of universals. It is a process of eliminating irrelevant elements. The hypothesis that color or shape or weight influences velocity may be experimentally disproved, thus permitting a progressive abstraction in what the physicist observes. From the standpoint of systematic relativism, then, induction is the process of abstracting from experience the elements relevant to a given system and of eliminating elements which are not relevant. . . .

This viewpoint with respect to the relativity of proof throws light, I think, on the problem of probability. No fact has, in itself, an assignable probability. It either exists or does not exist. And what is true of one fact is true, a thousand times, of a thousand

[17] Cf. Russell, pp. 221–23.

facts. The empirical frequency of a certain occurrence is a fact and not a probability. To be specific, there is no probability that I *as an individual* will live another ten years. Different insurance companies may assign different degrees of probability to this possible event, depending upon whether they classify me with respect to age, health, weight, occupation, and heredity, or disregard one or more of these factors, or weigh the factors differently. A degree of probability can be assigned only within a system that selects certain elements as relevant, disregards others, and deals with the characteristics of classes defined by these relevant elements. . . .

3. The Relativity of Classification

Applied to the notion of class, the viewpoint of systematic relativism suggests that classification is relative to context, that no entity contains within itself a unique principle of classification. Any entities may be grouped together in a class. If certain classes seem more "natural" than others, this is largely the result of language and habits of thought that change with changing cultures and vary in various contexts. Failure to recognize the relativity of classification to purpose or system is a fruitful source of empty argument. This people argue for or against the proposition that international law is a kind of law, or that the social sciences are sciences, or that man is an animal, as if these were propositions with a fixed meaning, true or false, and are continually surprised because such arguments never convince their adversaries. . . .

4. The Relativity of Causation

Applied to the notion of *cause,* the method of systematic relativism points to the plurality of systems in which lines of causation can be traced. If the question is asked, in the system of physics, "What causes the periodic rearrangement of these pages?" an answer in terms of my desire to get to the next page is quite irrelevant.

The notion of the relativity of causation throws light, I think, upon a central problem of jurisprudence. When we seek to impose a liability upon the person who has caused an injury, a science that utterly ignores ethics can never fasten responsibility upon any one individual. An event in society typically involves antecedent events by many persons, including persons no longer alive at the time of the event. If, as a matter of fact, we fasten the thread of causation to one person, it is because here is a point in the myriad strings of historical connectedness where social pressure accomplishes some approved social purpose.[20]

The relativity of causation implies the relativity of the accidental. The pure accident does not exist. A hurricane may be an accident in a social system, but not in a system of meteorology.

If causation is relative to system, the whole problem of chance and determinism must be reformulated. Any event is determinate within a system that postulates the sufficient conditions of the event, and indeterminate in any other system. The fact that an act of a human being is determined in the system of physical motion does not mean that the act is determined in another kind of system. No event is in itself determinate or indeterminate.

5. The Relativity of Individuality

I think that a good deal of confusion in political life as well as in philosophy has been caused by an absolutistic view of individuality. In the system of psychology, or at least in some systems of psychology, I am an individual. From the viewpoint of the biology of unicellular organisms, I suppose I am a cooperative society of several million members, the membership of which is constantly changing. From the sociologist's viewpoint, I suppose I am only a part of a community or society, perhaps a part of many concentric or overlapping societies.

[20] There is illumination in the comment of Judge Andrews in the case of Palsgraf *vs.* L. I. R. R. (248 N.Y. 339): "Each cause brings about future events. Without each the future would not be the same. Each is proximate in the sense it is essential. But that is not what we mean by the word. Nor on the other hand do we mean sole cause. There is no such thing. . . . We cannot trace the effect of an act to the end, if end there is. Again, however, we may trace it part of the way. . . . This is not logic. It is practical politics."

It is significant to ask whether I am *really* an individual or a great many individuals or only a part of some bigger individual? The thesis here advanced would require us to maintain that this question is invalid,[21] that individuality is relative to system, that any group may be an individual from some viewpoint, that any individual may be a group from some viewpoint.

This, of course, is merely an example of what might be called the relativity of number to the unit of operation. In its everyday forms, this relativity is accepted by common sense. A quart is two pints and is, at the same time, a fourth of a gallon. The same liquid thus partakes of plurality, unity, and partiality, with reference to different standards. So, when the monistic lamb in Professor Strong's philosophic fable, refusing to recognize a real distinction between the nutritious and the poisonous, told its mother that, after all, the universe is one, the lamb's mother, being a thoroughgoing systematic relativist, replied, "One what?"[22]

What we call a principle of individuation is, in effect, a formula for designating units of operation within a rational system. If alternative systems are valid, alternative principles of individuation are likewise valid.

This viewpoint dissolves a good many philosophic problems that seem otherwise insoluble. The metaphysical problem of the personality of groups which runs through political philosophy and jurisprudence vanishes once we recognize that the term "person" may be defined to cover various units in the segmentation of human activity. There remains the question of what definitions are useful for certain purposes, but this is no longer a problem of metaphysics.[23]

This notion of the relativity of the individual person or thing

[21] Cf. F. S. Cohen, "What is a Question?" *Monist,* 39 (1929): 350.

[22] C. A. Strong, *The Wisdom of the Beasts* (1921), p. 60 ("The Lamb and Its Mother"). The answer of the lamb, as reported by Professor Strong, was: "I am not quite sure; but if I have correctly understood my illustrious teachers, it is one Lamb."

[23] Cf. John Dewey, "Corporate Personality" in *Philosophy and Civilization* (1931); F. S. Cohen, *Ethical Systems and Legal Ideals* (1933), pp. 9–16.

suggests the thought that what is substance in one context may be quality or relation in another context. The distinction between essence and attribute, between substance and quality, between entity and relation, is, like the distinction between the individual and the society that includes the individual or the environment that surrounds the individual,[24] relative to the contextual system in which the distinction is drawn.

[24] "The 'problem of free will' is a product of two absolutistic fallacies: the notion that there is an absolute line of distinction between the individual and the environment, and the notion that there is a one-way causal relationship between the two. I have elsewhere suggested that there is an alternative view: . . . the human soul is neither the master nor the slave of its environment. The human soul *is* its environment, seen from within." F. S. Cohen, "The Socialization of Mortality," in Hook and Kallen, *American Philosophy Today and Tomorrow* (1935), p. 98.

HUMANITY AND THE LIMITS OF REASON*

Karl Jaspers

The universality of thought is not merely a fact of human nature, but a demand made by its freedom upon itself. But this universality can appear as a fatality because, through the formal priority of thought, everything can become evacuated into the mere form of the thinkable, and humanity can be dissolved into the empty play which universally touches upon everything without penetrating into anything, or becoming anybody. The originally positive aspect of opening up possibilities becomes in formalization something negative which destroys everything serious in reality. But now, if one turns against thought, the struggle can only succeed by thought. The destruction of thought always remains itself still thought, but now violent, simplistic, narrow, and self-binding thought. The fate of thought is the destiny of our humanity; the danger that lies therein is in the unceasing questioning over the path of fulfillment toward a reality which has come to itself and been awakened into development, possibilities first liberated by thought itself.

The formal priority of thought is destroyed in its formalization but is real in the priority of rational thought.

．　．　．　．

1. A. Rational A-logic; The Circle as a Necessary Form of Genuine Philosophy

We shall start with a Kantian idea. Kant conceived all objectivity as a material formed by the categories of the subject which was consciousness as such. We live in a world of appearance produced by us not, to be sure, in its empirical existence, but in its general

* Reprinted with the permission of Farrar, Straus & Giroux, Inc., from *Reason and Existenz* by Karl Jaspers, copyright © 1955 by The Noonday Press, pp. 109, 113–15, 119–21.

form. The thing-in-itself was absolutely hidden, a mere limiting concept implied by the phenomenality of empirical existents. Now the categories like unity, plurality, substance, causality, etc., were for Kant to be derived from the original unity of the thinking consciousness, the so-called unity of transcendental apperception which bound whatever we might encounter into the unity of an object. But Kant said, "this unity which precedes a priori all synthesizing concepts is not at all the category of unity." Kant thus requires us in thinking by categories—and, according to him, we cannot think otherwise—to grasp something which does not fall under the categories. This he had to do, since he wanted to touch the origin of all objectivity which itself could not be objective. Thus, I must think a nonobjectivity objectively, that which grounds the categories, including that of unity, under the category of unity. We arrive thus in formal logic either at a circle: unity is explained through unity; or at a contradiction: unity is not unity.

In all genuine philosophies we find such circles and contradictions at the decisive point, whether it is metaphysics, transcendental philosophy, or the clarification of Existenz. And everywhere one sees the critics at work triumphantly exposing these discrepancies and imagining the criticized philosophy thereby destroyed.

But it must be shown that such forms of thought are necessary in philosophy by the nature of things. And, in order to do this, we will first look at the process by which these circles and contradictions arise, according to a purely logical interpretation. To be sure, we shall not be interested in those many mistakes which can be corrected verbally without further change, but rather in errors which appear to be logically unavoidable and irresolvable.

There are many striking examples from antiquity. Epimenides the Cretan said, "All Cretans always lie when they speak." Thus, that which Epimenides, a Cretan, said is not true; thus his proposition, "All Cretans lie," is not true, etc. Or there is the story of the sophist Protagoras and his pupil Euathlus who took lessons from him but was to pay only when he had won his first lawsuit. But Euathlus took no cases. When Protagoras brought suit for his money, Euathlus explained: "If I win this suit, I need not pay, for the judgment is against you; and if I lose the suit, I also need not pay since our agreement was that I must pay only on winning my first suit." Or there is the argument of the crocodile: a crocodile stole a child from its mother and told the mother, "I will give it back to you if you will give me the right answer to the following question: Will I give you back your child?" The mother replied, "You will not return my child; and now you must give it back to me in either case. For if my answer was right, then you must return it according to our agreement. And also if it was wrong, for it would be wrong only if you did return my child." But the crocodile answered, "I cannot return the child in either case. For if your answer is wrong, then the child is not returned according to our agreement, and if your answer is right, then it is right only if I do return the child."

Without going into the particularities and necessarily more precise conceptions in these examples, we find as the general principle of the difficulties that in each case there is a so-called self-reflexivity. The lying Cretan says something whose content cancels the saying of it, which is then restored ad infinitum. The object of the trial of Euathlus and the content of the mother's assertion are both condition and conditioned. But we can only think meaningfully and unambiguously if in the content of our thought we have two terms to be related; thus, in the relation of condition, the conditioning and the conditioned must be distinct, and in the relation of object, the thing and its properties must be distinct. The error lies, not in the individual conclusions, but in the premises where only a single term is related to itself. As soon as two are distinguished, all the difficulties fall away, as well as the wit in these oddities invented by the Greeks. These striking examples are so easily grasped that the solution is easy. But we are interested not so much in these examples as in the principle to be grasped through them: of a limit to literal conceivability for us.

Now precisely in distinction from cognition of things in the world, in philosophizing something is thought which, if it is to be touched upon, can permit nothing outside of its being thought, since it is the fundamental origin; it may be Being itself, or the condition of all objectivity as in the Kantian philosophy, or it may be Existenz. We always have something which the understanding cannot grasp but which is decisive for our certainty of being, which is less before us than present in our thought.

. . . .

That the whole of my rationality rests upon the basis of non-reason—such a phrase does not assert that reason can be denied out of some general right drawn from existential philosophy. Nothing which lacks reason or which is contrary to reason can raise up argumentative claims out of itself, for precisely in this process it enters into the medium of rationality. Neither the positivity of mere empirical existence nor that of the existential basis has a right without reason. Every premise of justification enters into the realm of the rational. The truth of the nonrational is impossible unless reason is pushed to its limit.

Thus, the concepts of existential philosophy can become a medium which confuses Existenz instead of illuminating it. Every direct usage of these concepts as contents of assertions, instead of living under their appeal, is already on this path.

For example, it can be almost the extreme of merciless cruelty to demand freedom of others where it can never be released from its bonds by such direct volition, but only through the ripening prudence of a love which, however, is unrelentingly demanding. It is as when love is paralyzed and nothing is left but the deadly, abstract demands expressed in rationalistic existential concepts; it is perhaps a priest who is acting, prepared with the means of grace of his church, trying to be of some help even in the extremities. Likewise it is an existentially disastrous refusal if this love, become weak and self-satisfied, deceiving both the other and itself, justifies the other in his empirical existence and shrinks back from the danger of entering into a desperate situation. . . .

Thus the concepts of an existential philosophy can become the means by which the existential is lost more than ever in a delusive pretense. When I apply the concepts abstractly, I speak of something which is only further removed by my speech, for I am not really on its path. I speak correctly, and at the same time I am, myself, wholly false. Perhaps abstractly I say something decisive, but I say it in such a fashion that concretely it is not only irrelevant but destroyed. The abstract application no longer speaks in the situation.

The reason is that the truth of existential thought never lies in its content as such, but rather in what happens to me in the thinking of it: either in a passion for possibilities which prepares in advance and recalls, or in real communication where what was said comes forth as existentially true in ever unique ways, unplanned out of the absolute consciousness of love. There is always a misuse when what is intended through philosophic contents is used as though it were something known, to be applied and argued about in order to attain some end, instead of producing by such concepts in one self and in communication something which is man himself and not something meant by him. Such existential thought is either true, and then it is indissolubly connected with the being of the thinker; or it is a content to be known like any other, and then it is false. The concepts of existential philosophy are such that I cannot think them without being in them; scientific contents, on the other hand, are such that I can know them while I myself live in wholly different categories; what I am is irrelevant to scientific knowledge.

WHAT ARE VALUABLE SCIENTIFIC STUDIES OF MAN?*

John Somerville

Let us invoke philosophic license for a moment to suppose you receive the following letter:

"Dear Sir:

I am taking the liberty of calling upon you to be the judge in a dispute between me and an acquaintance who is no longer a friend. The question at issue is this: Is my creation, umbrellaology, a science? Allow me to explain this situation. For the past eighteen years, assisted by a few faithful disciples, I have been collecting materials on a subject hitherto almost wholly neglected by scientists, the umbrella. The results of my investigations to date are embodied in the nine volumes which I am sending to you under separate cover. Pending their receipt, let me describe to you briefly the nature of their contents and the method I pursued in compiling them. I began on the island of Manhattan. Proceeding block by block, house by house, family by family and individual by individual I ascertained (1) the number of umbrellas possessed, (2) their size, (3) their weight, (4) their color. Having covered Manhattan after many years, I eventually extended the survey to the other boroughs of the city of New York, and at length completed the entire city. Thus I was ready to carry forward the work to the rest of the state and, indeed, the rest of the United States and the whole known world.

"It was at this point that I approached my erstwhile friend. I am a modest man, but I felt I had the right to be recognized as the creator of a new science. He, on the other hand, claimed that umbrellaology was not a science at all. First, he said, it was silly to investigate umbrellas. Now this argument is false, because science scorns not to deal with any object, however humble and

* Reprinted from "Umbrellaology, or, Methodology in Social Science," *Philosophy of Science,* 8 (1941): 557–66. By permission of the Williams and Wilkins Company, Baltimore, and the author.

lowly, even to the 'hind leg of a flea.' Then why not umbrellas? Next he said that umbrellaology could not be recognized as a science because it was of no use or benefit to mankind. But is not the truth the most precious thing in life? And are not my nine volumes filled with the truth about my subject? Every word is true. Every sentence contains a hard, cold fact. When he asked me what was the object of umbrellaology, I was proud to say, 'To seek and discover the truth is object enough for me.' I am a pure scientist; I have no ulterior motives. Hence it follows that I am satisfied with truth alone. Next, he said my truths were dated and that any one of my findings might cease to be true tomorrow. But this, I pointed out, is not an argument against umbrellaology, but rather an argument for keeping it up to date, which is exactly what I propose. Let us have surveys monthly, weekly or even daily to keep our knowledge abreast of the changing facts. His next contention was that umbrellaology had entertained no hypotheses and had developed no theories or laws. This is a great error. In the course of my investigations, I employed innumerable hypotheses. Before entering each new block and each new section of the city, I entertained an hypothesis as regards the number and characteristics of the umbrellas that would be found there, which hypotheses were either verified or nullified by my subsequent observations, in accordance with proper scientific procedure, as explained in authoritative texts. (In fact, it is interesting to note that I can substantiate and document every one of my replies to these objections by numerous quotations from standard works, leading journals, public speeches of eminent scientists, and the like.) As for theories and laws, my work presents an abundance of them. I will here mention only a few by the way of illustration. There is the Law of Color Variation Relative to Ownership by Sex. (Umbrellas owned by women tend to great variety of color, whereas those owned by men are almost all black.) To this law I have given exact statistical formulation. (See Vol. 6, Appendix I, Table 3, p. 582.) There are the curiously interrelated Laws of Individual Ownership of Plurality of Umbrellas, and Plurality of Owners of Individual Umbrellas. The interrelationship assumes the form, in the first law, of almost direct ratio to annual income, and in the second, of almost inverse ratio to annual income. (For an exact statement of the modifying circumstances, see Vol. 8, p. 350.) There is also the Law of the Tendency toward Acquisition of Umbrellas in Rainy Weather. To this law I have given experimental verification in Chapter 3 of Volume 3. In the same ways I have performed numerous other experiments in connection with my generalizations.

"Thus I feel that my creation is in all respects a genuine science, and I appeal to you for substantiation of my opinion."

How should we reply to this letter? It merits our attention, because a thorough consideration of umbrellaology might explain much, first, about the natural sciences, second, about the social sciences. If the purpose of science were just to discover truth, so that any field of knowledge was a science in proportion to the amount of truth it accumulated about its subject matter, then umbrellaology would have quite as good a claim to the status of a science as physics or chemistry. In fact, if the amount of truth were the proper criterion, umbrellaology would be much more scientific than physics or chemistry because, in the pure sunlight of its unmistakable certainty, it actually possesses a far greater number of truths about umbrellas than physics, laboring in the twilight of partly verified hypotheses and almost established facts, possesses about its subject matter. Evidently it is not truth that makes a science, but, at best, a certain type or kind of truth.

Evidently there is something that must be called scientific truth which possesses at least certain differences from ordinary truth. It is evident also that, whatever the distinguishing characteristic of this scientific truth may be, it is not its absoluteness as truth. This fact is of incalculable importance to the advancement of the social sciences. A half-truth, or even an outright error "in the right direction," to speak vaguely for the moment, is very frequently of far more value to science than some unmitigated verity that doesn't go anywhere.

To deal more precisely with the problem, we have to address ourselves to the following question: what is possessed by the truths, or even the half-truths of physics, chemistry, or any established science, by virtue of which these fields are recognized as sciences, while at the same time this something is not possessed by umbrellaology? Or, to reformulate the question in quantitative terms, the only fruitful way to deal with it, what is it that is possessed in so much greater degree by physics and chemistry as to make them so much more scientific than umbrellaology? To answer in a word, the power to predict. The development of modern natural science suggests the following rule, which, however, must not be taken mechanically: Any body of doctrine or collection of truths is scientific to the extent that it yields the power to predict in relation to the subject matter of its choice. Of course, the extent or amount of the subject matter must be reckoned in. The amount of predictability, if it could be calculated mathematically, would equal the product of number of predictions and amount of subject matter. The amount of subject matter involves both extent and frequency of occurrence. Mathematically, it would be the product of the average extent of a single case times the number of cases. War, for example, takes place very seldom in comparison with tuberculosis. Predictions about both are very important, in regard to war, primarily because of the extent of what is involved in any single case, in regard to tuberculosis, primarily because of the number of cases.

Now the observations, experiments, hypotheses, and laws which, as we have seen, are possessed by umbrellaology, would indeed yield a certain amount of prediction. For instance, our umbrellaologist is able to foretell, with a high degree of accuracy, how many umbrellas will be owned by a family of such and such income, to which respective sexes the owners of a large black and a small red umbrella will be found to belong, what greater proportion of umbrellas will be acquired on a rainy than on a fair day, and other like interesting matters. However, his prognosis is severely limited to just such aspects of the umbrella. He cannot predict its behavior under various physical and social conditions, to what extent it helps to prevent disease, how it might perform its functions more effectively, what new materials might improve its construction, and so on. Most of these matters are already dealt with in existing branches of physics, chemistry, and other sciences. The amount of predictability that would actually be added by the new "science" is so slight as to be negligible. Thus umbrellaology, as conceived by its founder, may be said to be scientific to the extent that it yields predictability, and, by the same token, must be judged to be only slightly scientific.

Our conclusion here serves to emphasize the essentially quantitative rather than qualitative character of the whole problem. Very frequently we read and hear discussions of the question, "Is sociology a science?" Such formulation is probably based upon, and in any case cannot fail to encourage, the misleading presumption that the question is essentially a qualitative one, permitting a yes or no response. The problem that should be discussed is, "To what extent is sociology a science, and how can it be made more scientific?"

Granted the quantitative character of the question, "Why, in answering it, do we select predictability?" Why not one of the other factors, such as observation, experiment, law, or hypothesis? Certainly not because these other factors are thought unnecessary. On the contrary, it may be noted that in making this point we say that it is "any body of doctrine or collection of truths" which is a science to the extent that it gains the power to predict in relation to the subject matter of its choice. If we somehow possessed the power to predict, but could not embody and express this power in a collection of propositions, or, in other words, if it were not upon the basis of observations, calculations, and generalizations that we gained this power, that would not be science. While doctrine is naturally indispensable, it is nevertheless its contribution to prognosis which gives it scientific status. The more prediction that is yielded by laws and principles, the more scientific they are. However, we cannot say, the more laws and principles we have, the more prediction we have, or the more science we have. If we could, then umbrellaology would be just as scientific as physics. It ought perhaps to be emphasized that the concept of predictability itself must not be taken narrowly. What is meant is the predictability of a total body of doctrine over a sufficiently extended period of time.

If we thus emphasize predictability, do we not run the risk, it might be asked, of developing a type of social science which would be just as valueless as umbrellaology even though it might yield a high degree of prognosis? That is to say, might it not gain prediction over things which are not considered important? At the present stage in the development of social science, there would seem to be little such danger. To mankind taken generally, things are considered important in direct proportion to the frequency with which they occur, taken together with the extent of each occurrence. As it is exactly in these terms that we define amount of predictability, we can be certain that, in the vast majority of cases, the amount of predictability itself will be its own guarantee of the amount of importance which will be attached to it by society at large. It is important to emphasize that this principle is valid for mankind taken generally and on the average. Hence, individual exceptions do not materially affect it. It is a principle which might help to clarify the problem of values in science by raising factors often considered as hopelessly subjective to a more objective level.

Thus science increases or decreases, prospers or declines, not with truth as such, but with predictability. To "explain" something in science is, in the long run, to predict its behavior. Scientists habitually pass by whole clusters of propositions bursting with a wealth of absolute truth (like umbrellaology) to fasten lovingly upon some proposition admittedly less than full-fledged in truth, but rich in the power of prediction (like either the wave or corpuscular theory of light in physics). It need hardly be added that science never prefers error to truth of its own kind. The point is that it often prefers its own kind of error to another kind of truth, however pure. That is the sort of science we have been developing in the modern world. It is doubtful whether certain ancient or medieval philosophers would be quite satisfied with it, but we seem to like it very much. The basic reason is not far to seek: it is so useful. Where we can predict, we can always find a way to utilize, which is a type of control. We all know what is meant by saying that scientists are busy finding out how nature works. It would be just as true to say they are always busy finding out how to work nature.

Unfortunately, much of what we call social science bears only too strong a resemblance to umbrellaology. Isolated investigations which solve no important problem, laws or generalizations which yield no special predictions, uncoordinated projects which verify or nullify no important theory are, with notable exceptions, the order of the day. A primary condition of the advancement of the social sciences is the selection of problems that are scientific. What is a scientific problem? The best test is predictability: how much of that would it contribute if solved? It is frequently more difficult, especially in the beginning stages of a science, to find the right problems than it is to find the right solutions, the right questions to raise than the right answers once they are raised. However, by a peculiar process involved in the passage of time, after a science has become well established, the original difficulty seems to have been no difficulty at all. It seems that the problems were always at hand, and that the only difficulty that ever existed was finding the solutions. In short, the feeling disappears that there is any problem involved in finding the problems. To make it far worse, this lack of feeling then carries over to fields like the social sciences, which are still in their beginning stages (in point of growth, if not of time), and it operates there to produce the impression that the problems are all at hand, or, in short, that anything which occurs to one as a problem may without further consideration be regarded as worthy of scientific investigation.

The fact must somehow be brought home, perhaps especially to American social scientists that, speaking broadly, no problem is worth working on that does not involve a deliberately formulated hypothesis which has scientific implications beyond the original problem. What is meant by scientific implications? Mainly, value in promoting prediction. Just to find out "what the facts are," or just to feel that it would be "interesting" to know this or that, is not sufficient for the result to be of any value to science or to distinguish itself in any vital particular from umbrellaology. In other words, it cannot be assumed, as it so frequently seems to be, that conclusions, just because they are true and about society, are a contribution to the science of society.

A very important part of the method of any science is, of course, the set of concepts employed. They are not given by nature, but to nature, or, what is of more point here, not by society but to society. A word tags some part of the universe and, through its meaning, delimits, identifies, and to a certain extent explains this part. Now the parts of the universe, even those that come within range of our human experience, are probably infinite. They are not all tagged; only the minutest portion is. While it would be instructive to inquire on what principle this very severe selection has been made, we are here concerned with a different aspect of the matter. Concepts are methodological instrumentalities, and many of the best ones used in any science have been selected for formulation by that science itself. They were not there, as concepts, when it originally came upon the scene. This process has very little to do with making up names or words. It is first of all a matter of delimiting aspects, characteristics, things, classes; in a word, parts of the universe not previously delimited, although they may have been dealt with fragmentarily or conjointly by previous delimitations either greater or lesser in extent. This delimitation by science is not arbitrary but takes place in the light of its contribution to predictability. What any science needs, especially in its beginning stages, are strategic concepts, that is, concepts so located and so fashioned that they make it possible to solve the right problems. Concepts by themselves cannot do any more than that, but that is a great deal. Concepts, like problems, must be discovered. Society, mankind, gives to the scientist not problems but difficulties. The scientist must formulate these difficulties as problems. The stuff of his formulation is concepts. Not until the problem is properly formulated, or, better, not until the proper problem is formulated will the difficulty be overcome.

Our thesis is not that social science has never made progress, but rather that the progress it has made is owing to the operation, unfortunately still too restricted, of such factors as we have discussed. In addition to these, it must take more accurate and realistic stock of itself in terms of its connections and role in the actually existing complex of powerful social institutions. Unfortunate as the fact may be, the growth of a science is not something mankind makes easy for itself. The physical sciences won the right to live only at the cost of a prolonged and bitter struggle against interests and institutions which evidently felt themselves threatened by what those sciences represented. Had science then confined itself to what was acceptable to the militant protagonists of the status quo, we would not today possess the work of many a persecuted thinker. It frequently happens in science that he who gives mankind the most is himself made to pay the greatest price. It is certainly not because the human race is naturally sadistic, or because a series of especially malevolent persons happened to hold power, that we witness this tragic recurrence. It is because far-reaching intellectual discoveries often involve vital readjustments in the social structure. Wherever there are powerful forces that would stand to lose by these readjustments, they naturally fight them with the various weapons at their disposal.

If these conditions attended the development of physical science, can we expect them to be absent in the case of social science, which bears upon the social structure even more directly and pervasively? If history whispers, "Social scientists, be prepared to suffer," we may also be certain that this warning does not apply to umbrellaologists. They have little to fear. The road of prediction and control is the risky road, but it is also the only one that offers any prospect of scientific value.

In modern democratic civilization as we know it, the job of social science is to establish itself in the open market of ideas and grow strong enough to survive in the struggle. This is by no means an easy task. The market is open to both good and bad ideas, and the competition into which social science must enter against all forms of attractive superficiality, superstition, and vulgarity is extremely severe. Moreover, short-sighted holders of great power have a right, which they frequently exercise, to back with all their resources these very competitors of social science.

Certainly under these circumstances social science should neither carry a chip on its own shoulder, nor fail to distinguish deeds from words on the part of others. If it commits itself to the objective of predictability, it must at the same time be prepared to defend against attack, whatever gains it makes. Of course, it can easily avoid all such unpleasant struggles by abandoning the criterion of predictability. This way out, however, has its own price: it leads social science to a point where it must lose itself in either the Scylla of irresponsible metaphysical speculation or the Charybdis of mock-empirical umbrellaology.

INDEX